Traditionalism

Traditionalism

Religion in the light of the Perennial Philosophy

Harry Oldmeadow

SOPHIA PERENNIS
SAN RAFAEL, CA

© Harry Oldmeadow, 2000
First edition, The Sri Lanka Institute
of Traditional Studies, 2008
Second edition, Sophia Perennis, 2011
All rights reserved

Series editor: James R. Wetmore

No part of this book may be reproduced or transmitted,
in any form or by any means, without permission

ISBN 978-1-59731-131-1

For information, address:
Sophia Perennis, P.O. Box 151011
San Rafael, CA 94915
sophiaperennis.com

Design on cover by
Paul Goble
author of many books
on North American myths and legends

Contents

Introduction	viii

I The Traditionalists

1	The Traditionalist Attitude to Biography	2
2	René Guénon	10
3	Ananda Coomaraswamy	26
4	Frithjof Schuon	36
5	Other Traditionalists *and the forums of traditionalist thought*	44

II Tradition and the traditions

6	Tradition: *towards the definition of a principle*	58
7	The Transcendent Unity of Religions	68
8	Metaphysics, Theology and Philosophy	84
9	Symbolism and Sacred Art	102

III Traditionalism and Modernism

10	The Critique of Modernism	116
11	Counterfeit Spirituality	142
12	Criticisms of Traditionalism	164
13	The Phenomenology of Religion	186
14	Religious Pluralism and the Study of Religions	198

Epilogue	207
Selected Bibliographies	209
Acknowledgments	217
Index	219

Plates

facing page

René Guénon   6

Ananda Coomaraswamy   22

Frithjof Schuon   38

Titus Burckhardt   54

Marco Pallis   70

Martin Lings   86

Whitall Perry   102

Seyyed Hossein Nasr   118

Diagrams

page

The Exoteric-Esoteric Divide   76

The Centre and the Circumference   77

Abbreviations

AKC *BL*	A. Coomaraswamy	*The Bugbear of Literacy*
AKC *COPA*	A. Coomaraswamy	*Christian and Oriental Philosophy of Art*
AKC *SL*	A. Coomaraswamy	*Selected Letters of Ananda K. Coomaraswamy*
AKC *SPI*	A. Coomaraswamy	*Selected Papers Vol I, Traditional Art and Symbolism*
AKC *SPII*	A. Coomaraswamy	*Selected Papers Vol II, Metaphysics*
FS *CI*	F. Schuon	*Christianity/Islam: Essays on Esoteric Ecumenicism*
FS *DI*	F. Schuon	*Dimensions of Islam*
FS *EOPW*	F. Schuon	*Echoes of Perennial Wisdom*
FS *EPW*	F. Schuon	*Esoterism as Principle and as Way*
FS *EW*	F. Schuon	*The Essential Writings of Frithjof Schuon*
FS *FDH*	F. Schuon	*From the Divine to the Human*
FS *GDW*	F. Schuon	*Gnosis, Divine Wisdom*
FS *IPP*	F. Schuon	*Islam and the Perennial Philosophy*
FS *ITB*	F. Schuon	*In the Tracks of Buddhism*
FS *LAW*	F. Schuon	*Light on the Ancient Worlds*
FS *L&T*	F. Schuon	*Logic and Transcendence*
FS *LS*	F. Schuon	*Language of the Self*
FS *PM*	F. Schuon	*The Play of Masks*
FS *RHC*	F. Schuon	*Roots of the Human Condition*
FS *SME*	F. Schuon	*Survey of Metaphysics and Esoterism*
FS *SPHF*	F. Schuon	*Spiritual Perspectives and Human Facts*
FS *SVQ*	F. Schuon	*Sufism, Veil and Quintessence*
FS *SW*	F. Schuon	*Stations of Wisdom*
FS *THC*	F. Schuon	*To Have a Center*
FS *TM*	F. Schuon	*The Transfiguration of Man*
FS *TUR*	F. Schuon	*The Transcendent Unity of Religions*
FS *UI*	F. Schuon	*Understanding Islam*
JN *SG*	J. Needleman *ed*	*The Sword of Gnosis*
RG *CMW*	R. Guénon	*Crisis of the Modern World*
RG *RQ*	R. Guénon	*The Reign of Quantity and the Signs of the Times*
RF *UT*	R. Fernando *ed*	*The Unanimous Tradition*
RL *CLW*	R. Lipsey	*Coomaraswamy: His Life and Work*
SCR		*Studies in Comparative Religion*
SHN *K&S*	S.H. Nasr	*Knowledge and the Sacred*
RH	Nasr/W. Stoddart *ed*	*Religion of the Heart*
SS *ACRR*	S.D.R. Singam *ed*	*Ananda Coomaraswamy: Remembering and Remembering Again and Again*
WP *TTW*	W. Perry *ed*	*A Treasury of Traditional Wisdom*

Introduction

In his essay 'The Pertinence of Philosophy' Ananda Coomaraswamy[1] suggested that

> ... if we are to consider what may be the most urgent practical task to be resolved by the philosopher, we can only answer that this is ... a control and revision of the principles of comparative religion, the true end of which science ... should be to demonstrate the common metaphysical basis of all religions ...

This might well serve as a capsule statement of the agenda of a group of several contemporary thinkers who can be gathered together under the term 'traditionalists'. The traditionalist perspective was first publicly articulated by the French metaphysician, René Guénon. Since the time of Guénon's earliest writings, soon after the turn of the century, a significant traditionalist 'school' has emerged with Guénon, Ananda Coomaraswamy and Frithjof Schuon acknowledged within the group as the pre-eminent exponents of the age-long worldview of all pre-modern peoples.

The traditionalists, by definition, are committed to the explication of the *philosophia perennis* which lies at the heart of the diverse religions and behind the manifold forms of the world's different traditions. At the same time, they are dedicated to the preservation and illumination of the traditional forms which give each religious heritage its *raison d'être* and guarantee its formal integrity and, by the same token, ensure its spiritual efficacy.

The word 'tradition' has, of course, gathered all manner of political and sentimental accretions of which it must be cleansed if we are to understand its formative significance in the works of the writers with whom we are here concerned. The term 'traditionalist' calls for some preliminary comment. While Coomaraswamy occasionally used it in a straightforward way to describe an outlook in conformity with traditional principles, Guénon, on the other hand, applied it pejoratively to certain individuals (of whom there were apparently many at the time he was writing) who in reaction to the relentless march of modernism were calling for some kind of traditional restoration in the West although they were themselves unaware of the true nature of tradition: 'people who' as Guénon wrote, 'have only a sort of tendency or aspiration towards tradition without really knowing anything at all about it ....'.[2] He called these people 'traditionalists' and their vague objectives 'Traditionalism' which he contrasted with 'the true traditional spirit'.

It is important to note in this context that, at that time, a Guénonian 'school' guided by a proper understanding of tradition had not yet emerged, and by the time such a movement began to take shape in the fifties and early sixties, not only were both Guénon and Coomaraswamy no longer alive, but the war years had effectively put an end to such revivalist agitation as Guénon had in mind when he first used those terms. Therefore, some three decades later when the new traditional 'school' had established itself and attracted sufficient attention, it was inevitable that the term 'traditionalism' should be used to describe its message and its members be called 'traditionalists'. If the traditionalists themselves have used the term cautiously this is doubtless because they do not see themselves as a 'school', nor the principles they affirm as constituting any kind of '-ism'.[3] Personal references are conspicuously absent from their work and one looks in vain for any kind of self-appellation.

It might be argued that 'perennial philosophers' would be an apposite designation for these thinkers. They are indeed perennial philosophers but, as will be shown in some detail, certain commentators have hastily and indiscreetly used this classification as an umbrella term to cover disparate individuals who do not belong together, thus generating more confusion than it is worth. The traditionalists themselves have been at some pains to disassociate their vision of the perennial philosophy from those divergent points of view with which traditionalism has been confused. However, there are signs that the traditionalist position has recently come to be somewhat better understood in that the current American term 'perennialism' refers specifically to the views of the traditionalists. Insofar as these writers would concede the need for some kind of generic label for their thought most would probably find 'traditionalism' the least unsatisfactory. It does have the merit of spotlighting one of the central conceptions in their work.

The basic contentions of this study are these: that there exists a coherent and unified school of thought which can be called 'traditionalism'; that the writings of the traditionalists represent a profound and challenging vision deserving more attention from those concerned with the deepest questions to which we can address ourselves; that traditionalism constitutes a militant and powerful critique of the modern Western *Weltanschauung*; and that it carries vital implications for the study of religion.

While this book is intended as an introduction to traditionalism as a whole, it focuses on the work of Frithjof Schuon whose *oeuvre* constitutes the most accomplished and inclusive expression of the traditionalist outlook. Frequent reference will, however, be made to the writings of all the major traditionalists, especially those of Guénon and Coomaraswamy. In the main we shall be more interested in ideas than in personalities but some account of the lives of the foremost figures is given in the opening chapters. The first chapter offers some remarks about the traditionalist attitude to biography. The reasons why this has been chosen as a starting point will be plain enough in the reading.

---

[1] This essay by that distinguished scholar from Sri Lanka first appeared in S. Radhakrishnan & J. H. Muirhead (eds) *Contemporary Indian Philosophy* Allen & Unwin, London, 1952, rev. ed., see pp158–159; it has recently been republished in A. K. Coomaraswamy *What is Civilisation? and Other Essays* Golgonooza Press, Ipswich, 1989; pp13–32. For some discussion of this essay see A. L. Herman: 'A. K. C. and the Pertinence of Philosophy' in SS *ACRR* pp84–93.
[2] RG *RQ* pp251–252.
[3] FS *LT* p6. See also SHN *K&S* p104.

I

The Traditionalists

1

The Traditionalist Attitude to Biography

Put on the mantle of nothingness, and drink of the cup of annihilation, then cover your breast with the belt of belittlement and put on your head the cloak of non-existence
Attar [1]

In a traditional civilisation, it is almost inconceivable that a man should lay claim to the possession of an idea
René Guénon [2]

Truth is not and cannot be a personal affair *Frithjof Schuon* [3]

... All that is true, by whomsoever spoken, is from the Holy Ghost *St Ambrose* [4]

In Porphyry's *Life of Plotinus* we are told that the sage resisted all attempts to unravel his personal history:

> ... he could never be induced to tell of his ancestry, his parentage or his birthplace. He showed too, an unconquerable reluctance to sit to a painter or a sculptor, and when Amelius persisted in urging him to allow of a portrait being made he asked him 'Is it not enough to carry about this image in which nature has enclosed us? Do you really think I must consent to leave, as a desirable spectacle to posterity, an image of the image?'[5]

The episode is instructive. We see in this anecdote not only an attitude everywhere to be found amongst the wise and the pious but also, at least implicitly, the principle which informs it. The outer person, the egoic self with all its attendant contingencies, is of no lasting significance. It is only the Inner Self which matters and which is not a mere 'image'. An aversion to any preoccupation with purely personal and temporal considerations is, of course, a characteristic mark of the mystic. It is sometimes thought that a predilection for anonymity and self-effacement is 'Eastern' or 'oriental'. The simple fact is that such an attitude is common amongst those of high spiritual attainment wherever they be found.

Discussing this outlook a recent commentator remarked that,

> To an age which believes in personality and personalism, the impersonality of the mystics is baffling; and to an age which is trying to quicken its insight into history the indifference of mystics to events in time is disconcerting.[6]

Between the spiritual posture exemplified by Plotinus and the modern European mania for biographical anecdotage lies a veritable abyss. This is not the place for a detailed inquiry into the development of that voracious appetite, scholarly and otherwise, for all manner of biographical literature. However, a few general remarks will serve as a backdrop against which to sketch out the traditionalist attitude.

One of the most potent factors affecting the history of the modern world has been a humanistic individualism, the seeds of which were germinated in the Renaissance. The erosion of traditional Christian values by the Renaissance, the Scientific Revolution, the so-called Enlightenment, and the materialist ideologies of the 19th century has been matched by a corresponding growth of a secularist worldview which has helped to promote what can properly be called a pseudo-cult of individualism. Several other developments have also stimulated an interest in mundane biography. Historicism in its various guises (Marxism, for instance) has sharpened our awareness of 'events in time' and emphasized the influence of our social environment. More recently psychologism – so called because its practitioners are more often than not

---

1 Farid Ud-Din Attar *The Conference of the Birds* ed. & tr. C.S. Nott, Shambala, Boulder, 1971; pp124–125. (I have substituted the words 'mantle' and 'cloak' for Nott's 'khirk' and 'burnous'.)
2 RG *CMW* pp52–53.
3 FS *LAW* p34.
4 St Ambrose, quoted in Letter to *The New English Weekly*, January 1946, AKC *SL* p108.
5 Porphyry's 'On the Life of Plotinus...' in Plotinus *The Enneads* Faber, London, 1960, tr S. Mackenna; p1.
6 A reviewer in *The Harvard Divinity School Bulletin* XXXIX, 1942; p107.

dealing in a kind of ideology rather than in science proper – has focused attention on the apparently unique experience of each individual person.

European thought since the Renaissance has also been increasingly dominated by a totalitarian scientism, one bereft of any metaphysical basis and operating outside the framework of religious tradition. The impact of this scientism, conspiring with the ideologies of industrial capitalism, has done nothing to check the rise of secular humanism and individualism – quite the contrary. The implications of these changes in the European ethos have been profound and far-reaching. They have everything to do with the modern fascination with biography.[7]

Part and parcel of this intellectual and cultural change is the triumph of empiricism and of a wholesale philosophical relativism. All phenomena are reduced to a level where they can be investigated empirically and are situated on the plane of the 'natural' or the 'cultural'. This trend is writ large over the pages of Europe's recent history, evidenced by such characteristically modern systems of thought as philosophical rationalism, positivism, dialectical materialism, existentialism and the like. We can see a somewhat paradoxical expression of it in Enlightenment theories of 'natural religion'.[8] A recurrent set of assumptions about 'reality', 'human nature' and 'knowledge', embedded in this ideational network, has infiltrated almost every academic discipline and shaped our modern modes of inquiry. Scientistic reductionism pervades comparative religion as much as any of the other humane disciplines that have been herded together as 'social sciences': the term itself exposes the kinds of assumptions under discussion. The interest in biography is intertwined with these changes in the European mentality and is linked with the habit of mind which might be called the 'relativising impulse'. In the biographical field this appears as the tendency to see whatever a person thinks or believes as no more than a function of social background and personal experience. Whilst this has often been a healthy corrective to culture-bound and ethnocentric views of 'reality' and 'normality', it has also seduced many minds into an all-embracing relativism. In castigating this outlook Schuon has written that it '. . . will not ask whether it be true that two and two make four, rather it will ask from what social background the man has come who declares such to be the case.'[9] In other words, questions about a more or less accidental background take precedence over questions of truth and falsity. Once the objective nature of truth is compromised and everything is seen through the spectacles of relativism, then, of course, such a tendency becomes inevitable.

Psychologism is one of the components of this relativism which has now penetrated the European mentality to such an extent that it is more or less 'invisible', so much is it taken for granted. The interest in biography has been consolidated by a psychologistic outlook which is less interested in *what* a person believes than in *why* they believe it. One of the symptoms of a rampant psychologism is what has been called the 'psycho-genetic fallacy', namely, the belief that to explain the psychological motivation for an idea is to explain the idea itself. Some thinkers of a psychologistic

---

7 Scientism will be discussed in more detail in Chapter 10 and some scholarly support for these claims elaborated.
8 For some discussion of these theories and their historical matrix see E.J. Sharpe: 'Universal Religion for Universal Man', *Charles Strong Memorial Lecture* 1978; reprinted from *Colloquium – Journal of the ANZSTS* (Australian and New Zealand Society of Theological Studies) Melbourne, 1978.
9 FS *L&T* p8.

bent make the even graver error of supposing that if an idea or belief correlates with some 'subconscious wish' then, *ipso facto*, this invalidates the idea as such. However, as Erich Fromm points out, 'Freud himself states that the fact that an idea satisfies a wish does not mean necessarily that the idea is false ... The criteria of validity does [sic] not lie in the psychological analysis of motivation ...'.[10] No one will deny that there is an intimate nexus between a person's spatio-temporal situation and his or her beliefs, attitudes, values, ideas and so on. Most of us are creatures of our environment, mentally as well as in other ways. The issue at stake here is this: is this *all* we are? The traditionalist attitude to biography suggests a decisively negative response to this kind of question. However, before turning to the traditionalists we should remind ourselves of another trend in modern European thought.

There are those people who, it seems, 'invent' or 'discover' 'new' ideas – Newton, Darwin, Freud or Einstein, to name a few from the 'pantheon' of modern science. Similarly in the world of the arts: Michelangelo, or Beethoven, or Tolstoy, we are told, was a creative 'genius', a special kind of individual. What so impresses us about such figures is that they seem to have fashioned, out of their own subjective resources, some new idea, some original art form, some fresh and startling perception of the world. Our adulation of such figures is fuelled by a passion for what is, often improperly, called 'originality' ('novelty' would sometimes be more apt). There is no gainsaying the fact that the subjective resources of, say, a Michelangelo were considerable indeed. It is the emphasis on subjectivity which is interesting and revealing. As Coomaraswamy remarked, 'Individualists and humanists as we are, we attach an inordinate value to personal opinion and personal experience, and feel an insatiable interest in the personal experience of others ...'.[11] Thus we tend to identify an idea or an art-form with the personality which apparently first gave it expression. This tendency issues from a humanistic individualism and has come to colour the way in which we understand 'ideas'. It is certainly no accident that the very notion of 'genius' (in the sense in which it is now understood) is largely a product of Renaissance humanism. Again, there are links with the interest in biography.

The cultural pedigree of this web of ideas and values which we have signalled in a kind of short-hand by terms like 'individualism', 'humanism' and 'scientism' need not concern us here. At present the point which needs to be clearly established is this: the interest in biography has grown in a distinctive climate of ideas. There is, on the other hand, an attitude to biography quite at odds with some of these trends; it is the attitude evinced by Plotinus. Before turning to the traditionalists and to some of the principles which sponsor a distaste for biography, a personal reminiscence might not be out of place.

A few years ago a friend had the privilege of looking after a Tibetan lama and of introducing him to a culture which, to him, was strange indeed. One of the phenomena which most astonished the lama was the European interest in biography. He was amazed to learn that quite ordinary people should write about their own lives and those of others, and that there should be a sizeable market for such personal histories. For him the only biography which could be of any possible value or interest was the life of a saint or sage, an exemplary life rather than one made up of the

---

10 E. Fromm *Psychoanalysis and Religion* Victor Gollancz, London, 1951; p20fn.
11 AKC *COPA* pp61–62.

'paraphernalia of irrelevant living'.[12] Coming from what was until recently one of the last bastions of an authentic traditional culture, the lama was expressing a point of view which nowhere would have seemed idiosyncratic until modern times.

Traditionalism as a whole is sharply antagonistic to the predominant trends in European thought since the Renaissance. This can be seen in microcosm in the attitude of the traditionalists to biography and in their related perception of 'ideas' and 'truth'. When pressed to write his autobiography Coomaraswamy replied:

> I must explain that I am not at all interested in biographical matter relating to myself and that I consider the *modern* practice of publishing details about the lives and personalities of well-known men is nothing but a vulgar catering to illegitimate curiosity ... All this is not a matter of modesty but of *principle*.[13]

It was the same principle which left Coomaraswamy indifferent to the question of copyright in his own works.[14] Plotinus has already introduced us to the principle at hand: the plane of the individual human ego, of the conditioned, subjective personality and of its doings in the world, is the plane of *māyā*, of ephemerality and flux, of impermanence. Insofar as a person is no more than a 'product' of this environment, they are as nothing in the face of Reality. Likewise, any ideas, or for that matter any art, which grows out of purely subjective and conditioned resources are of no lasting moment. The highest and most urgent purpose of life is to free oneself from the limiting contingencies of one's spatio-temporal situation and from the fetters of the ego, to liberate one's Self from one's self, so to speak, or as Coomaraswamy put it, to become no one.

In one form or another this lies close to the heart of all the great religious teachings. As R.D. Laing observed,

> In fact all religious ... philosophies have agreed that such egoic experience is a preliminary illusion, a veil, a film of *māyā* – a dream to Heraclitus, and to Lao-Tzu, the fundamental illusion of all Buddhism, a state of sleep, of death, of socially accepted madness, a womb state to which one has to die, from which one has to be born.[15]

Such, of course, is precisely the point of Christ's teaching about the corn of wheat,[16] of the Prophet's 'Die before ye die',[17] and of an inexhaustible wealth of spiritual maxims of like intent from all over the world. Black Elk, the revered Lakota holy-man, espoused the same principle when he said, in the inimitable idiom of the Plains Indians,

---

12 The phrase is borrowed from Patrick White's novel *The Twyborn Affair* Jonathan Cape, London, 1979; p386.
13 Letter to S. Durai Raja Singam, May 1946, AKC *SL* p25.
14 See comments by Doña Luisa Coomaraswamy quoted in W. Perry: 'The Man and the Witness' in *SS ACRR* p6. See also N. Krsnamurti: 'Ananda Coomaraswamy' in the same volume, p172, and W. Perry: 'Coomaraswamy: The Man, Myth and History' *SCR* XI, iii, 1977; p160.
15 R.D. Laing *The Politics of Experience* Penguin, 1967; p113.
16 *St John* XII.24–25.
17 Quoted in M. Lings *A Sufi Saint of the Twentieth Century* Uni of California Press, Berkeley, 1971, rev. ed.; p160.

René Guénon

> ...what is one man that he should make much of his winters, even when they bend him like a heavy snow? So many other men have lived and shall live that story, to be grass upon the hills.[18]

The lack of historically accurate biographies of the great saints and sages, especially in the East, has sometimes been regretted by scholars. Often we hear talk about 'a lack of a sense of history'. This is to see the issue only in negative terms. Frithjof Schuon has commented on this question with reference to two of the great Eastern traditions:

> What characterises Buddhism, as also Hinduism and every other comparable doctrine is precisely this, namely that it likes to express ... its consciousness of the 'mythological' character attaching to all formal data; and that is also why it hardly troubles to give its symbols any semblance of historicity, indeed quite the contrary; it sets out to awaken a presentiment of the great rending of the veil that is to come and it tries to suggest from beforehand that facts themselves are nothing but 'emptiness'.[19]

We cannot plumb the depths of the philosophical and metaphysical issues involved here but the contrast with the modern European obsession with history is marked enough.[20] From a traditionalist point of view this obsession with history and the vogue of private biography are nothing other than symptoms of disproportion in the modern outlook, especially when these are pursued, as they usually are, in the context of profane scholarship. They signify a preoccupation with the worldly and ephemeral and an indifference to ultimate ends. (The emphasis on a sacred history, as in the Judaic tradition, is another matter altogether).

Closely associated with this stance is a further principle of crucial importance. It concerns the nature of 'ideas', of 'truth', and of our relationship to truth. Guénon stated the principle in striking and unequivocal terms:

> ... if an idea is true it belongs equally to all those capable of understanding it; if it is false there is no reason to be proud of having thought it. A true idea cannot be 'new', since truth is not a product of the human mind; the truth exists independently of ourselves, and it is for us simply to comprehend it; outside of this knowledge there can be nothing but error...[21]

Here Guénon is speaking, of course, of the principial domain and not of the realm of material exactitudes. In one of his early books Schuon remarked that, '... it will be useless to look for anything "profoundly human" in this book ... for the simple reason that nothing human is profound ...'.[22] He was re-stating the same principle.

The same principle of the independence and non-personal nature of truth is nothing new, being repeatedly affirmed within the religious traditions. Something of the traditionalist attitude to truth is anticipated in a passage such as this, from an early Buddhist Scripture:

---

18 J. Neihardt (ed) *Black Elk Speaks* Abacus, London, 1974; p13.
19 FS *ITB* p110. See also FS *GDW* pp20-23, 42.
20 For some discussion of the traditional Indian attitude to biography see Swami Tapasyananda's 'Introduction' to Madhava-Vidyaranya's *The Traditional Life of Sri Sankaracharya* Ramakrishna Math, Madras, 1978.
21 RG *CMW* p53.
22 FS *TUR* p15. Taken from the first English edition, Faber, London, 1953. (The passage was omitted from the revised edition of 1975.)

> Whether Buddhas arise, O monks, or whether Buddhas do not arise, it remains a fact and the fixed and necessary constitution of being, that all its constituents are transitory. This fact a Buddha discovers and masters, and when he has discovered and mastered it, he announces, teaches, publishes, proclaims, discloses, minutely explains, and makes it clear.[23]

We might compare this with the following passage from Coomaraswamy:

> There can be no property in ideas. The Individual does not make them but FINDS THEM; let him see to it that he really takes possession of them, and work will be original in the same sense that the recurrent seasons, sunset and sunrise are ever anew although in name the same.[24]

This is the only kind of 'originality' in which the traditionalists are interested.

The traditionalist disposition is also governed by certain moral and spiritual values, humility not the least of them. We might profitably pause to ponder the implications of a more or less random sample of maxims which affirm another one of the principles informing the traditionalist tendency to self-effacement.

> A man may receive nothing except it be given him from heaven. *St John*[25]

> ... no creature, howsoever rational and intellectual, is lighted of itself, but is lighted by the participation of eternal Truth. *St Augustine*[26]

> Outward existence can perform no act of itself; its acts are those of its Lord immanent in it. *Ibn 'Arabī*[27]

> ... no good thing can be done by man alone .... *Black Elk*[28]

Nothing could be further from the spirit of a humanistic individualism. We are free to take such teachings seriously or not, but in their light one begins to understand the moral dimension of the practice of anonymity in the eyes of the world. What Coomaraswamy called 'the invisibility proper to the complete philosopher'[29] is anchored in the virtue of humility, one which Schuon describes as 'as a state of emptiness in which our thoughts and actions appear as strangers to us'.[30]

Today the traditionalist posture – the distaste for personal biography, the affirmation of the non-personal nature of truth, the immunity to self-publicising, the refusal to identity ideas as one's 'own' – is far from common. Nevertheless, there remain those who resist all attempts to identify the ideas to which they give expression with themselves as individual persons, refusing to participate in a kind of 'capitalism' of ideas where these are seen as the 'creation' and 'property' of this or that thinker.

---

23 From *Anguttara Nikāya* III.134. Can one imagine the Buddha claiming that this ideas was 'his'? The notion is absurd.
24 Quoted in N. Krsnamurti *op.cit.*; p172. On his own role Coomaraswamy wrote, 'I regard the truth ... as a matter of certainty, not of opinion. I am never expressing an opinion or any personal view, but an orthodox one.' Letter to George Sarton, November 1934, AKC *SL* p31.
25 III.27.
26 per WP *TTW* p276.
27 per WP *TTW* p341.
28 in J. Neihardt *op.cit.*; p13.
29 in SS *ACRR* p223.
30 FS *SPHF* p198. See also p137.

(The copyright laws are, after all, not so different from those regulating patents!) Sarvepalli Radhakrishnan, explaining to his editor his reluctance to make public details of his private life, wrote '... there is a sense in which our writings, though born out of ourselves, are worth more than what we are.'[31] Thomas Merton disclaimed any 'originality' in his work, writing of one of his books, 'We sincerely hope that it does not contain a line that is new to Christian tradition.'[32] These remarks share something with the traditionalist position.

Traditionalists like Guénon and Coomaraswamy were quite unconcerned with any aspiration towards a personal 'creativity' or 'originality' in the sense in which these words are now understood. Their purpose was the re-expression of the *sophia perennis*, the timeless wisdom which is everywhere and always the same but which, according to the exigencies of the age, can be expressed anew in such a way as to bring humankind back to the truths it enshrines and the spiritual path which its realisation entails.

We can see, then, that the traditionalist attitude to biography is only one thread in a whole fabric of ideas and values. It is interwoven with principles and values concerning the nature of the human situation, truth, knowledge, the role of ideas and the traditionalists' view of their own function as writers. Any kind of 'intellectual individualism', if one might so put it, is out of the question. Thus Coomaraswamy, for instance, abjures any suggestion that he is propounding his own ideas:

> I am not a reformer or propagandist. I don't think for myself ... I am not putting forward any new or private doctrines or interpretations ... For me there are certain axioms, principles or values beyond question; my interest is not in thinking up new ones, but in the application of those that are.[33]

In other words, it is a matter of being a vehicle for the expression of ideas which belong to everyone and therefore to no one.

Already we can also see that traditionalism is antipathetic to what might loosely be called the spirit of modern European thought. Many of the antagonisms which have only been touched on in this introductory chapter will be thrown into sharper relief later in this study. In the context of the principles which have been adumbrated in this initial discussion we can now turn to the three most important figures of the traditionalist movement.

---

31 Letter to P.A. Schilpp, reproduced in P.A. Schilpp (ed) *The Philosophy of Radhakrishnan* Tudor, New York, 1972; p4.
32 T. Merton *New Seeds of Contemplation* New Directions, New York, 1972; pxiv.
33 Quoted in Rama P. Coomaraswamy 'Who speaks for the East?', *SCR* XI, ii, 1977. See also letter to Herman Goetz, AKC *SL* p33. and his remarks in 'The Seventieth Birthday Address', AKC *SPII* p434: '... the greatest thing I have learned is never to think for myself ... what I have sought is to understand what has been said, while taking no account of the "inferior philosophers".'

2
René Guénon

...there are those whose vocation it is to provide the keys with which the treasury of wisdom of other traditions can be unlocked, revealing to those who are destined to receive this wisdom the essential unity and universality and at the same the formal diversity of tradition and revelation
Seyyed Hossein Nasr[1]

In keeping with the principles discussed in the previous chapter, Ananda Coomaraswamy wrote that

> ... the least important thing about Guénon is his personality or biography ... The fact is he has the invisibility that is proper to the complete philosopher: our teleology can only be fulfilled when we really become no one.[2]

The American traditionalist, Whitall Perry, who knew Guénon personally, speaks of his 'outer anonymity' and of this 'austere yet benevolent figure ... ungraspable and remote'.[3] There is indeed something elusive and enigmatic about René Guénon the man. He left a formidable legacy of writings which testify to his achievements as a metaphysician but his personal life remains shrouded in obscurity. In France he has always commanded a small but dedicated following and academic interest in Guénon shows some sign of burgeoning there.[4] Elsewhere he remains a shadowy figure whose name occasionally crops up in reference to French occultism or his pioneering study (in the West) of *Advaita* Vedanta. The growing interest in Guénon has generated no small amount of controversy amongst French scholars about some aspects of his life, especially in the years from 1906 to 1912.[5] Here we shall confine ourselves to a biographical sketch which leaves aside some of these unresolved questions and includes only such material for which there appears to be persuasive evidence and reputable authority.[6] Furthermore, we shall only be interested in those aspects of his life which might shed light on his work.

René Guénon was born in Blois in 1886. He grew up in a strict Catholic environment and was schooled by Jesuits. As a young man he moved to Paris to take up studies in mathematics at the Collège Rollin. Maths remained a lifelong interest and a few years before his death he published a short mathematical treatise, *Les principes du calcul infinitésimal*. However, his energies were soon diverted from academic studies and in 1905 he abandoned his preparation for *Grandes Écoles*. For the next seven years, seized by what Anatole France called 'the vertigo of the invisible', Guénon submerged himself in *fin-de-siècle* French occultism.[7] He became a leading member in several secret societies – theosophical, spiritualistic, masonic and 'gnostic'.

Guénon's involvement in the occultist underground seems to have been somewhat indiscriminate. From the vantage-point of his later work it was a murky and bizarre period in his life, one of which he apparently did not care to be reminded. Neverthe-

---

1   S.H. Nasr *Sufi Essays* Allen & Unwin, London, 1972; p126.
2   Letter to Kurt Leidecker, November 1941, AKC *SL* pp49–50.
3   W. Perry: 'Coomaraswamy: the Man, Myth and History' *SCR* XI, iii,1977; p160 and 'The Man and the Witness' in SS *ACRR* p6.
4   See two reviews of some of the literature in *SCR* VII, iv, 1978; pp472–475.
5   Some of these controversies have been dispassionately discussed in J.P. Laurant: 'Le problème de René Guénon, ou Quelques questions posées par les rapports de sa vie et de son oeuvre' *Revue de l'Histoire des religions* CLXXIX, i, 1971; pp41–70.
6   The only English-language biography is R. Waterfield *René Guénon and the Future of the West* Crucible, London, 1987.
7   France's phrase is cited in M. Eliade: 'The Occult and the Modern World' in *Occultism, Witchcraft and Cultural Fashions* Uni of Chicago, 1976; p51.

less, Guénon learned a good deal in this period and indeed, he was eventually to become one of the most unsparing critics of these occultists movements.

In the context of the present study it is not necessary to unravel all the details of Guénon's participation in various secret societies. However, it is worth pausing to reflect on the significance of this period in his life. In its sociological dimension occultism provided, as doubtless it still does, a framework for the repudiation of the bourgeois ideologies and institutions of the day. Most of the occult groups turned to the archaic past in search of authentic spiritual values against which modern civilisation was measured and found wanting. As Mircea Eliade has observed,

> ... involvement with the occult represented for the French literary and artistic avant-garde one of the most efficient criticisms and rejections of the religious and cultural values of the West – efficient because it was considered to be based on historical facts.[8]

Although Guénon was to disown the philosophical and historical assumptions on which such movements were built and to contrast their 'counterfeit spirituality' with what he came to see as genuine expressions of esotericism, as a traditionalist he remained steadfastly opposed to contemporary European civilisation.

Some of the occult movements stimulated a study of ancient esoteric traditions in Egypt, Persia, India and China, and directed attention towards the sacred writings of the East. Precisely how Guénon came to a serious study of Taoism, Hinduism and Islam remains unclear but it seems likely that it was through his involvement in one of the occultist groups. Whitall Perry has suggested that the 'catalyzing element' was Guénon's contact in Paris with some Indians of the *Advaita* school.[9] The facts of the matter are far from clear and there is insufficient evidence to make speculation fruitful. Guénon always kept a cloak of secrecy tightly wrapped around his own spiritual life.

In June 1909, Guénon founded the occultist journal *La Gnose*, subtitled '*organe de l'Eglise gnostique universelle*'. It lasted a little over two years and carried most of his writings from this period which, although they exhibit some rationalistic and anti-religious bias, demonstrate a familiarity with Vedanta.

It can be said that Guénon's life certainly entered a new phase in 1912, one marked by his marriage to a devout Catholic. He emerged from the rather subterranean world of the occultists and now moved freely in an intensely Catholic milieu, leading a busy social and intellectual life. He was influenced by several prominent Catholic intellectuals of the day, among then Jacques Maritain, Fathers Peilleaube and Sertillanges, and one M. Milhaud who conducted classes at the Sorbonne on the philosophy of science. The years 1912 to 1930 were the most public of Guénon's life. He attended lectures at the Sorbonne, wrote and published widely, gave public lectures himself and maintained many social and intellectual contacts. He published his first books in the 1920s and soon became well known for his work on philosophical and metaphysical subjects.

Whatever Guénon's personal commitments may have been during this period his thought had clearly undergone a major shift away from occultism towards an interest

---

8   M. Eliade: *op.cit.*; p53.
9   W. Perry: 'The Revival of Interest in Tradition' in RF *UT* pp8–9.

in sapiential traditions within the framework of the great religions. One of the foci of interest for Guénon was the possibility of a Christian esotericism within the Catholic tradition. (He always remained somewhat ignorant of the esoteric dimensions of Eastern Orthodoxy.[10]) Olivier de Fremond, a friend of those years, wrote of Guénon's letters from this period, '*Les vieilles lettres que j'ai de lui respirent un parfait esprit catholique.*'[11] Guénon envisaged, in some of his work in this period, a regenerated Catholicism, enriched and invigorated by a recovery of her esoteric traditions and 'repaired' through a *prise de conscience*[12]. He contributed regularly to the Catholic journal *Regnabit*, the Sacré-Coeur review founded and edited by P. Anizan. These articles reveal the re-orientation of Guénon's thinking in which 'tradition' now becomes the controlling theme. Some of these periodical writings found their way into his later books.

The years 1927 to 1930 mark another transition in Guénon's life, culminating in his move to Cairo in 1930 and his open commitment to Islam. A conflict between Anizan (whom Guénon supported) and the Archbishop of Rheims, and adverse Catholic criticism of his book *Le roi du monde* (1927) compounded a growing disillusionment with the Church and hardened Guénon's suspicion that it had surrendered to the 'temporal and material'. In January 1928 Guénon's wife died rather abruptly. Following a series of fortuitous circumstances Guénon left on a three month visit to Cairo.[13] He was to remain there until his death in 1951.

In Cairo Guénon was initiated into the Sufic order of Shadilites and invested with the name Abdel Wahed Yahya. He married again and lived a modest and retiring existence.

> . . . such was his anonymity that an admirer of his writings was dumbfounded to discover that the venerable next door neighbour whom she had known for years as Sheikh Abdel Wahed Yahya was in reality René Guénon.[14]

A good deal of Guénon's energies were directed in the 1930s to a massive correspondence he carried on with his readers in Europe, often people in search of some kind of initiation, others simply pressing inquiries about subjects dealt with in Guénon's books and articles. Most of Guénon's published work after his move to Cairo appeared in *Études Traditionnelles* (until 1937 *Le Voile d'Isis*), a formerly theosophical journal which under Guénon's influence was transformed into the principal European forum for traditionalist thought.[15] It was only the war which provided Guénon with enough respite from his correspondence to devote himself to the writing of some of his major works including *The Reign of Quantity* (1945).

In his later years Guénon was much preoccupied with questions concerning initiation into authentic esoteric traditions. He published at least twenty-five articles

---

10 Guénon's view of Christianity has been discussed in P.L. Reynolds *René Guénon: His Life and Work* (unpublished) pp9ff. See also B. Kelly: 'Notes on the Light of the Eastern Religions' in *RH* pp160–161.
11 Quoted in J.P. Laurant: 'Le problème . . .' p57. (Trans: 'These old letters I have from him breathe a perfect Catholic spirit.')
12 *ibid.*; pp57–59. See RG *CMW* pp95–96.
13 J.P. Laurant: 'Le problème . . .' p60.
14 W. Perry: 'Coomaraswamy' p160.
15 See Chapter 5.

in *Études Traditionnelles* dealing with this subject from many different angles. Although he had found his own resting-place within the fold of Islam, Guénon remained interested in the possibility of genuine initiatic channels surviving within Christianity. He also never entirely relinquished his interest in Freemasonry and returned to this subject in some of his last writings. It was only shortly before his death that he concluded there was no effective hope of an esoteric regeneration within either masonry or Catholicism.[16]

The relationship between Guénon's life and his work has engaged the attention of several scholars. Jean-Pierre Laurant has suggested that his intellectual, spiritual and ritual life only achieved a harmonious resolution after his move to Cairo and within the protective embrace of Islam.[17] P.L. Reynolds has charted the influence of his French and Catholic background on his work.[18] Others, especially those committed to traditionalism themselves, have argued that Guénon's whole adult life represents a witness to an unchanging vision of the truth and that his participation in occultism was part of this function. Such commentators suggest that his thought does not 'evolve' but only shifts ground as Guénon responds to changing circumstances. Thus Michel Valsan, a collaborator on *Études Traditionnelles*, writes:

> *Il convient de préciser en l'occurrence que le privilège spécial qu'a cette oeuvre de jouer le rôle de critère de vérité, de régularité et de plénitude traditionnelle devant la civilisation occidentale dérive du caractère sacré et non-individuel qu'a revêtu la fonction de René Guénon. L'homme qui devait accomplir cette fonction fut certainement préparé de loin et non pas improvisé. Les matrices de la Sagesse avaient prédisposé et formé son entité selon une économie précise, et sa carrière s'accomplit dans le temps par une corrélation constante entre ses possibilités et les conditions cycliques extérieures.*[19]

Each of these kinds of claims carries some legitimacy. The shaping influence of his own background and period is obvious enough in his work. Nor is there any point in denying that, looked at as a whole, Guénon's thought does undergo a radical change between about 1910 and 1914. While much of his early work remains interesting and often illuminating it cannot be said to represent a strictly traditionalist view such as we find in his later works. Given Guénon's education and background he could not have come to a traditionalist understanding without passing through a period in which he would learn to shed some modernistic (which is to say, anti-traditional) views and assumptions. To borrow one of his own favourite images, his early work is not without fissures which left it vulnerable to some of the more fanciful theories of the occultists. However, if we leave aside a few jejune writings from these early years, Guénon's work does exhibit an arresting consistency, an apparently intuitive grasp of metaphysical and cosmological principles and an authoritative

---

16 Discussed in J.P. Laurant's article.
17 J.P. Laurant: *op.cit.*; pp66–69.
18 P.L. Reynolds: *op.cit.; passim*. These influences, Reynolds argues, account for various imbalances and inadvertencies in Guénon's work.
19 M. Valsan in the Special Issue of *Études Traditionnelles: Le Sort de l'Occident*, Nov 1951. (Trans: It is useful to clarify in the present case that the special privilege of truth which belongs to this work of playing the role of truth, regularity and traditional plenitude in the face of Western civilisation derives from the sacred and non-individual character that clothed the function of René Guénon. The man who had to accomplish this function would certainly have been prepared from long ago rather than improvising [his role]. The matrices of Wisdom had predisposed and formed his being according to a precise economy, and his career fulfilled itself in time by a constant correlation between his possibilities and the exterior cyclic conditions [of the age].)

explication of the *sophia perennis*. One commentator has observed that after the occultist period Guénon only revised his position on two substantial issues: the authenticity of Buddhism as an integral tradition and the initiatic possibilities of freemasonry.[20] If we add to this his changing attitude to the revival of Christian esotericism we have indeed catalogued all the radical revisions in Guénon's work in almost forty years. We shall return to this aspect of Guénon's achievement in discussing his own perception of the role he had to play.

Guénon was a prolific writer. He published seventeen books during his lifetime, and at least eight posthumous collections and compilations have since appeared. Here we shall take only an overview of his work. The *oeuvre* exhibits certain recurrent motifs and preoccupations and is, in a sense, all of a piece. Guénon's understanding of tradition is the key to his work. As early as 1909 we find Guénon writing of '... the Primordial Tradition which, in reality, is the same everywhere, regardless of the different shapes it takes in order to be fit for every race and every historical period.'[21] As the English traditionalist, Gai Eaton, has observed, Guénon

> believes that there exists a Universal Tradition, revealed to humanity at the beginning of the present cycle of time, but partially lost ... his primary concern is less with the detailed forms of this Tradition and the history of its decline than with its kernel, the pure and changeless knowledge which is still accessible to man through the channels provided by traditional doctrine ...[22]

The existence of a Primordial Tradition embodying a set of immutable metaphysical and cosmological principles from which derive a succession of traditions each expressing these principles in forms determined by a given Revelation and by the exigencies of the particular situation, is axiomatic in Guénon's work.[23] It is a first principle which admits of no argument; nor does it require any kind of 'proof' or 'demonstration', historical or otherwise.

Guénon's work, from his earliest writings in 1909 onwards, can be seen as an attempt to give a new expression and application to the timeless principles which inform all traditional doctrines. In his writings he ranges over a vast terrain – Vedanta, the Chinese tradition, Christianity, Sufism, folklore and mythology from all over the world, the secret traditions of gnosticism, alchemy, the Kabbalah, and so on, always intent on excavating their underlying principles and showing them to be formal manifestations of the one Primordial Tradition. Certain key themes run through all of his writings and one meets again and again with such notions as these: the concept of metaphysics transcending all other doctrinal orders; the identification of metaphysics and the 'formalisation', so to speak, of gnosis (or *jñāna* if one prefers); the distinction between the exoteric and esoteric domains; the hierarchic superiority

---

20 M. Bastriocchi: 'The Last Pillars of Wisdom' in SS *ACRR* p359, fn8. Seyyed Hossein Nasr writes of the lack of 'development' in Guénon's work that it was 'as if he had written them all [his books] at one sitting and then published them over the next few decades.' SHN *K&S* p101.
21 R. Guénon: 'La Demiurge' *La Gnose* 1909; per M. Bastriocchi: *op.cit.*; p351.
22 G. Eaton *The Richest Vein* Faber & Faber, London, 1949; pp188–189.
23 The relationship between the Primordial Tradition and the various traditions needs clarification in that while each tradition in fact derives its overall form and principal characteristics from a particular Revelation, it nevertheless carries over (in many of its aspects) certain essential features of the tradition which precedes it.

and infallibility of intellective knowledge; the contrast of the modern Occident with the traditional Orient; the spiritual bankruptcy of modern European civilisation; a cyclical view of Time, based largely on the Hindu doctrine of cosmic cycles; a contra-evolutionary view of history. Many of these key ideas will be explored in greater detail later in this study, especially as they have found expression in the work of Frithjof Schuon. Here we shall confine ourselves to a few general remarks and to a brief look at the Guénonian corpus.

Guénon gathered together doctrines and principles from diverse times and places but emphasized that the enterprise was a synthetic one which envisaged formally divergent elements in their principial unity rather than a syncretic one which press-ganged incongruous forms into an artificial unity. This distinction is a crucial one not only in Guénon's work but in traditionalism as a whole.[24]

Guénon repeatedly turned to oriental wisdoms, believing that it was only in the East that various sapiential traditions remained more or less intact. It is important not to confuse this Eastward-looking stance with the kind of sentimental exoticism nowadays so much in vogue. As Coomaraswamy noted,

> If Guénon wants the West to turn to Eastern metaphysics, it is not because they are Eastern but because this is metaphysics. If 'Eastern' metaphysics differed from a 'Western' metaphysics – one or the other would not be metaphysics.[25]

One of Guénon's translators made the same point in suggesting that if Guénon turns so often to the East it is because the West is in the position of the

> foolish virgins who, through the wandering of their attention in other directions, had allowed their lamps to go out; in order to rekindle the sacred fire, which in its essence is always the same wherever it may be burning, they must have recourse to the lamps still kept alight.[26]

The contrast between the riches of traditional civilisations and the spiritual impoverishment of modern Europe sounds like a refrain through Guénon's writings. In all his work

> Guénon's mission was twofold: to reveal the metaphysical roots of the 'crisis of the modern world' and to explain the ideas behind the authentic and esoteric teachings that still remained alive ... in the East.[27]

By way of an expedient we can divide Guénon's writings into five categories, each corresponding roughly with a particular period in his life: the occultist periodical writings of the pre-1912 period; the reaction against and critique of occultism, especially spiritualism and theosophy; writings on Oriental metaphysics; on aspects of the European tradition and on initiation; and, fifthly, the critique of modern civilisation. This is a rather arbitrary classification but it does help to identify some of the focal points in Guénon's work.

---

24 See R. Guénon *The Symbolism of the Cross* Luzac, London, 1958; pp. x-xi and RG *CMW* p9 & pp108ff.
25 Coomaraswamy in 'Eastern Wisdom and Western Knowledge', AKC *BL* pp72-73.
26 Quoted in Gai Eaton *op.cit.*; p199.
27 Jacob Needleman in his 'Foreword' to JN *SG* pp11-12.

Guénon's earliest writings appeared, as we have seen, in the organs of French occultism. In the light of his later work some of this periodical literature must be considered somewhat ephemeral. Nonetheless the seeds of most of Guénon's work can be found in articles from this period. The most significant, perhaps, were five essays which appeared in *La Gnose* between September 1911 and February 1912, under the title '*La constitution de l'être humain et son évolution selon le Védânta*'; these became the opening chapters of one of his most influential studies, *Man and His Becoming According to the Vedanta*, not published until 1925. Other writings from this period on such subjects as mathematics and the science of numbers, prayer and incantation, and initiation, all presage later work.

The shift in Guénon's intellectual orientation away from occultism is difficult to pinpoint precisely. However, as early as 1909 we find him attacking what he saw as the misconceptions and confusions abroad in the spiritualist movements.[28] Whilst his misgivings about many of the occultist groups were growing in the 1909–1912 period it was not until the publication of two of his earliest books that he mounted a full-scale critique: *Le théosophisme, histoire d'une pseudo religion* (1921) and *L'erreur spirite* (1923). The titles are suggestive: these were lacerating attacks not only on theosophy and spiritualism but also on the 'gnostic' groups founded by a certain Dr. Encausse (who achieved some celebrity as 'Papus'), and on movements such as Rosicrucianism. Guénon's exposé was not merely a polemical fusillade but a meticulously detailed analysis. Of the groups in which Guénon himself had been involved only the Masons escaped relatively unscathed. As Eliade has noted:

> The most erudite and devastating critique of all these so-called occult groups was presented not by a rationalist outside observer, but by an author from the inner circle, duly initiated into some of their secret orders and well acquainted with their occult doctrines; furthermore, that critique was directed, not from a sceptical or positivistic perspective, but from what he called 'traditional esotericism'. This learned and intransigent critic was René Guénon.[29]

The details of this demolition job need not concern us here but it is worth noting the main lines of Guénon's attack. The most fundamental part of Guénon's indictment was that such movements, far from preserving traditional esotericisms, were made up of a syncretic mish-mash of distorted and heterogeneous elements forced into a false unity, devoid of any authentic metaphysical framework. Thus they were vulnerable to the scientistic ideologies of the day and inevitably fell prey to the intellectual confusions rampant in Europe. One of the most characteristic confusions of such groups, to cite but one example, was the mistaking of the psychic for the spiritual.[30] Occultism as a whole he now saw as one of the 'signs of the times', a symptom of the spiritual malaise in modern civilisation. Guénon took up some of these charges again in later works, especially *The Reign of Quantity*.

Guénon's interest in Eastern metaphysical traditions had been awakened some time around 1909 and some of his early articles in *La Gnose* are devoted to Vedantic metaphysics. His first book, *Introduction générale à l'étude des doctrines hindoues* (1921)

---

28 R. Guénon: 'La Gnose et les Ecoles Spiritualistes', *LA GNOSE* December, 1909. See also P. Charconac: 'La vie simple de René Guénon' in the Special Issue of *ÉTUDES TRADITIONNELLES*, Nov. 1951; p321 and P.L. Reynolds: *op.cit.*; p3.
29 M. Eliade: *op.cit.*; p51.
30 For more detailed discussion on this see Ch. 10.

marked Guénon as a commentator of rare authority. It also served notice of Guénon's role as a redoubtable critic of contemporary civilisation. Of this book Seyyed Hossein Nasr has written,

> It was like a sudden burst of lightning, an abrupt intrusion into the modern world of a body of knowledge and a perspective utterly alien to the prevalent climate and world view and completely opposed to all that characterizes the modern mentality.[31]

However, Guénon's axial work on Vedanta was published in 1925, *L'homme et son devenir selon le Védânta*. Other significant works in the field of oriental traditions include *La métaphysique orientale*, delivered as a lecture at the Sorbonne in 1925 but not published until 1939, *La Grande Triade*, based on Taoist doctrine, and many articles on such subjects as Hindu mythology, Taoism and Confucianism, and doctrines concerning reincarnation. Interestingly, Guénon remained more or less ignorant of the Buddhist tradition for many years, regarding it as no more than a 'heterodox development' within Hinduism and without integrity as a formal religious tradition. It was only through the intervention of Marco Pallis, one of his translators, and Ananda Coomaraswamy, that Guénon revised his attitude to Buddhism.[32]

During the 1920s when Guénon was moving in the coteries of French Catholicism he turned his attention to some aspects of Europe's spiritual heritage. As well as numerous articles on such subjects as the Druids, the Grail, Christian symbolism and folkloric motifs, Guénon produced several major works in this field, including *L'esotérisme de Dante* (1925), *St Bernard* (1929), and *Le symbolisme de la croix* (1931). Another work, *Autorité spirituelle et pouvoir temporel* (1929), was occasioned by certain contemporary controversies. A collection of Guénon's writings on symbolism has recently appeared in English translation for the first time under the title *Fundamental Symbols of Sacred Science* (1995). The quintessential Guénon is to be found in two works which tied together some of his central themes: *La crise du monde moderne* (1927) and his masterpiece, *Le règne de la quantité et les signes des temps* (1945). The themes of these two books had been rehearsed in an earlier work, *Orient et Occident* (1924). Each of these books mounted an increasingly elaborate and merciless attack on the foundations of the contemporary European worldview. We shall turn to the last of these works in some detail.

The Reign of Quantity is a magisterial summation of Guénon's work. It is, characteristically, a difficult work. He was quite unconcerned with reaching a wide audience and addressed the book to those few capable of understanding it 'without any concern for the inevitable incomprehension of the others'.[33] He set out to challenge nearly all of the intellectual assumptions current in Europe at the time. The book, he writes, is directed to

> ... the understanding of some of the darkest enigmas of the modern world, enigmas which the

---

31 SHN *K&S* p101

32 This change in Guénon's attitude has been documented and discussed by several commentators. See Marco Pallis: Letter to the Editor, *SCR* VII, iv; p73; K.E. Steffens: Letter to the Editor, *SCR* XI, ii, 1977; pp116–117; J.M. Murray: Letter to the Editor, *SCR* XI, ii, 1977; pp191–192; W.Perry: 'The Man and the Witness' in SS *ACRR* p5 ;and M.Pallis: 'A Fateful Meeting of Minds: A.K. Coomaraswamy and René Guénon', *SCR* XII, iii & iv, 1978; pp180–181.

33 RG *RQ* p11.

world itself denies because it is incapable of perceiving them although it carries them within itself, and because this denial is an indispensable condition for the maintenance of the special mentality whereby it exists.[34]

At first sight the book ranges over a bewildering variety of subjects: the nature of time, space and matter as conceived in traditional and modern science; the philosophical foundations of such typically modern modes of thought as rationalism, materialism and empiricism; the significance of ancient crafts such as metallurgy; the nature of shamanism and sorcery; the 'illusion of statistics'; the 'misdeeds of psychoanalysis'; the 'pseudo-initiatic' pretensions of spiritualism, theosophy and other 'counterfeit' forms of spirituality; tradition and anti-tradition; the unfolding of cosmic and terrestrial cycles. Some study of the book reveals that these apparently disparate strands have been woven into a work of subtle design and dense texture. *The Reign of Quantity* is a brilliantly sustained and excoriating attack on modern civilisation. It has less polemical heat and moral indignation than some of his earlier works but is none the less effective for that. The book is a controlled and dispassionate but devastating razing of the assumptions and values of modern science. At the same time it is an affirmation of the metaphysical and cosmological principles given expression in traditional cultures and religions.

Guénon unfolds a startling thesis concerning the present terrestrial situation in the light of the doctrine of cosmic cycles. His vision is rooted in the Hindu conception of the *Kali-Yuga* but is not restricted to the purely Indian expression of this doctrine. There is a dark apocalyptic strain in the book which some readers are tempted to dismiss as the rantings of another doom-sayer. For Guénon the dire circumstances in which the modern world finds itself are largely to be explained through an elucidation of the cyclic doctrine whereby humankind is seen to be degenerating into an increasingly solidified and materialised state, more and more impervious to spiritual influences. Inversely, the world becomes increasingly susceptible to infernal forces of various kinds.[35] The forced convergence of different civilisations is the spatial correlate of the temporal unfolding of the present terrestrial cycle, moving towards an inexorable cataclysm.

Guénon took the inevitable end of the world absolutely seriously.[36] By the time of writing this book he believed there were no possible 'remedies', no escape from the apocalypse. To some readers this looks like a 'despairing pessimism' to which Guénon might have retorted that neither optimism nor pessimism had anything to do with the case. Moreover, what from one angle might be seen as a 'worldly pessimism', appears from another as a 'celestial optimism' since the end of a cycle marks its completion and the restoration of a true order.

Closely related to the doctrine of cycles is Guénon's profoundly challenging thesis about the nature of time, space and matter, one based on traditional cosmologies. Contrary to the claims of modern science, says Guénon, time and space do not constitute a kind of uniform continuum in the matrix of which events and material

---

34 *ibid.*
35 Herein, from the traditionalist viewpoint, lies the explanation for the modern excrescence of what Dr. Christopher Evans has called 'cults of unreason' – scientology, UFO-ism, Lobsang Rampa-ism and so on. See C. Evans *Cults of Unreason* Harrap, London, 1973 and J. Webb/*The Flight from the Rational* Macdonald, London, 1971.
36 See J.P. Laurant: *op.cit.;* p58.

phenomena manifest themselves. Rather, time-and-space is a field of *qualitative* determinations and differences. In other words, the nature of time and space is not a constant, fixed datum but is subject to both quantitative and qualitative change. Any exclusively quantitative and materialistic science such as now tyrannises the European mind cannot accommodate this principle. It strives rather to reduce qualitatively determined phenomena to the barren and mechanistic formulae of a profane system. (One might add that some of the 'discoveries' of physicists since Guénon's time have done nothing to disprove his thesis; indeed, to some minds, they give it more credibility. Guénon himself would have argued that metaphysical and cosmological principles such as he was applying could in no way be affected by empirical considerations.[37])

Guénon's critique of scientism – the ideology of modern science – is something quite other than just another attack on scientific reductionism, although that surely is part of his case. Nor is it a catalogue of the inadequacies of this or that scientific theory. Rather, it is a radical and disturbing challenge to almost every postulate of modern European science. The critique hinges on the contrast between sacred, traditional sciences on the one hand, and a profane, materialistic science on the other. In an earlier work Guénon had elaborated the basis of this contrast in uncompromising terms:

> Never until the present epoch had the study of the sensible world been regarded as self-sufficient; never would the science of this ephemeral and changing multiplicity have been judged truly worthy of the name of knowledge ... According to the ancient conception ... a science was less esteemed for itself than for the degree in which it expressed after its own fashion ... a reflection of the higher immutable truth of which everything of any reality necessarily partakes ... all science appeared as an extension of the traditional doctrine itself, as one of its applications, secondary and contingent no doubt ... but still a veritable knowledge none the less ...[38]

For Guénon and the other traditionalists, the notion of a self-sufficient, self-validating, autonomous material science is a contradiction, an incongruity, for all sciences must have recourse to higher and immutable principles and truths. Science must be pursued in a metaphysical and cosmological framework which it cannot construct out of itself. In another work Guénon wrote that modern science,

> in disavowing the principles [of traditional metaphysics and cosmology] and in refusing to re-attach itself to them, robs itself both of the highest guarantee and the surest direction it could have; there is no longer anything valid in it except knowledge of details, and as soon as it seeks to rise one degree higher, it becomes dubious and vacillating.[39]

---

37 For some discussion of the 'fissures' in modern science see J. Needleman *A Sense of the Cosmos* Doubleday, New York, 1975 and T. Roszak *Where the Wasteland Ends* Doubleday, New York, 1972. For a traditionalist critique which follows on from Guénon see Section 1 of T. Burckhardt *Mirror of the Intellect* Quinta Essentia, Cambridge, 1987/SUNY, Albany, 1987. On the 'new physics' see F. Capra *The Tao of Physics* Fontana, London, 1976. See also SHN *K&S* pp114ff, Wolfgang Smith *Cosmos and Transcendence* Sherwood Sugden & Co, La Salle, 1984 and *The Quantum Enigma*, 1995.

38 This passage is quoted in G. Eaton: *op.cit.;* p196. The source is not given but for a more extended discussion of precisely this contrast see RG *CMW* Ch. IV, 'Sacred and Profane Science'; pp37–50.

39 Quoted in W.T. Chan: 'The Unity of East and West' in W.R. Inge et al *Radhakrishnan: Comparative Studies in Philosophy Presented in Honour of His Sixtieth Birthday* Allen & Unwin, London, 1951; pp107–108. (This passage is from *Orient et Occident*).

These principles, of course, are quite alien to the modern mentality. They are likely to provoke all kinds of quite irrelevant responses about the material inadequacies of traditional cosmologies – geocentricism, for example. Later we shall see how the traditionalist vision of both traditional and modern science cannot be so easily brushed aside.

The Reign of Quantity also seeks to demonstrate the intimate connections between traditional metaphysics and the arts, crafts and sciences which are found in any traditional culture, and to show how many modern and profane sciences are really a kind of degenerated caricature of traditional sciences.[40] Such a demonstration turns largely on Guénon's explanation of the nature of symbolism and of the initiatic character of many traditional sciences.

What of the qualities of mind and temperament revealed in Guénon's writings? Marco Pallis wrote of Guénon

> ... a mind of phenomenal lucidity of a kind one can best describe as 'mathematical' in its apparent detachment from anything savouring of aesthetic or even moral considerations; his criteria of what was right and what was inadmissible remained wholly intellectual ones needing no considerations drawn from a different order of reality to reinforce them – their own self-evidence sufficed.[41]

Another commentator speaks of Guénon's exposition as 'so crystalline and geometric, so mathematically abstract and devoid of almost any human element'[42] while Gai Eaton notes that 'in him the blade of French intellectuality is tempered to a razor-sharp edge'.[43] Theodore Roszak writes of his 'keen, spiritual discrimination'[44] while Schuon, referring to the absence of any sentimental or even psychic dimension in Guénon's work, once used the image of 'an eye without a body'.[45]

These images of sharpness, of a finely-honed cutting edge, a mathematical precision and incisive penetration all testify to Guénon's clarity of thought in his metaphysical expositions and his pitiless exposure of the 'signs of the times'. Nonetheless, Guénon's work is by no means easy to assimilate. Gai Eaton, despite his admiration of Guénon, concedes that 'It is questionable whether anyone with the normal tastes and intellectual background of our day can approach Guénon's work for the first time without a sense of revulsion.'[46] Why so?

Firstly there is the substance of Guénon's work. It is not easy of access and, at first sight, often strange, startling, baffling. His premises are too radically at odds with conventional wisdom for him to gain any easy following. His critique of European civilisation is so ruthless, so unnerving in its implications that it often provokes a

---

40 See RG *RQ* p14.
41 M. Pallis: 'A Fateful Meeting of Minds' p178. The word 'intellectual' in this passage does not mean 'mental' but refers to the intellect as understood in medieval scholastcism, the faculty of transcendent realisation. See Chapter 8.
42 W. Perry: 'Coomaraswamy' p163. See also W. Perry: 'The Revival of Interest in Tradition' p11.
43 G. Eaton: *op.cit.;* p184.
44 T. Roszak: *Unfinished Animal* Harper & Row, New York, 1977; p15.
45 Quoted in W. Perry: 'Coomaraswamy' p163. For photographs of Guénon see P. Charconac: *op.cit.;* facing p320; SS *ACRR* p223; and in *TOMORROW* accompanying his article 'Oriental Metaphysics', Vol XII, i, 1964; pp10, 13, 15; and in RF *UT* pxv.
46 G. Eaton: *op.cit.;* p184.

kind of defensive reflex, an emotional and intellectual resistance which makes for a failure to engage with what is actually being said. Without the right kind of predisposition the reader is unlikely to recover from the initial shock. An acceptance of Guénon's general thesis also entails a drastic intellectual and existential adjustment for most readers which very few are willing to make. André Gide typified this kind of response to Guénon's work when he wrote:

> If only I had known Guénon is my youth! ... Now it is too late; the die is cast. My sclerosed mind has as much difficulty conforming to the precepts of that ancestral wisdom as my body has to the so-called 'comfortable' position recommended by the Yogis ... To tell the truth, I cannot even manage really to desire resorption of the individual into the Eternal Being they seek ... I cling desperately to my limits and feel a repugnance for the disappearance of those contours that my whole education made a point of defining ... I am and remain on the side of Descartes and of Bacon. None the less, those books of Guénon are remarkable ... [47]

This is very much to the point. Guénon's vision cannot be accepted 'a little'. One might, of course, disagree over details but his fundamental premises must be either accepted or rejected. There is nothing of the *smörgåsbord* in Guénon's writings.

Then, also, there is Guénon's claim to being a mouthpiece for a metaphysical vision or *theoria* which is beyond the reach of 'proof', even of debate. Take for instance, the following:

> Those who are qualified to speak in the name of a traditional doctrine are not required to enter into discussion with the 'profane' or to engage in polemics: it is for them simply to expound the doctrine such as it is, for the sake of those capable of understanding it, and at the same time to denounce error wherever it arises ... their function is not to engage in strife and in doing so to compromise the doctrine, but to pronounce the judgement which they have the right to pronounce if they are in effective possession of the principles which should inspire them infallibly.[48]

Such a passage is likely, to say the least, to stick in the craw of many contemporary scholars for reasons obvious enough. For Guénon a genuine understanding of metaphysical principles represented a 'permanent and changeless certitude' which left no room for debate: one either understood these principles or one did not. Guénon was not bent on 'proving' anything whatsoever, only on making traditional doctrines more intelligible.

Hand in hand with this perception of his role went a tone of implacable certitude, all too easily seen as a kind of intellectual arrogance. Roszak, for example, speaks of 'a mind whose very precision led to an aristocratic intolerance and an elitism that risked sterility'[49]. Roger Lipsey refers to Guénon's 'formidably intolerant'[50] attitude to the modern West while Pallis writes of his 'habitually hectoring tone ... adopted in regard to people whose views he disapproved of'.[51] Bernard Kelly refers to the

---

47 A. Gide *The Journals of André Gide* Vol IV, 1939–1949; Secker & Warburg, London, 1951, tr. J. O'Brien; entry for October, 1943; p226. I am grateful to Mr. Richard Forsaith for alerting me to this reference.
48 RG *CMW* p65.
49 T. Roszak: *op.cit.;* p15.
50 R. Lipsey *CLW* p273.
51 M. Pallis: Letter to the Editor, *SCR* I, i, 1967; pp47–48

Ananda K. Coomaraswamy

'withering, intransigent, unbending' tone of Guénon's writings.[52] Jacques Lacarriere has regretted Guénon's 'aristocratism, his exclusive attachment to esoterism, his arbitrary rejection – and at times indeed, his faulty knowledge – of contemporary philosophies, plus his ferocious intellectualism'.[53]

There is in Guénon's work an adamantine quality, an austerity and inflexibility, and a combative tone as well as his 'icy brilliance'.[54] He was not one to coax, cajole or seduce his readers. He wrote as a man convinced he was in possession of timeless truths and he will brook no compromises. There is no concession to alternative points of view, no sense of a dialogue with his readers, no hospitality to any ideas at odds with those he is expressing. Something of Guénon's unyielding posture is evinced in the following passage (and it needs be remembered that he is writing in the 1920s):

> ...hitherto, so far as we are aware, no one else beside ourselves has consistently expounded authentic Oriental ideas in the West; and we have done so ... without the slightest wish to propagandize or to popularize, and exclusively for the benefit of those who are able to understand the doctrines just as they stand, and not after they have been denatured on the plea of making them more readily acceptable...[55]

In an unusually personal vein he reprimanded a critic who had suggested that Guénon had 'passed' from Hinduism to Islam:

> We have never 'passed' from one thing to another, as all our writings abundantly prove; and we have no need to 'seek the truth' since we know (and we must insist upon this word) that it exists equally in all traditions...[56]

Doubtless, for many contemporaries such claims smack of extravagant confidence. However, the crucial point is this: to be offended by Guénon's 'arrogance' and to invalidate his message are two quite different matters. It is to the latter purpose that Guénon's would-be critics ought to address themselves. One should also perhaps add that in these times of a full-scale relativism any claim to certitude is likely to be dismissed, without any further consideration, as 'fanaticism' or some such. Looked at from another angle Guénon's militant posture is nothing other than an expression of his fierce commitment to the truth and it is precisely his refusal to compromise first principles which gives his work its power and integrity.[57]

Another factor helps to explain Guénon's comparative obscurity in the West: his methodology and his attitude to scholarship. We have already seen how, for Guénon, metaphysical principles were self-evident and self-authenticating. This poses a problem for the scholarly mind. However, the problem runs deeper than this. If it were simply a matter of Guénon working from the basis of certain clearly-stated premises there would be no more reason to reject his work than that of many a philosopher

---

52 B. Kelly: 'Notes on the Light of Eastern Religions' in *RH* p160.
53 J. Lacarriere *The Gnostics* Peter Owen, London, 1977; p126.
54 G. Eaton: *op.cit.;* p183.
55 RG *CMW* p103.
56 Quoted in G. Eaton: *op.cit.;* p185.
57 See I.R. Tucker: Letter to the Editor, *SCR* I, iii, 1967; pp141–144. (It was precisely Guénon's refusal to make concessions which Coomaraswamy much admired. See Letter to Paul Furfey, undated, AKC *SL* p158.)

or theologian. No, the fact is that Guénon was, in Whitall Perry's words, 'somewhat slipshod in scholarship':

> his certitude about principles lent a false sense of security on the factual level, where a little research would have sufficed to protect him from the barbs of orientalists who, if incognizant of metaphysical and spiritual truths, had at least done their homework.[58]

Guénon was never primarily a scholar. Father Sylvain Lévi, to whom Guénon submitted a draft of *Introduction générale* as a possible doctoral thesis, recommended its rejection on the grounds that

> Il entend exclure tous les éléments qui ne correspondent pas à sa conception ... tout est dans le Vedanta ... il fait bon marché de l'histoire et de la critique historique ... il est tout prêt à croire á une transmission mystique d'une vérité première apparue au génie humain dès les premiers âges du monde ...[59]

This is not unjust. However, while Guénon can reasonably be reproached with a failure to 'do his homework' on the empirical and historical level, we must remember that he was a metaphysician concerned with first principles. If his application of these principles to contingent phenomena sometimes left room for a more scrupulous scholarship then this is indeed regrettable but it leaves the principles themselves quite unaffected.[60] This is sometimes forgotten by those who wish to force Guénon into the mould of the historian, the sociologist, the anthropologist or the comparative religionist.

Guénon was quite out of sympathy with the prevailing ideals of academic scholarship. Nothing could have been further removed from the spirit of his work than the notion of scholarship for its own sake. 'Passion for research', he said, 'taken as an end in itself is mental restlessness without end and without issue'.[61] As Roger Lipsey remarked, Guénon kept his distance from the academic intelligentsia: 'he mistrusted the academic mind and received abundant mistrust in return'.[62]

All of these factors conspired to limit Guénon's appeal. However, while his influence remains fairly minimal in the Western academic community at large, he is *the* seminal influence in the development of traditionalism. Along with Coomaraswamy and Schuon he forms what one commentator has called 'the great triumvirate' of the traditionalist school.[63] By way of concluding this introduction to Guénon we shall briefly consider his own perception of his role and the way in which he is seen by other traditionalists.

For those who accept Guénon's premises his work is a voice crying in the European

---

58 W. Perry: 'Coomaraswamy' p160

59 Quoted in J.P. Laurant: *op.cit.;* p43. (Translation: He intentionally excludes all the elements which do not correspond to his conception ... all is in the Vedanta ... he lightly dismisses history and historical criticism ... he is entirely ready to believe in a mystical transmission of a primordial truth which appeared to humanity in the earliest ages of the world.)

60 Furthermore, as Schuon has pointed out, '... one may have an intuition for pure principles without having one for a given phenomenal order, that is to say, without being able to apply the principles spontaneously in such and such a domain'. FS *SVQ* p128.

61 From 'Orient et Occident' per WP *TTW* p. 732.

62 RL *CLW* p272.

63 E.J. Sharpe *Comparative Religion* Duckworth, London, 1975; p265.

wilderness. However, as both Schuon and Perry have stressed, Guénon's function cannot strictly be termed 'prophetic', the age of prophecy being over. Schuon:

> If on the doctrinal plane the Guénonian work has a stamp of unicity, it may not be useless to point out that this is owing not to a more or less 'prophetic' nature – a supposition that is excluded and which Guénon had already rejected beforehand – but to an exceptional cyclical conjuncture whose temporal aspect is this 'end of the world' in which we live, and whose spatial aspect is – by the same token – the forced convergence of civilisations.[64]

We have already met with Michel Valsan's contention to the same effect. Guénon himself did not doubt that he had access to the *sophia perennis* about which he wrote. In a conversation with Dr. Grangier in 1927 Guénon spoke of the wisdom to which he gave expression as '*impersonelle, d'origine divine, transmise par révélation, détachée et sans passion*'.[65] Although certain of his own intellectual realization of the truth Guénon never assumed the role of the spiritual master; he consistently refused those who requested initiation from him.[66]

Like other traditionalists, Guénon did not perceive his work as any kind of essay in creativity or personal 'originality', repeatedly emphasising that in the metaphysical domain there was no room for 'individualist considerations' of any kind. In a letter to a friend he wrote, 'I have no other merit than to have expressed to the best of my ability some traditional ideas.'[67] When reminded of the people who had been profoundly influenced by his writings he calmly replied, '. . . such disposition becomes a homage rendered to the doctrine expressed by us in a way which is totally independent of any individualistic consideration . . .'.[68] Like Coomaraswamy, Guénon certainly did not see himself building a new philosophy or creating a new school of thought. If it is sometimes necessary to speak of the traditionalist 'school' this is, from a traditionalist viewpoint, merely an expedient. For the traditionalists Guénon is the 'providential interpreter of this age'.[69] It was his role to remind a forgetful world, '"in a way that can be ignored but not refuted", of first principles and to restore a lost sense of the Absolute'.[70]

---

64 From F. Schuon: 'L'Oeuvre' per W.Perry: 'Coomaraswamy' p160. For some reflections by Frithjof Schuon on Guénon see 'Definitions' in *Sophia* I, ii, Winter 1995; and Schuon's contributions to *Les Dossiers H: René Guénon* ed. Pierre-Marie Sigaud, L'Age d'Homme, Lausanne, 1984, and *L'Herne: René Guénon* ed. Jean-Pierre Laurant, Les Editions de l'Herne, Paris, 1985 (which also includes a letter from Guénon to Schuon, 16th April, 1946).
65 From T. Grangier *Souvenirs sur René Guénon* quoted by J.P. Laurant: *op.cit.;* p58.
66 See J.P. Laurant: *op.cit.;* pp62–64. For a traditionalist understanding of the term 'spiritual master' see F. Schuon: 'Nature and Function of the Spiritual Master' *SCR* I, ii, 1967; pp50–59.
67 W. Perry: 'The Man and His Witness' p7.
68 M. Bastriocchi: *op.cit.;* p356.
69 F. Schuon: 'L'Oeuvre', quoted by M. Bastriocchi: *op.cit.;* p359.
70 W. Perry: 'Coomaraswamy' p163.

3

Ananda Coomaraswamy

He was one of the luminaries of scholarship from whom we have all learned. And by the immense range of his studies and his persistent questioning of the accepted values, he gave us an example of intellectual seriousness, rare among scholars today
Meyer Schapiro[1]

Ananda Coomaraswamy was a much more public figure than René Guénon. Despite his aversion to biography his life story has been told in some detail by Roger Lipsey. Whitall Perry has observed of this paradox:

> It nonetheless remains, as Coomaraswamy would doubtless have admitted, that biographies of great men are a source of inspiration ... While he understandably deplored the fashion of modern biography to 'psychoanalyse' the subject by dredging up and then distorting trivia, as 'a vulgar catering to illegitimate curiosity', this is but the perversion of a legitimate art ...[2]

The 'legitimate art' has been admirably pursued by Dr Lipsey in a model biography, sympathetic but clear-eyed and critical, painstakingly researched but not burdened with trivial detail, shunning any half-baked psychologising, narrated in elegant prose, and attuned to those aspects of the *oeuvre* to which Coomaraswamy himself would have wished attention to be drawn.[3]

Here we shall concern ourselves less with biographical matter than with an introduction to Coomaraswamy's ideas and writings. We will focus on certain intellectual and spiritual contours in Coomaraswamy's development, isolate some of the landmarks, and offer a few remarks about the influence and significance of his work. It should be said plainly at the outset that nothing less than a full-length study could do justice to the scope and depth of his work nor to the manifold influences issuing from it. By the end of his life Coomaraswamy was thoroughly versed in the scriptures, mythology, doctrines and arts of many different cultures and traditions. He was an astonishingly erudite scholar, a recondite thinker and a distinguished linguist. He was a prolific writer, a full bibliography running to upwards of a thousand items on geological studies, art theory and history, linguistics and philology, social theory, psychology, mythology, folklore, religion and metaphysics. He lived in three continents and maintained many contacts, both personal and professional, with scholars, antiquarians, artists, theologians and spiritual practitioners from all over the globe. The contributors to a memorial volume, some one hundred and fifty of them, included eminent scholars like A.L. Basham, Joseph Campbell and V.S. Naravane, writers such as T.S. Eliot and Aldous Huxley, art historians like Herman Goetz and Richard Ettinghausen, the distinguished Sanskritist Dr V. Raghavan – the list might go on.[4] Coomaraswamy was a widely known and influential figure. The contrast with Guénon is a marked one.

We can discern in Coomaraswamy's life and work three focal points which shaped his ideas and writings: a concern with social and political questions connected with

---

1 Letter to Doña Luisa Coomaraswamy, 12th September 1947, quoted in RL *CLW* p246.
2 W. Perry: 'The Bollingen Coomaraswamy Papers and Biography' *SCR* XI, iv, 1977; p212.
3 Lipsey's biography and two companion volumes of selected papers have been met with critical accalaim and have generated renewed interest in Coomaraswamy's work. For a sample of reviews see J.K. Galbraith in *The New York Times* 12th March, 1978; K. Raine: 'Seminal Influence' in *The Times* 18th May, 1978; p22; P. Rawson in *New York Review of Books* 22nd Feb, 1979; p15; V.S. Naipul in *New York Review of Books* 22nd March, 1979; p6; M. Eliade: 'Some Notes on the Theosophia Perennis: Ananda Coomaraswamy and Henry Corbin' *History of Religions* XIX, 1979; pp167–176; J. Rykwert: 'Ananda Coomaraswamy' *Religion* IX, 1979; pp104–115; H. Smith: Review article in *Philosophy East & West* XX, ix, 1979; pp347–356;
4 See SS *ACRR* pvii for a list of contributors.

the conditions of daily life and work, and with the problematic relationship of the present to the past and of the 'East' to the 'West'; a fascination with traditional arts and crafts which impelled an immense and ambitious scholarly enterprise; and thirdly, an emerging preoccupation with religious and metaphysical questions which was resolved in a 'unique balance of metaphysical conviction and scholarly erudition'.[5] Allowing for some over-simplification, we can distinguish three 'roles' in Coomaraswamy's intellectual life: social commentator and Indologist, historian of Indian art, perennial philosopher. Each of these roles was dominant during a certain period in his life: 1900 to 1917, 1917 to 1932, and 1932 to 1947 respectively. The three strands eventually became interwoven in Coomaraswamy's life and his work. However, his early concerns took on a different character when, following his encounter with the work of Guénon, Coomaraswamy arrived at a thoroughly traditionalist understanding.

Born in Ceylon in 1877 of a Tamil father and an English mother, Coomaraswamy was brought up in England following the early death of his father. He was educated at Wycliffe College and at London University where he studied botany and geology. As part of his doctoral work Coomaraswamy carried out a scientific survey of the mineralogy of Ceylon and seemed poised for a distinguished academic career as a geologist. However, under pressure from his experiences while engaged in his field work, his interests took another turn. He became absorbed in a study of the traditional arts and crafts of Ceylon and of the social conditions under which they had been produced. In turn he became increasingly distressed by the corrosive effects of British colonialism.

In 1906 Coomaraswamy founded the Ceylon Social Reform Society of which he was the inaugural President and moving force. The Society addressed itself to the preservation and revival not only of traditional arts and crafts but also of the social values and customs which had helped to shape them. The Society also dedicated itself, in the words of its Manifesto, to discouraging 'the thoughtless imitation of unsuitable European habits and custom'.[6] Coomaraswamy called for a re-awakened pride in Ceylon's past and in her cultural heritage. The fact that he was half-English in no way blinkered his view of the impoverishment of national life brought by the British presence in both Ceylon and India. In both tone and substance the following passage is characteristic of Coomaraswamy in this early period:

> How different it might be if we Ceylonese were bolder and more independent, not afraid to stand on our own legs, and not ashamed of our nationalities. Why do we not meet the wave of European civilisation on equal terms? ... Our Eastern civilisation was here 2000 years ago; shall its spirit be broken utterly before the new commercialism of the West? Sometimes I think the eastern spirit is not dead, but sleeping, and may yet play a greater part in the world's spiritual life.[7]

Prescient words indeed in 1905!

In the years between 1900 and 1913 Coomaraswamy moved backwards and forwards between Ceylon, India and England. In India he formed close relationships with the Tagore family and was involved in both the literary renaissance and the

---

5 From RL *CLW* quoted in W. Perry: *op.cit.*; p206.
6 Manifesto of the Ceylon Reform Society, almost certainly written by Coomaraswamy, quoted in RL *CLW* p22.
7 A.K. Coomaraswamy *Borrowed Plumes* 1905, quoted in W. Perry: *op.cit.*; p214, and in RL *CLW* p18.

swadeshi movement.[8] All the while in the subcontinent he was researching the past, investigating arts and crafts, uncovering forgotten and neglected schools of religious and court art, writing scholarly and popular works, lecturing, and organising bodies such as the Ceylon Social Reform Society and, in England, the India Society.

In England he found his own social ideas anticipated and given forceful expression in the work of William Blake, John Ruskin and William Morris, three of the foremost representatives of a fiercely eloquent and morally impassioned current of anti-industrialism.[9] Such figures had elaborated a trenchant critique of the ugliest and most dehumanising aspects of the industrial revolution and of the acquisitive commercialism which increasingly polluted both public and private life. They believed the new values and patterns of urbanisation and industrialisation were disfiguring the human spirit. These writers and others like Thomas Carlyle, Charles Dickens and Matthew Arnold, had protested vehemently against the conditions in which many were forced to carry out their daily work and living. Ruskin and Morris, in particular, were appalled by the debasing of standards of craftsmanship and of public taste. Coomaraswamy picked up a catch-phrase of Ruskin's which he was to mobilise again and again in his own writings: 'industry without art is brutality'.[10] This was more than a facile slogan and signals one of the key themes in Coomaraswamy's work. For many years he was to remain preoccupied with questions about the reciprocal relationships between the conditions of daily life and work, the art of a period, and the social and spiritual values which governed the civilisation in question.

The Arts and Crafts Movement of the Edwardian era was, in large measure, stimulated by the ideas of William Morris, the artist, designer, poet, medievalist and social theorist. Morris's work influenced Coomaraswamy decisively in this period and he involved himself with others in England who were trying to put some of Morris's ideas into practice. The Guild and School of Handicraft, with which Coomaraswamy had some connections, was a case in point.[11] Lipsey does not altogether grasp the moral values which underpinned the Arts and Crafts Movement's resistance to industrialism and speaks of Coomaraswamy's 'absurdly anachronistic' attitude on many social questions in this period.[12] This is facile. Lipsey has not been alone in making this kind of charge about Coomaraswamy's social thought; we shall return to it later.

We can catch resonances from the work of the anti-industrialists in a passage such as this, written by Coomaraswamy in 1915:

> If the advocates of compulsory education were sincere, and by education meant education, they would be well aware that the first result of any real education would be to rear a race who would

---

8   See RL *CLW* pp75ff.

9   For a chronological account of Coomaraswamy's involvement in English social reform movements and of the development of his own ideas under English intellectual influences see RL *CLW* pp105ff.

10 RL *CLW* p114. For a penetrating discussion of the anti-industrial movement in England see R. Williams *Culture and Society* Hogarth Press, London, 1990 (rev ed).

11 Lipsey offers a persuasive discussion of the the influence of Morris. For other material on this phase of Coomaraswamy's life and his involvement in the Arts and Crafts movement see W. Shewring: 'Ananda Coomaraswamy and Eric Gill' and A. Crawford: 'Ananda Coomaraswamy and C.R. Ashbee', both in SS *ACRR* pp89–90 and pp239–243. On Morris and his milieu there are several biographical studies, those by P. Henderson and E.P. Thompson amongst them. See also K. Clark *The Gothic Revival* Penguin, 1962.

12 Rl *CLW* p113. Lipsey likewise fails to fathom Coomaraswamy's attitude to modern art. See Ch 9 of this study.

refuse point-blank the greater part of the activities offered by present day civilised existence ... life under Modern Western culture is not worth living, except for those strong enough and well enough equipped to maintain a perpetual guerilla warfare against all the purposes and idols of that civilisation with a view to its utter transformation.[13]

This articulates a concern with the purposes of education which was to remain with Coomaraswamy all his life. The tone of this passage, ardent, vigorous, sharp-edged, is typical of Coomaraswamy's writings on social subjects in this period.

Later in life Coomaraswamy turned less often to explicitly social and political questions. By then he had become aware that 'politics and economics, although they cannot be ignored, are the most external and least part of our problem'.[14] However, he never surrendered the conviction that an urbanised and highly industrialised society controlled by materialistic values was profoundly inimical to human development. He was always ready to pull a barbed shaft from his literary quiver when provoked. As late as 1943 we find him writing to *The New English Weekly*, again on the subject of education, in terms no less caustic than those of 1915:

We cannot pretend to culture until by the phrase 'standard of living' we come to mean a qualitative standard ... Modern education is designed to fit us to take our place in the counting-house and at the chain-belt; a real culture breeds a race of men able to ask, What kind of work is worth doing?[15]

Coomaraswamy's work on social theory has, as yet, received scant attention.[16] It has been overshadowed by his work as an art historian and as a metaphysician. This is right and proper but it should be remembered that Coomaraswamy was profoundly concerned with social questions throughout his life. These came to be situated in a wider, and from a traditional viewpoint, more adequate perspective but his concern for a qualitative standard of living runs like a thread through his work. Here we have only touched on his social thought. However, a close inquiry into his fully developed ideas about education, literacy, social organisation and government would make a fascinating study.

Coomaraswamy's significance as a social commentator is not fully revealed until his later work when the political and social insights from the early period in his life found their proper place within an all-embracing traditional framework which allows him to elaborate what Juan Adolpho Vasquez has called 'a metaphysics of culture'.[17] In the years before he moved to America he was more significant as a propagandist and educator than as a theorist. In this respect he was almost certainly more important in India and Ceylon than in England where his voice was one amongst many. The seeds sown by Coomaraswamy in India and Ceylon, at first with his early writings and later through his mature work, have been a long time germinating. The harvest,

---

13 A.K. Coomaraswamy: 'Love and Art', 1915, quoted in RL *CLW* p105.
14 A.K. Coomaraswamy quoted in D. Riepe *Indian Philosophy and Its Impact on American Thought* Charles C. Thomas, Springfield, 1970; p126.
15 Letter to *The New English Weekly* April 1943, AKC *SL* p293.
16 Two of his most important essays in this field were re-published in *The Bugbear of Literacy* Perennial, London, 1979. A recent and welcome development has been the reprinting of *Spiritual Authority and Temporal Power in the Indian Theory of Government* Oxford University Press, New York, 1994.
17 See J. A. Vasquez: 'A Metaphysics of Culture' in SS *ACRR*.

if it does come, could be none the less rich for that. We should not imagine that because he at first received a lukewarm or even unfavourable response from his compatriots (an attitude which in some measure persists to this day) that this betokened any kind of failure but rather that his ideas were then, just as his later writings are now, from one point of view, 'ahead of their time'.[18] Ultimately Coomaraswamy's most important function as a social commentator lay in his insistence on relating social and political questions back to underlying religious and metaphysical principles. In this respect he anticipates some of the more percipient of present day social critics who realise that our most fundamental problems derive from a progressive etiolation of authentic moral and spiritual values.

In the context of the present study this period of Coomaraswamy's life is important for the ways in which some of his ideas and attitudes, later to be assimilated into a traditionalist vision, took shape. If Guénon's disillusionment with contemporary civilisation was first fashioned by French occultism, Coomaraswamy's was impelled by the contrast between the traditional and the modern industrial cultures of the two countries to which he belonged by birth. His thought was also imprinted with the social concerns and values of the great English anti-industrialists from Blake to Morris.

The second refrain which sounds through Coomaraswamy's life is closely related to his interest in social questions and became the dominant theme of his public career – his work as an art historian. From the outset Coomaraswamy's interest in art was controlled by much more than either antiquarian or 'aesthetic' considerations. For him the most humble folk art and the loftiest religious creations alike were an outward expression not only of the sensibilities of those who created them but of the whole civilisation in which they were nurtured. There was nothing of the *art nouveau* slogan of 'art for art's sake' in Coomaraswamy's outlook. His interest in traditional arts and crafts, from a humble pot to a medieval cathedral, was always governed by the conviction that something immeasurably precious and vitally important was disappearing under the onslaught of modernism in its many different guises. As his biographer remarks, '. . . history of art was never for him either a light question – one that had only to do with pleasures – or a question of scholarship for its own sake, but rather a question of setting right what had gone amiss partly through ignorance of the past.'[19] Coomaraswamy's achievement as an art historian can perhaps best be understood in respect of three of the major tasks which he undertook: the 'rehabilitation' of Asian art in the eyes of Europeans and Asians alike; the massive work of scholarship which he pursued as curator of the Indian Section of the Boston Museum of Fine Arts; the penetration and explanation of traditional views of art and their relationship to philosophy, religion and metaphysics. Again, for purposes of convenience we can loosely associate each of these tasks with the three main

---

18 To a sub-continent which despite a long struggle for political independence from colonial rule has now come to accept 'the counting house' and the 'chain belt' as desirable goals and to understand by a 'standard of living' a quantitative, and by no means a qualitative, standard, Coomaraswamy's mature work can have little appeal at the present time although paradoxically it is in India that almost all his books have long been in print. For a sample of the growing literature on Coomaraswamy by Indian scholars (most of it quite unsatisfactory) see M. Bagchee *Ananda Coomaraswamy* Bharata Manisha, Varanasi, 1977; K.C. Kamaliah *Ananda Coomaraswamy, Wise Man from the East* Madras, 1977 (no publisher given); P. Sastri *Ananda K. Coomaraswamy* Arnold-Heinemann, New Delhi, 1974.

19 RL *CLW* p20.

phases in his adult life whilst remembering that it was in the middle years (1917–1932) that he devoted himself almost exclusively to art scholarship.

In assessing Coomaraswamy's achievement it needs to be remembered that the conventional attitude of the Edwardian era towards the art of Asia was, at best, condescending, and at worst, frankly contemptuous. Asian art was often dismissed as 'barbarous', 'second-rate' and 'inferior' and there was a good deal of foolish talk about 'eight-armed monsters' and the like.[20] In short, there was, in England at least, an almost total ignorance of the sacred iconographies of the East. Such an artistic illiteracy was coupled with a similar incomprehension of traditional philosophy and religion, and buttressed by all manner of Eurocentric assumptions. Worse still was the fact that such attitudes had infected the Indian intelligentsia, exposed as it was to Western education and influences.

From the early days of his fieldwork in Ceylon Coomaraswamy set about dismantling these prejudices through an affirmation of the beauty, integrity and spiritual density of traditional art in Ceylon and India and, later, in other parts of Asia. He was bent on the task of demonstrating the existence of an artistic heritage at least the equal of Europe's. He not only wrote and spoke and organised tirelessly to educate the British but he scourged the Indian intelligentsia for being duped by assumptions of European cultural superiority. In studies like *Medieval Sinhalese Art* (1908), *The Arts and Crafts of India and Ceylon* (1913), and his earliest collection of essays, *The Dance of Shiva* (1918), Coomaraswamy combated the prejudices of the age and elaborated a vision of traditional Indian art and life which was inspiring, and adequate to the realities of the time. He revolutionised several specific fields of art history, radically changed others. His work on Sinhalese arts and crafts and on Rajput painting, though they can now be seen as formative in the light of his later work on Buddhist iconography and on Indian, Platonic and Christian theories of art, were nevertheless early signs of a prodigious scholarship. His influence was not only felt in the somewhat rarefied domain of art scholarship but percolated into other scholarly fields and eventually must have had some influence on popular attitudes in Ceylon, India, England and America.[21]

As a Curator at the Boston Museum Coomaraswamy performed a mighty labour in classifying, cataloguing and explaining thousands of items of oriental art. Through his professional work, his writings, lectures and personal associations Coomaraswamy left an indelible imprint on the work of many American galleries and museums and influenced a wide range of curators, art historians, orientalists and critics – Stella Kramrisch, Walter Andrae, and Heinrich Zimmer to name a few of the more well-known.[22]

Here we shall not rehearse Coomaraswamy's complex vision of traditional art but will only stress a few of the cardinal ideas. Traditional art, in Coomaraswamy's view,

---

20 See RL *CLW* pp60–61 and W. Perry: 'Bollingen Coomaraswamy' p214.
21 See Betty Heiman: 'Indian Art and Its Transcendence'; K.C. Kamaliah: 'Ananda Coomaraswamy's Assessment of Dravidian Civilisation and Culture'; A. Ranganathan: 'Ananda Coomaraswamy: Confluence of East and West'; B.N. Goswamy: 'Ananda Coomaraswamy as a Historian of Rajput Painting'; M.S. Randhava: 'Rediscovery of Kangra Painting' – all in SS *ACRR* pp24–26, 43–52, 53–58, 75–83, 201–204 respectively. For his impact on American thought see RL *CLW* passim and D. Riepe: *op.cit.*; see 'Coomaraswamy' in the Index.
22 See RL *CLW* pp206–231 and A. Ripley Hall: 'The Keeper of the Indian Collection: An Appreciation of Ananda Kentish Coomaraswamy' in SS *ACRR* pp106–124. This article includes a bibliography of Coomaraswamy's writings for the *Bulletin* of the Museum.

was always directed towards a twin purpose: a daily utility, towards what he was fond of calling 'the satisfaction of present needs', and towards the preservation and transmission of moral values and spiritual teachings derived from the tradition in which it appeared. A Tibetan tanka, a medieval cathedral, a Red Indian utensil, a Javanese puppet, a Hindu deity image, a piece of Shaker furniture – in such artefacts and creations Coomaraswamy sought a symbolic vocabulary. The intelligibility of traditional arts and crafts, he insisted, does not depend on a more or less precarious 'recognition', as does modern art, but on 'legibility'. Traditional art does not deal in the private vision of the artist but in a symbolic language.[23]

Modern art, which from a traditionalist perspective includes Renaissance and all post-Renaissance art, is by contrast, divorced from higher values, tyrannised by the mania for 'originality', controlled by 'aesthetic' (sentimental) considerations, and drawn from the subjective resources of the individual artist rather than from the well-springs of tradition. The comparison, needless to say, does not reflect well on modern art! An example:

> Our artists are 'emancipated' from any obligation to eternal verities, and have abandoned to tradesmen the satisfaction of present needs. Our abstract art is not an iconography of transcendental forms but the realistic picture of a disintegrated mentality.[24]

During the late 1920s Coomaraswamy's life and work somewhat altered their trajectory. The collapse of his third marriage, ill-health and a growing awareness of death, an impatience with the constrictions of purely academic scholarship, and the influence of René Guénon all cooperated to deepen Coomaraswamy's interest in spiritual and metaphysical questions.[25] He became more austere in his personal lifestyle, partially withdrew from the academic and social worlds in which he had moved freely over the last decade, and addressed himself to the understanding and explication of traditional metaphysics, especially those of classical India and pre-Renaissance Europe. (Coomaraswamy remarked in one of his letters that 'my indoctrination with the *Philosophia Perennis* is primarily Oriental, secondarily Mediaeval, and thirdly classic'.[26]) His later work is densely textured with references to Plato and Plotinus, Augustine and Aquinas, Eckhart and the Rhinish mystics, to Shankara and Lao-Tse and Nagarjuna. He also immersed himself in folklore and mythology since these too carried profound teachings. Coomaraswamy remained the consummate scholar but his work took on a more urgent nature after 1932. He spoke of his 'vocation' – and he was not one to use such words lightly – as 'research in the field of the significance of the universal symbols of the *Philosophia Perennis*' rather than as 'one of apology for or polemic on behalf of doctrines'.[27]

The influence of Guénon was decisive. Coomaraswamy discovered Guénon's writings through Heinrich Zimmer some time in the late twenties and, a few years later, wrote,

---

23 See AKC *COPA passim*.
24 'Symptom, Diagnosis and Regimen' in AKC *SP1* pp316–317.
25 See RL *CLW* pp161–175. On Coomaraswamy's move from 'descriptive iconography' towards metaphysics see his letter to Herman Goetz, June 1939 in AKC *SL* pp26–27.
26 Letter to Artemus Packard, May 1941, AKC *SL* p299.
27 A.K. Coomaraswamy: 'The Bugbear of Democracy, Freedom and Equality' *SCR* XI, iii, 1977; p134.

> ... no living writer in modern Europe is more significant than René Guénon, whose task it has been to expound the universal metaphysical tradition that has been the essential foundation of every past culture, and which represents the indispensable basis for any civilisation deserving to be so-called.[28]

Several commentators have detailed the creative reciprocal influences which flowed between Coomaraswamy and Guénon.[29] We shall not go over this ground again here. However, it is worth noting that Coomaraswamy told one of his friends that he and Guénon were 'entirely in agreement on metaphysical principles' which, of course, did not preclude some divergences of opinion over the applications of these principles on the phenomenal plane.[30]

The vintage Coomaraswamy of the later years is to be found in his masterly works on Vedanta and on the Catholic scholastics and mystics. Some of his work is labyrinthine and not easy of access. It is often laden with a mass of technical detail and with linguistic and philological subtleties which test the patience of some readers. Of his own methodology as an exponent of metaphysics Coomaraswamy wrote,

> We write from a strictly orthodox point of view ... endeavouring to speak with mathematical precision, but never employing words of our own, or making any affirmation for which authority could not be cited by chapter and verse; in this way making our technique characteristically Indian.[31]

Sometimes one wishes the chapter and verse documentation was not quite so overwhelming! Coomaraswamy was much more scrupulous than Guénon in this respect, the latter sometimes ignoring the niceties of scholarship at the cost of exposing some of his claims to scholarly criticism.

However formidable some of Coomaraswamy's later writings may be they demand close attention from anyone seriously interested in the subjects about which he wrote. There is no finer exegesis of traditional Indian metaphysics than is to be found in Coomaraswamy's later works. His work on the Platonic, Christian and Indian conceptions of sacred art is also unrivalled. Roger Lipsey has performed an invaluable service in bringing some of Coomaraswamy's finest essays on these subjects together in *Coomaraswamy, Vol II: Selected Papers, Metaphysics*. Special mention should be made of 'The Vedanta and Western Tradition', 'Sri Ramakrishna and Religious Tolerance', 'Recollection, Indian and Platonic', 'On the One and Only Transmigrant' and 'On The Indian and Traditional Psychology, or Rather Pneumatology' ... but it hardly matters what one picks up from the later period: all his mature work is stamped with rare scholarship, elegant expression and a depth of understanding which makes most of the other scholarly work on the same subjects look vapid and superficial. Of his later books three in particular deserve much wider attention: *Christian and Oriental Philosophy of Art* (1939), *Hinduism and Buddhism* (1943) and *Time and Eternity* (1947). *The Bugbear of Literacy* (1979) (first published in 1943 as *Am I my Brother's Keeper?*)

---

28 Quoted in RL *CLW* p170.
29 See W. Perry: 'The Man and the Witness' pp3–7; M. Pallis: 'A Fateful Meeting of Minds' pp176–182; and M. Bastriocchi: *op.cit.*; pp350–359.
30 W. Perry: 'The Man and the Witness' p5.
31 Quoted in V.S. Naravane: 'Ananda Coomaraswamy: A Critical Appreciation' in SS *ACRR* p206.

and two posthumous collections of some of his most interesting and more accessible essays, *Sources of Wisdom* (1981) and *What is Civilisation?* (1989), offer splendid starting-points for uninitiated readers.

In this introductory discussion of Coomaraswamy we have referred only briefly to some aspects of his work. However, it will be clear enough that he was a man of wide interests and achievements. From a traditionalist point of view and in the context of our present study we can unhesitatingly ratify Coomaraswamy's own words: 'I have little doubt that my later work, developed out of and necessitated by my earlier works on the arts and dealing with Indian philosophy and Vedic exegesis, is really the most mature and most important part of my work.'[32] However, we should remember that Coomaraswamy's influence radiated out in many directions. Even a severely attenuated list of some of the well-known figures on whom he exercised a significant influence testifies to his impact: Eric Gill, the English designer and writer; the judge, Christmas Humphreys, early populariser of Buddhism in England; the influential Indologist Heinrich Zimmer; Joseph Campbell, the Jungian student of the world's mythologies; René Guénon himself; Joseph Epes Brown who has helped to bring to light some of the esoteric traditions of the American Indians; the comparative religionist Mircea Eliade; and, of course, other traditionalists, including Titus Burckhardt, Marco Pallis and Whitall Perry.[33]

A tribute from his friend Eric Gill will leave us at an appropriate point to conclude this introduction:

> ... there was one person ... to whose influence I am deeply grateful; I mean the philosopher and theologian, Ananda Coomaraswamy. Others have written the truth about life and religion and man's work. Others have written good clear English. Others have had the gift of witty exposition. Others have understood the metaphysics of Christianity and others have understood the metaphysics of Hinduism and Buddhism. Others have understood the true significance of erotic drawings and sculptures. Others have seen the relationships of the true and the good and the beautiful. Others have had apparently unlimited learning. Others have loved; others have been kind and generous. But I know of no one else in whom all these gifts and all these powers have been combined ... I believe that no other living writer has written the truth in matters of art and life and religion and piety with such wisdom and understanding.[34]

Whatever we may think of Gill's commendations we can hardly doubt that the life and work of this 'warrior for dharma'[35] was a rare and precious gift to all those interested in the ways of the spirit.

---

32 in RL *CLW* p248.
33 For Coomaraswamy's influence on these figures see Index of RL *CLW* and SS *ACRR*.
34 E. Gill *Autobiography* London, 1940, p174.
35 M. Pallis: *op.cit.*; p187.

4

Frithjof Schuon

If Guénon was the master expositor of metaphysical doctrines and Coomaraswamy the peerless scholar and connoisseur of Oriental art who began his exposition of metaphysics through recourse to the language of artistic forms, Schuon seems like the cosmic intellect itself impregnated by the energy of divine grace surveying the whole of the reality surrounding man and elucidating all the concerns of human existence in the light of sacred knowledge

Seyyed Hossein Nasr[1]

With the person of Frithjof Schuon we move back into the shadows of a deliberate anonymity. Only such biographical facts as are pertinent to his work are publicly known.[2] Schuon was born of German parents in Basle in 1907. He was schooled in both French and German but left school at sixteen to work as a textile designer in Paris. From an early age he devoted himself to a study of philosophy, religion and metaphysics, reading the classical and modern works of European philosophy, and the sacred literatures of the East. Amongst the Western sources Plato and Eckhart left a profound impression while the *Bhagavad Gītā* was his favourite Eastern reading.[3] Even before moving to Paris Schuon came into contact with the writings of René Guénon 'which served to confirm his own intellectual rejection of the modern civilisation while at the same time bringing into sharper focus his spontaneous understanding of metaphysical principles and their traditional applications.'[4] The accent of this passage is important. Schuon, like Coomaraswamy, was not a disciple of Guénon whose writings helped to clarify an understanding already arrived at. (For this reason it is improper to label the thought of either Coomaraswamy or Schuon as 'Guénonian'. Indeed, in some respects, the latter figures surpass Guénon in their exposition of traditionalism.)

From his earliest years Schuon was also fascinated by traditional art, especially that of Japan and the Far East. In an unusual personal reference in one of his works he tells us of a Buddha figure in an ethnographical museum. It was a traditional representation in gilded wood and flanked by two statues of the Bodhisattvas Seishi and Kwannon. The encounter with this 'overwhelming embodiment of an infinite victory of the Spirit' Schuon sums up in the phrase 'veni, vidi, victus sum'.[5] One commentator has drawn attention to the importance of aesthetic intuition in accounting for Schuon's extraordinary understanding of traditional religious and social forms: 'It suffices for him to see ... an object from a traditional civilisation, to be able to perceive, through a sort of "chain-reaction", a whole ensemble of intellectual, spiritual and psychological ideas.'[6] This may seem an extravagant claim but those who have read Schuon's work will not doubt the gift to which this testifies.

After working for a time in Mulhouse, in Alsace, Schuon underwent a year and a half of military service before returning to his design work in Paris. There, in 1930, his interest in Islam led him to a close study of Arabic, first with a Syrian Jew and afterwards at the Paris mosque.[7] As in Guénon's case, Schuon's personal spiritual development is veiled in obscurity. We do not know when he formally committed himself to Islam but it seems probable that it was in this period.

In the 1930s Schuon several times visited North Africa, spending time in Algeria,

---

1 SHN *K&S* p107.
2 See *Frithjof Schuon, Metaphysician and Artist* World Wisdom Books, Bloomington, 1981 (hereafter *FSMA*). Fragmentary information can also be found in *The Essential Writings of Frithjof Schuon* ed. S.H. Nasr; Amity House, New York, 1986, and in S.H. Nasr: 'The Biography of Frithjof Schuon' in *RH* pp1–6.
3 *FSMA* p2.
4 *ibid.* See also W. Perry: 'The Revival of Interest in Tradition' in RF *UT* pp14–16.
5 FS *ITB* p121. See also *FSMA* p2.
6 *FSMA* p1.
7 *FSMA* p3.

Morocco and Egypt where he met René Guénon, with whom he had been corresponding for some years. In many respects Schuon's work was to be an elaboration of principles first given public expression by Guénon. Although, as already intimated, Schuon was not a disciple of Guénon in any strict sense of the word, there is, on the other hand, persuasive evidence to suggest that Schuon was, in fact, a disciple of the Shaikh Ahmad Al'Alawi, the Algerian Sufi sage and founder of the 'Alawi order.[8] Schuon has written of this modern saint:

> ... someone who represents in himself ... the idea which for hundreds of years has been the life-blood of that civilisation [the Islamic]. To meet such a one is like coming face to face, in mid-twentieth century, with a medieval Saint or a Semitic Patriarch.[9]

However, as Schuon himself has not seen fit to divulge the details of his own spiritual training we shall respect his reticence. What can be said without fear of contradiction is that Schuon's work is perfumed with the scents of Sufic spirituality and could not derive from any purely bookish learning.

The contemplative climate of India held a strong attraction for Schuon but a visit to the subcontinent was cut short by the outbreak of World War II which obliged him to return to Europe. Schuon served for some months in the French army before being captured by the Germans. His father had been a native of southern Germany while his mother had come from German-Alsatian stock. Such a background ensured some measure of freedom for Schuon but when the Nazis threatened to forcibly enlist Alsatians in the German army he seized an opportunity to escape to Switzerland. He was briefly imprisoned before being granted asylum. He settled in Lausanne and, some years later, took out Swiss nationality.[10]

In 1949 Schuon married Catherine Feer, the daughter of a Swiss diplomat. It was his wife who introduced him to the beauties of the Swiss Alps. Schuon's love of nature, which runs through his work like a haunting melody, was further deepened during two periods which he and his wife spent with the Plains Indians of North America. 'For Schuon, virgin nature carries a message of eternal truth and primordial reality, and to plunge oneself therein is to rediscover a dimension of the soul which in modern man has become atrophied.'[11] Schuon himself, writing in the context of Red Indian receptivity to the lessons of nature, said this:

> Wild Nature is at one with holy poverty and also with spiritual childlikeness; she is an open book containing an inexhaustible teaching of truth and beauty. It is in the midst of his own artifices

---

8 See M. Lings *A Sufi Saint of the Twentieth Century* Uni California Press, Berkely, 1971 and M. Valsan: 'Notes on the Shaikh al-'Alawi, 1869–1934' *SCR* V, i, 1971. There are branches of the 'Alawi order in England, France, the Netherlands, the Middle East, North Africa and the USA. There are references to the order in the following sources: J.S. Trimingham *The Sufi Orders in Islam* Clarendon, Oxford, 1971; pp113, 256; W.M. Watts's review of Lings in *Religious Studies* IX, 1973; p382; and 'Yemeni Arabs in Britain', *Geographical Magazine* (UK), August 1944. It has been suggested, wrongly, that Schuon was a 'disciple' of Coomaraswamy. See, for instance, E.J. Sharpe *Comparative Religion* Duckworth, London, 1975; p262, and R.C. Zaehner *At Sundry Times* Faber & Faber, London, 1958; p36fn2. Further, it needs to be remembered that 'To follow Guénon is not to follow the man, but to follow the light of traditional truth ...'; Bernard Kelly: 'Notes on the Light of the Eastern Religions' in *RH* pp160–161.
9 F. Schuon: 'Rahimahu Llah' *Cahiers du Sud* Aug-Sept 1935, quoted in M. Lings: *op.cit.*; p116; there is a moving portrait of the Shaikh by Schuon facing p160.
10 *FSMA* p3.
11 *ibid.*; p6.

Frithjof Schuon

that man most easily becomes corrupted, it is they who make him covetous and impious; close to virgin Nature, who knows neither agitation nor falsehood, he had the hope of remaining contemplative like Nature herself.[12]

Schuon and his wife had previously developed friendly contacts with visiting Indians in Paris and Brussels in the 1950s. During their first visit to North America in 1959, the Schuons were officially adopted into the Red Cloud family of the Lakota tribe, that branch of the Sioux nation from which came the revered 'medicine-man' Black Elk.[13] Schuon, Coomaraswamy and Joseph Epes Brown have all been instrumental in efforts to preserve the precious spiritual heritage of the Plains Indians.[14]

As well as making visits to America Schuon travelled in North Africa and the Middle East. He maintained on-going friendships with representatives of all the great religious traditions. Earlier he lived in reclusive circumstances in Switzerland but spent his later years in America until his death in May, 1998.

Schuon's published work forms an imposing corpus and covers a staggering range of religious and metaphysical subjects without any of the superficialities and simplifications which we normally expect from someone covering such a vast terrain. His works on specific religious traditions have commanded respect from scholars and practitioners within the traditions in question. As well as publishing over twenty books he was a prolific contributor to journals such as *Études Traditionnelles, Islamic Quarterly, Tomorrow, Studies in Comparative Religion* and *Sophia Perennis*. Most of his major works, written in French, have now been published in English.[15]

Schuon's works are all governed by an unchanging set of metaphysical principles. They exhibit nothing of a 'development' or 'evolution' but are, rather, re-statements of the same principles from different vantage points and brought to bear on divergent phenomena. More so than with either Guénon or Coomaraswamy, one feels that Schuon's vision was complete from the outset. The term 'erudition' is not quite appropriate: Schuon not only knows 'about' an encyclopedic range of religious manifestations and sapiential traditions but seems to understand them in a way which, for want of a better word, we can only call intuitive.

Much of Schuon's work has been explicitly directed to the Islamic tradition to which he has devoted four books: *Understanding Islam* (1963); *Dimensions of Islam* (1969); *Islam and the Perennial Philosophy* (1976); *Sufism: Veil and Quintessence* (1981). Both *Christianity/Islam: Essays on Ecumenic Esotericism* (1985) and *In the Face of the Absolute* (1989) focus on the Christian and Islamic traditions. Seyyed Hossein Nasr, himself an eminent Islamicist, wrote of *Understanding Islam*, 'I believe his work to be the most outstanding ever written in a European language on why Muslims believe in Islam and why Islam offers to man all that he needs religiously and spiritually.'[16] Nasr has been no less generous in commending later works.[17] Whilst all of Schuon's works have a Sufic

---

12 FS *LAW* p84.
13 For some account of the Schuons' personal experiences with the Plains Indians see FS *FS* Parts 2 & 3.
14 See RL *CLW* pp227–228.
15 For a full bibliography of Schuon's writings upto 1990 see *RH* pp299–327.
16 See S.H. Nasr *Ideals and Realities of Islam* Allen & Unwin, London, 1973; p10.
17 See his Prefaces to FS *DI* and FS *IPP* and his Introduction to FS *EW*.

fragrance his work has by no means been restricted to the Islamic heritage. Two major works focus on Hinduism and Buddhism: *Language of the Self* (1959) and *In the Tracks of Buddhism* (1969) (a revised and enlarged version of the latter was published by World Wisdom Books in 1993 as *Treasures of Buddhism*). He also frequently refers to Red Indian spirituality, to the Chinese tradition and to Judaism. His writings on the spiritual heritage of the Plains Indians have been collected, together with reproductions of some of his paintings, in *The Feathered Sun: Plains Indians in Art and Philosophy* (1990).

All of Schuon's work is concerned with a re-affirmation of traditional metaphysical principles, with an explication of the esoteric dimensions of religion, with the penetration of mythological and religious forms, and with the critique of a modernism which is indifferent to the principles which inform all traditional wisdoms. His general position was defined in his first work to appear in English, *The Transcendent Unity of Religions* (1953), a work of which T.S. Eliot remarked, 'I have met with no more impressive work on the comparative study of Oriental and Occidental religion.'[18] *Spiritual Perspectives and Human Facts* (1954) is a collection of aphoristic essays including studies of Vedanta and sacred art, and a meditation on the spiritual virtues. *Gnosis: Divine Wisdom* (1959), *Logic and Transcendence* (1976) and *Esoterism and Principle and as Way* (1981) are largely given over to extended and explicit discussions of metaphysical principles. The first includes a luminous section on the Christian tradition while *Logic and Transcendence* contains his most explicit refutation of some of the philosophies and ideologies of the modern West. Schuon suggested some years ago that *Logic and Transcendence* was his most representative and inclusive work. That distinction is perhaps now shared with *Esoterism as Principle and as Way* which includes Schuon's most deliberate explanation of the nature of esotericism,[19] and with *Survey of Metaphysics and Esoterism* (1986) which is a masterly work of metaphysical synthesis.

Stations of Wisdom (1961) is directed mainly towards an exploration of certain religious and spiritual modalities but includes 'Orthodoxy and Intellectuality', an essay of paramount importance in understanding the traditionalist position. *Light on the Ancient Worlds* includes a range of essays on such subjects as the Hellenist-Christian 'dialogue', shamanism, monasticism and the *religio perennis*. Schuon's most recent works are *To Have a Center* (1990), *Roots of the Human Condition* (1991), *The Play of Masks* (1992) and *The Transfiguration of Man* (1995). These later writings exhibit a masterly lightness of touch and a style that is increasingly synthetic and poetic. The title chapter of the first of these four collections is perhaps Schuon's only explicit statement concerning the literary and artistic 'culture' of the last two hundred years. Other essays in these books cover such subjects as intellection, prayer, integral anthropology and art. *Echoes of Perennial Wisdom* (1992) is an anthology of epigrammatic passages and apophthegms from many of Schuon's works. Perhaps the most remarkable event of recent years is the publication of *Road to the Heart* (1995), which contains nearly one hundred poems in English by Schuon. In these poems, the principles and insights expressed in his other writings find a lyric voice in the most simple and concise form.

In addition to these works there is an impressive array of articles in the journals

---

18 Cover of Harper & Row edition of 1975.
19 Schuon's tranlators often use the word 'esoterism'; I have preferred 'esotericism'. Schuon's comment about *Logic and Transcendence* is recorded in Whitall Perry's review in *SCR* IX, iv, 1975; p250.

already mentioned. Several of Schuon's most important essays were published in *The Sword of Gnosis* (Penguin, 1974). An event of signal importance was the publication of *The Essential Writings of Frithjof Schuon* (1986) which included some of the essays most pivotal in Schuon's work along with several pieces previously unpublished. The anthology was edited by Seyyed Hossein Nasr whose introduction identifies some of the recurrent themes and principles in Schuon's work and situates Schuon's work in a context intelligible to readers coming across a traditional outlook for the first time. A *festschrift* for Schuon's eightieth birthday, *Religion of the Heart*, was published in 1991 under the editorship of Nasr and William Stoddart, and includes a bibliography of Schuon's writings.

Guénon, Coomaraswamy and Schuon have played different but complementary roles in the development of traditionalism, each fulfilling a function corresponding to their distinct sensibilities and gifts. Guénon occupies a special position by virtue of being the first to articulate the fundamental metaphysical and cosmological principles through which the *sophia perennis* might be rediscovered and expressed anew in the West. We have already noted Schuon's recognition of Guénon as a 'providential interpreter, at least on the doctrinal level' for the modern West. In a like sense J.P. Laurant refers to Guénon's 'hieratic role'.[20] Guénon's critique of the 'reign of quantity' also provides the platform from which more detailed criticisms might be made by later traditionalists. His reaction to modernism was integral to his role and constitutes a kind of clearing of the ground.

Coomaraswamy brought to the study of traditional metaphysics, sacred art and religious culture an aesthetic sense and a scholarly aptitude not found in Guénon. The Frenchman had, as Reynolds observes, 'no great sensitivity for human cultures'.[21] Coomaraswamy, in a sense, brings the principles about which Guénon wrote, down to a more human level. His work exhibits much more of a sense of history, and a feel for the diverse and concrete circumstances of human experience. There is also a sense of personal presence in Coomaraswamy's writings which is absent in Guénon's work which, to some readers at least, must appear somewhat abstract and rarefied. As Gai Eaton put it, to move from Guénon's work to Coomaraswamy's is to '... descend into a far kindlier climate, while remaining in the same country ... The icy glitter is replaced by a warmer glow, the attitude of calm disdain towards all things modern by a more human indignation.'[22] Whitall Perry contrasts their roles through a metaphor which each would have appreciated:

> Guénon was like the vertical axis of a cross, fixed with mathematical precision on immutable realities and their immediate applications in the domain of cosmological sciences; whereas Coomaraswamy was the horizontal complement, expanding these truths over the vast field of arts, cultures, mythologies and symbolisms: metaphysical truth on the one hand, universal beauty on the other.[23]

---

20 J.P. Laurant: 'Le problème de René Guénon' *Revue de l'histoire des religions* CLXXIX, i, 1971; p63.
21 P.L.Reynolds *René Guénon: His Life and Work* (unpublished manuscript); p6.
22 Gai Eaton *The Richest Vein* Faber & Faber, London, 1949; p199.
23 W. Perry: 'The Man and the Witness' in SS *ACRR* p7.

Schuon combined in himself something of the qualities of both Guénon and Coomaraswamy. His work includes psychic, moral and aesthetic dimensions which are missing from Guénon's writings. As Jean Tourniac has remarked

> Un autre écrivian, M. Frithjof Schuon, devait, pour sa part, développer l'exégèse spirituelle des formes traditionnelles dans une série d'ouvrages d'un genre différent de ceux de Guénon, ourages de 'coloration' ... e mot n'est pas excessif, car la beauté et al couleur jouent un rôle particulier dans l'oeuvre de F. Schuon ... plus 'christique' que ceux de Guénon qui, eux, s'en tiennent d'abord, et essentiellement, à la définition des mécanismes principiels invariables.[24]

Schuon's work has a symmetry and an inclusive quality not found in the work of his precursors; there is a balance and fullness which give his writings something of the quality of a spiritual therapy. In this sense Schuon does not simply write about the perennial philosophy but gives it a direct and fresh expression proportioned to the needs of the age.

The contrast with Guénon can be clearly seen in the style and tone of language. If Guénon's expositions can be called 'mathematical', Schuon's might be described as 'musical', this, of course, not implying any deficiency in precision but rather the addition of a dimension of Beauty. As S.H. Nasr has observed of Schuon's writings, 'His authoritative tone, clarity of expression and an "alchemy" which transmutes human language to enable it to present the profoundest truths, make of it a unique expression of the ... *sophia perennis* ...'[25] Marco Pallis refers to what he rather loosely calls 'the gift of tongues': '... the ability, that is to say, both to speak and to understand the various dialects through which the Spirit has chosen to communicate itself ... the power to penetrate all traditional forms ....'.[26]

Like Guénon, Schuon appears to have an intuitive grasp of metaphysical and cosmological principles but he is less likely to subordinate facts to principles in a way which would leave his work vulnerable to scholarly attack. One sometimes senses in Guénon's work an impatience with and disdain for empirical and historical considerations. Schuon's commitment to first principles is no less steadfast but he is more sensitivite to the exigencies and diversities of human experience and to the spiritual textures of different civilisations. In this sense he is closer to Coomaraswamy with whom he also shares a discerning eye for the spiritual riches of traditional art. Although formidably learned Schuon's approach is less academic and scholarly than Coomaraswamy's, less burdened with technical minutiae and the ever-proliferating qualifications which often make Coomaraswamy's work something of an obstacle course. As a writer he is more discursive and fluid, and more poetic, than either Guénon or Coomaraswamy.

For Schuon the study of tradition has meant, primarily, the study of religion within a metaphysical framework. Guénon's work was fixed on questions of principle and on the esoteric repositories of metaphysical wisdom. Coomaraswamy's interests were

---

24 J. Tourniac *Propos sur René Guénon* Paris 1973; p16, quoted in P.L. Reynolds, p13. (Trans: 'Another writer, M. Frithjof Schuon, for his part, had to develop the spiritual exegesis of traditional forms in a series of works of a different kind to those of Guénon, works of high colour – this word is not excessive, for beauty and colour play a distinctive role in the work of F. Schuon – more "Christly" than those of Guénon which essentially hold themselves to defining the mechanisms of invariable principles.')
25 S.H. Nasr: Preface to FS *IPP* pviii.
26 M. Pallis *The Way and the Mountain* Peter Owen, London, 1960; p78.

wide-ranging indeed but, for the most part, underpinned by his preoccupation with the relationships of Truth, Beauty and Goodness. Schuon, on the other hand, moves in a boundless universe, being concerned with the spiritual life in all its aspects. He has written of religion in all its dimensions: doctrinal, ethical, psychological, historical, social, aesthetic and so on. He is equally at home with the most abstruse subtleties of, say, Eckhart's exposition of metaphysical knowledge, and the simple pieties of a European peasant. The explanation of the exoteric-esoteric distinction is fundamental in Schuon's work but, unlike Guénon, he does not restrict himself to the latter domain alone. His books are more attuned to the legitimate claims of religious forms and of theological orthodoxies than those of either of his precursors. He situates the exoteric and esoteric aspects of religion in a framework that gives to each its due.

Writing of the work of Guénon and Coomaraswamy, Whitall Perry suggested that

> The complement and copestone of this witness remained to be realised in the message of Schuon, coming freshly from the sphere of the *Religio Perennis*, in contradistinction to the *Philosophia Perennis* which was the legacy of the other two. His was the third pole, needed to complete the triangle and integrate the work on an operative basis.[27]

There is a nobility of spirit in Schuon's work which makes it something much more than a challenging and arresting body of ideas: it is a profoundly moving *theoria* which reverberates in the deepest recesses of one's being. He is the sublime metaphysician of the age. It is not without reason that Whitall Perry has recently compared Schuon's work to that of Plato and Shankaracharya.[28] In Schuon's work we find the richest, the most authoritative and the most resonant expression of the *sophia perennis* in modern times. One might borrow the following words, applied to Meister Eckhart but equally true of Schuon:

> Being wholly traditional in the truest sense, and therefore perennial, the doctrine he expounds will never cease to be contemporary and always accessible to those who, naturally unsatisfied with mere living, desire to know how to live, regardless of time or place.[29]

---

27 W. Perry: *op.cit.*; p7.
28 W. Perry: 'The Revival of Interest in Tradition' p15.
29 C.F. Kelley *Meister Eckhart on Divine Knowledge* Yale Uni Press, New Haven, 1977; pxv.

5

Other Traditionalists
and the forums of traditionalist thought

... there is a universally intelligible language, not only verbal but also visual, of the fundamental ideas on which the different civilisations have been founded ... We need mediators to whom the common universe of discourse is still a reality ...
Ananda Coomaraswamy[1]

The other important traditionalists have also been reticent about their personal lives and have maintained a silence concerning their own intellectual and spiritual development. We find scant reference to themselves in their work. Nor do their publishers offer readers anything beyond the most skeletal biographical facts. One finds the occasional fragment here and there, like a jigsaw piece. In the first part of this chapter we shall fit some of these pieces together and accompany our sketches of the other leading figures of the traditionalist or perennialist school with a few remarks about their published work.

Titus Burckhardt 1908–1984

In recent times the pre-eminent exponent of traditional thought, after Schuon, was Titus Burckhardt.[2] Born in Florence in 1908, he was the son of the Swiss sculptor Carl Burckhardt, and a member of a patrician family of Basel. Although he first followed in his father's footsteps as a sculptor and illustrator, he was from childhood attracted to medieval and oriental art. This early interest led Burckhardt to a theoretical study of medieval and Eastern doctrines and awoke in him a realisation of the metaphysical or intellectual principles that govern all traditional forms. For Burckhardt, the relationship between art and metaphysics finds perfect expression in the words of Plato: 'Beauty is the Splendour of Truth'. In the same vein a medieval artist had declared '*ars sine scientia nihil*' (art without science is nothing).[3] Following the same line of thought Burckhardt has shown how, in a traditional society, every art is a science, and every science an art. Given that the contemplation of God is the 'art of arts' and the 'science of sciences', one can see from the foregoing how intellectuality and spirituality are but two sides of the same coin, and how each is wholly indispensable. Without true intellectuality there can only be heresy; and without true spirituality there can only be hypocrisy. This, in a nutshell, is the doctrine which Burckhardt exemplified in his life's work.

As a young man, Burckhardt spent many years in North Africa where he mastered the Arabic language and assimilated the classics of Sufism in their original versions. In later years he was to share these treasures with a wider public through his irreplaceable translations of Ibn 'Arabi, Jili, and the eighteenth century Morrocan spiritual master Mulay al 'Arabi ad Darqawi.[4] During this period in North Africa Burckhardt received initiation into a Sufi order. Later, back in Switzerland, he was for several years a director of the publishing firm Urs Graf Verlag which specialised in producing facsimile editions of such outstanding medieval illuminated manuscripts as the *Book of Kells* and the *Lindisfarne Gospels*. These were the early days of fine book production, and the fascinating story – not without its humorous incidents – of how

---

1 AKC *BL* pp80 & 88.
2 For biographical information on Burckhardt see W. Stoddart: 'Right Hand of Truth' and M. Lings: 'Titus Burckhardt', both in the Titus Burckhardt Memorial Issue of *SCR* XVI, i & ii, 1984. This issue also includes contributions from Seyyed Hossein Nasr and Jean-Louis Michon.
3 See A.K. Coomaraswamy: '*Ars Sine Scientia Nihil*' in AKC *SPI* p229.
4 A full bibliography of Burckhardt's work can be found in *Mirror of the Intellect* pp255–262

this great printing and editing feat was accomplished is recounted by Burckhardt in *Von wunderbaren Büchern* (Urs Graf Verlag, 1963).

Burckhardt wrote principally in his native German. Most of his works have now been translated into English: *Introduction to Sufi Doctrine* (1959), *Sacred Art in East and West* (1967), *Alchemy: science of the cosmos, science of the soul* (1967), *The Art of Islam* (1976). He has written, in beautiful and evocative fashion, on sacred art, architecture and history, in a series of impressive monographs: *Sienna, City of the Virgin* (1960), *Moorish Culture in Spain* (1972), *Fez, City of Islam* (1992) and *Chartres and the Birth of the Cathedral* (1995). His masterly review of the deviations of modern science, 'Cosmology and Modern Science', was published in *The Sword of Gnosis* (1974), and is also included in Burckhardt's collected essays, *Mirror of the Intellect* (1987), edited by William Stoddart.

Burckhardt's work is in one sense a prolongation of that of Frithjof Schuon, but at every turn it also bears witness to his own spiritual originality and imposing gifts. Primarily a metaphysician, his works on sacred art and alchemy also testify to his gift for elucidating the cosmological principles that inform traditional arts and sciences. He was undoubtedly one of the most authoritative exponents of the traditional point of view. He died in Lausanne in 1984.

Marco Pallis *1895–1990*

The only Buddhist in what might be called the 'inner circle' of traditionalists was Marco Pallis.[5] He was born of Greek parents in Liverpool in 1895, educated at Harrow and Liverpool University, and served in the British army during the Great War. Later he studied music with Arnold Dolmetsch whose approach, Pallis tells us, was shaped by 'a radical rejection of the idea of "progress", as applied to the arts, at a time when the rest of the musical profession took this for granted.'[6] Dolmetsch himself was familiar with Coomaraswamy's work and it was through him that Pallis first heard of Coomaraswamy who was to become a decisive influence, with Guénon, in Pallis's intellectual and spiritual development.

In 1923 Pallis visited southern Tibet on a mountaineering trip. He returned to Tibet in 1936, consumed by an interest in its traditional culture. He returned for a third and more extended visit after the second World War when he lived and studied under Tibetan lamas near Shigatse and was initiated into one of the lineages with the Tibetan name of Thubden Tendzin.[7] On his way to Tibet in 1947 Pallis visited René Guénon in Cairo. He had already translated two of Guénon's books with his friend Richard Nicholson. He also visited Ceylon and South India, receiving the *darśan* of Ramana Maharshi at Tiravunnamalai. Whilst in India and Sikkim Pallis kept a protective eye on Ananda Coomaraswamy's son Rama who had been sent to India to study Hindi and Sanskrit. Pallis never met the elder Coomaraswamy but maintained a friendly correspondence with him and enlisted his aid in persuading

---

5 Information on Pallis taken from his own books, from his article 'A Fateful Meeting of Minds: A.K. Coomaraswamy and René Guénon' *SCR* XII, ii & iv, 1978; pp1175-188, and from T. Merton *Asian Journal* New Directions, New York, 1975; pp71-72.
6 'A Fateful Meeting of Minds' p176.
7 A. Desjardins *The Message of the Tibetans* Stuart & Watkins, London, 1969; p20.

Guénon to reconsider his attitude to Buddhism. Pallis returned to England in 1950 and, with Richard Nicholson and some other musicians, formed 'The English Consort of Viols', a group dedicated to the preservation of early English music. In a sense this completed the circle which began with his studies under Dolmetsch in the 1920s. Pallis made several concert tours with this group. On one such tour to the U.S.A. he met Thomas Merton with whom he had already opened a correspondence.[8]

Marco Pallis wrote two books deriving from his experiences in Tibet: *Peaks and Lamas* (1939) which was reprinted several times and became something of a bestseller, and *The Way and the Mountain* (1960), recently reprinted. They are a unique blend of travelogue, discursive essays on the Tibetan civilisation, and metaphysics. He also wrote a good number of articles for *Studies in Comparative Religion*, many of which are included in his last publication, *A Buddhist Spectrum* (1980). The work of Marco Pallis radiates a distinctively Buddhist ambience. The tone is less combative and more amiable than that found in the work of some of the other traditionalists but he is no less tough-minded. His writings on Buddhism fulfil a vital function, this tradition receiving comparatively little attention from other traditionalists. Marco Pallis died in 1990.

Martin Lings *b 1909*

The foremost English traditionalist, Martin Lings, was born in Burnage, Lancashire, in 1909.[9] After studying English at Oxford he was appointed Lecturer in Anglo-Saxon at the University of Kaunas. As with many of his fellow-traditionalists, an interest in Islam took him travelling to the Middle East and North Africa. A trip to Egypt in 1939 brought an appointment as Lecturer in Shakespeare at Cairo University. He spent many years in Cairo where he had a close association with Guénon.

In 1952 Lings returned to England to take out a doctorate in Arabic (in which he was already fluent) at London University. He worked for many years at the British Museum where he was Keeper of Oriental Manuscripts and Printed Books. He is an authority on Koranic manuscripts and calligraphy. His biography of the Shaikh Ahmad al-'Alawi, *A Moslem Saint of the Twentieth Century* (1961), was widely acclaimed. *The Book of Certainty* (1952), written under his Islamic name, Abu Bakr Siraj ad-Din, dealt with Sufic doctrines of faith, vision and gnosis while *What is Sufism?* (1975) is a more general and less technical work. In *Ancient Beliefs and Modern Superstitions* (1965) Lings took up certain themes from Guénon and Coomaraswamy to write a powerful indictment of modernism. He has also published a fascinating study of ten of Shakespeare's major plays, *The Secret of Shakespeare* (1966). More recent work includes the scholarly and authoritative *The Quranic Art of Calligraphy and Illumination* (1976), *Symbol and Archetype* (1991) and *The Eleventh Hour* (1993). Perhaps his most enduring work will be *Muhammad: his life based on the earliest sources* (1983) in which the Prophet's life is recounted with an authority and dignity appropriate to the subject. As well as his expertise in the field of Islamic studies Lings brings to traditionalism a cultivated English sensibility and a gift for expressing complex truths in simple language.

---

8   See M. Pallis: 'Thomas Merton, 1915–1968' *SCR* III, iii, 1969; pp138–146.
9   Information on Lings taken from his own publications.

Whitall Perry *b 1920*

The most authoritative traditionalist of American background is Whitall Perry.[10] He was born near Boston in 1920. His early intellectual interests included Platonism and Vedanta. He travelled in the Middle and Far East both before and after World War II with a brief interlude of study at Harvard University. He was one of several Harvard students who came under Coomaraswamy's influence in the 1940s, Joseph Epes Brown being another. Between 1946 and 1952 Perry and his wife lived in Egypt, at which time he developed close ties with René Guénon, after whose death he moved with his family to Switzerland. He was already a close associate of Frithjof Schuon with whom he returned to the United States in 1980.

Coomaraswamy once expressed the view that the time was ripe for someone well-versed in the world's great religious traditions and fluent in several languages to compile an encyclopedic anthology drawing together the spiritual wisdom of the ages in a single volume. This task was to be accomplished by Whitall Perry whose seventeen-year labour bore fruit in *A Treasury of Traditional Wisdom* (1971).[11] This is a work of singular importance. In his Introduction Perry invites the reader

> to enter upon a spiritual journey. In this book he will encounter the heritage he shares in common with all humanity, in what is essentially timeless and enduring and pertinent to his final ends. Out of this myriad mosaic of material emerges a pattern of the human personality in the cosmos that is unerringly consistent, clear and struck through with a resonance infallible in its ever renewed reverberations of the one same Reality.[12]

Thousands of quotations have been woven into an immense tapestry whose threads have been drawn from all the major religious and esoteric traditions. Each section of the book is introduced with a concise and acute commentary, usually referring to the works of Guénon, Coomaraswamy and Schuon to whom Perry acknowledges a debt of 'profound gratitude' and 'whose several roles', Perry tells us, 'have been altogether indispensable in the formation of this work'. While performing a valuable service in bringing the work of 'the great triumvirate' to the attention of a wider audience Perry has himself discharged an awesome labour in pulling together the many strands of traditional wisdom between the covers of a single volume in which the concrete reality of the *sophia perennis*, axiomatic in traditionalism, is revealed and documented. It would, of course, be impossible to uncover every manifestation of the Primordial Wisdom in all its plenitude but Perry has surely come close to such an ideal. It is a monumental and profoundly impressive achievement in the light of which the only remotely comparable book, Aldous Huxley's *The Perennial Philosophy* (1945), pales into insignificance.[13]

Perry is also the author of *Gurdjieff in the Light of Tradition* (1978), a work commissioned by the Editor of *Studies in Comparative Religion* to help dispel the miasma of

---

10 Material on Perry drawn from his own publications, especially 'The Man and the Witness' in SS *ACRR* pp5ff. Also from M. Pallis's Foreword to WP *TTW* pp7-11.
11 For a review of this anthology see P. Moore in *SCR* VI, i, 1972.
12 WP *TTW* p19.
13 We shall have more to say about Huxley's idiosyncratic view of the perennial philosophy in Chapter 11.

confusion that surrounds the Armenian thaumaturge. Recently he has published *The Widening Breach: Evolutionism in the Mirror of Cosmology* (1995) and *Challenges to a Secular Society* (1996), the latter a collection of essays on subjects such as drug-induced 'mysticism', reincarnation doctrines, psychotherapy, modern 'guru' figures, Shakespeare, cosmology and psychology. Perry's work is less well-known than that of some of the other traditionalists, perhaps because he has steered clear of any academic milieu and has lived in reclusion. However, *A Treasury* is arguably the single most important work in the traditionalist canon.

Seyyed Hossein Nasr *b 1933*

An eminent Islamicist and of the living traditionalists the most widely known in academic circles, Seyyed Hossein Nasr was born in Tehran.[14] As a young man he studied physics and the history of science at the Massachusetts Institute of Technology and at Harvard University, graduating from these institutions with a B.Sc., M.A. and Ph.D. He rapidly established himself as an authority on Islamic philosophy and science, and on Sufism. In 1958 he became Professor of Science and Philosophy at Tehran University and in 1964–65 occupied the first Aga Khan Chair of Islamic Studies at the American University at Beirut. Nasr became Chancellor of Aryamehr University in 1972 and was also the Founder President of the Imperial Iranian Academy of Philosophy which published the traditionalist journal *Sophia Perennis*. The purpose of the Imperial Academy, of which Nasr was the President, was stated thus:

> The goals of the Academy are the revival of the traditional intellectual life of Islamic Persia: the publication of texts and studies pertaining to both Islamic and pre-Islamic Persia; making the intellectual treasures of Persia in the field of philosophy, mysticism and the like known to the outside world; making possible extensive research in comparative philosophy; making Persians aware of the intellectual traditions of other civilisations in both East and West; encouraging intellectual confrontations with the modern world; and finally, discussing from the point of view of tradition various problems facing modern man.[15]

Since the political changes in Iran Nasr has lived in the U.S.A. and after some years in the Religious Studies Department at Temple University is now the University Professor of Islamic Studies at George Washington University. In 1962 and 1965 he was a visiting lecturer at Harvard University and at the University of Chicago in 1966. Nasr has lectured extensively not only in the U.S.A. but in Europe, the Middle East, Pakistan, India, Japan and Australia. He has published widely, being the author of some two dozen books and a frequent contributor to Islamic and traditionalist journals.[16]

---

14 Information about Nasr taken from notes accompanying his own publications, from Notes on Contributors in Y. Ibish & P.L. Wilson *Traditional Modes of Contemplation and Action* Imperial Iranian Academy of Philosophy, Tehran, 1977; p472, and from Notes on Contributors in several journals. A useful biographical sketch can be found in W. Chittick (ed) *The Works of Seyyed Hossein Nasr Through His Fortieth Birthday* Research Monograph No 6, Middle East Center, University of Utah, Salt Lake City, 1977. See also W. Stoddart's Introduction to T. Burckhardt *Mirror of the Intellect* Quinta Essentia, Cambridge/SUNY, Albany, 1987; pp3–9.

15 Quoted in the Editorial *SCR* X, i, 1976; pp3–4.

16 See Chittick for full bibliographical details upto 1977.

The hallmarks of Nasr's work are his rigorous scholarly methodology, his encyclopedic erudition about all matters Islamic, a robustness of critical thought, and a sustained clarity of expression. His most important works fall into three groups: those concerned with Islamic science and philosophy which include *An Introduction to Islamic Cosmological Doctrines* (1964), *Science and Civilisation in Islam* (1968), and *Islamic Science-An Illustrated History* (1976); works dealing with Islam more generally or with the mystical traditions of Sufism, *Three Muslim Sages* (1964), *Ideals and Realities of Islam* (1966), *Islamic Studies* (1967), *Sufi Essays* (1972), studies of Rumi and Sadr al-Din Shirazi, and *Islamic Art and Spirituality* (1987); and thirdly, books in which specifically modern problems are investigated in the light of traditional metaphysics: *The Encounter of Man and Nature* (1968), *Islam and the Plight of Modern Man* (1976), *Traditional Islam in the Modern World* (1987) and *Religion and the Order of Nature* (1996). Seyyed Hossein Nasr was the first non-European invited by Edinburgh University to give the prestigious Gifford Lectures in Natural Theology. This he did in 1981 and the lectures were subsequently published under the title *Knowledge and the Sacred*.

In recent times, these men – Burckhardt, Pallis, Lings, Perry and Nasr, along with Frithjof Schuon – have formed a kind of beneficent traditionalist sodality. Clearly there have been personal links between them as well as a shared philosophy. They have all written widely and any discussion of contemporary traditionalism must centre on this group. If an image of concentric circles be permissible we might say that Guénon, Coomaraswamy and Schuon occupy the inner circle of traditionalist thought, these men the next. Pursuing our image we could say that the persons in the next circle would include Lord Northbourne, Gai Eaton, Leo Schaya, Philip Sherrard, Joseph Epes Brown, Rama Coomaraswamy and William Stoddart whose works have been less seminal than those of the major figures. We shall confine our portraiture of these men to a few jottings.

Lord Northbourne was of the older generation of traditionalists.[17] He was born in 1896 and educated at Eton and Oxford. He played a role in the development of traditionalism in two ways: firstly as author of two comparatively simple but extremely useful books in which some of the central tenets of traditionalism are outlined, *Religion in the Modern World* (1963) and *Looking Back on Progress* (1970); and secondly, as the translator of that cardinal work, Guénon's *The Reign of Quantity*.

Gai Eaton was born in Switzerland and educated at Charterhouse and Cambridge.[18] He served as a young man in the British Army during World War II and later worked as a teacher, journalist and diplomat in Egypt, India and the Carribean. He was one of the first people to write in English about the work of René Guénon: *The Richest Vein*, a book commissioned by T.S. Eliot, includes an incisive essay on the writings of Guénon and Coomaraswamy which remains a valuable introduction to these two figures. More recently he published *King of the Castle* (1978), an inquiry into choice and responsibility in the modern world, and *Islam and the Destiny of Man*

---

17 Information on Lord Northbourne taken from his own books and from *Who's Who?* Adam and Charles Black, London, 1980.

18 Information on Eaton from his own books and from M. Pallis's review of *King of the Castle* in SCRXII, i & ii, 1978; pp119–123.

(1986), a work which directly confronts some of the political realities of the twentieth century.

Leo Schaya was, until his death some years ago, editor of the French journal *Études Traditionnelles*.[19] He was born in Switzerland in 1916 and later lived in France. He was an authority on Sufism and on the Kabbalah, subjects on which he published *La doctrine soufique de l'unité* (1962) – an English translation has been completed by Nancy Pearson – and *The Universal Meaning of the Kabbalah* (1971).

Joseph Epes Brown was the author of two important works: *The Spiritual Legacy of the American Indians* (1982) and *Animals of the Soul* (1992), which bring a fully traditionalist outlook to bear on the spiritual culture of the Plains Indians of North America. He also edited *The Sacred Pipe* (1953), based on Black Elk's account of the ritual forms of the Oglala Sioux. He was, until his recent death, a professor of Religious Studies at the University of Montana.

Philip Sherrard was a Lecturer in Orthodox Church History at London University and a member of the Greek Orthodox Church. As well as several fine works on aspects of the Orthodox tradition he published *The Rape of Man and Nature* (1987) – which, along with Nasr's *Man and Nature*, is one of the most far-reaching analyses of the ravages of modern scientism – *The Sacred in Life and Art* (1990), and *Human Image, World Image: the death and resurrection of sacred cosmology* (1992).

Rama Coomaraswamy, son of the illustrious Doctor, was born in Massachusetts in 1929 and educated in England at Wycliffe College.[20] He went with Marco Pallis to India to study Hindi and Sanskrit at the Haridwar Gurukul. He was there at the time of his father's death in the same year. He returned to America to study medicine and later practiced as a surgeon in Greenwich, Connecticut. He is a Roman Catholic and his book *The Destruction of the Christian Tradition* (1980) analyses the Catholic Church's deviation from its own traditions with the Second Vatican Council. With Alvin Moore Jnr he edited *Selected Letters of Ananda Coomaraswamy* (1987).

William Stoddart is the author of *Sufism, The Mystical Doctrines and Methods of Islam* (1976), *Outline of Hinduism* (1993) and *Outline of Buddhism* (1998), and contributed the chapter, 'Mysticism', to the traditionalist compendium *The Unanimous Tradition*, edited by Ranjit Fernando. He is the leading authority on the work of Titus Burckhardt four of whose books he has translated from the German. Originally from Britain, he now lives in Canada.

Anyone who has given more than cursory attention to the writings of these men will not doubt that they form a unified group. They share philosophical assumptions and adhere to a specific understanding of the perennial philosophy. Their works are shot through with the same ideas, principles and themes. The solidarity of the group is evident not only in the substance of their writings but in several superficial and more immediately obvious ways. They contribute to the same journals; they translate, review and preface each others' works; they all acknowledge a debt to the work of Guénon, Coomaraswamy and Schuon; they frequently refer to and commend writings by others in the traditionalist school. Guénon's translators include Marco Pallis

---

19 See Y. Ibish & P.L. Wilson: *op.cit.*; p475.
20 On Rama Coomaraswamy see M. Pallis: 'A Fateful Meeting of Minds' and RL *CLW* (see Index).

and Lord Northbourne, both of whom have also translated work by Schuon. Lord Northbourne also translated one of Burckhardt's books, as has William Stoddart, another of Schuon's translators. Doubtless there are many other reciprocal relationships, personal and intellectual, which are not visible to the public eye.

We are not concerned in this study with any kind of sociological or quasi-psychological analysis of the traditionalists as a group. For one thing the data is not available and for another our focus is on the works not the persons. The work of the later traditionalists has, in large measure, explored avenues opened up by Guénon, Coomaraswamy and Schuon. Certainly new fields of inquiry have been marked out but within the framework of traditionalism set up by these three. The traditionalist literature covers the whole field of metaphysics, cosmology, mythology, folklore and religion together with an implacable critique of the modern world.

To be a traditionalist is to be committed to one or another of the religious traditions. Traditionalism demands not merely a mental assent but an engagement of the whole person, evinced by a direct participation in a living tradition. It does not allow of any free-wheeling syncretism nor of any kind of factitious universalism such as would subvert the formal claims of any particular religious tradition. Fine scholars and linguists though some of the traditionalists are, their interest in religion always incorporates what we might call the experiential or existential dimension and goes beyond the purely academic. The traditionalists have studied and experienced religion 'in the field', as it were, not merely in the library.

There are, apart from the traditionalists themselves, several scholars whose work exhibits, in varying degree, a strong traditionalist influence. Mention should be made of Professors Huston Smith, Victor Danner (Indiana), the Rev Shojun Bando (Hawaii), Elémire Zolla (Italy), Toshihiko Izutsu (Japan), William Chittick (State University of New York), James Cutsinger (South Carolina), Wolfgang Smith (Oregon) and Adrian Snodgrass (Sydney).[21] The names of other traditionalists can be found in the pages of journals such as *Studies in Comparative Religion*, *Sophia Perennis*, *Études Traditionnelles*, *Sophia* and *Avaloka* (though it must be remembered that many contributors to these journals are in no way traditionalist).

A *fin-de-siècle* French theosophical journal, *Le Voile d'Isis*, founded in 1898, described itself as a '*revue . . . d'études ésoteriques, psychiques et divinatoires*'.[22] The title, reminiscent of Madame Blavatsky's famous work, signals something of the journal's initial orientation. It is not without some irony that this journal should become the voice-piece of European traditionalism. We have already charted the shift in Guénon's outlook. Under Guénon's influence something similar happened to *Le Voile d'Isis*. In 1929 the journal's subtitle was changed to '*revue mensuelle de Haute Science*' and its programme now described as '*l'étude de la Tradition et des divers mouvements du spiritualisme ancien et moderne*'.[23] Guénon had first contributed to this journal in the early 1920s but now

---

[21] For information on some of these figures see Notes on Contributors in Y. Ibish & P.L. Wilson: *op.cit.*; pp469–477. Professor Huston Smith has been singularly important in championing Schuon's work within the American academic establishment. For further information about Smith see A. Sharma (ed) *Fragments of Infinity: Essays in Religion and Philosophy*, A *Festschrift* in Honour of Professor Huston Smith, Prism, Dorset, 1991. See also Notes on Contributors in *RH* pp328–329.
[22] Most of the information following is taken from RL *CLW* pp270ff.
[23] Trans: 'The study of Tradition and the diverse movements of ancient and modern spirituality.'

started to exert an influence that was to result in a different philosophical slant, reflected in yet another subtitle change in 1932: *'La seule revue en language française ayant pour objet l'étude des doctrines traditionelles tant orientales qu'occidentales, ainsi que des sciences qui s'y rattachent.'*[24] Furthermore, the editors spoke quite unequivocally of *'LA TRADITION PERPETUELLE ET UNANIME, révélée tant par les dogmes et les rites des religions orthodoxes que par la langue universelle des symboles initiatiques.'*[25] The journal's platform was now that of traditionalism but it retained its original title until 1937 when it became *Études Traditionnelles*.

In England, the writings of the traditionalists first appeared mainly in *The Islamic Quarterly* published in London from 1954. It carried some important articles by Schuon, Burckhardt, Nasr and Martin Lings. However, this journal was to be completely overshadowed, as a traditionalist forum, by *Studies in Comparative Religion* which underwent a development parallel to that of *Études Traditionnelles*, and was to become an English-language journal given over exclusively to traditionalist thought. *Studies in Comparative Religion* was a direct descendant of *Tomorrow*, founded in the early 1940s as a parapsychological journal devoted to the ventilation of such subjects as spiritualism and mediumship, psychic healing, and telepathy. The first editor was Eileen J. Garrett, herself a well-known medium and President of the Parapsychology Foundation.[26] The critical shift took place in the early 1960s when the journal, now under the editorship of F. Clive-Ross, started to publish articles by traditionalists such as Whitall Perry, Titus Burckhardt and Marco Pallis. As with the French journal three decades earlier, a change in orientation was marked by a change in the subtitle, now 'The Journal of Parapsychology, Cosmology and Traditional Studies'. In the Autumn Issue of 1963 the editor announced that the journal would carry a series of articles by Guénon, originally published in *Études Traditionnelles*. He also welcomed Frithjof Schuon as a new contributor and expressed his 'satisfaction at being able to make available to readers some of the little writing that is of real importance in these troubled times.'[27] For a brief period traditionalists and spiritualists rubbed shoulders in the journals but by 1967 when the journal took on the title of *Studies in Comparative Religion* the transformation was an accomplished fact.[28] In ratifying the change the editor told readers that the journal '... is devoted to the exposition of the teachings, spiritual methods, symbols and other facets of the religious traditions of the world, together with the arts and sciences which have sprung from these religions.'[29] The subtitle also underwent a *post-eventum* change to 'Metaphysics, Cosmology, Tradition, Symbolism'. The periodical continued under this aegis until the early 1980s when the death of its editor, Mr. Francis Clive-Ross, and insurmountable financial difficulties spelled the end of a journal which for twenty years had provided

---

24 Trans: 'The only journal in French having as its object of study the traditional doctrines of East and West, as well as the sciences dependent on them.'

25 Trans: 'THE PERPETUAL AND UNANIMOUS TRADITION, revealed by the dogmas and rites of orthodox religions, no less than by the universal language of initiatic symbols.'

26 On Eileen Garrett and for something of the 'atmosphere' of the journal before the mid-60s see her own article 'The Nature of My Controls' *TOMORROW* XI, iv, 1963; pp324–328.

27 Editorial in the same issue; pp292–293.

28 This journal should not be confused with two other publications under the same title, one a series of apologetic pamphlets issued by the Catholic Truth Society in the 1930s, the other a series of scholarly monographs published in Stockholm. See E.J. Sharpe *Comparative Religion* Duckworth, London, 1975; p265.

29 Editorial *SCR* I, i, 1967; p1.

the most important forum for traditionalist writings in English. (The unique contribution made by Clive-Ross to both *Studies in Comparative Religion* and to the very important publishing program of Perennial Books in the 1960s and 70s should not go unremarked.) It was in *Studies* that many of Schuon's writings first appeared in English translation. *Studies* also performed an invaluable service in bringing translations of many works by Guénon and Coomaraswamy to new readers. Burckhardt, Nasr, Pallis, Perry, Lings and Rama Coomaraswamy were all regular contributors. Other regular but less frequent contributors included Donald Bishop, Gai Eaton, R.W.J. Austin, Angus MacNab, Kathleen Raine, Joseph Epes Brown, Victor Danner, Shojun Bando, Dorothea Deed and D.M. Matheson. The intellectual catholicity of traditionalism is reflected in the stated policy of the journal which, as the editor emphasized, 'is not sectarian and, inasmuch as it is not tied to the interests of any particular religious group, it is free to lay stress on the common spirit underlying the various religious forms.'[30]

In 1975 a new journal, *Sophia Perennis*, appeared in Tehran under the auspices of the Imperial Iranian Academy of Philosophy. Edited by Peter Lamborn Wilson and Karamat Ra'na-Hoseyni it appeared twice-yearly and carried articles in several languages, providing a more international forum for traditionalist thought. But in 1978, political events in Iran led to the closure of the Academy bringing the development of this journal to an untimely end.

Later, in 1981 a new periodical *Temenos* appeared in England. Edited by Kathleen Raine, Philip Sherrard, Keith Critchlow and Brian Keeble it proved to be a lively forum in which some discussion centered on the application of traditionalist principles in the sphere of the arts. Another journal carrying some traditionalist articles, *Avaloka*, also appeared in the 1980s under the editorship of Arthur Versluis but is now defunct. Mention should also be made of the American journal *Parabola* which has carried articles by traditionalists such as Coomaraswamy, Seyyed Hossein Nasr and Gai Eaton. Despite the demise of the Imperial Iranian Academy of Philosophy, the end of that decade and the early 80s witnessed the establishment of Institutes of Traditional Studies in Sri Lanka and Peru, and of the Foundation for Traditional Studies in the United States, which now publishes the new traditionalist journal *Sophia*.[31]

A few other developments which have helped to expose traditionalist thought to a wider audience should be noted. In the summer of 1973 an international colloquium was held at Rothko Chapel in Houston, on the theme 'Traditional Modes of Contemplation and Action'. The participants included several traditionalists and a good many scholars and religious leaders sympathetic to the traditionalist outlook. The papers from this important colloquium were published in 1977 by the Imperial Iranian Academy of Philosophy in a handsome volume, edited by Yusuf Ibish and P.L. Wilson, and introduced by Marco Pallis.

In 1976 the World of Islam Festival held in London occasioned the publication of four major works by eminent traditionalists: *Islam and the Perennial Philosophy* by

---

30 *ibid.*

31 Readers interested in *Sophia*, the journal of the Foundation for Traditional Studies should write to PO Box 370, Oakton, Virginia 22124, USA.

Titus Burckhardt

Frithjof Schuon, and a set of three lavishly-produced companion volumes, Burckhardt's *The Art of Islam*, Nasr's *Islamic Science, An Illustrated History* and *The Quranic Art of Calligraphy and Illumination* by Martin Lings.

In 1985 a conference on traditional themes was held in Lima, Peru, organised jointly by the Institute of Traditional Studies in Peru (Instituto Estudios Tradicionales) and the Foundation of Traditional Studies in Washington. It brought together a number of distinguished traditionalists from Europe and North America and scholars of Andean traditions. A collection of the papers delivered at the conference in English was later published by the Foundation of Traditional Studies under the title *In Quest of the Sacred* (1994), edited by Seyyed Hossein Nasr and Katherine O'Brien.

In 1974, as part of their Metaphysical Library, Penguin Books published an anthology of traditionalist writings entitled *The Sword of Gnosis*, edited by Jacob Needleman. For many years it remained the best general introduction to traditionalist thought. That distinction it now shares with *The Unanimous Tradition*, a collection of essays edited by Ranjit Fernando and published by the Sri Lanka Institute of Traditional Studies in 1991.

World Wisdom Books, based in Bloomington, Indiana, and in England *Golgonooza Press* of Ipswich and *Quinta Essentia* of Cambridge have emerged in the last decade as important publishers of traditionalist works. *Sophia Perennis et Universalis*, an information and book distribution centre in Ghent, New York, is now the largest stockist of traditionalist literature with its own publishing list of some of Guénon's out-of-print and long neglected works.[32]

Discussing the work of contemporary traditionalists, Gai Eaton observed that

> These books and articles present variety in unity, very different voices speaking from a single stand-point. Few readers respond to them in a neutral or tepid fashion. For some they open up new horizons, often with a sense of shock, discovery and delight, while others, who cannot bear to have their ingrained habits of thought and all the cherished assumptions of the age so ruthlessly challenged, are angered and outraged. They provoke ... a polarisation of perspectives which serves to clarify thought and to define the demarcation line between the basic tendencies of our time, the traditional and the modernist...[33]

In the following section of this study we shall turn to some of the principles and values which determine the traditionalist perspective.

---

[32] Readers interested in the extensive catalogue of works now available from *Sophia Perennis et Universalis* should write to Mr James Wetmore, RD2 Box 223, Ghent, NY 12075, USA.
[33] Gai Eaton: *op.cit.*; p219.

II

Tradition and the traditions

6

Tradition

towards the definition of a principle

... the very idea of tradition has been destroyed to such an extent that those who aspire to recover it no longer know which way to turn *René Guénon*[1]

Tradition, in the rightful sense of the word, is the chain that joins civilisation to Revelation *Lord Northbourne*[2]

Outside tradition there can assuredly be found some relative truths ... but outside tradition there does not exist a doctrine that catalyzes absolute truths and transmits liberating notions concerning total reality *Frithjof Schuon*[3]

One might embark on the controlling themes of traditionalist thought from any number of points but the idea of tradition itself is perhaps the most appropriate. It is a capital idea and in the traditionalist lexicon is freighted with a profound significance. As Roger Lipsey has observed,

> It implies a very specific vision of nearly everything, and is a fundamental idea that cannot be used 'a little' because it implies so many values and criticisms. It is rather a fixed idea – a content to be understood, not a content in evolution...[4]

The word 'tradition' thus becomes a short-hand or glyph for a whole world-view. Here we shall rehearse some of the primary meanings signified by the term.

St Augustine speaks of 'Wisdom uncreate, the same now as it ever was and ever will be'.[5] This timeless wisdom has carried many names: *philosophia perennis*, *Lex Aeterna*, *Hagia Sophia*, *Din al-Haqq*, *Akālika Dhamma* and *Sanātana Dharma* are among the better known. In itself and as such this truth is formless and beyond all conceptualisations. Any attempt to define it is, to borrow a metaphor, like trying to catch the wind in a bag. This universal wisdom, in existence since the dawn of time and the spiritual patrimony of all humankind, can also be designated as the Primordial Tradition. Guénon refers, in one of his earliest articles, to '... the Tradition contained in the Sacred Books of all peoples, a Tradition which in reality is everywhere the same, in spite of all the diverse forms it assumes to adapt itself to each race and period....'.[6] In this sense tradition becomes synonymous with a perennial philosophy which is eternal, universal and immutable.[7] This amounts, in the traditionalist view, to a first principle, the *sine qua non* of traditionalism. It is a principle that has met with a good deal of scepticism, even derision, in modern times. The credibility of the principle, if one might so put it, has been compromised by its exploitation by all manner of thinkers and groups claiming adherence to some kind of vague universalist essence without really understanding its nature. It is crucial to understand that those who apparently subscribe to this principle do not necessarily do so from the same intellectual base.

As to the idea of a primordial truth or wisdom, the traditionalists point out that all the great religious teachings, albeit in the differing vocabularies appropriate to the spiritual economy in question, affirm just such a principle. We remember Krishna's declaration, in the *Bhagavad Gītā*, of the pre-existence of his message, proclaimed at the dawn of time.[8] Likewise Christ, speaking in his cosmic function as incarnation of the Truth, states, 'Verily I say unto you, before Abraham was, I am'.[9] Affirmations

---

1   RG *RQ* p251.
2   Lord Northbourne *Religion in the Modern World* J.M. Dent, London, 1963; p34.
3   F. Schuon: 'No Activity Without Truth' in JN *SG* p36.
4   RL *CLW* p266.
5   Quoted in S. Radhakrishnan: 'Fragments of a Confession' in P.A. Schilpp (ed) *The Philosophy of Sarvepalli Radhakrishnan* Tudor, New York, 1952; p80.
6   R. Guénon in *La Gnose* 1909, quoted in WP *TTW* p20.
7   See 'Vedanta and Western Tradition' in AKC *SPII* p7. See also SHN *K&S* p74.
8   *Bhagavad Gītā* IV.5.i.
9   *St John* VIII.58. For a brief commentary see M. Pallis *A Buddhist Spectrum* Allen & Unwin, London, 1980; p157.

of the principle are to be found over and over in the integral religious traditions. A few examples:

The true doctrine has always existed in the world.   *Chou Li*[10]

That which is called the Christian Religion existed among the Ancients, and never did not exist, from the beginning of the human race.   *St Augustine*[11]

There must first be one from which the many arise. This one is competent to lend itself to all yet remain one ... this is identify in variety.   *Plotinus*[12]

'Tradition' in its most pristine sense is this primordial truth and as such takes on the status of a first cause, a cosmic datum or a kind of principial reality woven into the very fabric of the universe. As such it is not amenable to 'proof'. It is a self-evident, self-validating principle in the face of which it is possible only to understand or not understand. As Coomaraswamy points out, 'a first cause, being itself uncaused, is not probable but axiomatic'.[13] (By 'uncaused' Coomaraswamy here means unconditioned, outside the realm of phenomenal contingencies.) Thus the Primordial Tradition or *sophia perennis* is of supra-human origin and is in no sense a product or evolute of human thought: it is 'the birth-right of humanity'.[14] It is, in Marco Pallis's words, 'formless and supra-personal in its essence' and thus 'escapes exact definition in terms of human speech and thought'.[15]

This sense of tradition is seminal in Guénon's work but the word sometimes carries a different significance which can, for some readers, be the cause of confusion. Etymologically 'tradition' simply means 'that which is transmitted' and this is the key to the second meaning of the word in the contexts with which we are concerned. Here tradition cannot simply be equated with a formless and immutable Truth but is rather that Truth as it finds formal expression in the myths, rituals, symbols, doctrines, iconographies and other manifestations of different primal and religious civilisations, through the medium of a divine Revelation. The Truth as such is formless and so cannot be conveyed, as such, within forms: thus it is aspects of Truth, or partial truths, as it were, which are transmitted by traditional forms.

Thus far we have two related but distinct meanings for the word 'tradition': a timeless, formless and immutable wisdom revealed at the beginning of time; and the formal embodiment of this wisdom which is transmitted through time.[16] To these two senses can be added a third: 'tradition' may sometimes refer to the living process of the transmission itself. It may also refer, fourthly, to the channels of transmission. If we pause to establish a simple convention we shall perhaps avert some potential

---

10 in WP *TTW* p794.
11 Quoted in S. Radhakrishnan: *op.cit.*; p80.
12 in WP *TTW* p776.
13 A.K. Coomaraswamy *Time and Eternity* Artibus Asiae, Ascona, 1947; p42fn.
14 Coomaraswamy in Letter to Vasudeva Saharan Agrawala, March 1939, AKC *SL* p168.
15 Cited in RF *UT* p1.
16 A caution must here be issued against seeing any particular tradition as no more than a temporal continuity of the Primordial Tradition. Guénon's work sometimes leaves the way open for this kind of misunderstanding. For a definitive treatment of the relationship between Tradition and the traditions see SHN *K&S* Ch 2, esp. pp66–69, 74. See also W. Perry: 'The Revival of Interest in Tradition' in RF *UT*.

misunderstandings. **Tradition**: the primordial wisdom, or Truth, immutable and unformed; **tradition**: a formal embodiment of Truth under a particular mythological or religious guise which is transmitted through time; or the vehicle for the transmission of this formal embodiment; or the process of transmission itself. This is not as confusing as it might look: once the distinction between the first sense and the other three has been grasped then the meaning carried by the word becomes clear in the context in which it is used. We can follow the same kind of expedient to distinguish two meanings of 'truth': **Truth**: equatable with Tradition; **truth**: an expression of Truth and, as such, incomplete.

When Guénon uses the word 'tradition' he is more often than not referring to what we shall now call Tradition. As we have noted, Guénon was not much interested in history and was not particularly interested in the different historical traditions. However, the later traditionalists frequently use the word to refer to different religious and spiritual heritages as they are manifested in time. When they speak of a tradition they are referring to a channel for the transmission of truths of supra-human origin, couched in the forms which have been providentially adapted to suit the needs and receptivities of the peoples and civilisations in question. This can be re-stated in Marco Pallis's words:

> ... tradition ... namely an effective communication of principles of more-than-human origin ... through use of forms that will have arisen by applying those principles to contingent needs.[17]

Plainly tradition here means something quite other than the blind observance of custom and something more than a temporal continuity. It cannot simply be assimilated to any historical process. The word must be purged of its negative associations if it is to be properly understood in the traditionalist context. Brian Keeble makes a crucial point in writing,

> ... tradition is far beyond being merely an accumulation of human endeavour and invention even if it does have a history. Granting that the external characteristics and expression of a tradition are coloured by and reflect the passage of time, nonetheless, to equate tradition with a form of historical continuity is to ignore its supra-formal essence in the name of which it remains free and objective in relation to spatio-temporal determinations.[18]

The reference here to 'supra-formal essence' is, of course, the key to the relationship between Tradition and tradition and thus to the deciphering of the perennial philosophy. The emphasis on the supra-human origin of both Tradition and the traditions must be carefully marked. Guénon insists that '... there is nothing and can be nothing truly traditional that does not contain some elements of a superhuman order.'[19] Again, this is both an *a priori* postulate and a semantic ground rule. If it be accepted then all such looseness of expression as we find in phrases like 'the tradition of the English novel' or 'the European tradition of socialism' must be abandoned

---

[17] M. Pallis *The Way and the Mountain* Peter Owen, London, 1960; p203.
[18] B. Keeble: 'Tradition, Intelligence and the Artist' *SCR* XI, iv, 1977; p236. The same point is made by Nasr in SHN *K&S* p69.
[19] RG *RQ* p253.

for these refer to phenomena of entirely human provenance. It must always be remembered that

> Tradition cannot be improvised from human means for by the terms of a tradition the human state as such is by definition a mode of ignorance – a blindness that cannot, by merely having recourse to itself, overcome its own unknowingness.[20]

A further misconception must be forestalled here: tradition cannot simply be equated with religion which is one form of tradition but not exhaustive. A formulation such as the following from Schuon is suggestive: 'In all epochs and all countries there have been revelations, religions, wisdoms; tradition is a part of mankind, just as man is part of tradition.'[21] Thus 'tradition' is more inclusive than 'religion' though the relationship of the latter to the former is always intimate. A tradition may appear in a guise which cannot strictly be termed 'religious', this word implying the presence of certain formal elements which may be missing. A tradition may, for instance, be embedded in a mythico-ritual complex which might more properly be described as traditional rather than religious. Again, one might refer to an esoteric wisdom which may be associated with religious forms but which is distinct from them, as a tradition – one can speak, for example, of the Pythagorean tradition or the alchemical tradition.

However, these qualifications notwithstanding, we can say that in most cases where the word 'tradition' is used the writer has a religious tradition in mind. Marco Pallis provides us with a kind of working definition of tradition, one that covers the kinds of assumptions and significances that are built into the term. It will provide us with a springboard for further investigation:

> ...wherever a complete tradition exists this will entail the presence of four things, namely: a source of ... Revelation; a current of influence or Grace issuing from that source and transmitted without interruption through a variety of channels; a way of 'verification' which, when faithfully followed, will lead the human subject to successive positions where he is able to 'actualise' the truths that Revelation communicates; finally there is the formal embodiment of tradition in the doctrines, arts, sciences and other elements that together go to determine the character of a normal civilisation.[22]

Revelation, grace, a way of verification, formal embodiment: these four constituents of any integral tradition demand careful definition and amplification.

Revelation. We shall start with a metaphorical explanation – indeed, strictly speaking, no other kind is possible. In his study of Sufism Martin Lings articulates the 'idea' of Revelation in these terms:

> From time to time a Revelation 'flows' like a great tidal wave from the Ocean of Infinitude to the shores of our finite world ... From 'time to time': this is a simplification which calls for a commentary; for since there is no common measure between the origin of such a wave and its destination, its temporality is bound to partake, mysteriously, of the Eternal, just as its finiteness is bound to partake of the Infinite. Being temporal, it must first reach this world at a certain moment in history; but that moment will in a sense escape from time. 'Better than a thousand

---

20 B. Keeble: *op.cit.*; p239.
21 FS *LAW* p35. See also W. Perry: 'The Revival of Interest in Tradition' in RF *UT*.
22 M. Pallis *The Way and the Mountain* p9.

months' is how the Islamic Revelation describes the night of its own advent. There must also be an end which corresponds to the beginning; but that end will be too remote to be humanly foreseeable ... There is only one water but no two waves are the same. Each wave has it own characteristics according to its destination, that is, the particular needs of time and place towards which and in response to which it has providentially been made to flow.[23]

This passage gives rise to certain questions which will be put aside until the next chapter. However, one form of misunderstanding can easily be anticipated and should be countered now by recourse to a passage from Schuon, one which should be read as a kind of addendum to the account just given:

To say that Revelation is 'super-natural' does not mean that it is contrary to nature in so far as nature can be taken to represent, by exhaustion, all that is possible on any given level of reality, it means that Revelation does not originate at the level to which, rightly or wrongly, the epithet 'natural' is normally applied. This 'natural level' is precisely that of physical causes, and hence of sensory and psychic phenomena considered in relation to those causes.[24]

This leaves open the way for an understanding of Revelation compatible with whatever religious tradition is in question, not excluding Buddhism which, on the face of it at least, might appear to pose the most difficulties as far as the principle is concerned. In this context Schuon does not hesitate to speak of the Buddha's 'transcendent nature ... without which there could no question of the efficacy of his Law nor of the saving power of his name'.[25]

Two related errors must also be resisted in any consideration of Revelation. The first has been anticipated in the passage just quoted: Revelation is in no sense to be understood in any psychological sense.[26] This is a prejudice to which some of the neo-Hindus have been prone, failing as they sometimes do to respect the crucial distinction between the psychic and spiritual domains. The second fallacy, which is really the same misconception in different clothes, is the notion that Revelation can occur under the pressure of purely human initiatives. Here Revelation must be sharply distinguished from intellection and from inspiration; these terms will be explored in Chapter 8 in our discussion of the traditionalist view of metaphysics.[27] There is, then, no necessity to restrict the meaning of the term to its characteristic formulation in the Abrahamic traditions nor to identify it with the historic events pertaining to the successive Revelations wherein those traditions originated, namely the Sinaitic Revelation, the Incarnation, and the Descent of the *Koran*. Looked at from another angle – and this is the one usually taken by Guénon – Revelation can be understood as a 'remembering anew', through a divine unveiling, of the Primordial Tradition, in respect of a given branch of humanity. Schuon avails himself of this perspective in writing:

It has been said more than once that total Truth is inscribed, in an immortal script, in the very

---

23 M. Lings *What is Sufism?* Allen & Unwin, London, 1975; pp11–12. See also S.H. Nasr *Sufi Essays* Allen & Unwin, London, 1972; p30.
24 FS *LAW* p35. See also FS *SPHF* pp110–111.
25 FS *ITB* p120.
26 See FS *LS* pp56–59. and 'Keys to the Bible' in JN *SG* pp356–357.
27 On intellection or realisation and its relationship to Revelation see FS *LS* pp24ff. and FS *EPW* pp39ff.

> substance of our spirit; what the different Revelations do is to 'crystallize' or 'actualize', in differing degrees according to the case, a nucleus of certitudes...[28]

Revelation must take on some form whence we can say that it communicates truths rather than Truth, since to form is to limit. Nevertheless, and somewhat paradoxically, the Revelations, being of divine origin, also communicate something of the virtuality of Absolute Truth:

> Revelation speaks an absolute language because God is absolute, not because the form is; in other words, the absoluteness of the Revelation is absolute in itself, but relative *qua* form.[29]

To some mentalities this must remain something of a conundrum while to others it will be as clear as the day.

Secondly, in Pallis's formulation, there is the principle of Grace. This is related to but not exhausted by the technical and dogmatic senses of the word in the Christian and Islamic theological perspectives. It is a beneficent and protective influence which issues from the same source as the Revelation and which will be mediated through the form of the Revelation. If the primary principle of Revelation be accepted then this 'grace' follows as a corollorary. The idea of the uninterrupted flow of this influence is of critical import: the spiritual legacy derived from a Revelation must be handed down through an unbroken chain which may take various forms – initiatic, apostolic or some other. Hence the concern in all integral traditions with spiritual lineages.

The third factor characterising a tradition will be what Pallis calls a 'means of verification', which is to say a spiritual 'methodology' whereby one may conform one's being to the truths communicated by the Revelation and enshrined in the tradition. The tradition in question provides 'a method of concentrating upon the Real, of attaching oneself to the Absolute and living according to the Will of Heaven....'.[30]

Finally one finds the formal embodiments of which Pallis speaks, the formal elements which give expression to saving truths and which will be found in all branches of a traditional civilisation. In this context Gershom Scholem has written that tradition 'embodies the realisation of the effectiveness of the Word in every concrete state and relationship entered into by a society.'[31] Tradition is the 'application and full extension in every domain' of Revelation.[32] Thus the Revelation impinges on the arts and crafts, the sciences and the social life of a traditional civilisation, as well as on its theology and spiritual means. In this sense, then, tradition is indeed 'the chain that joins civilisation to Revelation'[33] and 'the mediator between time and eternity'.[34]

Of these many formal elements the traditionalists have paid especially close attention to sacred art. We shall devote a later chapter to this subject but for the moment

---

28 FS *LAW* p136... See also FS *L&T* p261 and FS *EPW* pp10-11.
29 FS *GDW* p30.
30 S.H. Nasr *Ideals and Realities of Islam* Allen & Unwin, London, 1966; p15.
31 G. Scholem: 'Tradition and Commentary as Religious Categories in Judaism' *SCR* III, iii, 1969; p148.
32 Whitall Perry: 'The Revival of Interest in Tradition' in RF *UT* p3.
33 Lord Northbourne: *op.cit.*; p34.
34 A.K. Saran: 'The Crisis of Hinduism' *SCR* V, ii, 1971; p93.

we can note the implications of a claim such as this, from Schuon: 'Traditions appear out of the Infinite like flowers; they can no more be invented than can the sacred art which is their witness and their proof.'[35]

Before turning to a consideration of Schuon's view of the nature of any traditional society we need to clarify a couple of points of no small importance. A tradition is not static, an unchanging datum that persists in a frozen state through time. Traditions are dynamic: if needs be, they can grow, branch out and blossom. However, the principle of continuity which preserves the link with the Revelation must always be respected if the tradition is to remain an integral one. Titus Burckhardt explains the principle of growth with the aid of the following image: 'The growth of a tradition resembles that of a crystal, which attracts homologous particles to itself, incorporating them according to its own laws of unity.'[36] In the final phrase we find the key to the principle of orthodoxy.

One of the implications of the principle of continuity and of the homogeneity of the spiritual economy in question is this: the great doctrinal elaborations which follow a Revelation, usually at some historical distance, do not, essentially, constitute an 'addition' to the tradition but an unfolding of principles and perspectives which until then have remained implicit. One thinks of a Nagarjuna, a Shankara, an Aquinas. Such figures disavow any personal 'originality', claiming only to be elaborating the spiritual teaching to which they are heirs. Burckhardt again: 'Doctrine grows, not so much by addition of new knowledge, as by the need to refute errors and to reanimate a diminishing power of intuition . . .'[37] For the traditionalists there is always something providential about the appearance of the great doctors of theology and metaphysics. Schuon has addressed this issue in terms which leave no room for misunderstanding. The principle involved is of sufficient importance to permit quotation at some length:

> It is therefore our increasing weakness, and therewith the risk of forgetfulness and betrayal, which more than anything else obliges us to externalise and to make explicit things that were at the beginning included in an inward and implicit perfection. St Paul had no need either of Thomism or of Cathedrals, for all profundities and all splendours were in himself, and all around him in the sanctity of the primitive community. And this, so far from supporting iconoclasts of all kinds, refutes them completely; more or less late epochs – the Middle Ages for example – are faced with an imperious need for externalisations and developments, exactly as the water from a spring, if it is not to be lost on its way, needs a channel made by nature or by the hand of man; and just as the channel does not transform the water and is not meant to do so – for no water is better than spring water – so the externalisations and developments of the spiritual patrimony are there, not to change that patrimony, but to transmit it as integrally and effectively as possible.[38]

Traditional cultures, then, are those in which we find the four characteristics outlined by Pallis. They are oriented towards our ultimate ends and governed by a coherent religious or mythological vision derived from a Revelation. This view of society has all manner of implications and applications. We shall mention a few.

---

35 FS *ITB* p120.
36 T. Burckhardt *Alchemy* Penguin, 1974; p17.
37 T. Burckhardt *An Introduction to Sufi Doctrines* Thorsons, Northamptonshire, 1976; p17.
38 FS *LAW* p11.

The traditionalists, unlike most modern social theorists, find no absolute or self-evident value in 'society' as such or, indeed, in what is called 'civilisation'. Nor are they susceptible to the 'demagogic obsession with purely "social" values' which is nowadays so widespread, even amongst believers.[39] As Schuon points out,

> When people talk about 'civilisation' they generally attribute a qualitative meaning to the term, but really civilisation only represents a value provided it is supra-human in origin and implies for the civilised man a sense of the sacred ... A sense of the sacred is fundamental for every civilisation because fundamental for man; the sacred – that which is immutable, inviolable, and so infinitely majestic – is in the very substance of our spirit and of our existence.[40]

Traditional societies are grounded in an awareness of this reality. Society itself represents nothing of permanent or absolute value but only insofar as it provides a context for the sense of the sacred and the spiritual life which it implies.[41] A traditional society will not necessarily be self-consciously aware of being 'traditional': the conditions pertaining to a traditional order will appear to be natural, no other possibility having intruded itself.

We can see that the traditionalist vision of a religious culture is radically opposed to the Durkheimian thesis about the relationship between religion and society. It is not society which fashions religion in its own image but religion which shapes the society whose whole rationale is embedded in the sense of which Schuon speaks. In traditional societies, 'It is the spiritual, not the temporal, which culturally, socially and politically is the criterion of all other values.'[42] It is from this platform that the traditionalists reaffirm the values of civilisations other than our own and from which the most trenchant critique of modernism can be mounted. Western civilisation is now, in Guénon's words, 'devoid of any traditional character with the exception of the religious element',[43] which itself is devastated on all sides.

Clearly there is a danger of the idea of tradition being turned to all sorts of over-simplifications. Coomaraswamy's biographer has noted the dangers of the using the idea as a simplistic device for separating the Blessed from the Cursed. One does sense, it must be admitted, the occasional over-schematisation in the social critiques of both Guénon and Coomaraswamy, necessitated no doubt by their pioneering roles, but this is not a charge that can be sustained against the later traditionalists. In any case, there is nothing of that rosy sentimentality which looks back to a romanticised past in any of these writers. The reproach of wanting to 'turn back the clock' is not one that anyone who has understood the traditionalist position would make. As Schuon remarks, a 'nostalgia for the past' is, in itself, nothing; all that is meaningful is 'a nostalgia for the sacred' which 'cannot be situated elsewhere than in the liberating "now" of God'.[44]

To appreciate the texture and density of the traditionalist view of a normal civilis-

---

39 FS *TM* p18.

40 FS *UI* p33. See also p48.

41 One of the most eloquent statements of this principle can be found in the Foreword to A. Govinda *The Way of the White Clouds* Shambala, Boulder, 1970; ppxi-xii.

42 F. Schuon: 'Usurpations of Religious Feeling' *SCR* II, ii, 1968; p66. See also FS *ITB* pp124ff; FS *LAW* p24; and Abu Bakr Siraj ad-Din: 'The Spiritual Function of Civilisation' in JN *SG* pp104ff.

43 R. Guénon, quoted in RL *CLW* p266.

44 F. Schuon: 'On the Margin of Liturgical Improvisations' in JN *SG* p353.

ation one must immerse oneself in their writings on this subject. This is especially true of Schuon's work: no amount of quotation can capture the cadences and resonances which grace his writings on this or, indeed, any other subject. The ideas he expresses are robbed of some of their richness when extracted from their matrices. Nevertheless, it will perhaps be useful to close this part of our inquiry with a rather lengthy quote from Schuon, one which deals with some of the issues that have been under consideration in this chapter.

> When the modern world is contrasted with traditional civilisations, it is not simply a question of seeking the good things and the bad things on one side or the other; good and evil are everywhere, so that it is essentially a question of knowing on which side the more important good and on which side the lesser evil is to be found. If someone says that such and such a good exists outside tradition, the answer is: no doubt, but one must choose the most important good, and it is necessarily represented by tradition; and if someone says that in tradition there exists such and such an evil, the answer is: no doubt, but one must choose the lesser evil, and again it is tradition that embodies it. It is illogical to prefer an evil which involves some benefits to a good which involves some evils.
>
> Nevertheless, to confine oneself to admiring the traditional worlds is to stop short at a fragmentary point of view, for every civilisation is a 'two-edged sword'; it is a total good only by virtue of those invisible elements that determine it positively. In certain respects every human society is bad; if its transcendent character is wholly eliminated – which amounts to dehumanising it since an element of transcendence is essential to man though always dependent on his free consent – then the whole justification of society's existence is removed at the same time, and there remains only an ant-heap ... It is one of the most pernicious of errors to believe, firstly, that the human collectivity as such represents an unconditional or absolute value, and secondly that the well-being of this collectivity represents any such value or any such end in itself.
>
> Religious civilisations, regarded as social phenomena and independently of their intrinsic value – though there is no sharp dividing-line between the two – are, despite their inevitable imperfections, like sea-walls built to stem the rising tide of worldliness, of error, of subversion, of the fall and its perpetual renewal ... The rejection of the traditional religious frameworks amounts to an assertion that the founders of religion did not know what they were doing, as well as that abuses are not inherent in human nature, and that they are therefore avoidable even in societies counting millions of men, and that they are avoidable through purely human means; no more flagrant contradiction than this could well be imagined.[45]

Clearly there is much in this passage that might call for comment, and we shall indeed return to some of the issues it raises in our discussion of the confrontation of traditionalism and modernism. For the moment we shall let the passage stand as it is and move on to an intimately related subject – the nature of religion. Our exposition of the traditionalist understanding of this term will help to situate the passage above in a fuller context.

---

45 FS *LAW* pp42-43. See also FS *THC* pp11-12.

7

The Transcendent Unity of Religions

Essentially all religions include decisive truths and mediators and miracles, but the disposition of these elements, the play of their proportions, can vary according to the conditions of the revelation and of the human receptacles of the revelation
Frithjof Schuon[1]

... orthodoxy is the principle of formal homogeneity proper to any authentically spiritual perspective ... *Frithjof Schuon*[2]

Exotericism consists in identifying transcendent realities with the dogmatic forms, and if need be, with the historical facts of a given Revelation, whereas esotericism refers in a more or less direct manner to these same realities
Frithjof Schuon[3]

If we can grasp the transcendent nature of the human being, we thereby grasp the nature of revelation, of religion, of tradition; we understand their possibility, their necessity, their truth. And in understanding religion, not only in a particular form or according to some verbal specification, but also in its formless essence, we understand the religions ... the meaning of their plurality and diversity; this is the plane of gnosis, of the *religio perennis,* whereon the extrinsic antinomies of dogmas are explained and resolved
Frithjof Schuon[4]

Amongst the traditionalists Schuon writes with sovereign authority on the subject of religion as such. We have already noted that his outlook is more attuned to religion in all its manifestations than that of either Coomaraswamy or Guénon. The traditionalist view of religion can best be understood by a close examination of Schuon's writings in this field. Four *leitmotifs* run through his work on religion. They are flagged by the quotes on the opposite page: the necessary diversity of Revelations and thus of religious forms; the principle of orthodoxy; the distinction between the exoteric and esoteric domains, and the relationship between these outer and inner dimensions of religion; and the transcendent unity of religions. He has repeatedly returned to these themes, to the exposition of the principles involved and their application to manifold religious phenomena.

Schuon's view of religion turns on the axiomatic notion of multiple and diverse Revelations; the principle is a kind of linch-pin in his work. In discussing it we shall have to tread carefully if we are not to stumble into the same confusions that have ambushed some of Schuon's critics. Schuon perceives humankind neither as a monolithic psychic entity nor as an amorphous agglomerate but as being divided into several distinct branches, each with its own peculiar traits, psychological and otherwise, which determine its receptivities to truth and shape its apprehensions of reality. Needless to say there is no question here of any kind of racialism or ethnocentricism which attributes a superiority or inferiority to this or that ethnic collectivity. Nor, however, is there any sentimental prejudice in favour of the idea that the world's peoples are only 'superficially' and 'accidentally' different. 'We observe the existence, on earth, of diverse races, whose differences are "valid" since there are no "false" as opposed to "true" races.'[5] Each branch of humanity exhibits a psychic and spiritual homogeneity which may transcend barriers of geography and biology. An example: that shamanism should extend through parts of Northern Europe, Siberia, Mongolia, Tibet and the Red Indian areas betokens, in Schuon's view, a certain spiritual temperament shared by the peoples in question, one quite independent of physical similarities and leaving aside the question of 'borrowings' and 'influences'.[6]

To the diverse human collectivities are addressed Revelations which are determined in their formal aspects by the needs and receptivities at hand. This is a crucial point. Thus

> ... what determines the differences among forms of Truth is the difference among human receptacles. For thousands of years already humanity has been divided into several fundamentally different branches, which constitute so many complete humanities, more or less closed in on

---

1 FS *SPHF* pp66–67.
2 FS *SW* P13.
3 FS *L&T* p144.
4 FS *LAW* P142.
5 FS *GDW* p32.
6 See FS *LAW* p72.

themselves; the existence of spiritual receptacles so different and so original demands differentiated refractions of the one Truth.[7]

This principle is of incalculable import. We have already met with the idea that Truth is one. Revelation marks a 'formalisation' of Truth and thus cannot be identical with it. This distinction must be maintained if the idea of multiple Revelations is to remain intelligible:

> Truth is situated beyond forms, whereas Revelation, or the Tradition that derives from it, belongs to the formal order, and that indeed by definition; but to speak of form is to speak of diversity, and thus of plurality . . .[8]

In a sense the Revelations are communicated in different divine languages. Just as we should baulk at the idea of 'true' and 'false' languages, so we need to see the necessity and the validity of multiple Revelations.[9] This is not to suggest that all 'religions' which claim to derive from a 'Revelation' do so in fact, nor that there is no such thing as a pseudo-religion. We shall turn to this issue presently.

The principle of multiple Revelations is not accessible to all mentalities and its implications must remain anathema to the majority of believers. This is in the nature of things. Nevertheless, from a traditionalist viewpoint, anyone today wishing to understand religion as such and the inter-relationships of the various traditions must have a firm purchase on this principle. It is one which can be supported by Scriptural and traditional authority though the penetration of the passages in question will again be beyond the reach of most believers. As the Semitic traditions have been the ones most prone to extravagant claims of exclusivism we shall cite a few passages from their Scriptures which are suggestive in the light of the foregoing:

> Other sheep have I which are not of this fold. *St John*[10]

> For each we have appointed a law and traced out a path, and if God had wished, verily He would have made you one people. *The Koran*[11]

> And we never sent a messenger save with the language of his folk, that he might make the message clear for them. *The Koran*[12]

Revelation must be carefully distinguished from other intuitions and disclosures of the divine. In the traditionalist vocabulary, 'Revelation' always signifies a formal

---

7 See FS *GDW* p29. For some mapping of these branches and some account of their differences see Schuon's essay 'The Meaning of Race' in FS *LS* pp173–200. This essay should be read in conjunction with 'Principle of Distinction in the Social Order' in the same volume. These essays can also be found in F. Schuon *Castes and Races* Perennial Books, London, 1982, the latter essay appearing under the title 'The Meaning of Caste'.
8 FS *GDW* p29.
9 *ibid.*; p30. The comparison of religions and languages is a common one. For some examples see M. Müller: 'Chips from a German Workshop' in J. Waardenburg (ed) *Classical Approaches to the Study of Religion* Mouton, The Hague, 1973; pp88–89; R. Zwi Werblowsky: 'Universal Religion and Universalist Religion' *International Journal for Philosophy of Religion* II, i, 1971; pp10–11.
10 X.16.
11 Sura V.53.
12 *ibid.*; XIV.4. See S.H. Nasr *Sufi Essays* Allen & Unwin, London, 1972; p126fn2.

Marco Pallis

source for a whole religious tradition. When Martin Buber wrote that 'Revelation is continual, and everything is fit to become a sign of revelation' he was using the word in a different sense.[13] Likewise Archbishop Temple in writing 'Unless all existence is a medium of revelation, no particular revelation is possible...'.[14] The referent here is what Eliade might call a 'hierophany' and what the traditionalists would describe as an 'archetypal illumination'.[15] In this study 'Revelation' will be used in the traditionalist sense and thus signalled by the use of the capital.

Furthermore, Revelation must be distinguished from 'inspiration' which can encompass all manner of workings of divine influence. This distinction has been scrupulously preserved in the Judaic, Islamic and Hindu traditions, which is not to suggest that it is one of which all the adherents of these traditions will be aware. The neglect of this distinction in some quarters has produced abuses too numerous to catalogue but the Nonconformist tendency to idolatrize Scripture is a case in point where the Revelation, Christ Himself, is confused with phenomena which are, in some cases, inspired.[16]

As each religion proceeds from a Revelation, it is, in Nasr's words, both

> ... *the* religion and *a* religion, *the* religion inasmuch as it contains within itself the Truth and the means of attaining the Truth, *a* religion since it emphasises a particular aspect of Truth in conformity with the spiritual and psychological needs of the humanity for whom it is destined.[17]

In other words each religion is sufficient unto itself and contains all that is necessary for man's sanctification and salvation. Nevertheless, it remains limited by definition. The recognition and reconciliation of these two apparently antagonistic principles is crucial to the traditionalist perspective. Schuon re-states the point made by Nasr in this way:

> A religion is a form, and so also a limit, which 'contains' the Limitless, to speak in paradox; every form is fragmentary because of its necessary exclusion of other formal possibilities; the fact that these forms – when they are complete, that is to say when they are perfectly 'themselves' – each in their own way represent totality does not prevent them from being fragmentary in respect of their particularisation and their reciprocal exclusion.[18]

This will be amplified in our discussion of esotericism and exotericism.

The diversity of Revelations raises the question of the 'status', so to speak, of the Messengers through whom the Revelations have been communicated. This is not a question which can be treated in any depth here but the following remarks from Schuon at least disallow some of the more obvious confusions which might arise:

> The great Messengers, if they are assuredly one by their principle, in their gnosis and in the Logos, are not however of necessity equal on the phenomenal plane, that of manifestation on earth; what are equivalent are the Messages when each is taken in its entirety. It is necessary, in any case, not

---

13 M. Buber *A Believing Humanism* Simon & Schuster, New York, 1967; p113.
14 From *Nature, Man and God*, quoted by J. Wach *The Comparative Study of Religions* Columbia Uni Press, New York, 1958; p44.
15 See M. Pallis *A Buddhist Spectrum* Allen & Unwin, London, 1980; p152.
16 On this distinction see M.Lings *op.cit.*; p25fn1; FS *SPHF* pp110–111, and FS *UI* P44fn1.
17 See S. H. Nasr *Ideals and Realities of Islam* Allen & Unwin, London, 1966; p15.
18 See FS *UI* p144. See also FS *DI* p136.

to confuse the phenomenal or cosmic with the spiritual reality; it is the latter which is one and the former which is diverse.[19]

Each Messenger fulfils the appropriate function in a certain modality, or spiritual key which determines the 'tone' of the tradition which is bound to flow from the Message. Thus it is that

> ... when one says *the* Prophet it means the prophet of Islam ... when one says *the* Incarnation it refers to Christ who personifies this aspect. And although every prophet and saint has experienced 'enlightenment', *the* Enlightenment refers to the experience of the Buddha which is the most outstanding and universal embodiment of this experience.[20]

Given this framework it hardly needs saying that the great religious founders must not be confounded with other religious figures, no matter how saintly or sagacious. Schuon goes to some lengths to point out why Vivekananda's sentimental trinity of Jesus, the Buddha and Ramakrishna is quite unacceptable from many different points of view – not because the sanctity of the latter is in any way in doubt but because his spiritual function is of a quite different order, Ramakrishna being as a river besides the oceanic nature of the other two.[21]

A question which has exercised many minds, often to no very good effect, is this: what is 'religion'? In the traditionalist perspective this question cannot be met without reference to Revelation and tradition. Within this framework we can identify two elements which must always be present: doctrine and method. Nasr gives a compact definition:

> ... every religion possesses two elements which are its basis and its foundation: a doctrine which distinguishes between the Absolute and the relative, between the absolutely Real and the relatively real ... and a method of concentrating upon the Real, of attaching oneself to the Absolute and living according to the Will of Heaven, in accordance with the purpose and meaning of human existence.[22]

Plainly this kind of definition is not acceptable to everyone. It is incompatible with many of the definitions which have been in vogue at one time or another amongst scholars from several different academic disciplines. It is no part of our present purpose to debate the merits of various formulations about religion but simply to make the traditionalist position clear. It hardly needs to be pointed out that there is a yawning chasm between the traditionalist view and those which reduce religion to something less than it claims to be.

By what means can it be established whether something deserves the dignity of the term 'religion'? The answer to this question has, in part, been suggested by much

---

19 FS *GDW* p14. See also FS *SW* pp92–93. For a discussion of the relationship between the Message and the Messenger in Buddhism see FS *ITB* pp24–28.
20 See S.H. Nasr *Ideals and Realities of Islam* p67.
21 See FS *UI* p87fn. Schuon's argument will be presented more fully in Chapter 11 which includes a traditionalist perspective on Vivekananda.
22 S.H. Nasr *Ideals and Realities of Islam* p15. For some account of the different conceptual approaches to 'religion' see J. Waardenburg: *op.cit.*; E.J. Sharpe *Comparative Religion* Duckworth, London, 1975; W.C. Smith *The Meaning and End of Religion* SPCK, London, 1978; M. Eliade *The Quest* Uni of Chicago Press, 1969; pp12–71; and W.E. Paden *Religious Worlds: the Comparative Study of Religion* Beacon Press, Boston, 1988.

that has already been said about tradition. Further ambiguities are dispelled by the principle of orthodoxy. Schuon articulates the principle thus:

> In order to be orthodox a religion must possess a mythological or doctrinal symbolism establishing the essential distinction between the Real and the illusory, or the Absolute and the relative ... and must offer a way that serves both the perfection of concentration on the Real and also its continuity. In other words a religion is orthodox on condition that it offers a sufficient, if not always exhaustive, idea of the absolute and the relative, and therewith an idea of their reciprocal relationships ...[23]

This is re-stated and expanded in another passage from Schuon:

> For a religion to be considered intrinsically orthodox – an extrinsic orthodoxy hangs upon formal elements which cannot apply literally outside their own perspective – it must rest upon a fully adequate doctrine ... then it must extol and actualise a spirituality that is equal to this doctrine and thereby include sanctity within its ambit both as concept and reality; this means it must be of Divine and not philosophical origin and thus be charged with a sacramental or theurgic presence ...[24]

The insistence on divine origin, adequate doctrine and an effective spiritual method is by now clear enough. How are these to be put to the test? There are several angles of approach here.

Firstly, the origin of the 'religion' in question: according to the traditionalists any claim to a Revelation such as would provide the impetus for a whole new religious tradition is out of the question in post-Koranic times.

> It is quite out of the question that a 'revelation', in the full sense of the word, should arise in our time, one comparable, that is to say, to the imparting of the great sutras or any other primary scriptures: the day of revelations is past on this globe and was so already long ago. The inspirations of the saints are of another order ...[25]

Neither the basis nor the ramifications of this claim can be rehearsed here except to say that it derives from the sacred Scriptures themselves, especially the *Koran*, and from the doctrine of cycles. The Koranic Revelation must needs be the last great Revelation in this cycle. Muhummad is the 'Seal of the Prophets', no later prophecies of this order being possible.[26] From the traditionalist point of view, history has only gone to confirm this claim.

Under this view there can, in fact, be no new religions as such: there can only be conformity to the traditional orthodoxies on one side or a surrender to the confusions of the age on the other. The traditionalists have been intractable in refusing to grant religious 'status', as it were, to the various heterodox and quasi-spiritual movements of which there has been such an efflorescence in recent times. Amongst the traditionalist targets are the movements of 'reformist' bent (neo-Hinduism, liberal theology, 'Christian Marxism' [sic]), those of syncretic intention and esoteric trappings (theos-

---

23 FS *LAW* p138.
24 FS *IPP* p14. See also commentary by Leo Schaya in Y. Ibish & P.L. Wilson (eds) *Traditional Modes of Contemplation and Action* Imperial Iranian Academy of Philosophy, Tehran, 1977; pp462ff.
25 F. Schuon: 'No Activity Without Truth' in JN *SG* p35. See also FS *SW* p17.
26 See S.H. Nasr *Ideals and Realities of Islam* pp33-36.

ophy), those centred on charismatic 'gurus' who are not faithful purveyors of any authentically traditional doctrine (Gurdjieff, Krishnamurti, Rajneesh) or those claiming a new divine dispensation (Mormonism, Subud).[27] Although these groups and persons are rarely mentioned by name in traditionalist writings it is clear that they fly in the face of the principles which the traditionalists espouse. It is clearly such movements that Schuon has in mind when he writes about heterodoxies which

> always tend to adulterate either the idea of the divine Principle or the manner of our attachment to it; they offer either a worldly, profane, or, if you like, 'humanist' counterfeit of religion, or else a mysticism with a content of nothing but the ego and its illusions.[28]

Secondly, the adequacy of the doctrine: this can only be determined by a metaphysical discernment, itself nurtured within the integral traditions. A third test of religion is offered by the Biblical maxim 'By their fruits ye shall know them'.[29] Any orthodox tradition, by being such, will necessarily bring forth from within itself saints and sages who are living testimony to the efficacy of the spiritual economy in question. Men indeed do not gather grapes from thorns nor figs from thistles. However, here again an acute metaphysical discernment and sensitivity is necessary to recognise spirituality in all its strange and sometimes scandalous guises. It might also be added that another fruit of tradition is a fully-fledged sacred art.

What of the attitude of one orthodoxy to another? We have already encountered Schuon's reference to 'formal elements which cannot apply literally outside their own perspective'. This provides the key. From the exoteric vantage point of any particular tradition there can only be one orthodoxy, ie. the one determining the outlook in question. Thus, for example, from a Hindu viewpoint Buddhism must appear as unorthodox, the test of orthodoxy here being the acceptance of Vedic authority. Here the Hindu viewpoint is both 'right' and 'wrong'. This paradox is resolved in an illuminating passage from Schuon:

> Traditional orthodoxy means being in accord with a doctrinal or ritual form, and also, and indeed above all, with the truth which resides in all revealed forms; thus the essence of every orthodoxy is intrinsic truth ... and not merely the internal logic of a doctrine that may turn out to be false. What makes the definition of orthodoxy rather troublesome is that it presents two principal modes, the one essential or intrinsic, and the other formal or extrinsic: the latter is being in accord with a revealed form, and the former the being in accord with the essential and universal truth, with or without being in accord with any particular form, so that the two modes sometimes stand opposed externally. To give an example, it can be said that Buddhism is extrinsically heterodox in relation to Hinduism, because it makes a departure from the basic forms of the latter, and at the same time intrinsically orthodox, because it is in accord with that universal truth from which both traditions proceed; on the other hand the Brahmo-Samaj, like every other variety of 'progressive' neo-Hinduism, is doubly heterodox, first in relation to Hinduism itself and secondly in relation to truth unqualified...[30]

---

27 For an interesting but uncritical account of some of these movements see J. Needleman *The New Religions* Pocket Books, New York, 1972.
28 FS *LAW* p138.
29 *St Matthew* VII.20.
30 FS *LS* p1. See also SHN *K&S* pp78–80.

Whilst on the subject of 'reformist' movements it might be as well to clarify a couple of points of some moment. There is a good deal of talk these days about the traditional religions being 'played out', 'inadequate to the problems of the age', 'irrelevant to contemporary concerns' and so on. 'New solutions' are needed, 'appropriate to the times'. This kind of thinking is by no means restricted to those who are openly hostile to religion; it is to be found amongst many people who, being deeply concerned about our spiritual welfare, sense that something has gone wrong. The traditionalists are the first to agree that we have indeed gone astray – our understanding of religion is in disarray. However, the solution is not to be found in any 'program' which has as its starting-point the belief that the religions must be 'reformed' in order to conform to the needs of 'our times'. Such thinking is part of the very problem which the reformers apparently want to solve.

Nothing is more likely to draw a combative response from the traditionalists than the suggestion that the plight of the modern world is to be explained in terms of the inadequacies of the traditional religions. This issue will be explored in some detail elsewhere in this study but it will be as well, at this point, to establish the traditionalist position in general outline. Again we can do no better than allow Schuon to speak directly to the issue:

> Nothing is more misleading than to pretend, as is so glibly done in our day, that the religions have compromised themselves hopelessly in the course of the centuries or that they are now played out. If one knows what a religion really consists of, one also knows that the religions cannot compromise themselves and they are independent of human doings ... The fact that a man may exploit a religion in order to bolster up national or private interests in no wise affects religion as such ... as for an exhausting of the religions, one might speak of this if all men had by now become saints or Buddhas. In that case only could it be admitted that the religions were exhausted, at least as regards their forms.[31]

It is we who are compromised by our failure to conform to the timeless truths which tradition preserves.

A concept of the utmost importance in the Schuonian perspective on religion is the distinction, first made explicit by Guénon, between the exoteric and esoteric dimensions of any religious tradition. Huston Smith has made this distinction a conceptual fortress from which to repel attacks on Schuon's view of religion.[32] This strategy is not without its dangers; one might do better, as far as polemic and debate are concerned, to take one's stand on the idea of tradition itself. The exoteric-esoteric distinction only makes sense in the context of several more inclusive principles. To focus on it as *the* key to Schuon's work, as Smith tends to do, is perhaps to court unnecessary trouble. Be that as it may, no one will deny that the distinction is pivotal in Schuon's work and is intimately related to his affirmation of the transcendent unity of religions.

If the distinction between these two dimensions of religion and the relationship

---

31 F. Schuon: 'No Activity Without Truth' p29. See also FS *SW* p11.
32 See H. Smith: 'Frithjof Schuon's *The Transcendent Unity of Religions*: Pro' *Journal of the American Academy of Religion* XLIV, iv, 11976; pp721–724. For some discussion of the exoteric-esoteric divide see M.Pallis *A Buddhist Spectrum* pp116–117.

between them is not precisely understood then the traditionalist perspective on the inner unity of the religions cannot be fully grasped. There has, after all, been no small number of people who have posited the 'essential' unity of the religions.[33] The supports for this claim have all too often been inadequate and open to demolition from both within and without the religious traditions themselves. We shall not find in Schuon's work or in the writings of other traditionalists any Procrustean attempt to find a unity on a plane where it does not exist nor an insipid universalism which posits a unity of no matter what elements as long as they lay some claim to being 'religious' or 'spiritual'.

Generally we are accustomed to drawing sharp dividing lines between the religious traditions. The differences are, of course, palpably real and Schuon has no wish to blur the distinctions. Indeed, his vigorous defence of the principle of orthodoxy should preclude any misunderstanding on this point. However, this notwithstanding, Schuon draws another kind of dividing line which in some senses is much more fundamental – that between the exoteric and esoteric. A diagrammatic representation of the idea may be helpful.[34]

TRUTH

Esoteric Domain

Exoteric Domain: the Formal Traditions

The Revelations

ORIGIN

---

33 For some discussion of such claims see P.J. Saher *Eastern Wisdom and Western Thought* Allen & Unwin, London, 1969. For one example amongst many see J. Stewart-Wallace: 'The World Religions One in Mysticism' *Hibbert Journal* L, 1951–2; pp107–112.

34 This is an elaborated version of a diagram offered by Huston Smith in his Introduction to FS *TUR* pxii.

There is no question here of the lines being blurred. They issue from a single point of origin and converge on their 'destination', at the far side of the exoteric domain. The apex of this diagram can be thought of as Truth, Reality, the Absolute. The point of origin and the point of 'arrival' or better, fulfilment, are in fact one and the same. In the exoteric domain, we see the separate, distinct religious traditions each cleaving to an ensemble of formal elements deriving from a Revelation. Above this, in the esoteric domain, the different traditions converge on the Truth through a variety of means – esoteric doctrines, initiations and spiritual disciplines, intellection, the plenary experience. The necessity and the formal integrity of the different traditions is in no way compromised under this view which fully respects the formal differences between the religions on the plane where such distinctions, even antagonisms, find their proper place. It is only through the exoteric realm that the esoteric can be reached. The universality of every great spiritual patrimony rests 'on a foundation of divinely instituted formal elements'.[35]

The diagram we have been considering can be complemented by the following representation which draws on the traditional symbolism of the circle.

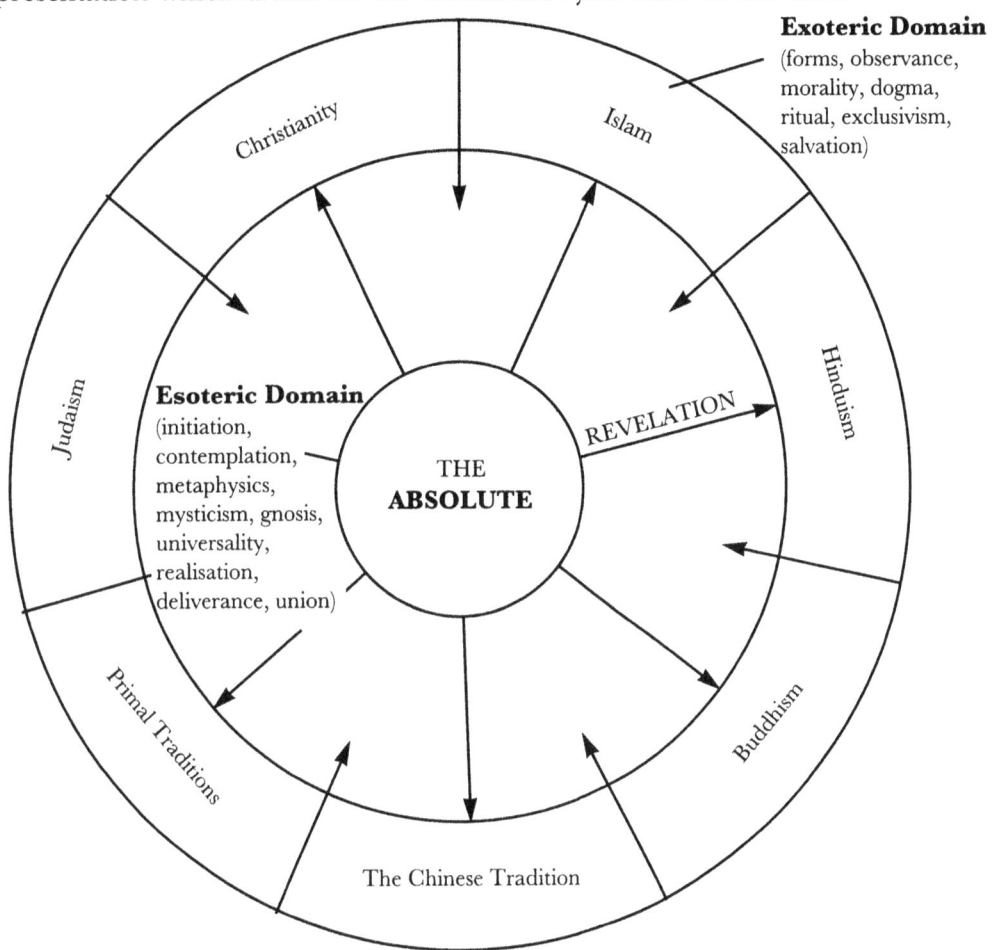

---

[35] FS *LAW* p137. It is, of course, precisely because the formal elements of tradition are divinely instituted that the traditionalist must treat them with such respect. See SHN *K&S* pp293–294.

A couple of points which this illustrates should not go unnoticed. The exoteric domain does not derive from the esoteric but from a Revelation. This in itself is sufficient to throw out of court any suggestion that exoteric forms can be dispensed with. *Within* the circumference of the formal exotericisms are to be found convergent esotericisms. At a time when it is sometimes suggested that the esoteric dimension can exist *in vacuo* or that it can be detached from the formal tradition in question, this is a point which needs some stressing.[36]

In discriminating between the exoteric and the esoteric we are, in a sense, speaking of 'form' and 'spirit'. Exotericism rests on a necessary formalism:

> Exotericism never goes beyond the 'letter'. It puts its accent on the Law, not on any realisation, and so puts it on action and merit. It is essentially a 'belief' in a 'letter', or a dogma envisaged in its formal exclusiveness, and an obedience to a ritual and moral Law. And, further, exotericism never goes beyond the individual; it is centred on heaven rather than on God, and this amounts to saying that this difference has for it no meaning.[37]

Huston Smith has offered a useful gloss on Schuon's elucidation of the exoteric-esoteric distinction in these terms:

> For the exoteric God's personal mode is his only mode; for the esoteric this mode resides in one that is higher and ultimately modeless ... For the exoteric the world is real in every sense; for the exoteric it has only a qualified reality ... For the exoteric God is primarily loved; for the esoteric He is primarily known; though in the end the exoteric comes to know what he loves and the esoteric to love what he knows.[38]

It follows that exotericism must thereby embody certain inevitable and in a sense therapeutic limits or 'errors' which from a fuller perspective can be seen in both their positive and negative aspects. Religion, in its formal aspect, is made up of what the Buddhists call *upāya*, 'skillful means' which answer the necessities of the case, what Schuon calls 'saving mirages' and 'celestial stratagems'.[39] The limiting definitions of exoteric formalism are 'comparable to descriptions of an object of which only the form and not the colours can be seen'.[40] Partial truths which might be inadequate in a sapiential perspective may be altogether proper on the formal exoteric plane:

> The formal homogeneity of a religion requires not only truth but also errors – though these are only in form – just as the world requires evil and as Diversity implies the mystery of creation by virtue of its infinity.

> Absolute truths exist only in depth, not as a surface.

> The religions are 'mythologies' which, as such, are founded on real aspects of the Divine and on

---

36 This kind of assumption is evident in the pretensions of people who claim to be 'Sufis' without being Muslims. See S.H. Nasr *Sufi Essays* p169fn11, and SHN *K&S* p77.
37 FS *LAW* p76.
38 Huston Smith in Introduction to FS *TUR* pxxvi. See also FS *UI* p110.
39 FS *SME* p185fn2. See also FS *TM* p8: 'In religious esoterisms, efficacy at times takes the place of truth, and rightly so, given the nature of the men to whom they are addressed.'
40 FS *UI* p80.

sacred facts, and thus on realities but only on aspects. Now this limitation is at the same time inevitable and fully efficacious.[41]

In other words the forms of exotericism represent certain accommodations which are necessary to bring various truths within the purview of the average mentality. As such they are adequate to the collective needs in question. Just as there exists within each tradition an exoteric and an esoteric dimension so too, as Huston Smith's commentary makes clear, there exist corresponding spiritual dispositions. It is in the nature of things that only a small minority will be blessed with the contemplative intelligence necessary to penetrate the formal aspects of religion. For the normal believer the exoteric domain is the only domain.

A specific example of an exoteric dogma might help to reinforce some of the points under discussion. In discussing the Christian dogmas about heaven and hell, Schuon has this to say:

> We are made for the Absolute, which embraces all things and from which none can escape; this truth is marvellously well presented in the monotheistic religions in the alternative between the two 'eternities' beyond the grave ... the alternative may be insufficient from the point of view of total Truth, but it is psychologically realistic and mystically efficacious; many lives have been squandered away and lost for the single reason that a belief in hell and in paradise is missing.[42]

The statements of a formal exotericism can thus be seen as partial truths, as intimations of Truth, as metaphors and symbols, as bridges to the formless Reality.[43] Herein lies the point of Schuon's repeated affirmations of orthodoxy, such as this one: 'Orthodoxy includes and guarantees incalculable values which man could not possibly draw out of himself.'[44] If 'exotericism consists in identifying transcendent realities with dogmatic forms' then esotericism is concerned 'in a more or less direct manner with these same realities'.[45] Esotericism is concerned with the apprehension of Reality as such, not Reality as understood in such and such a perspective and 'under the veil of different religious formulations'.[46] While exotericism sees 'essence' or 'universal truth' as a function of particular forms, esotericism sees the forms as a function of 'essence'.[47] To put it another way, exotericism particularises the universal, esotericism universalises the particular:

> What characterises esoterism to the very extent that it is absolute, is that on contact with a dogmatic system, it universalises the symbol or religious concept on the one hand, and interiorizes it on the other; the particular or the limited is recognised as the manifestation of the principial and the transcendent, and this in its turn reveals itself as immanent.[48]

---

41 FS *SPHF* p70.
42 FS *LAW* p22.
43 See FS *UI* p110.
44 FS *SPHF* p113. See also FS *IPP* p5.
45 FS *L&T* p144. See also FS *EPW* p37.
46 FS *EPW* p19.
47 *ibid.*; p37.
48 *ibid.*

Esotericism is 'situated' on the plane of mystical experience, of intellection and realisation. The traditionalist understanding of these terms will be expounded in the next chapter. However, a few points cannot go unmentioned here.

If gnosis as such is under consideration then the question of orthodoxy cannot arise, this being a principle which is only operative on the formal plane:

> If the purest esotericism includes the whole truth — and that is the very reason for its existence — the question of 'orthodoxy' in the religious sense clearly cannot arise: direct knowledge of the mysteries could not be 'Moslem' or 'Christian' just as the sight of a mountain is the sight of a mountain and not something else.[49]

Nevertheless, the two realms, exoteric and esoteric, are continually meeting and interpenetrating, not only because there is such a thing as a 'relative esotericism' but because 'the underlying truth is one, and also because man is one'.[50] Furthermore, even if esotericism transcends forms, it has need of doctrinal, ritual, moral and aesthetic supports on the path to realisation.[51]

What of the attitude, so to speak, of the exoteric to the esoteric? Given the factors which have been mentioned it is not surprising that the exoteric elements in a religious tradition should be preserved and protected by traditional representatives whose attitude to esotericism will be, at best, somewhat ambivalent, at worst openly hostile. In addressing itself to the defence of the *credo* and of the forms which appear as guarantors of truth the exoteric 'resistance' to esotericism is entirely positive. The esoteric can see and respect this guardianship of the 'incalculable values' of orthodoxy. On the other hand,

> ... the exoteric's assessment of the esoteric is likely to be less charitable, not because exoterics are less endowed with that virtue, but because a portion of the esoteric position being obscured from him, he cannot honour it without betraying the truth he does see.[52]

It is in this context that we should understand Coomaraswamy's remark, frequently made in his corresponsdence with 'exoterics': 'even if you are not on our side, we are on yours.'[53] Sometimes the exoteric defendants of orthodoxy overstep themselves and in doing so beget results that are both destructive and counter-productive, especially when a religious tradition is endangered by a preponderantly exoteric outlook:

> The exoteric viewpoint is, in fact, doomed to end by negating itself once it is no longer vivified by the presence within it of the esotericism of which it is both the outward radiation and the veil. So it is that religion, according to the measure in which it denies metaphysical and initiatory realities and becomes crystallized in literalistic dogmatism, inevitably engenders unbelief; the atrophy that overtakes dogmas when they are deprived of their internal dimension recoils upon them from outside, in the form of heretical and atheistic negations.[54]

---

49 FS *UI* p139. See also FS *SVQ* p112.
50 FS *EPW* p16.
51 *ibid.*; p29. See next chapter.
52 Huston Smith, Introduction to FS *TUR* pxv.
53 For one of many instances where Coomaraswamy uses this phrase see Letter to Joachim Wach, August 1947, AKC *SL* p113.
54 FS *TUR* p9.

How much of post-medieval Christian history bears witness to this truth![55] As to the theological ostracisms that have befallen some of the mystics and metaphysicians seeking to preserve the esoteric dimension within their respective religious traditions, Schuon reminds us of Aesop's fable about the fox and the grapes, a story which 'repeats itself in all sectors of human existence'.[56]

The principles which determine the transcendent unity of religions have already come into view. The supra-human origin of a religious tradition in a Revelation, an adequate doctrine concerning the Absolute and the relative, the saving power of the spiritual method, the esoteric convergence on the Unitive Truth – all these point to the inner unity of all integral traditions which are, in a sense, variations on one theme. However, there remain certain puzzling questions which might stand in the way of an understanding of the principial unity which the *religio perennis* discloses. If we need to repeat some of the considerations already outlined above, then no matter; their reiteration may consolidate some points which might otherwise remain precarious.

One frequently comes across formulations such as the following: 'It is sometimes asserted that all religions are equally true. But this would seem to be simply sloppy thinking, since the various religions hold views of reality which are sharply different if not contradictory.'[57] This kind of either/or thinking, characteristic of much that nowadays passes for philosophy, is in the same vein as a dogmatism which

> reveals itself not only by its inability to conceive the inward or implicit illimitability of a symbol, but also by its inability to recognise, when faced with two apparently contradictory truths, the inward connection that they apparently affirm, a connection that makes of them complementary aspects of one and the same truth.[58]

It is precisely this kind of incapacity which must be overcome if the transcendent unity of the religions is to be understood.

Let us rehearse some of the points made earlier through the following passage from Schuon:

> A religion is not limited by what it includes but by what it excludes; this exclusion cannot impair the religion's deepest contents – every religion is intrinsically a totality – but it takes its revenge all the more surely on the intermediary plane ... the arena of theological speculations and fervours ... extrinsic contradictions can hide an intrinsic compatibility or identity, which amounts to saying that each of the contradictory theses contains a truth and thereby an aspect of the whole truth and a way of access to this totality.[59]

---

55 A spiritually alert minority has recently given much thought to the implications of this principle. The intuition and affirmation of its lessons was perhaps the most important aspect of the work of the late Thomas Merton. Merton's work has too often been seen as an enterprise in dialogue, which indeed it was, without any thought as to what end this was to be directed. The end Merton had in view was, of course, precisely the revivification of the contemplative and esoteric dimension within the Catholic tradition.
56 FS *IPP* p46.
57 O. Thomas: 'Introduction' to *Attitudes to Other Religions* SCM, London, 1969, quoted by Huston Smith, Introduction to FS *TUR* pxiiifn.
58 FS *TUR* p3. See also SHN *K&S* p281.
59 FS *IPP* p46.

Examples of 'contradictory' truths which effectively express complementary aspects of a single reality can be found not only across the traditions but within them. One might instance, by way of illustration, the Biblical or Koranic affirmations regarding predestination and free will.[60]

From an esoteric viewpoint the exclusivist claims of one or another religion have no absolute validity. It is true that 'the arguments of every intrinsically orthodox religion are absolutely convincing if one puts oneself in the intended setting'.[61] It is also true that orthodox theological dogmatisms are entitled to a kind of 'defensive reflex' which makes for claims to exclusivism. However, and this is crucial,

> The exoteric claim to the exclusive possession of a unique truth, or of Truth without epithet, is ... an error purely and simply; in reality, every expressed truth necessarily assumes a form, that of its expression, and it is metaphysically impossible that any form should possess a unique value to the exclusion of other forms; for a form, by definition, cannot be unique and exclusive, that is to say it cannot be the only possible expression of what it expresses.[62]

The argument that the different religions cannot all be repositories of the truth because of their formal differences and antagonisms rests on a failure to understand this principle. The lesson to be drawn from the multiplicity of religious forms is quite different:

> The diversity of religions, far from proving the falseness of all the doctrines concerning the supernatural, shows on the contrary the supra-formal character of revelation and the formal character of ordinary human understanding: the essence of revelation – or enlightenment – is one, but human nature requires diversity.[63]

In connection with this need for diversity, which is explained by the fact that humanity is divided into different branches, we might mention in passing Junayd's maxim that '... the color of the water is the color of the vessel containing it'.[64] Or, if a more abstract formulation be preferred, this from Aquinas: '... the thing known is in the knower according to the mode of the knower'.[65]

Schuon has deployed several images to clarify the relationship of the religions to each other. He likens them to geometric forms. Just as it would be absurd to imagine that spatial extensions and relationships could only be expressed by one form so it is absurd to assert that there could be only one doctrine giving an account of the Absolute. However, just as each geometric form has some necessary and sufficient reason for its existence, so too with the religions. To affirm that the Truth informing all religious traditions is one and that they essentially all vehicle the same message in different forms is not to preclude qualitative discriminations concerning particular aspects of this and that tradition. Schuon extends the geometric analogy:

---

60 FS *TUR* p4.
61 FS *SPHF* p14.
62 FS *TUR* p17.
63 F. Schuon: 'No Activity Without Truth' p4. See also M. Pallis *A Buddhist Spectrum* p157.
64 Quoted in A.K. Coomaraswamy: 'Sri Ramakrishna and Religious Tolerance' in AKC *SPII* p37.
65 *ibid.*; p36.

The differentiated forms are irreplaceable, otherwise they would not exist, and they are in no sense various kinds of imperfect circles; the cross is infinitely nearer the perfection of the point ... than are the oval or the trapezoid, for example. Analogous considerations apply to traditional doctrines, as concerns their differences of form and their efficacy in equating the contingent to the Absolute.[66]

The inter-relationships of the religions today is an issue which has taken on a new urgency in the cyclical conditions in which we live. In former times, just as man appeared as 'man' and not as 'yellow man' or 'black man', and just as each language seemed to its practitioners to be language as such, so too each religion, for most believers, appeared as 'religion' without further qualification. To choose one example from a multitude of possibilities, the Tibetans referred to their beliefs and practices not as 'Mahāyāna Buddhism' but simply as 'the way', *tehen*.[67] The imperative need for an esoteric resolution of the apparent incompatibilities of the different religious traditions is a matter that will be taken up again in our final chapter.

We have now discussed the four themes in Schuon's work heralded at the beginning of this chapter. By way of a footnote to our discussion two other points deserve brief mention: Schuon's views with respect to the limits of religious expansion and the inclusive nature of the great traditions. A corollary to the principle of multiple Revelations is the notion that there are certain natural, or better, providential limits to the possible expansion of each tradition. Here we shall only mention the principle without exposing its supports. The principle of providential limits is confirmed, as it were, by the relative inefficiency of religious expansionism outside its own perimeters: 'if God were on the side of one religious form only, the persuasive power of this form would be such that no man of good faith would be able to resist it.'[68] Another thread in the same web is the idea that all the great religious traditions will include under their canopy different spiritual perspectives and methods necessary for different temperaments and dispositions. Beyond the characteristics and prevalent spiritual economy of any one tradition each

> ... particular spiritual perspective is commonly discoverable somewhere within the framework of a tradition that seems to exclude it; thus theism appears in a certain sense in the framework of Buddhism despite its non-theism...[69]

Here, of course, Schuon is referring primarily to the cult of the Buddha Amitabha in the Pure Land Schools. To attempt, as historians often do, to explain this away as a 'deviation' resulting from Nestorian influences is to fail to understand that analogous phenomena are bound to appear where circumstances are favourable and that '... no profound possibility of man's nature can fail to emerge in some form or another within so vast a framework as that offered by a great Revelation.'[70]

---

66 FS *LAW* p139.
67 A. Desjardins *The Message of the Tibetans* Stuart & Watkins, London, 1969; p20.
68 FS *TUR* p14. See Chapter 5 of *TUR* pp74–88. See also FS *IPP* p15.
69 FS *ITB* p18.
70 *ibid.*; p122.

8
Metaphysics, Theology and Philosophy

... truth is the ultimate goal of the whole universe and the contemplation of truth is the essential activity of wisdom ...
St Thomas Aquinas[1]

The proof of the sun is the sun: if thou require the proof, do not avert thy face
Rumi[2]

The possession of all the sciences, if unaccompanied by the knowledge of the best, will more often than not injure the possessor
Plato[3]

The Infinite is what it is; one may understand it or not understand it. Metaphysics cannot be taught to everyone but, if it could be, there would be no atheism
Frithjof Schuon[4]

'Metaphysics is the finding of bad reasons for what we believe upon instinct.'[5] This Bradleian formulation, perhaps only half-serious, signposts a modern conception of metaphysics shared by a good many people, philosophers and otherwise. There is, of course, no single modern philosophical posture on the nature and significance of metaphysics. Some see it as a kind of residual blight on the tree of philosophy, a feeding-ground for obscurantists and lovers of mumbo-jumbo. Others grant it a more dignified status.[6] It is one of those words, like 'dogma' or 'mystical', which has been pejorated by careless and ignorant usage. The word 'metaphysics' is so fraught with hazards, so hedged about with philosophical disputation, and so sullied by popular usage that we shall have to take some care if the proper sense in which the traditionalists use the word is to become clear. Some operational definitions of several crucial terms will provide the starting-point. The elucidation of the traditionalist conception of metaphysics will be structured around three questions: What is metaphysics? What is its relationship, in terms of procedures, criteria and ends, to philosophy? And to theology? Subsequently a subordinate question will come into focus: Why have the traditionalists seen fit to expose to the public gaze certain metaphysical principles and esoteric insights previously the exclusive preserve of those spiritually qualified to understand them?

Without a clear definition of terms certain misunderstandings will be more or less inevitable. The following words in the traditionalist vocabulary must be understood precisely: tradition, Revelation, inspiration, Intellect, gnosis, metaphysics, and mystical. The first three terms have been discussed in the two preceding chapters so let us turn to the others.

Intellect: Whenever the traditionalists use this word or its derivatives it is not to be understood in its modern and popular sense of 'mental power'. Rather, it is a precise technical term taken from the Latin *intellectus* and from mediaeval scholasticism: that faculty which perceives the transcendent.[7] The Intellect receives intuitions and apprehends realities of a superphenomenal order. We remember Meister Eckhart's statement: 'There is something in the soul which is uncreated and uncreatable ... this is the Intellect'.[8] It is, in Schuon's words, 'a receptive faculty and not a productive power: it does not "create"; it receives and transmits. It is a mirror.'[9] The Intellect is an impersonal, unconditioned, receptive faculty, whence the objectivity of intellection. It is 'that which participates in the divine Subject'.[10] Marco Pallis reminds us

---

1 St. Thomas Aquinas, quoted in FS *UI* p133fn2.
2 Rumi in WP *TTW* p750.
3 Plato in WP *TTW* p731.
4 FS *SPHF* p50.
5 From F.H. Bradley *Appearance and Reality* quoted by S. Radhakrishnan: 'Reply to My Critics' in P.A. Schilpp (ed) *The Philosophy of Sarvepalli Radhakrishnan* Tudor, New York, 1952; p791.
6 For some discussion of this term by a modern philosopher see J. Hospers *An Introduction to Philosophical Analysis* Routledge and Kegan Paul, London, 1956; pp211ff.
7 See M. Lings *What is Sufism?* Allen & Unwin, London, 1975; p48.
8 Quoted in M. Lings *A Sufi Saint of the Twentieth Century* Uni California Press, Berkeley, 19171; p27.
9 FS *SW* p21.
10 *ibid.*; p88.

that the belief in this transcendent faculty, capable of a direct contact with Reality, is to be found in all traditions under various names.[11]

Gnosis: 'The word gnosis ... refers to supra-rational and thus purely intellective, knowledge of metacosmic realities.'[12] It must not be confused with the historical phenomenon of gnosticism, the Graeco-Oriental syncretism of latter classical times.[13] Its Sanskrit equivalent is *jñāna*, knowledge in its fullest sense, what Eckhart calls 'divine knowledge'.

Metaphysic: We shall turn to this term in some detail presently but for the moment the following capsule definition from Nasr will suffice: 'Metaphysics, which in fact is one and should be named metaphysic ... is the science of the Real, of the origin and end of things, of the Absolute and in its light, the relative'.[14] Similarly 'metaphysical': 'concerning universal realities considered objectively'.[15]

Mystical: 'concerning the same realities considered subjectively, that is, in relation to the contemplative soul, insofar as they enter into contact with it'.[16]

As Guénon observed more than once, metaphysics cannot properly and strictly be defined, for to define is to limit, while the domain of metaphysics is the Real and thus limitless. Consequently, metaphysics 'is truly and absolutely unlimited and cannot be confined to any formula or any system'.[17] Its subject, in the words of John Tauler, is 'that pure knowledge that knows no form or creaturely way'.[18] This must always be kept in mind in any attempt at a 'definition' which must needs be provisional and incomplete. Let us return to the passage in which Nasr explains the nature of metaphysics:

> It is a science as strict and as exact as mathematics and with the same clarity and certitude, but one which can only be attained through intellectual intuition and not simply through ratiocination. It thus differs from philosophy as it is usually understood. Rather, it is a *theoria* of reality whose realisation means sanctity and spiritual perfection, and therefore can only be achieved within the cadre of a revealed tradition. Metaphysical intuition can occur everywhere – for the 'spirit bloweth where it listeth' – but the effective realisation of metaphysical truth and its application to human life can only be achieved within a revealed tradition which gives efficacy to certain symbols and rites upon which metaphysics must rely for its realisation.
>
> This supreme science of the Real ... is the only science that can distinguish between the Absolute and the relative, appearance and reality ... Moreover, this science exists, as the esoteric dimension within every orthodox and integral tradition and is united with a spiritual method derived totally from the tradition in question.[19]

11 M. Pallis quoted in WP *TTW* p733.
12 FS *UI* p115.
13 See FS *THC* pp67–68. See also FS *RHC* pp10–11.
14 S.H. Nasr *Man and Nature* Allen & Unwin, London, 1976; p81.
15 FS *L&T* p204fn9.
16 *ibid.* Schuon is, of course, not unaware of the linguistic and connotative ambiguites surrounding this term. See FS *SPHF* p86fn. See also S.H. Nasr *Sufi Essays* Allen & Unwin, London, 1972; p26 fn5. For an extended traditionalist discussion see W. Stoddart: 'Mysticism' in RF *UT* pp89–95.
17 R. Guénon: 'Oriental Metaphysics' in JN *SG* pp43–44.
18 Quoted in C.F. Kelley *Meister Eckhart on Divine Knowledge* Yale Uni Press, New Haven, 1977; p4.
19 S.H. Nasr *Man and Nature* pp81–82. See also Coomaraswamy's undated letter to 'M', AKC *SL* p10: '...traditional Metaphysics is as much a single and invariable science as mathematics.'

Martin Lings

This view of metaphysics accords with the traditional but not with the modern conception of philosophy – of *philo-sophia*, love of wisdom as a practical concern. In India, for example, philosophy was never only a matter of epistemology but an all-embracing science of first principles and of the true nature of Reality, and one wedded to the spiritual disciplines provided by religion. The ultimate reality of metaphysics is the Supreme Identity in which all oppositions and dualities are resolved, those of subject and object, knower and known, being and non-being; thus a Scriptural formulation such as 'The things of God knoweth no man, but the Spirit of God'.[20] As Coomaraswamy remarks, the philosophy, or metaphysics, provided the vision, and religion the way to its effective verification and actualisation in direct experience.[21] The cleavage between metaphysics and philosophy only appears in modern times.

The nature of metaphysics is more easily grasped through a contrast with philosophy and theology. However, several general points need to be established before we proceed. Because the metaphysical realm lies 'beyond' the phenomenal plane the validity of a metaphysical principle can be neither proved nor disproved by any kind of empirical demonstration, by reference to material realities.[22] The aim of metaphysics is not to prove anything whatsoever but to make doctrines intelligible and to demonstrate their consistency.

Secondly, metaphysics is concerned with a direct apprehension of reality or, to put it differently, with a recognition of the Absolute and our relationship to it. It thus takes on an imperative character for those capable of metaphysical discernment.

> The requirement for us to recognise the Absolute is itself an absolute one; it concerns man as such and not man under such and such conditions. It is a fundamental aspect of human dignity, and especially of that intelligence which denoted 'the state of man hard to obtain', that we accept Truth because it is true and for no other reason.[23]

Furthermore, because metaphysics is attuned to the sacred and the divine it demands something of those who would unlock its mysteries:

> If metaphysics is a sacred thing, that means it could not be ... limited to the framework of the play of the mind. It is illogical and dangerous to talk of metaphysics without being preoccupied with the moral concomitances it requires, the criteria of which are, for man, his behaviour in relation to God and to his neighbour.[24]

Thirdly, metaphysics assumes man's capacity for absolute and certain knowledge:

> The capacity for objectivity and for absoluteness is an anticipated and existential refutation of all the ideologies of doubt: if man is able to doubt this is because certitude exists; likewise the very

---

20 *1 Corinthians* II.11. The Absolute may be called God, the Godhead, *nirguna Brahman*, the Tao, and so on, according to the vocabulary at hand. See FS *LAW* pp96-9fn1 for a commentary on the use of 'God' and FS *L&T* for a similar discussion of 'Allah'.
21 A.K. Coomaraswamy: 'A Lecture on Comparative Religion' quoted in RL *CLW* p275. Also see 'Vedanta and Western Tradition' in AKC *SPII* p6.
22 See R. Guénon: *op.cit.*; p53.
23 FS *ITB* p33.
24 FS *SPHF* p173.

notion of illusion proves that man has access to reality ... If doubt conformed to the real, human intelligence would be deprived of its sufficient reason and man would be less than an animal, since the intelligence of animals does not experience doubt concerning the reality to which it is proportioned.[25]

Metaphysics, therefore, is immutable and inexorable, and the 'infallible standard by which not only religions, but still more "philosophies" and "sciences" must be "corrected" ... and interpreted'.[26] Metaphysics can be ignored or forgotten but not refuted 'precisely because it is immutable and not related to change *qua* change'.[27] Metaphysical principles are true and valid once and for all and not for this particular age or mentality, and could not, in any sense, 'evolve'. They can be validated directly in the plenary and unitive experience of the mystic. Thus Martin Lings can write of Sufism – and one could say the same of any intrinsically orthodox traditional esotericism – that it

> ... has the right to be inexorable because it is based on certainties and not on opinions. It has the obligation to be inexorable because mysticism is the sole repository of Truth, in the fullest sense, being above all concerned with the Absolute, the Infinite and the Eternal; and 'If the salt have lost its savour, wherewith shall it be salted?' Without mysticism, Reality would have no voice in the world. There would be no record of the true hierarchy, and no witness that it is continually being violated.[28]

One might easily substitute the word 'metaphysics' for 'mysticism' in this passage, the former being the formal and objective aspect of the 'subjective' experience. However, this is not to lose sight of the fact that any and every metaphysical doctrine will take it as axiomatic that every formulation is 'but error in the face of the Divine Reality itself; a provisional, indispensable, salutary "error" which, however, contains and communicates the virtuality of the Truth'.[29] With these considerations to the forefront we can turn to a comparison, firstly, of metaphysics and philosophy.

In a discussion of Shankara's *Advaita* Vedanta Coomaraswamy exposed some of the crucial differences between metaphysics and modern philosophy:

> The Vedanta is not a 'philosophy' in the current sense of the word, but only as the word is used in the phrase *Philosophia Perennis*.... Modern philosophies are closed systems, employing the method of dialectics, and taking for granted that opposites are mutually exclusive. In modern philosophy things are either so or not so; in eternal philosophy this depends upon our point of view. Metaphysics is not a system, but a consistent doctrine; it is not merely concerned with conditioned and quantitative experience but with universal possibility.[30]

Modern European philosophy is dialectical, which is to say analytical and rational in its modes. From a traditionalist point of view it might be said that modern

---

25 FS *L&T* p13. See also FS *EPW* pp15ff.
26 Letter to J.H. Muirhead, August 1935, in AKC *SL* p37.
27 S. H. Nasr *Sufi Essays* p86. See also FS *SW* p42.
28 M. Lings *What is Sufism?* p93.
29 FS *SPHF* pp162–163. Cf. A.K. Coomaraswamy: '... and every belief is a heresy if it be regarded as the truth, and not simply as a signpost of the truth.' 'Sri Ramakrishna and Religious Tolerance' in AKC *SPII* p38. See also FS *SVQ* p2.
30 A.K. Coomaraswamy: 'Vedanta and Western Tradition' p6.

philosophy is anchored in a misunderstanding of the nature and role of reason; indeed, the idolatry of reason could hardly have otherwise arisen. Schuon spotlights some of the strengths and deficiencies of the rational mode in these terms:

> Reason is formal by its nature and formalistic in its operations; it proceeds by 'coagulations', by alternatives and by exclusions – or, it can be said, by partial truths. It is not, like pure intellect, formless and fluid 'light'; true, it derives its implacability, or its validity in general, from the intellect, but it touches on essences only through drawing conclusions, not by direct vision; it is indispensable for verbal formulations but it does not involve immediate knowledge.[31]

Titus Burckhardt likens reason to 'a convex lens which steers the intelligence in a particular direction and onto a limited field'.[32] Like any other instrument it can be abused. Much European philosophy, adrift from its religious moorings, has surrendered to a kind of totalitarian rationalism, to what Blake called 'Single Vision'.[33] In so doing it has violated a principle which was respected wherever a metaphysical tradition and a religious framework for the pursuit of wisdom remained intact – the principle of adequation, articulated thus by Aquinas: 'It is a sin against intelligence to want to proceed in an identical manner in typically different domains – physical, mathematical, metaphysical – of speculative knowledge.'[34] This, it would seem, is precisely what modern philosophers are bent on. No less pertinent in this context is Plotinus's well-known maxim 'knowing demands the organ fitted to the object'.[35] The grotesqueries of modern philosophy spring, in large measure, from an indifference to this principle. The situation is exacerbated further by the fact that many philosophers have been duped by the claims of a totalitarian scientism and thus suffer from a drastically impoverished view of reality and of the avenues by which it might be apprehended. The words of the Moravian alchemist, Michael Sendivogius, seem more apposite than ever: 'philosophers are men whom too much [profane] learning and thought have made mad'.[36]

The place of reason, of logic and dialectic, in metaphysics is altogether more subordinate as the following sample of quotes make clear. It is worth mobilising several quotations as this issue is so often misunderstood, with bizarre results. From Schuon:

> In the intellectual order logical proof is only a quite provisional crystallisation of intuition, the modes of which ... are incalculable. Metaphysical truths are by no means accepted because they are merely logically clear, but because they are ontologically clear and their logical clarity is only a trace of this imprinted on the mind.[37]

Or again:

---

31 FS *UI* p24. See also FS *SW* pp18ff.
32 T. Burckhardt *Alchemy* Penguin, 1971; p36fn1.
33 For a discussion of Blake's critique of rationalism see T. Roszak *Where the Wasteland Ends* Doubleday, New York, 1972; pp142–177.
34 Quoted in S. H. Nasr *Man and Nature* p35.
35 Quoted in E.F. Schumacher *A Guide for the Perplexed* Jonathan Cape, London, 1977; p49.
36 per WP *TTW* p735.
37 FS *SPHF* p10.

Metaphysics is not held to be true – by those who understand it – because it is expressed in a logical manner, but it can be expressed in a logical manner because it is true, without – obviously – its truth ever being compromised by the possible shortcomings of human reason.[38]

Similarly Guénon:

... for metaphysics, the use of rational argument never represents more than a mode of external expression and in no way affects metaphysical knowledge itself, for the latter must always be kept essentially distinct from its formulation...[39]

Metaphysical discernment proceeds more through contemplative intelligence than through ratiocination. Metaphysical formulations depend more on symbol and on analogy than on logical demonstration, though it is a grave error to suppose that metaphysics has any right to irrationality.[40] What many modern philosophers apparently fail to understand is that thought can become increasingly subtle and complex without approaching any nearer to the truth. An idea can be subdivided into a thousand ramifications, fenced about with every conceivable qualification and supported with the most intricate and rigorous logic but, for all that, remain purely external and quantitative for 'no virtuosity of the potter will transform clay into gold'.[41] Furthermore,

... that a reasoning might simply be the logical and provisional description of an intellectual evidence, and that its function might be the actualisation of this evidence, in itself supralogical, apparently never crosses the minds of pure logicians.[42]

Analytical rationality, no matter how useful a tool, will never, in itself, generate metaphysical understanding. Metaphysicians of all ages have said nothing different. Shankara, for instance: '... the pure truth of *Ātman* ... can be reached by meditation, contemplation and other spiritual disciplines such as a knower of *Brahman* may prescribe – but never by subtle argument.'[43] The Promethean arrogance of much modernist thought, often bred by scientistic ideologies, is revealed in the refusal to acknowledge the boundaries beyond which reason has no competence or utility. This has, of course, prompted some quite ludicrous claims about religion and religious phenomena. As Schuon remarks,

The equating of the supernatural with the irrational is characteristic ... it amounts to claiming that the unknown or the incomprehensible is the same as the absurd. The rationalism of a frog living at the bottom of the well is to deny the existence of mountains: this is logic of a kind but it has nothing to do with reality.[44]

The intelligibility of a metaphysical doctrine may depend upon a measure of faith in

---

38 FS *EPW* p28.
39 R. Guénon quoted in FS *SW* p29fn1.
40 See FS *EPW* p28.
41 FS *UI* p149.
42 FS *L&T* p37.
43 *Shankara's Crest Jewel of Discrimination* tr & ed. Swami Prabhavananda & C. Isherwood, Mentor, New York, 1970; p73.
44 FS *L&T* p42

the traditional Christian sense of 'assent to a credible proposition'. As Coomaraswamy observes

> One must believe in order to understand and understand in order to believe. These are not successive, however, but simultaneous acts of the mind. In other words, there can be no knowledge of anything to which the will refuses its consent...[45]

This mode of apprehension is something quite other than the philosophical thought that

> ...believes it can attain to an absolute contact with Reality by means of analyses, syntheses, arrangements, filtrations and polishings – thought that is mundane by the very fact of this ignorance and because it is a vicious circle which not merely provides no escape from illusion, but even reinforces it through the lure of a progressive knowledge which in fact is inexistent.[46]

It is in this context that we can speak of modern philosophy as 'the codification of an acquired infirmity'.[47] Unlike modern philosophy, metaphysics has nothing to do with personal opinion, originality or creativity – quite the contrary. It is directed towards those realities which lie outside mental perimeters and which are unchanging. The most a metaphysician will ever want to do is to reformulate some timeless truth so that it becomes more intelligible in the prevailing climate.[48] A profane system of thought, on the other hand, is never more than a portrait of the person who creates it, an 'involuntary memoir' as Nietzsche put it.[49]

The metaphysician does not seek to invent or discover or prove a new system of thought but rather to crystallize direct apprehensions of Reality insofar as this is possible within the limited resources of human language, making use not only of logic but of symbol and analogy. Furthermore, the science of metaphysics must always proceed in the context of a revealed religion, protected by the tradition in question which also supplies the necessary supports for the full realisation or actualisation of metaphysical doctrines. The metaphysician seeks not only to formulate immutable principles and doctrines but to live by them, to conform his or her being to the truths they convey. In other words, there is nothing of the 'art for art's sake' type of thinking about the pursuit of metaphysics: it engages the whole person or it is as nothing.[50] As Schuon states,

> The moral exigency of metaphysical discernment means that virtue is part of wisdom; a wisdom without virtue is in fact imposture and hypocrisy... plenary knowledge of Divine Reality presupposes or demands moral conformity to this Reality, as the eye necessarily conforms to light; since the object to be known is the sovereign Good, the knowing subject must correspond to it analogically...[51]

---

45 A.K. Coomaraswamy: 'Vedanta and Western Tradition' p8. See also SHN *K&S* p6.
46 FS *L&T* p34.
47 FS *TM* p4.
48 Here we are at the opposite end of the spectrum not only from the philosophical relativists but from those who hold a 'personalist' or 'existentialist' view of truth.
49 Friedrich Nietzsche in *Beyond Good and Evil*, taken from *A Nietzsche Reader* Penguin 1977, ed R.J. Hollingdale; Extract 13. See also FS *L&T* p34 and FS *TM* p4. (For an iulluminating passage on both the grandeur and the 'dementia' of Nietzsche's work see FS *THC* p15.)
50 See A.K. Coomaraswamy: 'Vedanta and Western Tradition' p9.
51 FS *RHC* p86.

A point often overlooked: metaphysics does not of necessity find its expression only in verbal forms. Metaphysics can be expressed visually and ritually as well as verbally. The Chinese and Red Indian traditions furnish pre-eminent examples of these possibilities. Moreover,

> ... the criterion of metaphysical truth or of its depth lies not in the complexity or difficulty of its expression, having regard to a particular capacity of understanding or style of thinking. Wisdom does not lie in any complication of words but in the profundity of the intention; assuredly the expression may according to the circumstances be subtle and difficult, or equally it may not be so.[52]

One is irresistibly reminded of the Buddha's Flower Sermon.

By way of a digression it might be noted that because the fundamental distinction between reason and Intellect has been obscured in recent European thought, then similarly, '... the basic distinction between metaphysics as a *scienta sacra* or Divine Knowledge and philosophy as a purely human form of mental activity has been blurred or forgotten.'[53] In the field of comparative religion this has led to a good deal of confusion. As S.H. Nasr has noted, to speak of Hindu or Chinese philosophy and rationalistic European philosophy in the same breath is a contradiction in terms unless the word 'philosophy' is used in two quite different senses. A failure to draw the necessary distinctions has

> ... made a sham of many studies of comparative philosophy and has helped to reduce to nil the real significance of Oriental metaphysics ... To say that this or that statement of Hegel resembles the Upanisads or that Hume presents ideas similar to Nagarjuna's is to fall into the worst form of error, one which prevents any type of profound understanding from being achieved, either for Westerners wanting to understand the East or vice versa.[54]

Let us summarise the most significant differences between metaphysics and modern philosophy. The latter is, generally speaking, analytical, rationalistic and quantitative; it is concerned with relationships and contingencies accessible to rational inquiry, or at least to the workings of the normal mind, these including imagination which is no less a mental process than ratiocination; European philosophers tend to see the development of philosophy as progressive, driven forward by the work of this or that philosopher who creates or discovers new insights, fresh perceptions, a different vocabulary of discourse, and so on; philosophy is usually seen as self-validating, not requiring any justification outside itself. Metaphysics, by contrast, is concerned with supra-mundane, transcendent and unconditioned realities; it is qualitative, symbolical and synthetic in its modes and is rooted in certain immutable principles; it is indifferent to the question of 'proofs' and the metaphysician's purpose is not the resolution of some 'problem' but the demonstration of something already intellectually evident; it does not evolve or progress; it is intimately linked with spiritual disciplines and depends for its realisation on the presence of elements which could only be drawn from an integral tradition; it is a practical pursuit which has as its end gnosis, transformation and sanctification.

---

52 FS *UI* p111.
53 S.H. Nasr: 'Conditions for a meaningful comparative philosophy' *Philosophy East and West* XXII, i, 1972; p54.
54 *ibid.*; p55 and p58.

Metaphysics, Theology and Philosophy

The relationship between metaphysics and theology is more subtle, complex and problematic. Under the traditionalist view, a Divine Revelation is always the fountainhead of any orthodox religion while metaphysical insight derives from intellection. The dichotomy here is more apparent than real, Revelation taking the place of intellection for the human collectivity in question. This is a principle not easily grasped but without it the apparent antagonisms of theology and metaphysics cannot be resolved. Schuon defines the relationship between Revelation and intellection in this way:

> ... in normal times we learn *a priori* of divine things through Revelation, which provides for us the symbols and the indispensable data, and we have access *a posteriori* to the truth of these things through Intellection, which reveals to us their essence beyond received formulations, but not opposing them ... Revelation is an Intellection in the Macrocosm, while Intellection is a Revelation in the microcosm; the *Avatāra* is the outward Intellect, and the Intellect is the inward *Avatāra*.[55]

It might be said, then, that intellection appears in a more 'subjective' mode, but only with this qualification:

> It is subjective because empirically it is within us. The term 'subjective', as applied to the intellect, is as improper as the epithet 'human'; in both cases the terms are used simply in order to define the way of approach.[56]

The traditionalists, always alert to the dangers of a reductionist psychologism, insist that the truth to which intellection gives access is beyond all spatio-temporal determinations. As Schuon points out, Biblical formulations such as 'the Kingdom of Heaven is within you' certainly do not mean that heaven, God or Truth are of a psychological order but simply that access to these realities is to be found through the centre of our being.[57]

Religion itself, flowing from the Divine, must contain within itself principial or metaphysical knowledge but this will be veiled by the forms in question. For instance,

> The message of Christ, like that of the Bible, is not *a priori* a teaching of metaphysical science; it is above all a message of salvation, but one that necessarily contains, in an indirect way and under cover of an appropriate symbolism, metaphysics in its entirety.[58]

The metaphysical emphasis varies from one tradition to another. Buddhism, for example, is primarily a spiritual therapy rather than a metaphysical system but one which of necessity requires a metaphysics while Hinduism is, in the first place, a metaphysics which implies, under the same necessity, a spiritual therapy.[59] Doubtless there are those who will be quick to asseverate that Buddhism is indifferent to metaphysics, pointing to the Buddha's refusal to answer the indeterminate questions. The traditionalists would simply remind us of Nagarjuna's statement that the Buddha

---

55 FS *EPW* p10. See also SHN *K&S* pp148–149.
56 FS *UI* p57fn2.
57 F. Schuon: 'Keys to the Bible' in JN *SG* pp356–358.
58 FS *L&T* p86.
59 See FS *SPHF* p55.

taught two levels of truth and that an understanding of the distinction, not possible without a metaphysical doctrine, is preconditional to a full understanding of the *dharma*.[60] 'There is no science of the soul,' says Schuon, 'without a metaphysical basis to it and without spiritual remedies at its disposal.'[61]

The relationship of theology to metaphysics is that of exotericism to esotericism. Exotericism is 'unable of itself to take cognisance of the relationships whereby, at one and the same time, it is justified in its claims and limited in its scope.'[62] Theological dogmatism is characterised by its insistence on elevating a particular point of view, or aspect of reality under a specific formal guise, to an absolute value with exclusive claims. As we have seen already, what characterises a metaphysical esotericism, on the other hand, is its discernment of the universal in the particular, of the essence in the form. This distinction can be hinged on the terms 'belief' and 'gnosis', or similarly, 'faith' and 'certitude'. The difference between these, writes Schuon, is

> ... comparable to the difference between a description of a mountain and direct vision of it; the second no more puts us on top of the mountain than the first but it does inform us about the properties of the mountain and the route to follow; let us not however forget that the blind man who walks without stopping advances more quickly than a normal man who stops at each step.[63]

Elsewhere Schuon refers to the theologies as taking upon themselves the contradiction of being 'sentimental metaphysics':

> ... being ignorant of the differentiation of things into aspects and standpoints they have therefore to operate on the basis of arbitrarily rigid data, the antinomies of which can only be solved by going beyond their artificial rigidity; their working has moreover a sentimental slant and this is described as 'thinking piously'.[64]

Such remarks should not be construed as an attack on the theological perspective but only as a caution about the limits of dogmatism and the dangers of a theological totalitarianism when it enters an arena where it is inadequate. As Marco Pallis so neatly puts it,

> What one always needs to remember is that traditional forms, including those bearing the now unpopular name of dogmas, are keys to unlock the gate of Unitive Truth; but they are also (since a key can close, as well as open a gate) possible obstacles to its profoundest knowledge ...[65]

In a felicitous metaphor Schuon compares the religions to the beads of rosary, gnosis being the cord on which they are strung. In other words, the religious orthodoxies, or more specifically theologies, are only able to fulfil their function when they remain attached to the principial knowledge which is preserved in the esoteric dimension of each tradition.

The hierarchic superiority of gnosis to all other forms of knowledge and of meta-

---

60 *ibid.*
61 FS *L&T* p14.
62 FS *ITB* p46.
63 FS *UI* p148.
64 FS *IPP* p39.
65 M. Pallis: 'Foreword' to WP *TTW* p10.

physical doctrine to all other kinds of formulations should not be allowed to obscure the inter-dependent relationship of the esoteric and the exoteric, of the metaphysical domain and the rest of any religious tradition. Three general points need to be made in this context. They concern the ineffectiveness of intellection outside a traditional framework, the distinction between doctrinal understanding and realisation, and the relationship between metaphysical discernment and the spiritual life in general.

There are, writes Schuon,

> no metaphysical or cosmological reasons why, in exceptional cases, direct intellection should not arise in men who have no link at all with revealed wisdom, but an exception, if it proves the rule, assuredly could not constitute the rule.[66]

In more normal cases

> Intellection has need of tradition, of a Revelation fixed in time and adapted to a society, if it is to be awakened in us and not go astray ... the importance of orthodoxy, of tradition, of Revelation is that the means of realising the Absolute must come 'objectively' from the Absolute; knowledge cannot spring up 'subjectively' except within the framework of an 'objective' divine formulation of Knowledge.[67]

Thus, although intellection can occur as 'an isolated miracle' anywhere, it will have neither authority nor efficacy outside tradition.[68] (In this context the case of Ramana Maharishi is not without interest, remembering how the sage had to cast his own mystical insight into the moulds of classical Vedanta in order to be able to communicate it.[69])

The distinction between doctrinal understanding and even intellection itself on the one hand, and realisation on the other, is a crucial one. Contemplative intelligence and metaphysical insight do not, in themselves, save, 'do not prevent Titans from falling'.[70] There must be a participation of the will in the intelligence, or as one scholar glossed Meister Eckhart, 'The intellective center is not truly known without involving the volitive circumference.'[71] Here the will can be defined as 'a prolongation or a complement of the intelligence'[72] while intelligence itself refers to a contemplative receptivity rather than any mental cleverness, an intelligence which 'differs as much from mental virtuosity as the soaring flight of an eagle differs from the play of a monkey'.[73] Morality and the virtues, love, faith – these must be integrated with metaphysical insight if full realisation is to occur, which is to say there must be a merging of intellectual and volitive elements in a harmonized unity. It should also be remembered that although the Intellect is

---

66 FS *SPHF* p15.

67 FS *UI* p130.

68 FS *SW* p57.

69 The best introductory account of the life of the sage is T.M.P. Mahadevan *Ramana Maharshi, The Sage of Arunacala* Allen & Unwin, London, 1977. See also FS *SPHF* p122.

70 FS *SPHF* p138.

71 C.F. Kelley: *op.cit.* (Kelley's book clearly owes a great deal to Schuon whose aphorisms are repeated almost word for word but nowhere in the book can we find any acknowledgment of Schuon or any of the other traditionalists.)

72 FS *LAW* p136. See also FS *L&T* p199.

73 S.H. Nasr *Ideals and Realities of Islam* p21.

situated beyond sentiment, imagination, memory and reason . . . it can at the same time enlighten and determine all of these since they are like its individualized ramifications, ordained as receptacles to receive the light from on high and to translate it according to their respective capacities.[74]

The spiritual life, which can only be lived in conformity with a way provided by tradition, forms both a precondition and a complement to intellection. As Aquinas put it, 'By their very nature the virtues do not necessarily form part of contemplation but they are an indispensable condition for it.'[75] Moreover, sanctity itself may or may not be accompanied by metaphysical discernment: one may be a saint but no metaphysician, as history repeatedly demonstrates. To expect, as a necessity, metaphysical wisdom of the saint is to confuse different modes of spiritual perfection. As Schuon reminds us,

> To say 'man' is to say *bhakta*, and to say spirit is to say *jñānin*; human nature is so to speak woven of these two neighbouring but incommensurable dimensions. There is certainly a *bhakti* without *jñāna*, but there is no *jñāna* without *bhakti*.[76]

The perspectives of Ramanuja and Shankara might be cited as an illustrative example of this principle.[77]

If metaphysical discernment is to transform one's being then intellection alone is insufficient for 'Human nature contains dark elements which no intellectual certainty could, *ipso facto*, eliminate.'[78] Here the role of faith is of critical importance:

> A man may possess metaphysical certainty without possessing 'faith' . . . But, if metaphysical certainty suffices on the doctrinal ground, it is far from being sufficient on the spiritual level where it must be completed and enlivened by faith. Faith is nothing other than our whole being clinging to Truth, whether we have of truth a direct intuition or an indirect idea. It is an abuse of language to reduce 'faith' to the level of 'belief'.[79]

In another context Schuon emphasises this point in even more unequivocal terms. The following passage is, in my view, one of the most arresting in the whole Schuonian corpus, one made all the more so by the uncharacteristic personal reference:

> One can meditate or speculate indefinitely on transcendent truths and their applications (that is moreover what the author of this book does, but he has valid reasons for doing it, nor does he do it for himself). One can spend a whole lifetime speculating on the suprasensorial and the transcendent, but all that matters is 'the leap into the void' which is the fixation of spirit and soul in an unthinkable dimension of the Real . . . this 'leap into the void' we can call . . . 'faith' . . .[80]

The planes on which philosophy, theology and metaphysics are situated can be identified by comparing their respective approaches to 'God'. For the philosopher

---

74 FS *TM* p25.
75 Quoted in FS *UI* p133fn2.
76 FS *EPW* p22.
77 See FS *SPHF* pp103ff. For a European example of '*bhakti* without *jñāna*' one might cite St Theresa of Lisieux – but the history of Christianity furnishes many examples.
78 FS *SPHF* p139.
79 *ibid.*; p127. On the relationship of intellection and realisation see also SHN *K&S* pp310ff.
80 FS *L&T* p202.

'God' is a 'problem' to be resolved and His existence or non-existence a question to be approached rationally, as if human reason could prove no matter what!; the theologian will be less concerned with proofs, the existence and reality of God being a revealed and thus axiomatic datum, than with belief and its moral concomitances; the metaphysician is concerned neither with rational argument nor with belief but with an Intellectual Evidence which brings an absolute certitude. To put it another way one might say that philosophy trades in opinions and ideas, theology focuses on beliefs and moralities, and metaphysics formulates doctrines which are the fruit of intellection. Or, again, one might say that the philosopher is intent on constructing a mental system, the theologian on discovering and living by the 'will of heaven', and the metaphysician on a gnosis and transformation which will conform his being to Reality unqualified.

We can recapitulate some of the central points made in our discussion of the relationships between philosophy, theology and metaphysics through a passage from Schuon's *The Transcendent Unity of Religions*:

> ...intellectual or metaphysical knowledge transcends the specifically theological point of view, which is itself incomparably superior to the philosophical point of view, since, like metaphysical knowledge, it emanates from God and not from man; but whereas metaphysics proceeds wholly from intellectual intuition, religion proceeds from Revelation... in the case of intellectual intuition, knowledge is not possessed by the individual insofar as he is an individual, but insofar as in his innermost essence he is not distinct from the Divine Principle... the theological point of view, because it is based in the minds of believers on a Revelation and not on a knowledge that is accessible to each one of them... will of necessity confuse the symbol or form with the naked and supraformal Truth while metaphysics... will be able to make use of the same symbol or form as a means of expression while at the same time being aware of its relativity... religion translates metaphysical or universal truths into dogmatic language... What essentially distinguishes the metaphysical from the philosophical proposition is that the former is symbolical and descriptive... whereas philosophy... is never anything more than what it expresses. When philosophy uses reason to resolve a doubt, this proves precisely that its starting point is a doubt it is striving to overcome, whereas... the starting point of a metaphysical formulation is always something intellectually evident or certain, which is communicated to those able to receive it, by symbolical or dialectical means designed to awaken in them the latent knowledge that they bear unconsciously, and it may even be said, eternally within them.[81]

Our discussion of these inter-relationships has necessarily had to gloss over some issues, skirt round others. Some fundamentally important principles and distinctions had to be expounded within a short compass. Before closing this discussion it will be as well to offer some qualifications to the argument elaborated above which has drawn heavily on Schuon's *The Transcendent Unity of Religions*. As Schuon points out in a more recent work,

> In our first book... we adopted the point of view of Ghazali regarding 'philosophy': that is to say, bearing in mind the great impoverishment of modern philosophy, we simplified the problem, as others have done before us, by making 'philosophy' synonymous with 'rationalism'.[82]

---

81 FS *TUR* ppxxviii-xxx.
82 FS *SVQ* p123fn10.

We have followed more or less the same procedure here and will only modify it with two brief points. Firstly, the term 'philosophy' in itself 'has nothing restrictive about it'; the restrictions which we have imposed on it in this discussion have been expedient rather than essential. Schuon has laid bare some of the issues raised by both the ancient and modern use of the term in an essay entitled 'Tracing the Notion of Philosophy'.[83] Secondly, it must also be admitted that our discussion of the relationships of philosophy, theology and metaphysics has been governed by some necessary oversimplifications. From certain points of view the distinctions we have established are not as clear-cut nor as rigid as our discussion has suggested. As Schuon himself writes

> In a certain respect, the difference between philosophy, theology and gnosis is total; in another respect, it is relative. It is total when one understands by 'philosophy' only rationalism; by 'theology', only the explanation of religious teachings; and by 'gnosis', only intuitive and intellective, and thus supra-rational, knowledge; but the difference is only relative when one understands by 'philosophy' the fact of thinking, by 'theology' the fact of speaking dogmatically of God and religious things, and by 'gnosis' the fact of presenting pure metaphysics, for then the genres interpenetrate.[84]

We live in anomalous times. Nowhere is this more graphically demonstrated than in the fact that in the most irreligious and impious period in human history the esoteric wisdoms preserved by the religious traditions are more widely and easily accessible than ever before. Sapiential truths which previously had remained extrinsically inexpressible and which had been protected by those few capable of understanding them are now on public display, as it were. The traditionalists themselves have played a significant role in bringing esoteric wisdoms within the purview of a greater number of people. This calls for some explanation.

The erosion of the protective barriers which previously enclosed traditions has, in part, been caused by historical factors which, in a sense, are 'accidental'. One might cite the exposure of the Upanisadic Scriptures as a case in point; here certain historical factors, such as the introduction into India of cheap printing presses, combined with a degree of imprudence on the part of some of the 'reformers' of Hinduism to subvert the esoteric status of these Scriptures which became available to anyone and everyone. There are also innumerable cases where a garbled version of half-understood secret doctrines has been thoughtlessly and carelessly put into public circulation. The Biblical verse 'For there is nothing covered, that shall not be revealed . . .' has sometimes been taken as a licence for all manner of excesses in the popularising of esoteric doctrines. The warnings about false prophets might often be more to the point.

In the case of the traditionalists the unveiling of some esoteric teachings has been considered and prudent. What sorts of factors have allowed this development? Firstly, there are certain cosmic and cyclic conditions now obtaining which make for an unprecedented situation. In discussing the fact that what was once hid in the darkness is now being brought into the light, Schuon writes,

---

83 *ibid.*; p115–128. See also FS *TM* p3.
84 *SVQ* p125.

there is indeed something abnormal in this, but it lies, not in the fact of the exposition of these truths, but in the general conditions of our age, which marks the end of a great cyclic period of terrestrial humanity – the end of a *mahā-yuga* according to Hindu cosmology – and so must recapitulate or manifest again in one way or another everything that is included in the cycle, in conformity with the adage 'extremes meet'; thus things that are in themselves abnormal may become necessary by reason of the conditions just referred to.[85]

Secondly, from a more expedient point of view,

> ... it must be admitted that the spiritual confusion of our times has reached such a pitch that the harm that might in principle befall certain people from contact with the truths in question is compensated by the advantages that others will derive from the self-same truths.[86]

Schuon reminds us of the Kabbalistic adage that 'it is better to divulge Wisdom than to forget it.'[87] And thirdly there is the fact already mentioned: esoteric doctrines have, in recent times, been so frequently 'plagiarised and deformed' that those who are in a position to speak with authority on these matters are obliged to give some account of what 'true esoterism is and what it is not'.[88]

From another perspective it can be said that the preservation, indeed the very survival, of the formal exotericisms may depend on the revivifying effects of an esotericism more widely understood:

> exoterism is a precarious thing by reason of its limits or its exclusions: there arrives a moment in history when all kinds of experiences oblige it to modify its claims to exclusiveness, and it is then driven to a choice: escape from these limitations by the upward path, in esoterism, or by the downward path, in a worldly and suicidal liberalism.[89]

At a time when 'the outward and readily exaggerated incompatibility of the different religions greatly discredits, in the minds of most of our contemporaries, all religion',[90] the exposure of the underlying unity of the religions takes on a deep urgency. This task can only be achieved through esotericism. The open confrontation of different exotericisms, the extirpation of traditional civilisations, and the tyranny of secular and profane ideologies all play a part in determining the peculiar circumstances in which the most imperious needs of the age can only be answered by a recourse to traditional esotericisms. There is perhaps some small hope that in this climate and given a properly constituted metaphysical framework in which to affirm the 'profound and eternal solidarity of all spiritual forms',[91] the different religions might yet 'present a singular front against the floodtide of materialism and pseudo-spiritualism'.[92]

The hazards and ambiguities attending the exposure of esoteric doctrines to an audience in many respects ill-equipped to understand them have posed the same

---

85 FS *TUR* pxxxi.
86 *ibid.*
87 FS *TM* p10.
88 *ibid.*
89 FS *EPW* p19.
90 FS *TUR* pxxxi.
91 *ibid.*
92 FS *GDW* p12. See also WP *TTW* p22fn.

problems for representatives of traditional esotericisms the world over. Joseph Epes Brown writes of the disclosure of traditional Lakota wisdom, to choose one example, in terms very similar to those used by Schuon:

> ... in these days those few old wise men still living among them say that at the approach of the end of a cycle, when men everywhere have become unfit to understand and still more to realise the truths revealed to them at the origin ... it is then permissible and even desirable to bring this knowledge out into the light of day, for by its own nature truth protects itself against being profaned and in this way it is possible it may reach those qualified to penetrate it deeply.[93]

It is no accident that the few remaining holy men amongst the American Indians and traditionalists like Schuon should see this matter in the same terms.

---

93 J.E. Brown *The Sacred Pipe* Uni Oklahoma Press, 1953; pxii. (This passage was omitted from the Penguin edition.) See also Schuon's 'Human Premises of a Religious Dilemma' in *SVQ* pp97–113.

9
Symbolism and Sacred Art

...sacred art is the form of what lies Beyond Form, it is the image of the Uncreated, the language of Silence
Frithjof Schuon[1]

Traditional art derives from a creativity which combines heavenly inspiration with ethnic genius, and which does so in the manner of a science endowed with rules and not by way of individual improvisation *Frithjof Schuon*[2]

When standing before a cathedral, a person really feels he is placed at the centre of the world; standing before a church of the Renaissance, Baroque or Rococo periods, he merely feels himself to be in Europe *Frithjof Schuon*[3]

Whitall Perry

In former times the doctrine of archetypes was espoused the world over. No integral tradition has been able to do without it though the language in which it is clothed may speak not of archetypes but of 'essences', 'universals', 'Divine Ideas' and so on.[4] Plato gave the doctrine its most definitive European expression but there is nothing peculiarly Occidental about it as such.[5] It lies at the root of all traditional art. By way of introduction, let us consider the following sample of suggestive quotations:

> A form is made in the resigned will according to the platform or model of eternity, as it was known in God's eternal wisdom before the times of this world. *Jacob Boehme*[6]

> All forms of being in this corporeal world are images of pure Lights, which exist in the spiritual world. *Suhrawardi*[7]

> The Sages have been taught of God that this natural world is only an image and a copy of a heavenly and spiritual pattern; that the very existence of this world is based upon the reality of its celestial archetypes. *Michael Sendivogius*[8]

> Crazy Horse dreamed and went out into the world where there is nothing but the spirits of things. That is the real world that is behind this one, and everything we see here is something like a shadow from that world. *Black Elk*[9]

> Things in every instance involve universals ... If there were no universals we could not speak of things as things. *Kung-sun Lung*[10]

Formulations of this kind could be multiplied more or less indefinitely but their burden is clear enough. Meister Eckhart provided a concise statement of the doctrine in writing 'Form is revelation of essence'.[11]

Everything that exists, whatever its modality, necessarily participates in universal principles which are uncreated and immutable essences contained, in Guénon's words, in 'the permanent actuality of the Divine Intellect'. Consequently, all phenomena, no matter how ephemeral or contingent, 'translate' or 'represent' these principles in their own fashion at their own level of existence. Without participation in the immutable, they would 'purely and simply be nothing'.[12] The doctrine of archetypes

---

1   FS *LS* p107. Cf. a formulation by Walter Andrae quoted in A.K. Coomaraswamy: '*Ars Sine Scientia Nihil*' in AKC *SPI* p231.
2   F. Schuon: 'The Degrees of Art' *SCR* X, iv, 1976; p194 (hereafter FS:'DA').
3   FS *TUR* p61fn. See also FS *LAW* p13.
4   One is not suggesting only that the doctrine of archetypes was implicit in the religious traditions but that it was an explicit doctrine, consciously held. Examples from the Hindu and Buddhist traditions can be found in theories of the mandala. One might also cite classical Hindu ideas about the Vedas as an earthly reflection of a divine model.
5   Jung's ideas about 'archetypes' do not constitute a metaphysical doctrine but a hypothesis about certain psychic phenomena.
6   per WP *TTW* p671.
7   per WP *TTW* p673.
8   per WP *TTW* p672.
9   In J. Neihardt (ed) *Black Elk Speaks* Abacus, London, 1974; p67.
10 per WP *TTW* p670.
11 per WP *TTW* p673. For an explication of Eckhart's view of art see A.K. Coomaraswamy *The Transformation of Nature in Art* Dover, New York, 1956; pp59-96.
12 R. Guénon *Autorité spirituelle et pouvoir temporel* in WP *TTW* p302.

thus also implies the multiple states of being and a hierarchic structure of the cosmos. Thus Abu Bakr Siraj ad-Din writes:

> ... if a world did not cast down shadows from above, the worlds below it would vanish altogether, since each world in creation is no more than a tissue of shadows entirely dependent on the archetypes in the world above.[13]

The analogies between the archetypes or 'Divine Ideas' and the transitory material forms of this world, 'this changing and ephemeral multiplicity' as Guénon calls it, give to phenomena certain qualitative significances which render them symbolic expressions of higher realities. A contemporary Buddhist, not himself a member of the traditionalist 'school' but thoroughly versed in the wisdom tradition of one of the Tibetan lineages, stated the principle precisely:

> If we look at the world with ... the eyes of the spirit we shall discover that the simplest material object, nay anything that is formed, be it by man or by nature, is a symbol, a glyph of a higher reality and a deeper relationship of universal and individual forces ...[14]

The same idea is implicit in Eliade's claim that *homo religiosus* is also, necessarily, *homo symbolicus*.[15]

The traditionalist understanding of sacred art is predicated upon a very precise understanding of the nature of symbolism. A symbol may generally be defined as a reality of a lower order which participates analogically in a reality of a higher order of being. Therefore, a properly constituted symbolism rests on the inherent and objective qualities of phenomena and their relationship to spiritual realities. It follows that the science of symbolism is a rigorous discipline which can only proceed through a discernment of the *qualitative* significances of substances, colours, forms, spatial relationships and so on. This is crucial. Schuon:

> ... we are not here dealing with subjective appreciations, for the cosmic qualities are ordered both in relation to being and according to a hierarchy which is more real than the individual; they are, then, independent of our tastes ...[16]

So important is this principle that it deserves re-stating, this time in the words of Seyyed Hossein Nasr:

> The symbol is not based on man-made conventions. It is an aspect of the ontological reality of things and as such is independent of man's perception of it. The symbol is the revelation of a higher order of reality in a lower order through which man can be led back to the higher realm. To understand symbols is to accept the hierarchic structure of the Universe and the multiple states of being.[17]

---

13 Abu Bakr Siraj ad-Din *The Book of Certainty* Samuel Weiser, New York, 1974; p50. This book gives an account of the doctrine of archetypes and of the multiple states of being from a Sufic perspective. See also R. Guénon *The Multiple States of Being* Larson, New York, 1984, tr. J. Godwin.
14 A. Govinda *Creative Meditation and Multi-Dimensional Consciousness* Quest, Illinois, 1976; p102.
15 See M. Eliade: 'Methodological Remarks on the Study of Religious Symbolism' in M. Eliade & J. Kitagawa (eds) *The History of Religions: Essays in Methodology* Uni Chicago Press, 1959; p95.
16 FS *GDW* p110.
17 S.H. Nasr *Sufi Essays* Allen & Unwin, London, 1972; p88. See also G. Eaton *The Richest Vein* Faber & Faber, London, 1949; pp186ff. and M. Pallis *A Buddhist Spectrum* Allen & Unwin, London, 1980; pp144–163.

Symbolic significances cannot be invented or imputed. Thus the traditionalists give no credence to the idea that a religious symbolism depends on nothing more than a kind of cultural consensus, a collective agreement that such and such a phenomena can be thought of as 'representing' this or that reality. This is to make of symbolism an altogether too random and subjective an affair. It also fails to take account of the universality of a whole host of ever-recurring symbols. Furthermore, it fails to see that the symbol partakes of the reality which is its referent. This is important in any consideration of sacred art which, in a sense, is not separate from the reality to which it gives access and which it manifests on a particular plane. Thus, 'the function of every symbol is to break the shell of forgetfulness that screens the knowledge immanent in the Intellect'.[18]

Traditional symbolism, then, is an objective language which is conceived not according to the impulses of individual or collective 'taste' but in conformity with the nature of things. It will take account not only of 'sensible beauty' but 'the spiritual foundations of this beauty'.[19] Because of its precision and objectivity a traditional symbolism may be called a 'calculus' or 'algebra' for the expression of universal ideas.[20] The conception of symbolism as an objective language is axial in Coomaraswamy's mature work, much of which was directed towards reawakening a proper understanding of the symbolic vocabulary of traditional arts. A characteristic formulation:

> Symbolism is a language and a precise form of thought; a hieratic and a metaphysical language and not a language determined by somatic or psychological categories. Its foundation is in analogical correspondences ... symbolism is a calculus in the same sense that an adequate analogy is a proof.[21]

The study of traditional symbols therefore demands methods no less rigorous or sensitive than those of the philologist. Nothing could be more ill-conceived than a subjective interpretation of traditional symbols which are no more amenable to guess-work than is an archaic language. As Coomaraswamy points out, the study of such symbolisms is no easy business, not only because the same symbol may be deployed in different senses but because we are no longer familiar with the metaphysical burden which it once carried.[22]

The science of symbolism is a kind of objective analogue of the gift of 'seeing God everywhere', that is, the awareness of the transparency of phenomena and of the transcendent dimension which is present in every cosmic situation.[23] Rama-

---

18 FS *EPW* p11. See also FS *SPHF* p40. For some discussion of how this principle is applied in the traditional iconography of Tibetan Buddhism see Tarthang Tulku *Sacred Art of Tibet* Dharma, Berkeley, 1972 (no pagination; see section 'Consecration of Dieties'). See also J.E. Brown: 'Modes of Contemplation through Actions' in Y. Ibish & P.L. Wilson (eds) *Traditional Modes of Contemplation and Action* Imperial Iranian Academy of Philosophy, Tehran, 1977; p237.
19 F. Schuon: 'Foundations of an Integral Aesthetics' *SCR* X, iii, 1976; p130 (this article hereafter referred to as FS:'FIA'). See also B. Keeble: 'Tradition, Intelligence and the Artist' *SCR* XI, iv, 1977; pp240–241.
20 See M. Pallis *The Way and the Mountain* Peter Owen, London, 1960; p16.
21 A.K. Coomaraswamy: 'The Nature of Buddhist Art' in AKC *SPII* pp174–175. See also Coomaraswamy's undated letter to an anonymous recipient in AKC *SL* pp210–212, and Letter to Robert Ulich, July 1942, pp214–215.
22 A.K. Coomaraswamy: 'The Iconography of Durer's "Knots" and Leonardo's "Concatenation"' *The Art Quarterly* VII, ii, 1944; p125. Quoted in WP *TTW* p305.
23 See FS *GDW* pp106–121 and S.H. Nasr *Man and Nature* Allen & Unwin, London, 1976; p131.

krishna, who could fall into ecstasy at the sight of a lion, a bird, a dancing girl, exemplified this gift though in his case, Schuon adds, it was not a matter of deciphering the symbolism but of 'tasting the essences'.[24] Mircea Eliade, approaching the whole question from a different angle, has noted how, for *homo religiosus*, everything in nature is capable of revealing itself as a 'cosmic sacrality', as a hierophany. He also observes that for our secular age the cosmos has become 'opaque, inert, mute; it transmits no message, it holds no cipher'.[25]

The universality of certain recurrent symbols is adequately explained by the principles which have been under discussion. It is quite unnecessary to resort to fanciful diffusionist theories to explain this phenomena. W.J. Perry's pan-Egyptian hypothesis, now thoroughly discredited, is a conspicuous example of looking for the key to a universal symbolism in the wrong place.[26] It might also be noted that even when a diffusionist theory may have some limited historical validity, tracing the spatio-temporal genealogy of a particular symbol and explaining its metaphysical and cosmological significance are two quite different matters.[27] In general, diffusionist theories do little more than pile up, albeit unwittingly, material evidence of the existence of a universal symbolism.[28]

The study of symbolism has in recent times been much influenced by the work of Carl Jung. This is not the place to engage in a discussion of his hypotheses concerning symbols. Suffice it to say that from a traditionalist point of view there is much that is illuminating in Jung's researches provided one is not seduced by the temptation to reduce the provenance and the field of symbolism to a purely psychic level where symbols must take on something of a fugitive and phantasmic nature. Furthermore, insofar as Jung capitulated to a view of metaphysics which sees it as some kind of evolute of psychic forces he was reinforcing the anti-spiritual tendencies of the age – this despite his apparently sympathetic attitude to religion and traditional spiritualities. Psychism is always infra-intellectual and thus anti-spiritual.[29]

The doctrine of archetypes and the attendant understanding of symbolism form the foundation on which traditional theories of art and the art itself has been built. The traditionalists perceive in the sacred art of normal civilisations a recurrent set of principles, functions and characteristics which vary in their material applications but which are everywhere fundamentally the same.

Firstly there is the intimate nexus between the ideals of truth, goodness and beauty. The inter-relationships of the three are more or less inexhaustible and there is no

---

24 FS: 'FIA' p135fn. See also C. Isherwood *Ramakrishna and His Disciples* Advaita Ashram, Calcutta, 1974; pp61ff.
25 M. Eliade *The Sacred and the Profane* Harcourt, Brace & Jovanovich, New York, 1959; p12 and p178.
26 See W.J. Perry *The Origin of Magic and Religion* Methuen, London, 1923 and *The Primordial Ocean* Methuen, London, 1935.
27 See M. Eliade: 'Methodological Remarks' p93.
28 See G. Eaton: *op.cit.*; p187.
29 See letter from Schuon to Titus Burckhardt, reproduced in T. Burckhardt: 'Cosmology and Modern Science' in JN *SG* p177. See also Burckhardt's discussion of Jung in the same essay, pp167–178. These passages can also be found in Titus Burckhardt's *Mirror of the Intellect* Quinta Essentia, Cambridge/SUNY, Albany, 1987; pp45–67. For other critiques, from a more less traditionalist point of view, see P. Sherrard: 'An Introduction to the Religious Thought of C. G. Jung' *SCR* III, i, 1969; P. Novak 'C.G. Jung in the Light of Asian Philosophy' *Religious Traditions* XIV, 1991; H. Oldmeadow *Mircea Eliade and Carl Jung: 'Priests Without Surplices'?* Studies in Western Traditions Occasional Papers No 1, La Trobe University Bendigo, 1995.

end to what might be said on this subject. Here we shall establish only a few general points, taking the nature of beauty as our point of departure. Marsilio Ficino, the Renaissance Platonist, defined beauty as 'that ray which parting from the visage of God, penetrates into all things'.[30] Beauty, in most traditional canons, has this divine quality. It is a manifestation of the Infinite on a finite plane and so introduces something of the Absolute into the world of relativities. Its sacred character 'confers on perishable things a texture of eternity'.[31] Schuon:

> The archetype of Beauty, or its Divine model, is the superabundance and equilibrium of the Divine qualities, and at the same time the overflowing of the existential potentialities in pure Being ... Thus beauty always manifests a reality of love, of deployment, of illimitation, of equilibrium, of beatitude, of generosity.[32]

It is distinct but not separate from truth and virtue. As Aquinas affirmed, beauty relates to the cognitive faculty and is thus connected with wisdom.[33] The rapport between beauty and virtue allows one to say that they are but two faces of the one reality: 'goodness is internal beauty, and beauty is external goodness' or, similarly, 'virtue is the beauty of the soul as beauty is the virtue of forms'.[34] The relationships of beauty, truth and goodness explain why, in the Oriental traditions, every *avatāra* embodies a perfection of Beauty. It is said of the Buddhas they save not only by their doctrine but by their superhuman beauty. As Schuon notes, the name 'Shunyamurti' – manifestation of the void – applied to a Buddha, is full of significance.[35]

Schuon gathers together some of these principles in the following passage:

> ... the earthly function of beauty is to actualise in the intelligent creature the Platonic recollection of the archetypes ... there is a *distinguo* to make, in the sensing of the beautiful, between the aesthetic sensation and the corresponding beauty of soul, namely such and such a virtue. Beyond every question of 'sensible consolation' the message of beauty is both intellectual and moral: intellectual because it communicates to us, in the world of accidentality, aspects of Substance, without for all that having to address itself to abstract thought; and moral, because it reminds us of what we must love, and consequently be.[36]

This passage, so alien to any modernist aesthetic, arms us with the conceptual tools with which to penetrate the nature of sacred art.

The harmony of truth, beauty and virtue will find its richest expression in explicitly sacred art. However, as Schuon and Coomaraswamy both note, in a traditional society there can be no profane art, properly speaking, but rather what might be called 'extra-liturgical' art – the making of mundane implements and utensils, for example, or the ornamentation of clothing.[37]

---

30 Quoted in R.J. Clements *Michelangelo's Theory of Art* New York University Press, 1971; p5.
31 FS *UI* p48.
32 FS *L&T* p241. For some traditional formulations on the nature of Beauty see WP *TTW* p659–670.
33 See A.K. Coomaraswamy: 'The Mediaeval Theory of Beauty' in AKC *SPI* pp211–20, and two essays, 'Beauty and Truth' and 'Why Exhibit Works of Art?' in AKC *COPA* pp7–22 (esp. pp16–18) and pp102–109.
34 FS *L&T* pp245–246. See also FS *EPW* p95.
35 FS *SPHF* p25fn. See also FS *ITB* p121.
36 FS: 'FIA' pp131–132.
37 See FS: 'DA' pp194–197. On the distinction between traditional and sacred art see SHN *K&S* p275,fn1.

Traditional arts are marked by their objectivity: they are constituted by elements prescribed by tradition according to a set of changeless principles and rules. In a traditional society it matters not whether one is fashioning a water container, painting an icon or a *tanka*, or designing a stained glass window, whether one is painter or potter or smith: in each case the artist (or artisan – the distinction has little meaning in the present context) works under the creative constraints, if one might so express it, of tradition. Here we might recall the stipulation of the Second Council of Nicea:

> art [the integral perfection of the work] alone belongs to the painter, while ordinance [the choice of subject] and disposition [the treatment of the subject from the symbolical as well as the technical and material points of view] belong to the Fathers.[38]

Sacred art formed part of the Christian liturgy and could not therefore be left to any arbitrary impulses. Like any traditional religious art it had to be sacred in content, symbolic in detail and hieratic in treatment. These 'restraints' conferred qualities of depth and power such as the individual artist could not have drawn out of purely personal resources.[39] The anonymity of the traditional artist also testifies to the subordination of individual tastes and impulses to the dictates of tradition.

The notion of 'art for art's sake' is inconceivable in a traditional context where art, of whatever kind, is always directed to a use – spiritual or mundane, or often both. The modern distinction between the beautiful and the useful could not flourish in a traditional climate. In the case of a sacred art the uses are spiritual and realised through a symbolic language. St Augustine voiced the traditional view when he dismissed as a 'madness' the idea that any art worthy of the name could have no other purpose than to please.[40] As Schuon emphasises:

> Apart from their intrinsic qualities forms of art correspond to a strict utility. In order that spiritual influences may be able to manifest without encumbrance they have need of a formal setting which corresponds to them analogically ... in the soul of a holy man they can shine in spite of everything, but not everyone is a saint and a sanctuary is made to facilitate resonances of the spirit, not to impede them. Sacred art ... is made at the same time for God, for angels and for man; profane art on the other hand exists only for man and by that fact betrays him.[41]

If we move from sacred art as such to the arts and crafts of everyday life we can see that in traditional societies they always serve a double purpose: that of immediate physical utility, and secondly, a teaching function. The relationship of utility and symbolic significance is obvious enough in much religious art – in ritual supports for example. The sacred pipe of the American Indians furnishes an instance of an apparently simple and useful artefact carrying a whole complex of ritualistic and metaphysical significances.[42] However, the symbolic vocabulary of mundane arts and crafts often escapes the modern eye, jaundiced as it is by a prejudice in favour of aesthetic considerations to the exclusion of everything else. Much of Coomara-

---

38 Quoted in FS *TUR* p70. (Interpolations are Schuon's.) See also FS *GDW* p127.
39 FS *LS* p107 and FS *SPHF* pp36–37. See also SHN *K&S* p254.
40 See A.K. Coomaraswamy: 'Beauty and Truth' pp108–109.
41 See FS *SPHF* pp28–29 and FS *LS* pp103–104.
42 See J.E. Brown *The Sacred Pipe* Penguin, 1971; pp6–9.

swamy's work is given over to the deciphering of traditional symbolic languages which found their expression not only in the glories of religious iconographies but in the most unassuming arts of everyday life. He found a symbolic density, and thus a teaching, in the most diverse productions of traditional cultures – in Shaker furniture, a Javanese puppet, Indian Gupta seals, in traditional oriental dress, to name but a few examples from amongst hundreds.[43]

In *The Reign of Quantity* Guénon devotes a fascinating chapter to the 'degeneration of coinage' whereby coins have been robbed of the spiritual significance they once carried through their symbolism – yet another sign of the increasing 'quantification' and 'profanisation' of everyday life.[44] Marco Pallis has shown how the daily implements of Tibetan life were once charged with spiritual significance.[45] Coomaraswamy and Mircea Eliade have both directed attention to the symbolisms once inherent in the simplest house or dwelling-place.[46] In this light we can see how the modern distinctions between 'fine' and 'applied' arts, between arts and crafts, between artist and artisan, between the beautiful and the useful, make little sense in a traditional framework.

One of the least understood aspects of traditional art is its indifference to the claims of naturalism. Confusion over the principles involved here has sometimes inveigled art historians and others into ignorant talk about 'the lack of sophistication' of much traditional art, evinced, for example, by a putative inability to master the demands of perspective. Needless to say the purveyors of such views usually subscribe to some kind of evolutionist or progressivist view of art. Such views would be laughable did they not encourage a view of the past which is both impudent and condescending.

Schuon reminds us that a more or less exact observation of nature may find a place in traditional art, as it does, for example, in that of Pharonic Egypt. However, the attempt to 'imitate' nature could never be an end in itself in traditional art which generally, being concerned with analogical relationships and symbolisms, will not seek to reproduce the surfaces and appearances of the material world in any 'realistic' fashion. The revelation of the transparent and transcendental aspects of phenomena sits awkwardly with naturalism:

> ... there is a relative but not irremediable incompatibility between the spiritual content or radiance of a work and an implacable and virtuosic naturalism: it is as if the science of the mechanism of things killed their spirit.[47]

Artistic naturalism proceeds from an exteriorising mentality which, more often than not, also lacks 'the instinct of sacrifice, sobriety, restraint',[48] and which could not be normative in a traditional civilisation. Rather, a traditional art will tend to

> ... combine intelligent observation of nature with noble and profound stylisations in order, first,

---

43 For a sample of his work in this field see AKC *SPI*.
44 RG *RQ* Ch XVI, pp133–139.
45 M. Pallis: 'Introduction to Tibetan Art' *SCR* I, i,1967; pp22–35.
46 See A.K. Coomaraswamy: 'The Symbolism of the Dome' in AKC *SPI* pp422ff. and M. Eliade *The Sacred and the Profane* Ch 1, pp20–67.
47 FS: 'DA' p202.
48 FS *TM* p47.

to assimilate the work to the model created by God in nature and secondly, to separate it from physical contingency by giving it an imprint of pure spirit, of synthesis, of what is essential.[49]

Naturalism on the other hand is

> ... clearly luciferian in its wish to imitate the creations of God, not to mention its affirmation of the psychic element to the detriment of the spiritual, and above all, of the bare fact to the detriment of the symbol.[50]

Beauty can be either an open or a closed door: when it is identified only with its earthly support it leaves man vulnerable to idolatry; it brings us closer to God when 'we perceive in it the vibrations of Beatitude and Infinity, which emanate from Divine Beauty'.[51] As an accessory to wisdom sacred art takes account of the fact that intellectual certitude depends not on the ability to give an exhaustive account of the external characteristics of phenomena but on the discernment of their essences.[52] Lama Govinda, drawing on the traditional Tibetan conception of art, affirms the same principle in writing: 'while using the forms of the external world, [art] does not try to imitate nature, but to reveal a higher reality by omitting all accidentals, thus raising the visible form to the value of a symbol.'[53] Thomas Merton alerts us to the dangers of a naturalism which now obtrudes on the liturgy of the Roman Church, and contrasts it with a properly constituted symbolism:

> Symbolism fortifies and concentrates the spirit of prayer, but illustration [i.e. naturalism] tends rather to weaken and dissipate our attention. Symbolism acts as a very efficacious spiritual medium. It opens the way to an intuitive understanding of mystery – it places us in the presence of the invisible. Illustration tends rather to become an obstacle, to divert and to amuse rather than to elevate and direct. It tends to take the place of the invisible and to obscure it.[54]

Sacred art fulfils functions of incalculable importance in a traditional civilisation by conveying transcendental values through an 'intelligence' which is lacking in the human collectivity as a whole. Bypassing the pitfalls of abstract thought it is accessible to the humblest mentality in evoking a sense of the sacred. Through its symbolism sacred art addresses itself to the whole person rather than to the mind alone and thereby helps to actualise the teachings of the tradition in question. In this respect most people have far more need of a sacred art than they do of abstract metaphysical formulations.[55] It brings into the reach of the ordinary person values and truths which remain intelligible only to a few when couched in the language of the philosophers and theologians. We need to remember that 'The cathedral is as much an exposition of

---

49 FS *LS* p119.
50 FS *TUR* p72. For a more extended discussion of these issues see A.K. Coomaraswamy: 'The Mediaeval Theory of Beauty', 'Imitation and Expression' and 'Figures of Speech or Figures of Thought?' in AKC *SPI* pp189–228, 276–285, 20–25.
51 FS: 'FIA' p135.
52 See B. Keeble *op.cit.*; p242. The attempt to give an exhaustive account of the external characteristics of phenomena is, of course, precisely the agenda of modern science.
53 A. Govinda *op.cit.*; p152.
54 T. Merton: 'Absurdity in Sacred Decoration' in *Disputed Questions* Noonday Press, New York, 1977; p251.
55 FS *LS* pp107 & 110.

medieval Christianity as the *Summa* of Thomas Aquinas'.[56] Sacred art is both the witness and the proof of an authentic tradition.[57]

The initiatic and esoteric possibilities of traditional arts, crafts and sciences warrant a few brief remarks. A principle often invoked by the traditionalists is *ars sine scientia nihil* (art without science is nothing). These were the words of the Parisian Master, Jean Mignot, directed during the building of the Cathedral of Milan as a riposte to another view which was then just beginning to take shape – *scientia est unum et ars aliud* (science is one thing and art another).[58] The arts, crafts and sciences all interpenetrate one another – masonry (craft), geometry (science) and architecture (art) in the building of a cathedral for example.[59] All provided arenas for the exploration of analogical relationships and for the application of symbolic languages. The relationships between material forms and spiritual realities provided an initiatic point of entry into many different esoteric disciplines. This is something often misunderstood – the dismissal of the alchemists as 'charcoal burners' and 'primitive chemists', for example, betrays an ignorance of its essential nature which was that of an esoteric spiritual discipline.[60] This is a difficult and enigmatic field into which have intruded all manner of incompetent theorisers who have no grip on the principles involved.[61] Mention should be made of the invaluable work done on initiatic arts, sciences and crafts by men like Guénon, Burckhardt and Nasr.[62]

The traditionalist vision of sacred art carries an implicit repudiation of modern art and of most of the prevailing aesthetic theories. Modern European art, for the most part, ignores the cognitive, moral and utilitarian functions proper to art and is governed rather by aesthetic, sensory and subjective factors (here we are talking primarily of the visual arts). The traditionalist arraignment of modern art has been executed primarily by Coomaraswamy and Schuon. The prosecution has been by no means lenient, the charges being serious ones. For the traditionalists the defining characteristic of post-mediaeval art is its anti-traditionalism. Some of the tell-tales: an undisciplined individualism; a pre-occupation with novelty and 'originality'; an aestheticism indifferent to the moral, intellectual and spiritual functions of art; stylistic

---

56 From C. Morey *Christian Art* 1935, quoted in A.K. Coomaraswamy: 'Beauty and Truth' p104.

57 FS *ITB* p120. (To reinforce a point made earlier in this study: the need for sacred art, like the need for Scriptural exegesis and commentary, does not arise simultaneously with the Revelation but only some time later.)

58 See A.K. Coomaraswamy: '*Ars Sine Scientia Nihil*' in AKC *SPI* p229. See also Letter to *Art News*, May-August 1939, AKC *SL* pp378–380.

59 On this subject see T. Burckhardt: 'Perennial Values in Islamic Art' in JN *SG* p313.

60 The definitive study is T. Burckhardt *Alchemy: Science of the Cosmos, Science of the Soul* Penguin, 1971, tr. W. Stoddart. For a mis-understanding of alchemy one can consult almost any encyclopedia or history of Western science!

61 The occultists who see this as one of their special provinces are no exception. One can find all manner of grotesqueries in popular occultist writings in the field.

62 Amongst their most important works are RG *RQ* and R Guénon *Initiation and the Crafts* Golgonooza Press, Suffolk, 1974; T. Burckhardt *Mirror of the Intellect* Quinta Essentia, Cambridge, 1987, *Mystical Astrology According to Ibn'Arabi* Beshara Publications, Sherborne, 1977, and *The Art of Islam* World of Islam Festival, London, 1976; S.H. Nasr *Science and Civilisation in Islam* Allen & Unwin, London, 1976, *Man and Nature* Allen & Unwin, London, 1968, *Islamic Science, An Illustrated History* World of Islam Festival, London, 1976, and 'The Traditional Sciences' in RF *UT* pp129–144. See also FS *LAW* pp72–88 for an exposition of shamanic practices which activate some of the principles which govern many initiatic sciences. For an informed and well illustrated study of Sufic art see L. Bakhtiar *Sufi: Expressions of the Mystic Quest* Thames & Hudson, London, 1976. See also P.L. Wilson *Angels* Thames & Hudson, London, 1980.

excesses veering from a pedantic naturalism on one side to an inhuman surrealism on the other. The critique is implicit in much that has already been said and need not be laboured here. Rather we will touch on a few central points.

European art since the Renaissance has not sprung from a tradition regulated by the kinds of principles under consideration but from an increasingly secular and individualistic view of art, one of its central components being the notion of 'genius'.[63] During the Renaissance European civilisation in general and Christian art in particular were robbed of their traditional character by 'a sort of posthumous revenge on the part of classical antiquity'.[64] This marked a triumph for the alliance of rationalism and naturalism which had shaped the art of classical Greece. On this subject the views of the traditionalists part company, to say the least, with those of most modern art historians who still fall into a euphoria at the mere mention of the 'Golden Age' of classical Greek art. Schuon:

> ... the whole of the so-called miracle of Greece amounts to a substitution of one-side reason for intelligence; apart from the rationalism which inaugurated it, artistic naturalism would have been inconceivable. Extreme individualism results from the cult of 'form', of form envisaged as something finite and not as 'symbol'; reason indeed regulates the science of the finite, of limits and of order, so that it is only logical that an art which is directed by reason should share with reason itself a flatness refractory to all mystery.[65]

European art, since that 'Caesarism of bourgeois and bankers'[66] known as the Renaissance, has been less and less illuminated by any spirituality, and placed at the mercy of the individual artist. Its source is no longer the font of tradition but the subjective, psychic resources of the individual. These may be considerable as in the case of say, a Leonardo or a Michelangelo, but a fundamental change has taken place whereby art ceases to 'exteriorise either transcendent ideas or profound virtues'[67] and, instead, communicates a private vision of the artist. We remember Vasari's commendation of Michelangelo's role in this change: '... the craftsmen owe him an infinite and everlasting obligation, he having broken down the bonds and chains by reason of which they had always followed a beaten path in the execution of their works.'[68] For Vasari this marked a liberation of individual creativity; from a traditionalist perspective it is the beginning of the end:

> The modern conception of art is false in so far as it puts creative imagination ... in the place of qualitative form, or in so far as a subjective and conjectural valuation is substituted for an objective and spiritual one.[69]

---

63 For some discussion of the changes in the prevailing European view of art in the Renaissance see A. Blunt *Artistic Theory in Italy 1500–1600* London, 1965, and R.J. Clements: *op.cit.*
64 FS *TUR* p65
65 FS *LS* p121.
66 FS *SPHF* p38.
67 *ibid.*; p33.
68 G. Vasari *Lives of the Painters* quoted in A. Blunt *op.cit.*; p75.
69 FS *LS* pp126–127. See also WP *TTW* p660. There is a telling anecdote in Mircea Eliade's journal *No Souvenirs* Harper & Row, New York, 1977; p133: 'I met Henri Michaux. He talked about Padre Pio, whose mass he had attended several times. Extraordinary impression: Padre Pio speaks with God; for him God is *there*. At the end of three days he left for fear of being converted. "My path is entirely different," he told me, "I'm an artist. I have my personal experiences." This hardly needs a commentary.'

Schuon concedes that the art of the Renaissance retained some qualities of 'intelligence and grandeur' but the Baroque style which followed it 'could hardly express anything but the spiritual poverty and the hollow and miserable turgidity of its period'.[70] Inexorably the humanistic conception of art sponsored the mania for novelty (which later came to be regarded as 'originality') until today this becomes almost a litmus test for the value and validity of any artistic creation. The relentless pursuit of 'originality' could lead only to an anarchic art which must increasingly seek out the bizarre, the abnormal, the monstrous – thus surrealism. The 'liberation' of the Renaissance ends in the grotesqueries of a Dali! As Schuon remarks, 'the ambition of artistic creation which seeks to start from zero, as though man too could create *ex nihilo* . . . ends in the subhuman aberrations of surrealism'.[71]

Plato claimed that any art directed solely towards pleasure can produce nothing but 'toys'.[72] Under a traditionalist view this, at best, is the status of much modern art which serves nothing but aesthetic purposes which is to say the stimulation if not always the pleasing of our senses. The traditional vinculum between the ideals of truth, beauty and goodness, between the cognitive, aesthetic and moral domains, has been abandoned. Arts and crafts which were once rooted in a vocational pursuit which simultaneously served the needs of both the body and the spirit have been replaced by a dehumanising industry on the one hand, a sterile aestheticism on the other. 'The fact that the Industrial West . . . has now to reap the bitter harvest sown by its materialist assumptions is due in no small measure to its refusal to acknowledge the interdependence of making and knowing.'[73] A sense of beauty has become not a matter of truths but of tastes and the 'emancipation of the artist' is nothing other than the 'freedom' to ignore the claims of any ideal higher than 'self-expression'.[74]

These changes, says Coomaraswamy, have also infected our understanding of traditional arts:

> Our 'aesthetic' approach can be compared only to that of a traveller who, when he sees a signpost, proceeds to admire its elegance, asks who made it, and finally cuts it down and takes it home to be used as a mantelpiece ornament.[75]

> Let us then admit that the greater part of what is taught in the fine arts departments of our universities, all of the psychologies of art, all the obscurities of modern aesthetics, are only so much verbiage, only a kind of defence that stands in the way of our understanding of the wholesome art, at the same time iconographically true and practically useful, that was once to be had in the marketplace or from any good artist . . . our aesthetic is nothing but a false rhetoric, and a flattery of human weakness by which we can account only for the arts that have no other purpose than to please.[76]

A characteristic Coomaraswamy passage! If the traditionalist view of the tenets of sacred art are accepted then Coomaraswamy's contentions are irrefutable and his plea irresistible.

---

70 FS *SPHF* p33.
71 *ibid.*; p31.
72 Quoted in A.K. Coomaraswamy: 'Figures of Speech or Figures of Thought?' p20.
73 B. Keeble: 'Perennial Values Against Modern Decadence' *SCR* XIII, i & ii, 1979; p57.
74 See 'What is the Use of Art Anyway?' in AKC *COPA* pp89–101.
75 Quoted in E.S. Bremer: 'Some Implications for Literary Criticism from the Aesthetic Theory of Ananda Coomaraswamy' in SS *ACRR* p39.
76 'Figures of Speech or Figures of Thought?' p41.

III

Traditionalism and Modernism

10

The Critique of Modernism
scientism, evolutionism, psychologism and humanism

There can be no triumph over error through the sacrifice of any of the rights of truth
St Irenaeus[1]

That which is lacking in the present world is a profound knowledge of the nature of things; the fundamental truths are always there, but they do not impose themselves because they cannot impose themselves on those unwilling to listen
Frithjof Schuon[2]

Our ignorance of the few things that matter is as prodigious as our knowledge of trivialities
Gai Eaton[3]

... if you ever really enter into this other world ... you may never again be contented with what you have been accustomed to think of as 'progress' and 'civilisation'
Ananda Coomaraswamy[4]

Modernism: this term we may loosely define as the prevalent assumptions, values and attitudes of a world-view fashioned by the most pervasive intellectual and moral influences of recent European history, an outlook in conformity with the *Zeitgeist* of the times. One might classify the constituents of modernism under any number of different schema. Lord Northbourne typifies modernism as 'anti-traditional, progressive, humanist, rationalist, materialist, experimental, individualist, egalitarian, free-thinking and intensely sentimental'.[5] S.H. Nasr gathers these tendencies together under four general marks of modern thought: anthropomorphism (and by extension, secularism); evolutionist progressivism; the absence of any sense of the sacred; an unrelieved ignorance of metaphysical principles.[6] 'Modernism' then, is a portmanteau word.[7] We shall, in this part of our inquiry, uncover some of the significances it carries and examine these from a traditionalist point of view.

For the traditionalists modernism is nothing less than a spiritual disease which continues to spread like a plague across the globe, decimating traditional cultures wherever they are still to be found. Although its historical origins are European, modernism is now tied to no specific area or civilisation. Its symptoms can be detected in a wide assortment of inter-related 'mind sets' and '-isms', sometimes involved in cooperative co-existence, sometimes engaged in apparent antagonisms but always united by the same underlying principles. Scientism, rationalism, relativism, materialism, positivism, empiricism, psychologism, individualism, humanism, existentialism: these are some of the prime follies of modernist thought. The pedigree of this family of ideas can be traced back through a series of intellectual and cultural upheavals in European history and to certain vulnerabilities in Christian civilisation which left it exposed to the subversions of a profane science.[8] The Renaissance, the Scientific Revolution and the Enlightenment were all incubators of ideas and values which first ravaged Christendom and then spread throughout the world like so many bacilli. Behind the somewhat bizarre array of ideologies which have proliferated in the last few centuries the traditionalists discern a growing and persistent ignorance concerning ultimate realities and an indifference, if not always an overt hostility, to the eternal verities conveyed by tradition.

In books like *The Reign of Quantity* and *The Crisis of the Modern World* René Guénon detailed an unsparing critique of the philosophical foundations of modernism. Coomaraswamy's work, be it on art or on philosophy and metaphysics, repeatedly reminds us of the chasm which separates normal civilisations from the absurdities and anomalies of our own times. In most of Schuon's work the explication of

---

1 St Irenaeus quoted in F. Schuon: 'On the Margin of Liturgical Improvisations' in JN *SG* p353.
2 F. Schuon: 'No Activity Without Truth' in JN *SG* p28.
3 Gai Eaton, cited as an epigraph in *TOMORROW* XII, iii, 1964; p191.
4 A.K. Coomaraswamy: 'Philosophy of Mediaeval and Oriental Art' in AKC *SPI* pp46–47.
5 Lord Northbourne *Religion in the Modern World* J.M. Dent, London, 1963; p13.
6 S.H. Nasr: 'Reflections on Islam and Modern Thought' *The Islamic Quarterly* XXIII, iii, 1979; pp119–131.
7 It will already be clear to the reader that we are not here using 'modernism' in its restricted meaning, signalling various 'experimental' early twentieth century movements in the arts, but in a much more wide-ranging sense.
8 For a profound analysis of this process see S.H. Nasr *Man and Nature* Allen & Unwin, London, 1976, esp. Chs 1&2, pp17–80. See also Whitall Perry *The Widening Breach: Evolutionism in the Mirror of Cosmology* Quinta Essentia, Cambridge, 1995.

metaphysic and the penetration of religious forms remains his central purpose; censures of modernism, tangential to this purpose, tend to be launched through a series of asides. In three works, *Light on the Ancient Worlds*, *Logic and Transcendence* and *To Have a Center*, and in several essays, Schuon has dealt more explicitly and in magisterial fashion with some of the pretensions of the modernist *weltanschauung*.[9] His work as a whole represents an unyielding resistance to modernism and an even more damaging critique than that found in Guénon's frontal assaults.

The scope of the present work precludes any comprehensive rehearsal here of the traditionalist critique of modernism, on either the principial or the phenomenal level. We have already encountered some of the specific elements in the traditionalist indictment, and a good deal more can be inferred from the explanation of traditionalist principles rehearsed earlier. Rather than striving for any kind of inclusive treatment we shall isolate a few strands in the skein of modernism and scrutinise them from a traditionalist viewpoint. After some introductory remarks about scientism and its false claims to 'objectivity' we shall turn to three especially insidious manifestations of modernism: evolutionism, psychologism and humanism. We shall spend a good deal of time on the first of these as this is one of the most destructive and typical of modern illusions. However, even here a few well-aimed shafts will have to suffice to indicate the lines along which a full-scale devaluation of evolutionism might be mounted. In the next chapter the comparison of traditionalism with various contemporary counterfeit forms of spirituality and a discussion of some divergent views of the perennial philosophy will give the traditionalist critique of modernism more weight and specificity.

It has become increasingly clear, to some thinkers at least, that modern European science is not simply a disinterested and, as it were, a detached and 'objective' mode of inquiry into the material world; it is an aggregate of disciplines anchored in a bed of very specific and culture-bound assumptions about the nature of reality and about the proper means whereby it might be explored, explained and controlled. It is, in fact, impossible to separate the methodologies of modern science from their ideological base. This base we can signal by the term 'scientism'. Perhaps the central plank in the scientistic platform is the assumption that modern science contains within itself the necessary and sufficient means for any inquiry into the material world and that it can and should be an autonomous and self-validating pursuit answerable to nothing outside itself. Science and scientism are, if still distinct at all, certainly not separable in the modern context. This is an important preliminary point in protecting any debate about modern science from the rather transparent tactics used by some of its apologists.

The scientistic ideology does not hold the intellectual field unchallenged but few would dispute that it is the key to post-medieval European thought. Bacon, Galileo, Copernicus, Descartes, Newton, Locke, Voltaire, Darwin, Freud, Einstein – these are some of the luminaries of modernist thought, each making a seminal contribution

---

9 Apart from several essays which will be cited shortly mention should be made of the following: 'Usurpations of Religious Feeling' *SCR* II, i, 1968; 'Concerning the Proofs of God' *SCR* VII, i, 1973; 'The Contradictions of Relativism' *SCR* VII, ii, 1973; 'Letter on Existentialism' *SCR* IX, ii, 1975; 'To Be Man is to Know' *SCR* XIII, i & ii, 1979; and 'To Have a Center' in FS *THC*.

Seyyed Hossein Nasr

The Critique of Modernism

to the triumph of scientism. Modern science is flanked on one side by philosophical empiricism which provides its intellectual rationale, and by technology and industry on the other, a field for its applications.[10] It is rational, analytical and empirical in its procedures, materialistic and quantitative in its object, and utilitarian in application. By its very nature modern science is thus unable to apprehend or accommodate any realities of a suprasensorial order. Science becomes scientism when it refuses to acknowledge the limits of its competence, denies the authority of any sources which lie outside its ambit, and lays claim, at least in principle, to a comprehensive validity as if it could explain no matter what, and 'as if it were not contradictory to lay claim to totality on an empirical basis'.[11] As to the much vaunted empiricism of modern science Schuon remarks, 'there is no worse confession of intellectual impotence than to boast of a line of thought because of its attachment to experiment and disdain for principles and speculations'.[12] Schuon states the nub of the case against modern science directly:

> ... modern science is a totalitarian rationalism that eliminates both Revelation and Intellect, and at the same time a totalitarian materialism that ignores the metaphysical relativity – and therewith the impermanence – of matter and the world. It does not know that the supra-sensible, situated as it is beyond space and time, is the concrete principle of the world, and consequently that it is also at the origin of that contingent and changeable coagulation we call 'matter'. A science that is called 'exact' is in fact an 'intelligence without wisdom', just as post-scholastic philosophy is inversely a 'wisdom without intelligence'.[13]

Critiques of scientism are much in vogue these days both from within the scientific community and from without. Scientists and others are increasingly becoming aware of the dangers of an ideology of science which is inadequate. The insecure philosophical foundations of modern science, its epistemological ambiguities, its inability to accommodate its own findings within the Cartesian-Newtonian frame, the consequences of a Faustian pursuit of knowledge and power, the diabolical applications of science in the military industry, the dehumanising reductionisms of the behavioural sciences – all of these have come under attack in recent times. Recent 'discoveries' by physicists and the paradoxes of quantum theory throw conventional assumptions about time, space and matter into disarray: Heisenberg's Uncertainty Principle cuts the ground from under the 'objectivity' on which science has so much prided itself; mechanistic conceptions and indeed the very language of a materialist science, are found to be useless in the face of bewildering phenomena to which it has until now been blind.[14] Everywhere cracks are appearing in the scientific edifice.

Social commentators have become more alert to the dangers of this rationalist-materialist totalitarianism and its attendant technology. We see that rationality has been allowed to become man's definition instead of his tool. We sense that the disfigurement of the environment mirrors our internal state, that the ecological crisis

---

10 See P. Sherrard *The Rape of Man and Nature* Golgonooza Press, Ipswich, England, 1987, esp. Ch 3. (Asian Edition published by the Sri Lanka Institute of Traditional Studies, Colombo, 1987, and the American edition published by Lindisfarne Press under the title *The Eclipse of Man and Nature*.) See also FS *LAW* p111.
11 FS *LAW* p34.
12 FS *SW* p40.
13 FS *LAW* p117.
14 Some of these developments are discussed in F. Capra *The Tao of Physics* Fontana, London, 1976.

is, at root, a spiritual crisis which no amount of science and technology can, of itself, remedy.[15] We know the truth of Victor Frankl's claim that,

> The true nihilism of today is reductionism ... Contemporary nihilism no longer brandishes the word nothingness; today nihilism is camouflaged as *nothing-but-ness*. Human phenomena are thus turned into mere epiphenomena.[16]

We are awakening to the consequences of a science which is answerable to nothing but itself. Mary Shelley's nightmare vision in *Frankenstein* becomes a paradigm for our times. Commentators like Huston Smith, Theodore Roszak, E.F. Schumacher, R.D. Laing, Michael Polanyi, Jacob Needleman, Mircea Eliade and Bryan Appleyard awaken us to the provincialism of modern science and to the dangers of 'Single Vision'.[17]

The traditionalist critique subsumes many of the criticisms of modern science and scientism made by figures such as the ones just mentioned. What marks the traditionalist position off from other animadversions of science is that the traditionalists do not appeal to some kind of vague humanism nor do they entertain a vision of a 'reformed' science. Their impeachment of modern science is authorised by a set of clearly articulated metaphysical principles and by the truths and values enshrined in religious traditions.

Much of the traditionalist repudiation of modern science is predicated on the distinction we have already met in Guénon's work. We can recall it through Whitall Perry's words:

> Traditional learning is basically qualitative and synthetic, concerned with essences, principles and realities behind phenomena; its fruits are integration, composition and unity. Profane academic learning – whether in the arts or sciences – is quantitative and analytical by tendency, concerned with appearances, forces and material properties; its nature is to criticize and to decompose; it works by fragmentation.[18]

---

15 As well as the works by S.H. Nasr and Philip Sherrard already cited in this chapter see S.H. Nasr *Sufi Essays* Allen & Unwin, London, 1972, Ch10; W. Smith *Cosmos and Transcendence* Sherwood Sugden, La Salle, 1984, esp Ch2.; and K. Klostermaier: 'World Religions and the Ecological Crisis' *Religion* III, 1973. A useful starting point for an understanding of the 'ecological crisis' is the following observation from Kenneth Cragg: '... nature is the first ground and constant test of the authentically religious temper – the temper which does not sacralize things in themselves nor desecrate them in soul-less using and consuming. Between the pagan and the secular, with their contrasted bondage and arrogance, lies the reverent ground of a right hallowing where things are well seen as being for men under God, seen for their poetry, mystery, order and serviceability in the cognizance of man, and for their quality in the glory of God.' *The Mind of the Qur'an* Allen & Unwin, London, 1973; p148.

16 Quoted in E.F. Schumacher *A Guide for the Perplexed* Jonathan Cape, London, 1977; p15. For a chilling account of the brutalities to which scientific reductionism inevitably leads see T. Roszak *Where the Wasteland Ends* Doubleday, New York, 1972.

17 These critics of scientism have been chosen because their positions overlap with that of the traditionalists to a greater extent than those of many other commentators whose lines of attack only exacerbate the confusion. For a sample of the work of these commentators see works by Schumacher and Roszak already cited, and H. Smith: *Forgotten Truth* Harper & Row, New York, 1977; *Beyond the Post-Modern Mind* Quest, Wheaton, 1982; R.D. Laing *The Politics of Experience* Penguin, 1967; M. Polanyi *Personal Knowledge* Uni Chicago Press, 1958; J. Needleman *A Sense of the Cosmos* Doubleday, New York, 1974; M. Eliade *The Sacred and the Profane* Harcourt, Brace & Jovanovich, New York, 1974; B. Appleyard *Understanding the Present: Science and the Soul of Modern Man* Picador, London, 1992. See also Kathleen Raine: 'The Underlying Order: Nature and the Imagination' in A. Sharma (ed) *Fragments of Infinity: Essays in Religion and Philosophy* Prism, Bridport, 1991; pp198–216.

18 WP *TTW* p731. S.H. Nasr makes a more explicit distinction between modern and traditional science: '... modern science studies change with respect to change, where a traditional science studies change *vis-à-vis* permanence through the study of symbols, which are nothing but reflections of permanence in the world of change.' *Sufi Essays* p88.

The Critique of Modernism

Furthermore, traditional learning proceeds within a larger framework, that of religious values and of cosmological and metaphysical principles derived from Revelation and gnosis. Modern science, by contrast, asserts a Promethean autonomy and scorns all other avenues of knowledge. This is the crux of the problem. Here we shall address two issues: the cleavage between religion and science; and the epistemological limits of a materialistic science.

It is nowadays a commonplace that many of the ills of our time stem from the rift between 'faith' and 'science' but few people have suggested any convincing means of reconciling the two. Certainly the effusions and anxious compromises of the liberal theologians and 'demytholgizers' are of no help, marking little more than a thinly-disguised and often self-deceiving capitulation of religion to science. As Schuon remarks,

> ... the tragic impasse reached by the modern mind results from the fact that most men are incapable of grasping the *compatibility* between the symbolic expressions of tradition and the material discoveries established by modern science.[19]

This is a vital point. It is important to understand that the disapprobations of the traditionalists do not fall on the findings of science as such – they are not obscurantists – but on the absence of such principles as would situate these discoveries in a context which could preserve the incomparably more important truths enshrined in tradition. A concrete example will give the point more weight:

> According to the observations of experimental science, the blue sky which stretches above us is not a world of bliss, but an optical illusion due to the refraction of light by the atmosphere and from this point of view it is obviously right to maintain that the home of the blessed does not lie up there. Nevertheless it would be a great mistake to assert that the association of ideas between the visible heavens and the celestial Paradise does not arise from the nature of things, but rather from ignorance and ingenuousness mixed with imagination and sentimentality; for the blue sky is a direct and therefore adequate symbol of the higher and supersensory degrees of Existence; it is indeed a distant reverberation of those degrees and it is *necessarily* so since it is truly a symbol consecrated by the Sacred Scriptures and by the unanimous intuition of peoples ... The fact that the symbol itself may be no more than an optical illusion in no way impairs its precision or efficacy, for all appearances, including those of space and of the galaxies, are strictly speaking only illusions created by relativity.[20]

In the light of this kind of metaphysical understanding many of the apparent contradictions between 'science' and 'religion' simply evaporate. It is not necessary, to say the least, to throw religious beliefs on the scrapheap because they are 'disproven' by modern science; nor is it necessary to gainsay such facts as modern science does uncover, provided always that what science presents as facts are so indeed and not merely precarious hypotheses.

No one will deny that, from one point of view, the earth is not the centre of the solar system; this is no reason for jettisoning the more important truth which was carried by the geocentric picture of the universe.[21] (A heliocentric cosmology could

---

19 FS *SW* pp8–9 (emphasis mine). See also Lord Northbourne *Looking Back on Progress* Perennial Books, 1970; pp23–41.
20 FS *LAW* pp36–37 (emphasis mine).
21 See FS *THC* pp171–177.

also have been the vehicle for the same truth.[22]) Indeed, without the protective truths of traditional symbolisms such material discoveries as do issue from a profane science are likely to be more or less useless or positively destructive. Another example: it is preferable to believe that God created the world in six days and that heaven lies in the skies above the flat surface of the earth than it is to know precisely the distance from one nebula to another whilst forgetting the truth embodied in this symbolism, namely that all phenomena depend on a higher Reality which determines us and gives our human existence meaning and purpose.[23] A materially inaccurate but symbolically rich view is always preferable to the reign of brute fact.

Though modern science has doubtless revealed much material information that was previously unknown it has also supplanted a knowledge which infinitely outreaches it. We see the fruits of this tendency in the complacencies and condescensions of those scientists who like to suppose that we have 'outgrown' the 'superstitions' of our ancestors. Here is a random example from a prestigious contemporary scientist:

> I myself, like many scientists, believe that the soul is imaginary and that what we call our mind is simply a way of talking about the function of our brains ... Once one has become adjusted to the ideas that we are here because we have evolved from simple chemical compounds by a process of natural selection, it is remarkable how many of the problems of the modern world take on a completely new light.[24]

Here indeed is an 'intelligence without wisdom' or what Roszak calls a 'well-informed foolishness'. This kind of materialism is presently 'the reigning orthodoxy among philosophers of the mind'.[25]

In falling under the tyranny of a fragmentary, materialistic and quantitative outlook modern science is irremediably limited by its epistemological base. The apparent 'impersonality' and 'objectivity' of modern science should not for a moment blind us to the fact that it is and must be anthropomorphic in its foundations. No matter how inhuman may be its depictions of both man and the universe it remains true that '... the criteria and instruments which determine this science are merely and purely human. It is the human reason and the human senses which determine modern science.'[26] Of the realities to which faith, Revelation and intellection give access modern science knows and can know absolutely nothing. As Schuon observes

> There is scarcely a more desperately vain or naïve illusion – far more naïve than is Aristotelian astronomy! – than to believe that modern science, in its vertiginous course towards the 'infinitely small' and the 'infinitely great', will end up by rejoining religious and metaphysical truths and doctrines.[27]

The ways in which the triumph of scientism has contributed to man's dehumanisa-

---

22 See FS *RHC* p27.
23 *ibid.*; pp38-39.
24 F. Crick *Molecules and Men*, quoted in T. Roszak: *op.cit.*; p188. For an almost identical profession by a scientific popularizer see C. Sagan *The Dragons of Eden* Ballantine Books, New York, 1978; p10. For some commentary on this kind of thinking see H. Smith *Forgotten Truth* pp60ff; T. Roszak: *op.cit.*; pp178-219; FS *EPW* p17, and FS *SPHF* p49fn.
25 Daniel Dennett quoted in H. Smith: *Beyond the Post-Modern Mind* pp135-136.
26 S.H. Nasr: 'Reflections on Islam and Modern Thought' p121.
27 FS *DI* p156. See also FS *RHC* pp15ff.

tion have been written about a good deal in recent years. It matters not a jot how quick contemporary scientists now are to disown discredited 'facts' which stood between man and any true self-awareness – the mechanistic theories of the seventeenth century for instance – on the grounds that these were, after all, only provisional hypotheses which a more 'humane' scientific vision can now abandon. The simple fact is that modern science cannot be 'humanised' or 'reformed' from within itself because it is built on premises which are both inadequate and inhuman, not to say immoral. (To suggest that there is a contradiction between the fact that science is purely anthropomorphic and that it is inhuman betokens a failure to understand the issue: it is inhuman precisely because it is exclusively anthropomorphic. The same can be said of all the philosophies of 'humanism': by denying the transcendent dimension of man they betray him.)

By now it should be clear enough why it is a dangerous prejudice to believe that a materialistic science is harmless enough if it be confined to its own domain – the material world. This realm does not exist *in vacuo* and to pretend that it does only breeds trouble, as the history of modern science so convincingly demonstrates. Titus Burckhardt, one of the most authoritative traditionalists in this field, exposes some of the issues involved here in writing

> ... modern science displays a certain number of fissures that are not only due to the fact that the world of phenomena is indefinite and that therefore no science could come to the end of it; those fissures derive especially from a systematic ignorance of all the noncorporeal dimensions of reality. They manifest themselves right down to the foundations of modern science, and in domains as seemingly 'exact' as that of physics; they become gaping cracks when one turns to the disciplines connected with the study of the forms of life, not to mention psychology, where an empiricism that is relatively valid in the physical order encroaches strangely upon a foreign field. These fissures, which do not affect only the theoretical realm, are far from harmless; they represent, on the contrary, in their technical consequences, so many seeds of catastrophe.[28]

These fissures might be probed at some length. However, enough has been said to provide a framework within which we can examine two manifestations of the scientistic spirit, evolutionism and psychologism. Among the reasons why these two have been chosen is the fact that they each have a tenacious grip on the mentality of most Europeans and they have been especially malignant in their effects on the study of religion.

Evolutionism is one of the most beguiling and most treacherous of scientistic ideologies. For the moment it may be defined as the concurrence of certain palaeontological and biological facts, assumptions and speculations wedded to a cluster of philosophical and socio-political ideas and values. Contemporary evolutionism is far more deep-seated than a mere lingering residue of the crude social Darwinism promulgated by Herbert Spencer and others. Many people are now sensitive to the pitfalls of extrapolating from the biological to the social plane although there are still a host of 'naked

---

28 T. Burckhardt: 'Cosmology and Modern Science' in JN *SG* p131. Some of these fissures are dealt with in RG *RQ* esp Ch XXIV and following. See also P. Sherrard: 'Science and the Dehumanisation of Man' *SCR* X, i, 1976; pp74ff., and Gai Eaton *King of the Castle* Bodley Head, London, 1977; pp142–164.

ape' theories, supported by the pseudo-science of ethology, which fly in the face of any scientific prudence – the theories of Konrad Lorenz, Robert Ardrey and Desmond Morris are of this ilk.[29] No, the roots of the problem strike much deeper than this: the biological theory itself, one of the props of modern science, is riddled with contradictions, anomalies, absurdities and lacunae.

Before turning to the traditionalist dissent a couple of preliminary points are in order. Evolutionism is under attack from several directions. Some critics take their stand on entirely the wrong ground and not all critiques carry the same authority although they do share the basic intuition that evolutionism is, in the words of one of its critics, 'a hoax'. We shall have to take care to maintain several crucial distinctions both between the biological hypothesis and the social ideology of evolutionism, and between well-attested scientific facts and the extravagant interpretations to which they have sometimes been turned. Michael Negus expresses the traditionalist viewpoint when issuing the following caution:

> There is a need to avoid two errors: the first is the error of rejecting adequately established scientific fact, eg. the age of the earth or the space-time dimensions of the universe. This is the trap into which the biblical fundamentalists fall. The second error is that of accepting pseudo-doctrines like evolutionary progress with all its implications and thereby subverting Tradition. This is the trap into which the followers of Teilhard de Chardin fall.[30]

The balance, from a traditionalist perspective, lies in first of all acknowledging the supremacy of traditional doctrines over any profane science whatsoever but at the same time accepting, within appropriate limits, such facts as scientific inquiry has uncovered even though these often have no relevance to man's spiritual destiny.[31] The denial of such facts only taints legitimate opposition to evolutionism with the suspicion of crankiness and obscurantism. It is crucial not to confuse the traditionalist position with a literalist fundamentalism which goes on insisting, in the face of incontrovertible evidence, that the earth is only a few thousand years old or that all life was created in a few days.[32] No traditionalist wishes to evade or cover up scientific discoveries but only to separate fact from fiction and to situate the former in a framework which allows of an adequate interpretation.

The traditionalists repudiate both the biological hypothesis and the social ideology of evolutionism. We shall take the biological theory first. Amongst the traditionalists, Titus Burckhardt, Martin Lings and Michael Negus have taken issue with the theory on purely scientific grounds. Such objections by no means exhaust the case but they are an important component of it. These traditionalists point to the growing body of literature by reputable scientists – palaeontologists, botanists, zoologists, geneticists and others – which throws many of the central tenets in the Darwinian hypothesis into very serious question. Scientific critiques of evolutionary theory by men like

---

29 For a sample from this disturbing genre of pseudo-scientific 'research' see K. Lorenz *On Aggression* Methuen, London, 1969; R. Ardrey *African Genesis* Collins, London, 1961; D. Morris *The Naked Ape* Jonathan Cape, London, 1967. For some critiques see F.A. Montague *Man and Aggression* OUP, New York, 1968.

30 M. Negus: 'Reactions to the Theory of Evolution' *SCR* XII, iii & iv, 1978; p194. See also SHN *K&S* pp 205–214, esp. p205.

31 *ibid*.

32 Nor is it of much use to put forward counter-theories of a quasi-scientific kind which are even less credible than those of the evolutionists. See Michael Negus's review of Anthony Fides's *Man's Origins* in *SCR* XIII, i & ii, 1979; pp126–127.

Douglas Dewar, Evan Shute, Guiseppi Sermonti, Roberto Fondi and L. Bournoure proceed through the premises and methodologies of modern science itself; the theory is being white-anted from within.[33] The debate hinges on some very complex biological and palaeontological evidence which cannot be reviewed here. Rather, we shall mention a few lines of approach taken by some of the scientific critics of the biological theory. We shall consider three aspects of the theory that have been assailed by traditionalists and scientists alike: the evolutionary conception of life's beginnings, the transformationist thesis of 'mega-evolution' whereby one species evolves into another, and the notion of man's primate ancestry. We shall, for the moment, consider these matters from a material and logical point of view.

The conception of life's beginnings and its subsequent development as presented by the evolutionists is quite illogical and defies all common sense. A contemporary psychiatrist has this to say:

> If we present, for the sake of argument, the theory of evolution in a most scientific formulation we have to say something like this: 'At a certain moment of time the temperature of the earth was such that it became most favourable for the aggregation of carbon atoms and oxygen with the nitrogen-hydrogen combination, and that from random occurrences of large clusters molecules occurred which were most favourably structured for the coming about of life, and from that point it went on through vast stretches of time, until through processes of natural selection a being finally occurred which is capable of choosing love over hate, and justice over injustice, of writing poetry like that of Dante, composing music like that of Mozart, and making drawings like those of Leonardo.' Of course, such a view of cosmogenesis is crazy. And I do not mean crazy in the sense of slangy invective but rather in the technical meaning of psychotic. Indeed such a view has much in common with certain aspects of schizophrenic thinking.[34]

Now, this passage itself is by no means beyond criticism but it does expose the fundamental illogic of the evolutionist conception. There is no empirical method of either verifying or falsifying the hypothesis outlined above: we are then, from a scientific point of view, thrown back onto the resources of logic and commonsense. Can life emerge from inert matter? Can consciousness develop from non-consciousness? Can Shakespeare derive, in any amount of time, from a primeval algal slime? Can the effect be divorced from its cause? Wherein lies the cause of life? These are questions to which the evolutionist response will seem plausible only to those already indoctrinated into accepting the hypothesis as established fact — and this is only the beginning of the embarrassment to which evolutionism can be subjected.

A keystone in the evolutionary theory is the notion that one species can, over time, be transformed into another. This process we shall call mega-evolution. The testimony of many reputable scientists on this subject calls for our attention. Martin Lings, drawing on the work of Evan Shute, points out that,

---

33 For some of this literature see D. Dewar *The Transformist Illusion* Dehoff, Tenn., 1957; L. Bournoure *Determinisme et finalite double loi de la vie* Paris, 1957; E. Shute *Flaws in the Theory of Evolution* Craig Press, New Jersey, 1961; P. Moorehead & M. Kaplan (eds) *Mathematical Challenges to the neo-Darwinian Interpretation of Evolution* Wistar Institute Press, Philadelphia, 1967; G. Fremondi & R. Fondi *Dopo Darwin* Rusconi, Milan, 1980. For an academic lawyer's critique of evolutionism see Phillip E. Johnson *Darwin on Trial* Intervarsity Press, 1993. See also Michael Denton *Evolution: A Theory in Crisis* Adler & Adler, 1996.

34 Karl Stern quoted in E.F. Schumacher: *op.cit.*; pp127–128.

> The only evolution that has been scientifically attested is on a very small scale and within narrow limits. To conclude from this 'micro-evolution', which no one contests, that there could be such a thing as 'mega-evolution' – that for example, the class of birds could have evolved from the class of reptiles – is not merely conjecture but perverse conjecture... micro-evolution demonstrates the presence in nature of all sorts of unseen barriers that ensure the stability of the various classes and orders of animals and plants and that invariably cause transformation, when it has run its little course, to come to a dead-end.[35]

Jean Rostand, the French biologist:

> The world postulated by transformism is a fairy world, phantasmagoric, surrealistic. The chief point, to which one always returns, is that we have never been present at one authentic phenomenon of evolution ... we keep the impression that nature today has nothing to offer that might be capable of reducing our embarrassment before the genuinely organic metamorphosis implied in the transformist thesis.[36]

Evan Shute:

> Mega-evolution is really a philosophy dating from the days of biological ignorance; it was a philosophic synthesis built up in a biological kindergarten.[37]

Lemoine and other European scientists have shown how the palaeontological record on which the evolutionists base their arguments in fact contradicts the transformist hypothesis.[38] The geological record shows, for example, the abrupt appearance of whole new species which flatly contradicts the conventional scenario of adaptation and natural selection. Not all evolutionists have been able to turn a blind eye to this evidence and so, rather than questioning the whole theory, have developed new hypotheses which are somehow assimilated into the Darwinian framework. Having scorned the idea of the Creator some evolutionists now find themselves endowing nature itself with powers of instantaneous creation – thus we have, for example, Schindewolf's theory of 'explosive evolution' or Severtzoff and Zeuner's theory of 'aramorphosis', or again the theory of 'quanta of evolution' or 'tachygenesis',[39] or recent 'neo-Darwinian' speculations about 'organicistic revolutions'.[40] All of these theories involve what is, from an empirical viewpoint, so much hocus-pocus concealed however by the technical jargon which insulates such speculations from the inquiries of any lay person trying to follow the logic of the argument.[41]

The mega-evolution and transformist thesis is, of course, the platform for the idea that there is an essential continuity between man and the animals and that *homo sapiens* is a highly-evolved primate. This is open to question from any number of angles and we shall turn to some of these presently. For the moment we shall focus

---

35 M. Lings: 'Signs of the Times' in JN *SG* p113.
36 J. Rostand *Le Figaro Littéraire* quoted in T. Burckhardt: 'Cosmology and Modern Science' p143.
37 E. Shute quoted in M. Lings *op.cit.*; p113.
38 See S.H. Nasr *Man and Nature* pp125ff and SHN *K&S* pp238ff.
39 See M. Lings *Ancient Beliefs and Modern Superstitions* Allen & Unwin, London, 1980; pp77–78; and T. Burckhardt: 'Cosmology and Modern Science' pp146–147; and S.H. Nasr *Man and Nature* p126.
40 See S.H. Nasr *Man and the Order of Nature* Oxford University Press, 1966, p146.
41 M. Lings *Ancient Beliefs and Modern Superstitions* pp78–80.

on one phenomenon only: man's ability to create an extraordinary number of artefacts. Now, according to the Darwinian theory of natural selection and adaptation this skill must evolve in response to environmental pressures; it represents an adaptation necessary for survival. In most species we find that an animal has only 'evolved' the skills necessary to manufacture one artefact – say a nest in the case of a bird. (We will leave aside for now the awkward fact that where evidence is available it suggests that the species in question appeared with this skill ready-made: spiders, for example, were, as far as we can tell, always able to spin webs. There is not an iota of evidence to suggest that this 'adaptation' 'evolved' over a period of time.[42]) In the case of man we are asked to swallow the same explanation for the fact that he is capable of making not one or even half-dozen different artefacts but hundreds of thousands if not millions. Wherein is the explanation of this singularity? Howbeit that man alone can evolve these skills in what, from a geological point of view, must have been a minuscule period of time in his prehistory? The radical disjunction between man's unprecedented cultural achievements and the theory of adaptation and natural selection is one that no evolutionist has been able to explain in terms which have the slightest plausibility.

The debate about the 'missing link' between man and the other primates now takes on the characteristics of farce. The spectacle of evolutionists falling over each other in their attempts to find this link shows no sign of ending. Nor is another vexing question any closer to solution: what precisely are the criteria which distinguish humans from apes? Why are scientists unable to answer these questions? In this context we might also note the words of an American palaeontologist:

> You can, with equal facility, model on the Neanderthaloid skull the features of a chimpanzee or the lineaments of a philosopher. These alleged restorations of ancient types of man have very little, if any, scientific value, and are likely only to mislead the public.[43]

That there are certain similarities between men and apes no one will deny: what is at issue is the significance of these similarities. We return to this question when we come to a metaphysically-based critique of evolutionism.

If the evolutionary hypothesis is far from being supported by the palaeontological and biological evidence why, it might reasonably be asked, has it survived for so long? Why does it still command the support of the overwhelming majority of scientists and of nearly everyone else? The answer is simple: evolutionism has taken on the status of a pseudo-religion with its own inviolable dogmas. This fact was remarked by the distinguished entomologist F.R.S. Thompson over half a century ago:

> The concept of organic Evolution is very highly prized by biologists, for many of whom it is an object of genuinely religious devotion, because they regard it as a supreme integrative principle. This is probably the reason why the severe methodological criticism employed in other departments of biology has not yet been brought to bear against evolutionary speculation.[44]

---

42 See T. Burckhardt: 'Cosmology and Modern Science' pp144–146.
43 E.A. Hooton quoted in M. Lings: 'Signs of the Times' p113fn7.
44 F.R.S. Thompson *Science and Common Sense* London, 1937; p229, quoted in S.H. Nasr *Man and Nature* p139fn20. See also SHN *K&S* pp234–235.

Rather than discarding a hypothesis with which the facts do not conform the evolutionists go on endlessly modifying, qualifying and hedging their theories with ever more subtlety and ingenuity whilst all the time clinging to the basic premises on which the whole edifice of evolutionary theory rests. As Murray Eden observes, 'Neo-Darwinian evolutionary theory has been modified to the point that virtually every formulation of the principles of evolution is a tautology.'[45] It may be that the tide is turning. Certainly evolutionary theory has been subjected to more rigorous and penetrating criticism in the last quarter of a century and increasing numbers of people, scientifically trained and otherwise, are no longer prepared to accept the evolutionary account of life.

The traditionalists, as we have seen, have made some forays into the *scientific* debate about evolutionary theory. However, this is really only a side-show. The most fundamental grounds for a rejection of evolutionism are philosophical and metaphysical. The theory contradicts certain axiomatic principles; this fact alone robs it of any credibility. If it is in direct opposition to these principles then it could not be valid from any point of view, scientific or otherwise.

The whole evolutionary conception rests on the metaphysically absurd notion that the greater can emerge from the lesser. Whitall Perry sums up the basic article of faith in evolutionism thus: 'In the beginning was flesh ... and the flesh was made Word.'[46] Schuon anathematizes this 'dogma' in the severest possible terms:

> ... the evolutionary leap from matter to intelligence is the most arbitrary, the most inconceivable and the most foolish hypothesis possible, in comparison with which 'simple faith' seems like a mathematical formula.

He goes on to elaborate the support for such a claim from a metaphysical point of view:

> People accept transformist evolution as a useful and provisional postulate just as they are ready to accept no matter what on condition that they do not have to accept the primacy of Spirit. And yet, starting from this immediately tangible mystery which is subjectivity or intelligence, it is easy to understand that the origin of the Universe is not inert and unconscious matter, but a spiritual Substance which, from coagulation to coagulation and from segmentation to segmentation – and other projections, both manifesting and limiting – finally produces matter by causing it to emerge from a more subtle substance, but one that is already distant from principial Substance.[47]

We are not here concerned with alternative explanations of the origin of life and matter but this passage gives the clue. Furthermore, the cosmogonies in the different religious traditions do not contradict this account although they necessarily approach the problem from a more limited perspective.[48] The evolutionist position involves

---

45 M. Eden: 'Inadequacies of neo-Darwinian Evolution as Scientific Theory' in P. Moorehead and M. Kaplan: *op.cit.*; p109. See also SHN *K&S* p237.

46 W. Perry in a review of R.C. Zaehner *Evolution in Religion* in *SCR* V, iii, 1971; p192. This book is an example of the lengths to which some thinkers have gone in their attempts to reconcile religious faith and evolutionism. Zaehner is quite oblivious to the possibility that the evolutionary hypothesis is wrong.

47 F. Schuon: 'Consequences Flowing from the Mystery of Subjectivity' *SCR* XI, iv, 1977; pp197-198. See also SHN *K&S* p235.

48 For an explanation of the lines along which the apparent antinomies between traditional doctrines on this issues – Semitic creationism and Hindu or Platonic emanationism for instance – can be metaphysically resolved see FS *L&T* pp85ff. See also RG *RQ* p213 & pp331–333.

either an unabashed materialism wherein life and consciousness are evolutes of matter or some kind of mental contortionism whereby an attempt is made to reconcile the irreconcilable. On cannot accept both the primacy of Spirit and the evolutionist hypothesis about life's beginnings.

The notion of organic transformation, of mega-evolution, is from the outset quite incompatible with the doctrine of archetypes which finds one of its applications in the animal realm. Metaphysically, each species '... is an archetype, and if it is only manifested by the individuals belonging to it, it is nonetheless as real and indeed incomparably more real than they are.'[49] Titus Burckhardt's discussion of the doctrine of archetypes as it applies to life forms concludes this way:

> ... it follows that a species in itself is an immutable 'form'; it could not evolve and become transformed into another species, although it can include variants, all these being 'projections' of a single essential form from which they will never become detached.[50]

Darwinism postulates such variants to be 'buds' of new species, a quite illegitimate assimilation and one that does nothing to hide either the gaps in the palaeontological 'succession' of species or the fact that whole new species appeared abruptly. The facts which palaeontology has uncovered, in themselves indisputable, are amenable to a quite different interpretation, as Burckhardt demonstrates.

> All that palaeontology proves to us is that the various animal forms such as are shown by fossils preserved in successive layers of the earth made their appearance in a vaguely ascending order, going from relatively undifferentiated organisms – but not simple ones – to ever more complex forms, without this ascension representing, however, a univocal and continuous line. It seems to move in jumps; that is to say, whole categories of animals appear at once, without real predecessors. What means this order, then? Simply that on the material plane, the simple or relatively undifferentiated always precedes the complex and differentiated. All 'matter' is like a mirror that reflects the activity of the essences by inverting it; that is why the seed comes before the tree, and the leaf bud before the flower, whereas in the principial order perfect 'forms' pre-exist. The successive appearance of animal forms according to an ascending hierarchy therefore in no wise proves their continual and cumulative genesis.[51]

All traditional teachings affirm that there is a radical discontinuity between humankind and other life forms. The fact that some oriental exotericisms understand this distinction in terms of *karma* rather than ontologically in no wise affects the principle itself. The privileged and axial position of man in the cosmos is completely ignored by evolutionism which would have it that man is a kind of superior ape. How can the similarities between man and the primates be explained without resort to evolutionary speculations?

The anatomical similarities between men and apes are always explained tendentiously by evolutionists. However, if we start from the doctrine of archetypes and

---

49 T. Burckhardt: 'Cosmology and Modern Science' p141. See also M. Pallis *A Buddhist Spectrum* Allen & Unwin, London, 1980; p150.
50 T. Burckhardt: 'Cosmology and Modern Science' p141. See also S.H. Nasr *Man and Nature* p124.
51 T. Burckhardt: 'Cosmology and Modern Science' pp143–144. One might add that the evolutionary hypothesis also depends on a linear and one-dimensional view of time. Nasr has discussed the effects of neglecting the doctrine of cosmic cycles. See SHN *K&S* pp209ff.

the multiple states of being, these physical correspondences appear in a completely different light.

> However paradoxical this may seem, the anatomical resemblance between man and the anthropoid apes is precisely explainable by the difference, not gradual but essential, separating man from all other animals. Since the anthropoid form is able to exist without that 'central' element that characterises man – and that moreover is manifested anatomically by his vertical position, among other things – that form must exist; in other words there cannot but be found, at the purely animal level, a form that realises in its own way – that is to say, according to the laws of its own level – the very plan of the human anatomy. It is in this sense that the monkey is a prefiguration of man, not as an evolutionary phase, but in virtue of that law that decrees that at every level of existence analogous possibilities will be found.[52]

It is, of course, for this very reason that it is impossible to define the differences between the apes and man in purely physiological terms. Man's especial estate is not due to the fact 'that he has two hands which he manipulates or that he can make planes that fly or calculating machines that perform difficult mathematical operations in a short time. These and other abilities are no more than accidental to his real nature'.[53] This real nature is something about which a materialistic science can tell us nothing.

There are plenty of other puzzles concerning early man which embarrass evolutionary science. To think clearly about these matters involves balancing the modern scientific preoccupation with time, matter and change with traditional conceptions of space, Substance and Eternity. One then has a more comprehensive framework within which to work and all sorts of new possibilities present themselves. To give but one example: it is possible that the first humans in this particular terrestrial cycle left no solid traces, either because their bodies were not yet so materialised or because the spiritual state normal in those times, together with the cosmic and cyclic conditions then obtaining, made possible a resorption of the physical into the subtle body at the moment of death.[54] One mentions this possibility only to indicate how these questions can be approached from many different angles and not only from those proposed by modern science. So deeply is evolutionism embedded in the modern consciousness that it is no easy matter to explore different modalities of thought on the questions with which evolutionary theory deals.

Darwin's biological hypothesis became something of a Pandora's Box for nineteenth century social theory. His work was pillaged for new tools of social and historical analysis and for new categories of thought. The evolutionist schema and its methodology soon came to be applied to non-biological categories such as classes, races and nations, even religions. The original authors of what came to be known as 'Social Darwinism' were E.B. Tylor and Herbert Spencer. The earliest formulation of their ideas actually preceded Darwin's *Origin of Species*; in its earliest form social evolutionism was not an illegitimate offspring of Darwinism but an elder cousin who later exploited the family name. Indeed, it was Spencer rather than Darwin who coined the term 'survival of the fittest', a slogan under which all manner of social,

---

52 T. Burckhardt: 'Cosmology and Modern Science' pp149–150.
53 S.H. Nasr *Ideals and Realities of Islam* Allen & Unwin, London, 1975; p23.
54 See T. Burckhardt: 'Cosmology and Modern Science' p150.

The Critique of Modernism

racial and imperial brutalities were to be justified. The ideology of Social Darwinism was to be harnessed to a wide range of purposes: the assertion of Anglo-Saxon racial and cultural superiority; the colonial exploitation of other countries and peoples; the justification, in pseudo-scientific terms, of a rapacious capitalism and of various policies of social and economic *laissez-faire*; the shoring up of nationalist and racist ideologies, not only in Britain but in Europe and America as well.

> More than most theories, Darwinism lent itself to such stratagems of persuasion, enjoying not only the prestige and authority attached to science, but also the faculty of being readily translated into social terms. That this translation was rather free and loose was an added advantage, since it gave licence to a variety of social gospels.[55]

The story of the growth of Social Darwinism is a dismal one which need not be narrated here.[56] Rather we shall pinpoint a few social and political ideas which it has sponsored.

The traditionalists have been concerned, in the main, with the effects of evolutionism on attitudes to religion, to the past, to tradition; in all these areas they find evolutionism's bequeathals to be malign. The enervating effects of both biological and social Darwinism on attitudes to the Christian faith are well-known. E.F. Schumacher echoes the traditionalist position in writing:

> Evolutionism is not a science; it is a science fiction, even a kind of hoax ... that has imprisoned modern man in what looks like an irreconcilable conflict between 'science' and 'religion'. It has destroyed all faiths that pull mankind upward and has substituted a faith that pulls mankind down ... it is the most extreme product of the materialistic utilitarianism of the nineteenth century.[57]

Through its connections with a false gospel of Progress, evolutionism has seeped into our way of looking at history and has subverted the whole idea of tradition. Although social Darwinism has been thoroughly discredited on a theoretical and scholarly level the average mentality is still very much under its sway. The idea of progress maintains a tenacious hold; it is, after all, one of the most comfortable of illusions. It is still not uncommon to find formulations such as this one from a very well-known and influential anthropological theorist: 'Man has made objective progress in improving his society and ... we in the West seem at this stage to have the best society in recorded history.'[58] This is a staggering claim. It is a measure of the influence of the idea of progress, buttressed by evolutionism, that this kind of statement will be swallowed without demur by many people today. Nor did a popular television programme entitled *The Ascent of Man*, compered by Jacob Bronowski, raise

---

55 G. Himmelfarb *Darwin and the Darwinian Revolution* Chatto & Windus, London, 1959; p340.

56 Several important works in this field are: J.W. Burrow *Evolution and Society: A Study in Victorian Social Theory* Cambridge Uni Press, 1966; T.K. Penniman *A Hundred Years of Anthropology* Duckworth, London, 1952; R. Hofstadter *Social Darwinism in American Thought* Uni Philadelphia Press, 1945; W.H. Simon: 'Herbert Spencer and the "Social Organism"' *Journal of the History of Ideas* XXI, 1960; J.H. Randall: 'The Changing Impact of Darwin on Philosophy' *Journal of the History of Ideas* XXII, 1961. I have anatomized the pernicious effects of both biological and social Darwinism on attitudes to the Australian Aborigines in an unpublished work *The Science of Man: Scientific Opinion on the Australian Aborigines in the Late Nineteenth Century* BA Honours Thesis, Australian National University, 1968. See also my article 'The Religion of the Australian Aborigines' in A. Sharma: *op.cit.*.

57 E. F. Schumacher *op.cit.*; pp129-130.

58 I.C. Jarvie *The Revolution in Anthropology* Henry Regnary, Chicago, 1969; p14.

many eyebrows. One could catalogue a more or less endless list of the tokens of evolutionist assumptions in almost every aspect of contemporary thought.

The idea of progress and of evolution finds not a whit of support in any of the traditional doctrines concerning man and time in terms of any spiritual criteria — quite the contrary.

> All the traditional doctrines agree in this: From a strictly spiritual point of view, though not necessarily from other much more relative and therefore less important points of view, mankind is becoming more and more corrupted; the ideas of 'evolution', of 'progress' and of a single 'civilisation' are in effect the most pernicious pseudo-dogmas.

The intention impelling Schuon in such a passage is not merely critical but positive and affirmative, calling as it does for a rehabilitation of our attitudes to the past:

> We say not that evolution is non-existent but that it has a partial and most often quite external applicability; if there be evolution on one hand, there are degenerations on the other, and it is in any case radically false to suppose that our ancestors were intellectually, spiritually or morally our inferiors. To suppose this is the most childish of 'optical delusions'; human weakness alters its style in the course of history, but not its nature.[59]

We are left, in Shakespeare's words, to 'commit the oldest sins the newest kinds of ways'.[60]

The ideal of Progress is by now looking very tawdry to those who see our present situation clear-eyed. Theodore Roszak accents the incongruity of the idea when considered against our present global circumstances:

> The Last Days were announced to St John by a voice like the sound of many waters. But the voice that comes in our day summoning us to play out the dark myth of the reckoning is our meager own, making casual conversation about the varieties of annihilation ... the thermonuclear Armageddon, the death of the seas, the vanishing atmosphere, the massacre of the innocents, the universal famine to come ... Such horrors should be the stuff of nightmare ... They aren't. They are the news of the day ... we have not stumbled into the arms of Gog and Magog; we have *progressed* there.[61]

Evolutionist ideas not only distort our attitudes to the past but prepare the soil for sentimental Utopianisms of one sort and another. One might have thought that twentieth century history would have immunised us once and for all against the seductions of Utopianism but no, they still abound.[62] Utopian scenarios pre-date evolutionism but they received a new fillip when the theory of evolution was wedded to Enlightenment theories about the perfectibility of man and nineteenth century optimism about the inexorability of progress. The worldly Utopia — so often a grotesque parody of Augustine's 'City of God' but now a 'City of Man' — is dangled before the credulous in many guises: the classless society of the Marxist fantasy, the

---

59 F. Schuon: 'No Activity Without Truth' in JN *SG* pp38–39.
60 *King Henry IV* Pt II, Act IV, Sc 5.
61 T. Roszak: *op.cit.*; pix. As Gai Eaton observes, 'A superstitious faith in progress endures even when the dogma of progress has been exposed as an illusion.' *King of the Castle* p10.
62 Utopianism: 'impossible ideal schemes for the perfection of social conditions.' OED.

The Critique of Modernism

anarchist dream of the 'free' society, the pseudo-spiritual effusions of the 'cosmic consciousness' pundits, the quasi-theological aberrations of a Teilhard de Chardin. Each of these Utopianisms, by definition, is a form of profane humanism envisaging a human destiny which leaves no room for the transcendent, the divine, the sacred, the traditional – in a word, no room for God. As one representative of Russian Orthodoxy put it, 'All the tragedy of man is in one word, "godlessness".'[63]

It is a sign of the times that an anti-traditional, evolutionist Utopianism should find its way into domains where it should not for a moment have been countenanced. The work of Teilhard de Chardin is a conspicuous example of what results when one tries to reconcile the platitudes of evolutionist ideology with a traditional theology. The attempt is ingenious, even subtle if somewhat opaque, but the result is none the less dangerous for that. Kurt Almqvist has rightly pilloried it as a '... pseudo-metaphysical synthesis of neo-modernism, where evolutionist and pantheist materialism substitutes itself for religion by means of subversion and parody.'[64] That the Catholic hierarchy should, however uneasily, allow this to be passed off as 'Catholic' thought in any sense whatsoever is in itself a sad commentary. Would that we could still confidently accede to G.K. Chesterton's remark that 'the Church is the only thing that saves us from the degrading slavery of becoming children of our times'.[65] In this context we might also recall Coomaraswamy's question, 'What becomes of the spiritual power, if she cannot or does not speak with *authority*, but takes part in a discussion with profane teachers as if on equal terms? It is not for the Church to argue, but to *tell*.'[66]

Before leaving the subject of evolutionism let us remember these sobering words from Schuon:

> ... evolutionism – that most typical of all the products of the modern spirit – is no more than a kind of substitute: it is a compensation 'on a plane surface' for the missing dimensions. Because one no longer admits ... the supersensible dimensions ... one seeks the solution to the cosmogonic problem on the sensory plane and one replaces true causes with imaginary ones which, in appearance at least, conform with the possibilities of the corporeal world ... In doing this, one forgets what man is, and one forgets also that a purely physical science, when it reaches vast proportions, can only lead to catastrophe ...[67]

Psychologism is another view of man built on the sands of a profane science, and as such, another symptom of modernism. Its intrusion into the religious realm has been attended by consequences no less disturbing than those coming in the train of evolutionism. As Coomaraswamy so neatly put it, 'While nineteenth century materialism closed the mind of man to what is above him, twentieth century psychology

---

63 Metropolitan Anthony of Sourzah *God and Man* Hodder & Stoughton, London, 1974; p68.
64 K. Almqvist: 'Aspects of Teilhardian Idolatry' *SCR* XII, iii & iv, 1978; p195. For traditionalist commenatry on Teilhard see also SHN *K&S* pp240-244; T. Burckhardt: 'Cosmology and Modern Science' pp150-153; P. Sherrard: 'Teilhard and Christian Vision' *SCR* IV, iii, 1970; pp150-175; W. Smith *Teilhardism and the New Religion* Tan, Rockford, 1988. On the plight of the Roman Church since Vatican II see Rama P. Coomaraswamy *The Destruction of the Christian Tradition* Perennial Books, 1980; M. Pallis: 'The Catholic Church in Crisis' in JN *SG* pp57-80. See also FS *EPW* pp201-204.
65 Quoted in a review by W. Perry in *SCR* XII, iii & iv, 1978; p247.
66 Letter to Paul Furfey, August 1935, AKC *SL* p315.
67 FS *DI* pp153-154.

opened it to what is below him.'[68] Psychologism, as Schuon notes, is both an end-point and a cause, being a 'logical and fatal ramification and natural ally' of other profane and materialistic ideologies like evolutionism.[69]

Psychologism can be described as the assumption that man's nature and behaviour are to be explained by psychological factors which can be laid bare by a scientific and empirical psychology. Before we proceed any further an extremely important distinction must be made between modern psychology and traditional pneumatologies with which it shares some superficial similarities. The latter derived from radically different principles, applied different therapies and pursued different ends. Just as it is misleading to talk about modern European philosophy and traditional metaphysic in the same breath and under the same terms, so too with modern psychology and traditional pneumatology. A good deal of confusion would be averted if people would resist such terms as 'Buddhist psychology' or 'Zen psychotherapy'. It would also help clarify the issues at stake if many of the amateurish 'experts' in this field would abandon the extraordinary notion that the techniques of Western psychology can lead to the 'liberation' spoken of in the Eastern traditions.[70] This is to confuse two quite different planes of experience.

Modern psychology can be censured against the backdrop of traditional doctrines in this fashion:

> Psycho-analysis doubly deserves to be called an imposture, firstly because it pretends to have discovered facts which have always been known ... and secondly and chiefly because it attributes to itself functions that in reality are spiritual, and thus in practice puts itself in the place of religion.[71]

Psychology of the modern kind defines itself by its inability to distinguish between the psychic plane, the arena in which the more or less accidental subjectivities of the individual ego come into play in the depths of the subconscious, and the infinite realm of the spirit which, in terms of the human individual, is signalled by the capacity for the plenary experience and which is thus marked by an 'inward' illimitation and transcendence. The muddling of the psychic realm of the subconscious with the mystical potentialities of the human soul and the infinite reaches of the Intellect has given birth to all manner of confusions. There is indeed a science which reveals the way in which the play of the psyche can communicate universal realities; this is one of the fields of traditional pneumatologies. But, and the proviso is crucial, such a science cannot flourish outside a properly-constituted metaphysic and cosmology. In this context the following passage from Burckhardt deserves the closest attention:

> The connection with the metaphysical order provides spiritual psychology with qualitative criteria such as are wholly lacking in profane psychology, which studies only the dynamic character of phenomena of the psyche and their proximate causes. When modern psychology makes pretensions

---

68 Quoted in W. Perry in 'Drug-Induced Mysticism' *TOMORROW* XII, iii, 1964; p196. (Coomaraswamy was paraphrasing Guénon.)

69 F. Schuon: 'The Psychological Imposture' *TOMORROW* XIV, ii, 1966; p98.

70 On this issue see P. Novak; 'C.J. Jung in the Light of Asian Philosophy' *Religious Traditions* XIV, 1991, and J.M. Reynolds *Self-Liberation through seeing with naked awareness* Station Hill Press, Barrymore, 1989; Appendix 1.

71 F. Schuon: 'The Psychological Imposture', p98.

to a sort of science of the hidden contents of the soul it is still for all that restricted to an individual perspective because it has no real means for distinguishing psychic forms which translate universal realities from forms which appear symbolical but are only vehicles for individual impulses. Its 'collective subconscious' has most assuredly nothing to do with the true source of symbols; at most it is a chaotic depository of psychic residues somewhat like the mud of the ocean bed which retains traces of past epochs.[72]

The confusion of the psychic and the spiritual, which in part stems from the artificial Cartesian dualism of 'body' and 'mind', was discussed by René Guénon at some length in *The Reign of Quantity*. The confusion, he said,

> appears in two contrary forms: in the first, the spiritual is brought down to the level of the psychic; in the second, the psychic is ... mistaken for the spiritual; of this the most popular example is spiritualism ...[73]

The first form of the confusion thus licenses a degrading reductionism and relativism, often as impertinent as it is inadequate. The 'sinister originality' of psychologism lies in its 'determination to attribute every reflex and disposition of the soul to mean causes and to exclude spiritual factors.'[74] This tendency is often partner of a relativism whereby everything becomes

> ... the fruit of a contingent elaboration: Revelation becomes poetry, the Religions are inventions, sages are 'thinkers' ... infallibility and inspiration do not exist, error becomes a quantitative and 'interesting' contribution to 'culture' ... there is ... a denial of every supernatural, or even suprasensory, cause, and by the same token of every principial truth.[75]

Like evolutionism, psychologism attempts to explain the greater in terms of the lesser and excludes all that goes beyond it own limits. In this sense, historicism, relativism and psychologism are all cut from the same cloth:

> The mentality of today seeks to reduce everything to categories connected with time; a work of art, a thought, a truth have no value in themselves and independently of any historical classification ... everything is considered as an expression of a 'period' and not as having possibly a timeless and intrinsic value; and this is entirely in conformity with modern relativism, and with a psychologism ... that destroys essential values. In order to 'situate' the doctrine of a scholastic, or even a Prophet, a 'psycho-analysis' is prepared – it is needless to emphasize the monstrous impudence implicit in such an attitude – and with wholly mechanical and perfectly unreal logic the 'influences' to which this doctrine has been subject are laid bare. There is no hesitation in attributing to saints ... all kind of artificial and even fraudulent conduct; but it is obviously forgotten ... to apply the same principle to oneself, and to explain one's own supposedly 'objective' position by psychological

---

[72] T. Burckhardt *An Introduction to Sufi Doctrine* Thorsons, Northamptonshire, 1976; p37. See also S.H. Nasr *Sufi Essays* pp46ff, and A.K. Coomaraswamy 'On the Indian and Traditional Psychology, or Rather Pneumatology' in AKC *SPII* pp333–378. Coomaraswamy: 'The health envisaged by the empirical psychotherapy is a freedom from particular pathological conditions; that envisaged by the other is a freedom from all conditions and predicaments, a freedom from the infection of mortality ... Furthermore, the pursuit of the greater freedom necessarily entails the attainment of the lesser ...' p335.
[73] RG *RQ* p286. See Chapters XXXIV-XXXV, 'The Misdeeds of Psychoanalysis' and 'The Confusion of the Psychic and the Spiritual', pp273–290.
[74] F. Schuon: 'The Psychological Imposture' p99.
[75] FS *DI* pp154–155.

considerations: sages are treated as being sick men and one takes oneself for a god ... it is a case of expressing a maximum amount of absurdity with a maximum amount of subtlety.[76]

As Schuon remarks elsewhere, relativism goes about reducing every element of absoluteness to a relativity while making a quite illogical exception in favour of this reduction itself.[77]

Clearly these strictures do not apply with the same force to each and every attempt by scholars to detect and explain historical and psychological factors relating to particular religious phenomena. It is possible, for example, to take these kinds of considerations into account in a sympathetic and sensitive way without falling prey to a reductionist relativism. Nevertheless, Schuon's general point remains valid. It can hardly be denied that a kind of iconoclastic psychologism runs through a good deal of the scholarly literature on religion. In addition to the many schools, cliques, factions and splinter groups marching behind the various banners of Freud, Jung, Adler, Maslow, Skinner et. al., a new and militant psychologism is abroad in Academe – a 'feminist psychology' bent on reducing religious manifestations to the camouflaged machinations of an oppressive patriarchy.[78] It is true that feminist scholarship has opened up some new vistas, articulated new questions, and uncovered much hitherto neglected material but much of the enterprise is disfigured by a wholesale sociological and psychologistic reductionism.

A psychologism unrestrained by any values transcending those of a profane science can help to corrode religious forms by infiltrating the religious sphere itself. Schuon notes, by way of an example, the part psychologism has played in discrediting the cult of the Holy Virgin:

> ... only a barbarous mentality that wants to be 'adult' at all costs and no longer believes in anything but the trivial could be embarrassed by this cult. The answer to the reproach of 'gynecolatry' or the 'Oedipus complex' is that, like every other psycho-analytic argument, it by-passes the problem; for the real question is not one of knowing what the psychological factors conditioning an attitude may be but, something very different, namely, what are its results.[79]

The practice of dragging spiritual realities down to the psychological plane can everywhere be seen when religion is reduced to some kind of psychological regimen. Some of the neo-yogic, meditation, 'self-realisation' and 'New Age' movements are of this kind.

> One of the most insidious and destructive illusions is the belief that depth-psychology ... has the slightest connection with spiritual life, which these teachings persistently falsify by confusing inferior elements [psychic] with superior [spiritual]. We cannot be too wary of all these attempts to reduce the values vehicled by tradition to the level of phenomena supposed to be scientifically controllable. The spirit escapes the hold of profane science in an absolute fashion.

---

76 FS *LAW* pp32–33.
77 FS *L&T* p7.
78 See for example M. Daley *Gyn-ecology* The Women's Press, London, 1979, esp pp73–107. For an even more reckless reductionism see P. Chessler *About Men* The Women's Press, London, 1978; pp3–33. For a counter-view see FS *EPW* pp129–146. See also J. Cutsinger: 'Femininity, Hierarchy and God' in *RH* pp110–131.
79 F. Schuon: 'The Psychological Imposture' p101.

Similarly,

> It is not the positive results of experimental science that one is out to deny ... but the absurd claim of science to cover everything possible, the whole of truth, the whole of the real; the quasi-religious claim of totality moreover proves the falseness of the point of departure.[80]

Of course the traditionalists are not alone in unmasking 'the misdeeds of psychoanalysis'. Thomas Merton, for instance:

> Nothing is more repellent than a pseudo-scientific definition of the contemplative experience ... he who attempts such a definition is tempted to proceed psychologically, and there is really no adequate 'psychology' of contemplation ...[81]

Lama Govinda, more alert to this danger than some of his colleagues now in the West, warns of the 'shallow-mindedness' of those who teach a kind of 'pseudo-scientific spirituality'.[82] Mircea Eliade makes a more general point in writing,

> Psychoanalysis justifies its importance by asserting that it forces you to look at and accept reality. But what sort of reality? A reality conditioned by the materialistic and scientific ideology of psychoanalysis, that is, a historical product: we see a thing in which certain scholars and thinkers of the nineteenth century believed.[83]

Psychologistic reductionism, has ramifications on both the practical and the theoretical level: on the one hand we have the notion that psychological techniques and therapies can take the place of authentic spiritual disciplines; on the other, the pretension that psychological science can 'explain' religious phenomena. Both of these are related to the first form of the confusion of the psychic and the spiritual.[84] Let us turn briefly to the obverse side, that of falsely elevating the psychic to the spiritual. There is a vast spiritual wasteland here which we cannot presently explore but Whitall Perry identifies some of its inhabitants in writing of those occultist, psychic, spiritualistic and 'esoteric' groups who concern themselves with

> spirits, elementals, materialisations, etheric states, auric eggs, astral bodies, ids, ods and egos, ectoplasmic apparitions, wraiths and visions, subliminal consciousness and collective unconsciousness, doublings, disassociations, functional disintegrations, communications, obsessions and possessions, psychasthenia, animal magnetism, hypnoidal therapeutics, vibrations, thought-forces, mind-waves and radiations, clairvoyances and audiences and levitations, telepathic dreams, premonitions, death lights, trance writings, Rochester knockings, Buddhic bodies, and sundry other emergences and extravagances of hideous nomenclature ...[85]

---

80 F. Schuon: 'No Activity Without Truth' p37. See also FS *SW* p38 and FS *LAW* pp34ff.
81 T. Merton *New Seeds of Contemplation* New Directions, New York, 1972; pp6–7.
82 A. Govinda *Creative Meditation and Multi-Dimensional Consciousness* Quest, Illinois, 1976; p70.
83 M. Eliade *No Souvenirs* Harper & Row, New York, 1977; p269.
84 For some traditionalist literature in this field see, as well as the sources cited, D.M. Matheson: 'Psychoanalysis and Spirituality' *TOMORROW* XIII, ii, 1965; and W. Perry: 'The Revolt against Moses: A New Look at Psycho-analysis' *TOMORROW* XIV, i, 1966.
85 WP *TTW* p437. What Coomaraswamy said of the individual subconscious can be applied to the psychic realm as a whole: it is 'a sink of psychic residues, a sort of garbage pit or compost heap, fitted only for the roots of "plants", and far removed from the light that erects them.' Cited by Perry, p437.

all the while imagining that these are the stuff of the spiritual life. Much of Guénon's work was directed to reasserting the proper distinctions between psychic phenomena and spiritual realities and to sounding a warning about the infernal forces to which the psychic occultists unwittingly expose themselves. As Schuon remarks, '... modern occultism is by and large no more than the study of extrasensory phenomena, one of the most hazardous pursuits by reason of its wholly empirical character and its lack of any doctrinal basis.'[86] Without the protective shield of traditional doctrines and disciplines, such as those which guarded the shamans, any incursions into these realms are fraught with perils of the gravest kind. In a traditional discipline the psychic can be reintegrated with the spiritual but without the necessary metaphysical framework and religious supports psychism becomes wholly infra-intellectual and anti-spiritual.

The anti-traditional temper of modernism can also be gauged in one of its most typical off-spring, namely humanism. Humanism is not, of course, a single-headed monster but an ideological hydra stalking the modern world seeking whom it may devour. The humanisms of such representative figures as say, Bertrand Russell, Julian Huxley and Jean-Paul Sartre, present different philosophical countenances, some more unattractive than others.[87] However, we can isolate a defining characteristic in all these secularist humanisms be they atheistic or agnostic, 'optimistic' or 'pessimistic', Marxist or existentialist or 'scientific': the insistence that man's nature and purpose is to be defined and understood purely in terms of his terrestrial existence. This amounts to a kind of first principle in humanism wherein man is seen as an autonomous, self-sufficient being who need look no further than himself in 'explaining' the meaning of life and who need pay homage to nothing beyond himself. We may take Marx's dictum as a kind of central 'dogma' of secular humanism: 'Man is free only if he owes his existence to himself.'[88] Man, in other words, is indeed the measure of all things.

Such a principle blatantly contradicts the teachings of all the religious traditions without exception and is the most fundamental point at issue between humanism and traditionalism. Schuon states the traditionalist position plainly enough:

> To say that man is the measure of all things is meaningless unless one starts from the idea that God is the measure of man ... nothing is fully human that is not determined by the Divine, and therefore centered on it. Once man makes of himself a measure, while refusing to be measured in turn ... all human landmarks disappear; once cut off from the Divine, the human collapses.[89]

Or, more succinctly, 'to find man, one must aspire to God'.[90] As one commentator recently observed, 'If anything characterises "modernity", it is a loss of faith in

---

86 FS *L&T* p1. See also R. Guénon: 'Explanation of Spiritist Phenomena' *TOMORROW* XIV, i, 1966; RG *RQ passim*; S.H. Nasr *Sufi Essays* pp40–41.
87 For a sample of humanist writings see J. Huxley (ed) *The Humanist Frame* Allen & Unwin, London, 1961. See especially Huxley's own introductory essay; pp13–48.
88 Quoted by S. Radhakrishnan in P.A. Schilpp (ed) *The Philosophy of Sarvepalli Radhakrishnan* Tudor, New York, 1952; p50.
89 FS *SW* p47.
90 FS *PM* p16.

The Critique of Modernism

transcendence, in a reality that encompasses but surpasses our quotidian affairs.'[91] Humanism is both cause and result of this loss of faith.

One of the most implausible tenets of humanism, explicitly avowed or not – it is inescapable – is that God is a fiction which has played our ancestors false. To this Schuon makes the following reply:

> There are those who claim that the idea of God is to be explained only by social opportunism, without taking account of the infinite disproportion and the contradiction involved in such a hypothesis: if men such as Plato, Aristotle or Thomas Aquinas – not to mention the Prophets, or Christ, or the sages of Asia – were not capable of remarking that God is merely a social prejudice or some other dupery of the kind, and if hundreds and thousands of years have been based intellectually on their incapacity, then there is no human intelligence, and still less any possibility of progress, for a being absurd by nature does not contain the possibility of ceasing to be absurd.[92]

Humanism often goes hand-in-hand with an evolutionist perspective on the past which suggests that we have 'progressed' beyond the superstitions and obscurations which blinkered our ancestors.

> Opinions now current prove that people think themselves incomparably more 'realistic' than anyone has ever been, even in the recent past. What we call 'our own times' or 'the twentieth century' or 'the atomic age' seems to hover, like an uprooted island or a fabulously clear-headed monad, above millennia of childishness and fecklessness. The contemporary world is like a man ashamed of having had parents and wanting to create himself, and to recreate space, time and all physical laws as well, and seeking to extract from nothing a world objectively perfect and subjectively comfortable, and all this by means of a creative activity independent of God. The unfortunate thing is that attempts to create a new order of Being can only end in self-destruction.[93]

So much does the humanist philosophy depend on this condescension to the past that it is difficult to imagine any contemporary humanism divorced from the evolutionism which supports it.

The humanist failure to recognise the transcendent dimension in human life and its indifference or hostility to the very idea of God has all manner of ramifications: it impoverishes our view of reality, breeds all kinds of false definitions of man, and produces a chimerical 'humanitarianism', as well as encouraging negative attitudes to the past and to tradition itself. Humanists, by definition, are sceptical about the claims of the great religious teachings. The humanist outlook is seen, by its exponents, as 'open-minded', 'sane', unfettered by 'prejudices' and 'superstitions'. It seems not to occur to humanists that their own attitudes are simply the prejudices of a modernist rationalistic materialism, nor that scepticism may be a function of ignorance rather than knowledge.[94] As Schuon remarks,

---

91 A reviewer (name not given) in H. Smith: 'Excluded Knowledge: A Critique of the Western Mind Set' *Teachers College Record* LXXX, iii, 1981; p432, fn17.
92 FS *SW* p36. Also see pp19–20.
93 FS *LAW* p100.
94 FS *SW* pp19–20.

> Men think they have 'solid earth' under their feet and that they possess a real power; they feel perfectly 'at home' on earth and attach much importance to themselves, whereas they know neither whence they came nor whither they are going and are drawn through life by an invisible cord.[95]

The denial of God and of the transcendent leads to a debased understanding of human nature and to corrupting definitions of 'man'. Pressed to define 'man' the humanist will more often than not resort to some evasive evolutionist tactic. Man, we might be told, is a large-brained and exceptionally intelligent animal, or a tool-making or game-playing or language-using or self-conscious or rational or political animal. To the traditionalist ear such definitions simply sound inane: as Schumacher remarks, one might just as well define a dog as a 'barking plant' or a 'running cabbage'.[96] Furthermore,

> Nothing is more conducive to the brutalisation of the modern world than the launching, in the name of science, of wrongful and degraded definitions of man, such as 'the naked ape'. What could one expect of such a creature . . . ?[97]

The fabrication of dehumanising social forms on the external plane depends on our assent to thought-forms which deny or distort our real nature. Here humanism is more part of the problem than the solution.[98]

The social idealism and 'humanitarianism' on which humanists pride themselves is a sentimental illusion which is fed by an ignorance concerning man's true nature and his ultimate ends. The humanists would have us forget the first of Christ's two great commandments and have us pursue the second as a kind of social principle or ideal. But, as Schuon points out,

> Love of God could not defraud creatures: we may forget men in loving God without thereby lacking charity towards them, but we cannot, without defrauding both men and ourselves, forget God while loving men.[99]

In this context it might be noted that humanist values have played a part in perforating the fabric of Christianity and in denaturing it into a kind of sentimental humanitarianism which envisages the Kingdom of God as a kind of earthly Super Welfare State.[100]

All of the '-isms' that have been under discussion in this chapter, as well as countless other modernist ideologies with which they consort, amount to bogus philosophies because they betray our real nature. Let us end this chapter with a reminder from S.H.Nasr as to wherein lies the key to man's real nature. Nasr's statement is one that would be endorsed in all the religious traditions and one which, by the same token, would be rejected by humanists:

---

95 FS *LAW* p112.
96 E.F. Schumacher: *op.cit.*; p31.
97 *ibid.*
98 See P. Sherrard: 'Modern Science and the Dehumanisation of Man' p79.
99 FS *SW* p109. 'If Rousseau and other "idealists" had forseen all the outcomes of their inane philanthropy they would have become Carthusian monks.' *ibid.* p111 fn1. See also FS *EPW* pp104, 154 & 162, and FS *DI* p131.
100 See Lord Northbourne *Religion in the Modern World* p16 and Gai Eaton *King of the Castle* pp16ff.

> Man's central position in the world is not due to his cleverness or his inventive genius but because of the possibility of attaining sanctity and becoming a channel of grace for the world around him ... the very grandeur of the human condition is precisely that he has the possibility of reaching a state 'higher than the angels' and at the same time of denying God.[101]

It is the latter choice which gives modernism its essential character.

---

101 S.H. Nasr *Ideals and Realities of Islam* pp24–25. See also FS *EPW* p34.

11

Counterfeit Spirituality

Truth does not deny forms from the outside but transcends them from within
Frithjof Schuon [1]

Syncretism is never an affair of substance: it is an assembling of heterogeneous elements into a false unity...
Frithjof Schuon [2]

Freedom from self requires a method ... and recourse to cosmic principles that transcend the limitations of the human individuality ... And yet there are those who would vanquish the ego while obstinately refusing submission to a legitimate traditional form ... Autodetermination in spiritual matters amounts to intellectual anarchy
Whitall Perry [3]

... the worst of these false idealisms are, in certain respects, those which annex and adulterate religion   *Frithjof Schuon* [4]

A good deal of misunderstanding has been sponsored by the notion that all those thinkers and groups which espouse some kind of 'perennial philosophy' can be gathered together under this insignia: theosophists, anthroposophists, Gurdjieffians, neo-Hindu universalists, neo-Deists, pseudo-mystical romantics, syncretists, and occultists are herded together with traditionalists like Coomaraswamy and Schuon to rub shoulders under this philosophical canopy. P.J. Saher, for instance, groups together Aldous Huxley, Radhakrishnan, Gerald Heard, Herman Hesse, Christopher Isherwood, Ramakrishna, Coomaraswamy, Vivekananda and Aurobindo, amongst others.[5] However, even a modest inquiry will reveal that the similarities between such thinkers are superficial, the differences quite radical. While all these figures may indeed affirm some kind of timeless, universal wisdom they do so from different philosophical and metaphysical vantage points, elaborate quite divergent conceptions of what the perennial philosophy comprises, and educe quite different 'programs' from it. We remember Guénon's misgivings about the pseudo-traditionalists of his day — how much more appalled he would have been to find the ideas to which he gave expression lumped together with some of the reckless and bizarre claims made under the aegis of 'perennial philosophy'!

Our central concern in this chapter is the exposure of the divergences between traditionalism and some other perspectives with which it has been confused. We shall not confine ourselves to the ideas of thinkers who have sometimes been hailed as 'perennial philosophers' but will also consider the 'new consciousness' movements and the misnamed 'new religions' from a traditionalist viewpoint. The discussion will open with some general remarks about a number of the fundamental differences between the traditionalists and representatives of various other schools of thought which have become popular in recent times. We shall then turn to the 'consciousness' movements in a general kind of way, making some reference to Alan Watts and Jiddu Krishnamurti, and to neo-Hinduism. The latter part of the chapter will focus attention on four figures: Swami Vivekananda, Sarvepalli Radhakrishnan, Aldous Huxley, and Georgi Ivanovitch Gurdjieff. The intention here is to show that despite some apparent similarities there is no common measure between the ideas of these men and those to which the traditionalists give voice.

The traditionalist position can often be marked off from others by a clear definition of its stance *vis-à-vis* religious forms, syncretism and the possibilities of a universal religion. Although its position on these questions should be apparent from our earlier discussion it might be as well to reiterate some of the central principles involved. It

---

1 FS *SPHF* p112.
2 FS *LAW* p123.
3 WP *TTW* p271.
4 FS *THC* p30.
5 See P.J. Saher *Eastern Wisdom and Western Thought* Allen & Unwin, London, 1969; pp123–162. A less injudicious but nevertheless misleading association of the traditionalists and neo-deists, neo-Hindus and the Huxleyan vision of the perennial philosophy is made in E.J. Sharpe *Comparative Religion* Duckworth, London, 1975; pp262–263. For a similar confusion see G. Parrinder *Comparative Religion* Allen & Unwin, London, 1962; pp79–91, and R.S. Ellwood: book review in *Journal of the American Academy of Religion* XLV, 1977; p256. Another reviewer confounds traditionalism with theosophy. See F. H. Heinemann's otherwise intelligent review of FS *TUR* in *Journal of Theological Studies* VI, 1955; p338. These are only a few examples from amongst many.

is impossible both in principle and in fact to construct a new, universal religion. The traditionalists are intent on demonstrating the universal content of each religious tradition. This demonstration also situates the formal antagonisms between different exotericisms in a perspective which allows those capable of doing so to perceive 'the transcendent unity of religions' – the use of the qualifying adjective is crucial. At the same time traditionalism seeks to preserve the formal embodiments of each religious tradition, of each spiritual economy, these being self-sufficient and entirely adequate in providing all things needful to the civilisations in which they have appeared. The traditionalists envisage no universal religion but a gnosis which resolves the formal antinomies of the exoteric domain. This is in no way an attempt to dispense with or bypass the exotericisms as such or to down play the importance of the religious orthodoxies which have providentially been manifested in response to the differing needs of various human collectivities. Rather it is an attempt to discern the universal content of each religion and thereby demonstrate both its sufficiency and its essential unity with all other orthodox religions. In this sense it might be called synthetic, which is to say that it 'starts from principles ... from that which is innermost; it goes, one might say, from the centre to the circumference'.[6] This could not provide the platform for a new or universal religion; the use of either adjective with the word 'religion' is, in a traditionalist context, a contradiction in terms. The traditionalist insistence on a single Unitive Truth at the heart of each religious tradition in no way implies any syncretistic possibility whatsoever.

Syncretism, in Guénon's words, is

> ... the juxtaposition of elements of diverse origin, assembled 'from the outside' ... without any principle of a more profound order to unify them ... such a conglomeration cannot constitute a doctrine, any more than a pile of stones can constitute a building.[7]

Such syncretism should not be confused with a legitimate eclecticism whereby ideas and principles hitherto alien are assimilated into a tradition to illuminate and corroborate the spiritual perspective in question. The integration of Platonism into Christianity is a case in point.

Any syncretic attempt to fashion a 'universal religion' is bound to issue, says Coomaraswamy, in nothing but 'a mechanical and lifeless monstrosity' and 'a sort of religious Esperanto'.[8] S.H. Nasr articulates the traditionalist response to all such syncretisms:

> Not only do they not succeed in transcending forms but they fall beneath them, opening the door to all kinds of evil forces affecting those who are unfortunate enough to be duped by their so-called universalism.[9]

Elsewhere Nasr spells out some of the principles which render any kind of syncretistic universalism illegitimate:

---

6 R. Guénon quoted in G. Eaton *The Richest Vein* Faber & Faber, London, 1949; p181.
7 *ibid*. See also RG *RQ* pp296–297, and FS *L&T* pp3–4.
8 'Sri Ramakrishna and Religious Tolerance' in AKC *SPII* pp39–40. See also RL *CLW* p277.
9 S.H. Nasr *Sufi Essays* Allen & Unwin, London, 1972; p147fn38.

> The relation between man and God, or the relative and the Absolute, is central in every religion. Only each religion emphasises a certain aspect of this relationship, while inwardly it contains the Truth as such in its teachings whatever the limitations of its forms might be. That is why to have lived any religion fully is to have lived all religions and there is nothing more meaningless or even pernicious than to create a syncretism from various religions with a claim to universality while in reality one is doing nothing less than destroying the revealed forms which alone make the attachment of the relative to the Absolute, of man to God, possible.[10]

This censure can be directed not only against syncretists but against all those who imagine they can depart from traditional forms with impunity. Indeed the question of religious forms provides an acid test for separating the traditionalists from most of the other so-called perennial philosophers whose hackles are likely to rise at the mere mention of words like 'dogmas' or 'orthodoxy'!

There has recently been a good deal of talk about a 'spiritual revolution' in the West, one which 'promises to transform everything modern man has thought about God and human possibility'.[11] Jacob Needleman is one of many commentators who have written about this 'spiritual explosion' which is evidenced by a proliferation of movements which, we are told, turn 'toward the religions of the East and toward the mystical core of all religion'.[12] Much is made of this 'mystical core' to which all manner of groups claim access.

Amongst the movements surveyed in Needleman's *The New Religions* are 'American Zen', Transcendental Meditation, neo-Vedanta, Subud, 'Humanistic Mysticism' (sic), and groups devoted to the teachings of figures like Meher Baba, Gurdjieff and Krishnamurti. The 'revolution' is, of course, not confined to the U.S.A.: all over the Western world such movements and 'pop gurus' like Alan Watts, Rajneesh and Idries Shah have attracted the loyalties of millions of people. More recently we have had the burgeoning 'New Age' and 'Aquarian' movements. Then too, there is the veritable plague of occultists and 'esoteric' movements ranging from theosophy and Lobsang-Rampaism to black witchcraft and scientology.[13] What are we to make of all this from a traditionalist perspective?

We have already seen how the traditionalists deny the possibility of any new religion whatsoever: a religion finds its source in a divine Revelation and the age of such Revelations has long since passed in the present cycle. This disqualifies any claims to a new dispensation. Movements like Mormonism, Baha'ism or Subud, to

---

10 S.H. Nasr *Ideals and Realities of Islam* Allen & Unwin, London, 1975; p16. (Compare with Max Müller's claim that 'To know one religion is to know none.' From *Introduction to the Science of Religions* (1873) in J. Waardenburg (ed) *Classical Apporaches to the Study of Religion* Mouton, The Hague, 1973; p95.

11 J. Needleman *The New Religions* Pocket Books, New York, 1972; p1.

12 *ibid.*

13 On the 'new religions' see also a later collection edited by Jacob Needleman et al. *Understanding the New Religions* and T. Roszak *The Making of the Counter Culture* Faber & Faber, London, 1970; Ch IV; Mark Hayes: 'The New Consciousness Movement' *Religious Traditions* I, i, 1978; pp43–48; A, Bancroft *Twentieth Century Mystics and Sages* Heinemann, London, 1976 (includes chapters on Huxley, Watts, Teilhard, Krishnamurti, Gurdjieff, Subud, Maharishi Mahesh Yogi and Rudolf Steiner). On occultism and pseudo-spiritual 'esoteric' movements see C.R. Evans *Cults of Unreason* Harrap, London, 1973 (includes sections on scientology, Gurdjieff, 'black box' cults, UFO-ism, and Lobsang Rampa). It is interesting to note that it was two traditionalists, Marco Pallis and Richard Nicholson, who exposed 'Lobsang Rampa' as none other than Mr Cyril Hoskins, plumber, of Thames Ditton, Surrey. See W. Perry's review of Evans in *SCR* IX, iii, 1975; p185. On twentieth century occultism see also M. Eliade *Occultism, Witchcraft and Cultural Fashion* Uni Chicago Press, 1976; pp47–68.

name a few, are for the traditionalists 'signs of the times', symptoms of a spiritual hunger which looks for nourishment in all sorts of implausible places. They could not be authentic and integral religions as such.[14] However, a more serious threat to the teachings of tradition comes from idiosyncratic 'adaptations' of traditional teachings and from those who would overthrow tradition itself.

In a caustic but considered essay Whitall Perry has elaborated a traditionalist critique of some of the characteristics shared by many of the teachings of the 'prophets' of a 'new consciousness'. Amongst the people he mentions as representing 'the tip of the iceberg' are Aldous Huxley, Gerald Heard, R.C. Zaehner, Teilhard de Chardin, Aurobindo, Gopi Krishna, Alan Watts and Krishnamurti – the list is obviously representative rather than exhaustive.[15] Clearly Perry has to deal in this essay with generalities which will apply with varying emphases according to the case at hand but the tendencies to which he takes exception in the work of such people are these:

> ...a patent individualism, a scientific and moralistic humanism, evolutionism, a relativistic 'intuitionism', inability to grasp metaphysical and cosmological principles and the realities of the Universal Domain, a mockery (latent or overt) of the sacred, a prodigal dearth of spiritual imagination, no eschatological understanding, a pseudo-mysticism in the form of a 'cosmic consciousness'.[16]

Shortly we will turn our attention to several other figures to whom such admonitions also apply. For the moment we shall amplify a few of these points with reference to the ideas of Alan Watts and Krishnamurti.

The 'patent individualism' of people like Watts and Krishnamurti is attested by their refusal to submit to any traditional doctrine or spiritual discipline. Watts' flirtation with Zen can hardly pass muster while Krishnamurti was an unabashed iconoclast. Instead of conforming themselves and their ideas to an orthodoxy which would take them past the limitations of individualism they remained locked into various intellectual and existential stalemates which stem from the conflict between an aspiration to 'selflessness' and the absence of any traditional doctrine or method.

In the case of Watts this is plain enough in his later writings which are marked by an ambivalent attitude to the status of the ego. In a searching study of Watts' work Louis Nordstrom and Richard Pilgrim have demonstrated how his self-professed 'spiritual materialism' (his own term) ends, and can only end, in an affirmation of the human ego.[17] No amount of Watts' literary wizardry nor his amiable wit could camouflage the fact. What we find in Watts' later work is indeed what Schuon calls 'the disordered subjectivism of a personal mysticism'.[18] None of this, perhaps, would much matter were it not for the fact that Watts was often seen as a spokesperson for a kind of mystical rapprochement of the different religions. A good many people

---

14 On Subud see E. Van Hien *What is Subud?* Rider, London, 1963. On Baha'i see Sayyid Ali Raza Naqavi: 'Babism and Baha'ism: A Study of their History and Doctrine' *Islamic Studies* XIV, iii, 1975; pp185–217; and J. Nijenhuis: 'Baha'i: World Faith for Modern Man?' *Journal of Ecumenical Studies* X, 1973;pp532ff.

15 W. Perry: 'Anti-Theology and the Riddles of Alcyone' *SCR* VI, iii, 1972; pp176–192 (hereafter referred to as WP: 'ATRA'). For material on Teilhard see references in last chapter.

16 WP: 'ATRA' p186.

17 L. Nordstrom & R. Pilgrim: 'The Wayward Mysticism of Alan Watts' *Philosophy East and West* XXX, iii, 1980; p381–399.

18 F. Schuon: 'Nature and Function of the Spiritual Master' *SCR* I, ii, 1967; p54.

would endorse the claim that Watts 'has done more perhaps than any other writer to open the eyes of the West to the spiritual significance of Eastern religions and philosophies and to show that Truth is not the monopoly of any one school.'[19] Watts indeed affirmed that 'the Paths are many but their end is One'.[20] Insofar as this principle governed Watts' enterprise we can applaud it but the real question is whether he was qualified to understand and interpret traditional doctrines. The traditionalist judgement must be that he was not: his interpretation of traditional doctrines was too idiosyncratic to carry any authority. The title of his autobiography, *In My Own Way*, is a more fitting epitaph than he realised.

The Krishnamurti fiasco is a well-known chapter in the history of the theosophical movement. However, despite his disavowal of the Messianic role envisaged for him, Krishnamurti has since '... done nothing to dispel the illusion that he has a crucial message for mankind about the inner transformation of the individual with its consequent outward transformation of society.'[21] Perry has exposed some of the central contradictions which hide behind a 'smoke screen of sophistries' in Krishnamurti's work. We shall not rehearse Perry's case here: it is there for those who care to find it. Suffice it to note that Krishnamurti's wholesale rejection of 'dogma, religion, church and all that immature nonsense' stamp him as an inveterate anti-traditionalist.[22] It is perhaps worth noting Perry's condign remark that

> ... the man is in fact a victim of the very thought conditioning he would reject, being a product of the Brahmanic heritage from which he has deviated. The violence of his reaction to religion is a manifestation of exactly the sort of antagonism, resistance, opposition and conflict which he pretends to be rejecting.[23]

The subjective orientation of the thinkers targeted in Perry's essay goes hand-in-hand with what he calls a 'prodigal dearth of spiritual imagination' which signals another anti-traditional tendency:

> For a few very bright gentlemen of our century ... to speak as if they have discovered spiritual truths of which the entire humanity of the world was hitherto been in ignorance – that untold millions of Hindus, Buddhists, Taoists, Confucianists, Shintoists, Jews, Christians, Muslims, plus countless other ethnic groups have all shared in common the same errors ... and for these personages to hold forth as though there had never been Solomon, Shankara, Plato, Ibn 'Arabi, Eckhart, Nagarjuna, Chuang-tse and the rest – for such a phenomenon to be possible surely the politest explanation one can give is lack of imagination.[24]

This attitude is also often supported with a kind of evolutionism which suggests that man is now on the brink of a 'new consciousness'. The 'scientific and moralistic humanism' to which Perry refers exposes itself in the tendencies towards a Utopian vision of the possibilities of a science and technology wedded to a 'new consciousness'

---

19 L. Watts: 'Foreword' to A. Watts *In My Own Way* Random House, New York, 1972; ppvii-viii.
20 *ibid.*
21 WP: 'ATRA' p182.
22 Krishnamurti in *Talks and Dialogues, Saanen, 1967* Sevire, Netherlands, 1969, quoted in WP: 'ATRA' p183.
23 WP: 'ATRA' p184. See also P.T. Raju *Idealistic Thought of India* Allen & Unwin, London, 1953; p399-400. (This sort of comment has also been made, with some justice, about Freud's attitude to religion.)
24 WP: 'ATRA' p191. See also FS *LAW* pp95-101.

towards which we have 'evolved'. It was the Canadian R.M. Bucke who, through a book of that name, brought the term 'cosmic consciousness' into popular parlance. Bucke spoke of '... an intelligent enlightenment which alone would place the individual on a new plane of existence – would make him almost a member of a new species...'.[25] The evolutionist bias of this kind of thinking is plain enough and contrasts sharply with the traditionalist insistence that 'the ontological situation of man in the total scheme of things is always the same'.[26] As Perry notes, for most of these self-styled anti-dogmatists evolutionism is a 'dogma' of the most inviolable and inflexible kind.[27]

'Cosmic consciousness' has become a kind of catch-all wherein a vague and sentimental 'mysticism' consorts with a pseudo-scientific evolutionism. The working premise behind many of the 'cosmic consciousness' outpourings, of which Watts' *The Book of the Taboo Against Knowing Who You Are* (1973) is a characteristic example, is that the self and the universe are identical and that when the self perceives the identity there is 'enlightenment' or 'cosmic consciousness'. There is, of course, an echo of the Upanisadic *Ātman-Brahman* formulation here but usually in prostituted guise, wrapped up in quasi-psychological jargon, unsupported by any metaphysical rigour and unverified by authentic mystical experience and gnosis. One might also point out a fact frequently overlooked: in the Vedantic metaphysic, *Brahman* is by no means identical or equatable with the universe and the very term 'cosmic consciousness' implies a view still entrapped in *māyā*.[28]

Theodore Roszak issues a timely warning about the need for a genuine spiritual discrimination amidst the plethora of 'consciousness' movements:

> The power to tell the greater from the lesser reality, the sacred paradigm from its copies and secular counterfeits ... without it, the consciousness circuit will surely become a lethal swamp of paranormal entertainments, facile therapeutic tricks, authoritarian guru trips, demonic subversions.[29]

For the traditionalists, less sanguine than Roszak, these words serve better not as a warning but as a picture of present reality.

As Arvind Sharma has noted, a distinctive approach to religious pluralism has been associated with Hinduism, at least since the appearance of Swami Vivekananda at the World Parliament of Religions in Chicago in 1893. This approach has variously been described as 'accommodating, catholic, universal, open, assimilative, synthetic, hospitable, liberal, syncretistic, and above all tolerant'.[30] The neo-Hindu renaissance associated with such figures as Rammohan Roy, Keshab Chandra Sen, Swami Vivekananda, the Tagores, Aurobindo Ghose, and more recently Sarvepalli Radha-

---

25 Quoted in M. Hayes: *op.cit.*; p45.
26 S.H. Nasr *Sufi Essays* p93.
27 WP: 'ATRA' p187.
28 See M. Hiriyana *Essentials of Indian Philosophy* Allen & Unwin, London, 1978; pp15ff.
29 T. Roszak *Unfinished Animal* Faber & Faber, London, 1975; p13.
30 A. Sharma: 'All religions are – equal? one? same?: A critical examination of some formulations of the neo-Hindu position' *Philosophy East and West* XXIX, i, 1979; p59.

krishnan, has exhibited a strong universalist strain which, at certain points, coincides with traditionalism. It is not our present purpose to explicate Hindu approaches to religious pluralism[31] nor to address any questions concerning its philosophical, historical or social sources.[32] Rather we shall focus on a general question which will take on more specificity through a detailed discussion of Vivekananda and Radhakrishnan: what are some of the characteristic attitudes and values of neo-Hinduism which are most sharply at odds with traditionalism?

A shaping factor in the emergence of neo-Hinduism was the Western education to which most of its architects were exposed.[33] Inevitably they assimilated many of the prevailing European prejudices of the day, most notably the over-valuation of rationality and the potentialities of science, the belief in progress and the evolutionist assumptions which coloured nearly every aspect of late nineteenth century European thought, the notion that religious traditions were 'outmoded', the emphasis on the social and ethical aspects of religion to the neglect of the doctrinal and metaphysical. All of these were stock-in-trade for the Hindu reformers. It is, of course, no accident that the two figures who really exemplify the Hindu tradition in recent times, Ramakrishna and Ramana Maharshi, were innocent of these Western assumptions.[34] Western education did not necessarily disqualify one from either an orthodox Hindu or a traditionalist outlook as we see in the case of Coomaraswamy. Generally, however, the exposure to Western ideas, allied with an awareness of a decadence within contemporary Hinduism, produced in the reformers an attitude to tradition that was at best ambivalent. Movements like the Brahmo-Samaj were aggressively iconoclastic and served to erode the belief in Vedic authority, the *sine qua non* of Hindu orthodoxy, and to elevate the authority of reason, common sense, personal intuition or conscience. The whole idea of the supra-human origin and the authority of tradition was thus jeopardized. The traditionalist position hinges on these two principles. Many of the neo-Hindus did affirm a kind of perennial philosophy. Indeed Agehananda Bharati sees 'all religions are one' as the key notion of the Hindu Renaissance.[35] Nonetheless, without any firm commitment to the principle of Revelation, the similarities to traditionalism remain more apparent than real.

The modern Hindu attitude to other religions sometimes looks rather like an indiscriminate hospitality to anything and everything. This, of course, has its positive aspects when based on a proper metaphysical discernment but more often the 'accommodating' position of the neo-Hindus looks more like a kind of 'liberalism'. Consider, for instance, the implications of a formulation such as this, from Radhakrishnan:

---

31 See A. Sharma: *op.cit.; passim.*

32 See A. Sharma: 'Some Misunderstandings of the Hindu Apporach to Religious Plurality' *Religion* VIII, 1978; pp133ff.

33 For an introduction to neo-Hinduism see V.S. Naravane *Modern Indian Thought* Asia Publishing House, Bombay, 1964, and V.S. Naravane & R.S. McDermott *The Spirit of Modern India* Thomas Crowell, New York, 1974 (an anthology including selections from Roy, Keshub, Vivekananda, Aurobindo, Radhakrishnan, Gandhi, Rabindranath Tagore and Vinoba Bhave). For traditionalist commentary see A.K. Saran: 'The Crisis of Hinduism' *SCR* V, ii, 1971; pp92-110 and FS LS Chs1-4.

34 For serviceable introductions to these two figures see T.M.P. Mahadevan *Ramana Maharshi, the Sage of Arunacala* Allen & Unwin, London, 1977, and C. Isherwood *Ramakrishna and His Disciples* Advaita Ashrama, Calcutta, 1974.

35 A. Bharati: 'The Hindu Renaissance and Its Apologetic Patterns' *Journal of Asian Studies* XXIX, 1970; p278. For some discussion of 'tradition' and 'modernity' in India see M. Chatterjee: 'Tradition and Modernity with Respect to Religion in India'; F. Streng: ' "Sacred" and "Secular" as Terms for Interpreting Modernisation in India'; A.K. Saran: 'The Meaning and Forms of Secularism: A Note' – all in *Religious Traditions* II, i, 1979; pp14-20, 21-29 and 38-51 respectively.

'We may measure true spiritual culture by the comprehension and veneration we are able to give to forms of thought and feeling which have influenced masses of mankind.'[36] At first sight this looks like an entirely estimable attitude of tolerance and open-mindedness. However, a little reflection reveals it as a woolly platitude. Which 'forms of thought and feeling'? Do we include such aggressively anti-spiritual movements as fascism and communism? Should we 'venerate' an acquisitive materialism which presently influences 'masses of mankind'? If Radhakrishnan is talking of the different religions, how adequate a description is 'forms of thought and feeling'? The vagueness of this kind of 'open-mindedness' is characteristic. Furthermore, let us not forget that

> To tolerate the opinions of other people does not necessarily imply respect; it can also go hand in hand with a neutrality not untinged with contempt; the emphasis here is subjective, the supposed right to hold whatever opinions one pleases; an objective appreciation of those opinions as such hardly enters in.[37]

There is also in neo-Hinduism, as the term implies, a suspicion of tradition as such, of the religious and social forms which it carried. Doubtless some of the reforms advocated by the neo-Hindus could be justified as a return to traditional norms or as an attempt to cleanse Indian society of abuses which had no traditional legitimacy. More often, however, the reforming impulse was impelled not by traditional principles but by social and political values imported from the West.[38] In this context the terms 'Westernisation' and 'modernisation', the one implying an imitation of a spatially identified culture and the other an adherence to a temporally restricted mentality, are both appropriate.

As with many quasi-spiritual modernist movements, neo-Hinduism decisively parts company with traditionalism over the question of religious forms. In the writings of people like Vivekananda and Radhakrishnan we repeatedly find the idea that traditional religious and social forms (dogmas, rites, myths, institutions like caste) can be abandoned in the name of some apparently higher ideal – 'truth', 'social justice', 'reason', 'science' and such. Vivekananda's assertion that 'Temples and churches, books and forms are simply the kindergarten of religion . . .' is typical: it is justified in the name of 'realisation'.[39] The traditionalists would agree, of course, that realisation takes precedence over all other claims but this is no reason to capitulate to the 'mystical prejudice' that nothing counts in the spiritual life except 'states' – a prejudice widespread in India.[40] What Vivekananda does not add, as any traditionalist would, is the necessity and value of forms which must remain inviolate for the vast majority of believers. Schuon's cautionary words could not be more pertinent:

> When a man seeks to escape from 'dogmatic narrowness' it is essential that it should be 'upwards'

---

36 S. Radhakrishnan: 'Fragments of a Confession' in P.A. Schilpp (ed) *The Philosophy of Sarvapelli Radhakrishnan* Tudor, New York, 1952; p72.
37 M. Pallis *A Buddhist Spectrum* Allen & Unwin, London, 1980; p111.
38 See A.K. Coomaraswamy: 'The Bugbear of Literacy' and 'The Bugbear of Democracy, Freedom and Equality' in AKC BL.
39 Vivekananda quoted in A.R. Wadia in 'Swami Vivekananda's Philosophy of Religion' in R.C. Majumdar (ed) *Swami Vivekananda's Memorial Volume* Swami Vivekananda Centenary, Calcutta, 1963; p257.
40 See FS *TM* p9.

and not 'downwards': dogmatic form is transcended by fathoming its depths and contemplating its universal content, and not by denying it in the name of a pretentious and iconoclastic 'ideal' of 'pure truth'.[41]

Vivekananda did not, in fact, deny forms altogether but his attitude to them is condescending and irreverent. In view of the fact that many 'modern Hindus derive their knowledge of Hinduism from Vivekananda',[42] one can only wonder at the possible consequences of such an attitude.

A final general point before turning to Vivekananda in more detail: the traditionalists affirm a *sophia perennis* at the heart of each integral tradition without bias towards any particular tradition and without any wish to synthesize or distil any 'universal' or 'new' religion; some of the neo-Hindus tend to the view that almost anything which claims to be religious (no matter what the criteria!) has something to offer but that *Advaita* Vedanta (as understood by themselves) provides a platform on which can be mounted some kind of universal religion. This, for example, from Vivekananda: 'Vedanta, and Vedanta alone can become the universal religion of man ... no other is fitted for that role.'[43] Now, Schuon himself is the first to affirm that Shankara's perspective is 'one of the most adequate expressions possible of the *philosophia perennis* or sapiential esoterism'.[44] But we will certainly not find him indulging in loose talk about a 'universal religion' nor claiming that Vedanta is the sole possible expression of what it expresses: there are, for instance, no essential differences between Vedanta and Platonism save that the latter is more concerned with cosmology.[45]

A useful starting point for any traditionalist assessment of Vivekananda is his relationship with Ramakrishna. Schuon has written eloquently about the *Paramahamsa* and his mission:

> In Ramakrishna there is something which seems to defy every category: he was like the living symbol of the inner unity of religions; he was, in fact, the first saint to wish to penetrate foreign spiritual forms, and in this consisted his exceptional and in a sense universal mission ... In our times of confusion, disarray and doubt he was the saint called to 'verify' forms and 'reveal', if one can so express it, their single truth ... His spiritual plasticity was of a miraculous order.[46]

While leaving no doubt as to Ramakrishna's sanctity and the spiritual radiance which emanated from his person, Schuon notes several vulnerabilities in his position *vis-à-vis* an emergent neo-Hinduism: a *jñāna* extrinsically ill-supported because of his almost exclusive faith in the spiritual omnipotence of love, whence 'an inadequate integration of the mind in his perspective'; a universalism 'too facile because purely bhaktic'; an absence of safeguards against the dissolving influences of a modernism which left the saint himself untouched but which pervaded the milieu in which he found himself and which, in a sense, took a posthumous revenge through the influence of

---

41 FS *SW* p16.
42 A. Bharati: *op.cit.*; p278.
43 Quoted in P. Atmaprana: 'Swami Vivekananda on Harmony of Religions and Religious Sects' in R.C. Majumdar: *op.cit.*; p311.
44 FS *EPW* p21.
45 *ibid.*; p22.
46 FS *SPHF* pp115 & 119.

Vivekananda.[47] Ramakrishna, although instinctively suspicious of movements like the Brahmo-Samaj, was not altogether cognizant of the dangers posed by modernism. Furthermore, he attributed to his disciple Narendra 'a genius for ontological and plastic realisation which he neither had nor could have'[48], Narendra (later Swami Vivekananda) being a person in the grip of certain 'dynamic' mental tendencies which precluded any kind of realisation comparable to that of the Master himself.[49]

In a traditional framework which was 'entire, closed and without fissures' the potentialities for heterodoxy which lurked in Vivekananda's make-up might well have been 'rectified, neutralised and compensated'. However, as it was, Vivekananda's development was shaped not only by the *Paramahamsa* but an 'Occidentalism which was unknown and incomprehensible to Ramakrishna but which stimulated in the disciple exactly those tendencies the development of which had at times been feared by the master.'[50] One such development, of which Ramakrishna had some premonition, was the founding of a sect or order, a function which he explicitly rejected as being outside Vivekananda's proper vocation.[51] It might also be noted that Ramakrishna could not have foreseen the consequences of causes which he himself had not conceived – the fact, for instance, that Vivekananda's interpretation of Vedanta was to be filtered through a screen of misconceptions and prejudices which derived not only from his own disposition but from modernist influences.

Schuon concedes that the enigma of Vivekananda can perhaps be explained in terms of the fact that Hindu-Indian nationalism was inevitable and that the Swami was its predestined champion. In order to fulfil such a role Vivekananda had need of a certain anti-traditional mental dynamism and of some of the ideological premises of the modern West:

> In 'modernising' Hinduism Vivekananda did at the same time 'Hinduize' modernism, if one may so put it, and by that means neutralised some of its destructive impetus ... if it was inevitable that India should become a 'nation' it was preferable that it should become so in some way under the distant auspices of Ramakrishna rather than under the sign of a modernism that brutally denied all that had given India its reason to live for thousands of years past. [52]

This notwithstanding, the fact remains that much of Vivekananda's teaching was anti-traditional, both intrinsically and extrinsically. It is as clear as the day from his own writings that his conception of tradition was of the vaguest kind, that he had scant understanding of the reciprocal relationships of the exoteric and esoteric dimensions of religion, that he was less than vigilant in preserving 'the incalculable values of orthodoxy', that much of his talk about 'universal religion' is of the sentimental variety, that his understanding of Vedanta is compromised by modernist ideas, and that he had none of his master's genius for penetrating foreign religious forms. In

---

47 *ibid.*; pp116–118.
48 *ibid.*; p119.
49 *ibid.*; p124.
50 *ibid.*; p118.
51 See Swami Vireswarananda's *Life of Shri Ramakrishna* cited by Schuon in *SPHF* pp188–189fn. Incidentally, Schuon does point out that 'there are contemplatives of the line of Ramakrishna whose spirituality is impeccable' and who transmit 'a perfectly regular doctrine ... whatever may be their feelings on the subject of Vivekananda.' Swami Brahmananda is one such. See p120fn.
52 *ibid.*; p121.

brief, there is no common measure between Ramakrishna and Vivekananda.[53] None of this is to gainsay the Swami's prodigious talents, his personal charisma, or his effectiveness as a spearhead for the Hindu Renaissance: such considerations are not germane to our present purposes.

Vivekananda's penchant for the facile formulation and his disregard for traditional proprieties is suggested by his equation of Jesus, the Buddha and Ramakrishna. It is worth rehearsing Schuon's objections to this 'trinity':

> It is unacceptable, first, because it is impossible in a truly Hindu perspective to put Buddha and Christ in a trinity to the exclusions of Rama and Krishna; secondly because Christ is foreign to India; thirdly, because, if non-Hindu worlds are taken into account, there is no reason for taking only Christ into consideration still, of course, from the point of view of Hinduism; fourthly because there is no common measure between the river Ramakrishna and the oceans that were Jesus and the Buddha; fifthly, because Ramakrishna lived at a period in the cycle which could in any case no longer contain a plenary incarnation of the amplitude of the great Revealers; sixthly, because, in the Hindu system there is no room for another plenary and 'solar' incarnation of Divinity between the ninth and the tenth Avataras of Vishnu – the Buddha and the future *Kalki-Avatāra*. 'A single Prophet', such is the teaching of Et-Tahawi, 'is more excellent than the whole number of all the friends of God' (the saints).[54]

This reproach is made in a footnote to a discussion of Muhummad, more or less as an aside. It might be thought that to quote it at such length over what some will see as a minor point, is disproportionate. However, this is an illuminating passage in several respects: it demonstrates the principial rigour which always shapes Schuon's work; it alerts us to the fact that Schuon is more conversant than Vivekananda with the claims and proprieties of Hindu tradition; the recourse to another tradition to corroborate a point is typical of Schuon's *modus operandi*; and the passage reminds us again of the dangers of a 'hospitality' offered at the expense of doctrinal rigour and discrimination.

A small sample of quotes will be sufficient to expose the most absurd errors and incomprehensions of Vivekananda's thought. No traditionalist would be capable, in any circumstances whatever, of giving voice to anything like the following:

> The visions of Moses are more likely to be false than our own because we have more knowledge at our disposal and are less subject to illusion. (from *Inspired Talks*)[55]

A whole chain of prejudices lies behind this kind of formulation. Certainly no traditionalist would dream of comparing him/herself with Moses nor succumb to the ignorant complacency implied by the reference to our own 'enlightened' times. Another example:

> The Buddhas and Christs we know are heroes of second grade compared with those greater ones of which the world knows nothing. (from *Karma Yoga*)

---

53 On this question see F. Matchett: 'The Teaching of Ramakrishna in Relation to the Hindu Tradition and as Interpreted by Vivekananda' *Religion* XI, 1981; pp171–184.
54 FS *UI* p87fn.
55 This passage and the two following are cited without comment by Schuon. They speak for themselves! FS *SPHF* pp124–125.

– as if the perfections of Christ and the Buddha were a matter of degree which could be surpassed, and leaving aside the humanistic implications of 'heroes'. This sort of thing one might expect from a humanist but hardly from a man of Vivekananda's pretensions. Such an utterance is absolutely inconceivable in the mouth of Ramakrishna. And yet another statement even more astonishing, if that be possible:

> We have seen that the theory of a personal God who created the world cannot be proved. Is there today a single child who could believe in it? ... Your personal God, Creator of this world, has he ever succoured you? This is the challenge flung down by modern science. (from *Conference on the Vedanta*)

One hardly knows where to start in excavating the prejudices buried in this – the importing of considerations ('proof') into a domain where they do not apply, the brutal insolence of such condescension to countless millions of theists, both in India and elsewhere, the incomprehension of the spiritual economy of theistic perspectives, the utterly irrelevant appeal to modern science – all this from a man whose effusive apologists do not hesitate to compare him to Shankara!

Lest the reader imagine that such statements are unrepresentative we can only direct them to Vivekananda's writings about other religions. For a quite extraordinary agglomeration of self-contradictions, half-baked ideas and extravagant assertions one need look no further than the essay 'Buddhistic India'.[56] However, a scrutiny of almost any of Vivekananda's writings will expose the Trojan Horse of modernism, one which is likely to discharge some of its unattractive occupants at any turn. One can only sympathise with Mircea Eliade's reaction to Vivekananda's work: 'I was later to receive Vivekananda's books. But they didn't win me over. I was already immune to spiritualistic rhetoric, to popularised neo-Vedantic fervour; all that seemed shoddy to me.'[57]

Sarvepalli Radhakrishnan, along with Aldous Huxley, is perhaps the best-known of recent 'perennial philosophers'. At first glance he has a good deal in common with Ananda Coomaraswamy: both were Hindus having strong links with Western institutions of learning; both were committed to enriching European understanding of India's cultural and spiritual heritage; each championed a view of life which might be described as 'religious'; each was a scholar of cosmopolitan erudition and formidable reputation. However, closer inquiry into their work reveals men of very different mien. A comparison of some of their most characteristic ideas will identify Radhakrishnan's divergence from the traditionalist understanding of the *philosophia perennis*.

In 1942 Coomaraswamy reviewed Radhakrishnan's *Eastern Religions and Western Thought*, the *locus classicus* of some of his central ideas. Coomaraswamy found the book deeply offensive. It was, he said, the work of one 'who has forgotten what it is to be a Hindu, and has become an "Orientalist"'.[58] It exhibited 'essentially a

---

56 Reproduced in R.C. Majumdar: *op.cit.*; ppxxi-xliv.
57 M. Eliade *No Souvenirs* Harper & Row, New York, 1977; p134.
58 A.K. Coomaraswamy: Review of Radhakrishnan's book in *The Review of Religion* VI, Jan 1942; p140, quoted in K. Stunkel: 'The Meeting of East and West in Coomaraswamy and Radhakrishnan' *Philosophy East and West* XXIII, iv, 1973; p518. All references to the review article hereafter as AKC: 'Radhakrishnan' and to Stunkel's article which quotes excerpts from this review as 'Stunkel'.

European rather than an Indian mentality'.[59] The real issue at stake was the tension between traditionalism, identified here with India and Hinduism, and modernism, equated by Coomaraswamy with post-mediaeval European thought. The vocabulary in which Coomaraswamy couches his criticisms should not be allowed to suggest that he was some kind of reactionary Indian patriot with xenophobic tendencies: the dividing line between Coomaraswamy and Radhakrishnan has nothing to do with national boundaries or ethnic groupings; it has everything to do with attitudes to tradition as such.

It was precisely those features of Radhakrishnan's work which have been so frequently extolled by his Western admirers – what Kenneth Stunkel calls his 'modified secularism', his 'provisional rationalism', 'his willingness to concede value, dignity and importance to Western philosophy and science', and 'his spirit of conciliation' – that Coomaraswamy found objectionable.[60] Let us consider some of Coomaraswamy's specific criticisms before moving on to a more general consideration of Radhakrishnan.

Nothing is more likely to arouse the ire of traditionalists than a kind of historicist evolutionism. Coomaraswamy finds that Radhakrishnan

> ... accepts without hesitation the current academic notion of a human 'progress' with the correlative 'development' of 'systems' of 'religious philosophy', not realising what India has known so well, that there are things to which the historical method, valid only for the classification of facts and not for the elucidation of principles, does not apply.[61]

We shall not here enter into debate about the unfolding of religious philosophy in India but the general point remains. It is not difficult to identify the evolutionist assumptions that stalk through Radhakrishnan's work. Take this, for instance: 'Looking back on the millions of years of the steady climb of life on the path of evolution, it seems presumptuous for us to imagine that with thinking man evolution has come to an end.'[62] Or this: 'Man is yet in his infancy and has a long period ahead of him on this planet. He will work out a higher integration and produce world-minded men and women.'[63] In view of our discussion of the traditionalist critique of evolutionism it is hardly necessary to point out why this sort of thinking cannot be reconciled with traditionalism.

Coomaraswamy also finds, rightly, that the whole tenor of Radhakrishnan's work is not metaphysical but philosophical in the modern sense. It proceeds, that is to say, through dialectical, logical and analytical modes rather than issuing from a grasp of immutable principles and doctrines. It is the product of rationalistic thought rather than the formulation of the insights of intellection and gnosis. This, in itself, could hardly be a reproach against Radhakrishnan. What is unsettling is that although his work sometimes gives the appearance of being a kind of metaphysic Radhakrishnan himself appears to be unaware of this distinction. Certainly no traditionalist could

---

59 AKC: 'Radhakrishnan' p134 per Stunkel p518.
60 Stunkel p518.
61 AKC: 'Radhakrishnan' p134 per Stunkel p519.
62 S. Radhakrishnan: 'Fragments of a Confession' p29.
63 *ibid.*; p82.

endorse Charles Moore's imprudent claim that 'Radhakrishnan is the Thomas Aquinas of the present age'.[64] Coomaraswamy again:

> The essential distinction of the East from the modern West, and one that involves all other differences, is that the East referred to in Radhakrishnan's book has still preserved and is still conscious of the metaphysical bases of its life, while the modern West is almost completely ignorant of traditional metaphysics (which it confuses with 'philosophy', as does Radhakrishnan himself) and is at the same time actively and consciously anti-traditional.[65]

Radhakrishnan's 'modified secularism' and 'provisional rationalism' find expression in his somewhat impatient attitude to traditional forms as if these were nothing more than the more or less useless accretions of the centuries which, like the barnacles on a ship, would be better swept away.

> Radhakrishnan is thoroughly un-Indian [ie. anti-traditional] when he speaks ... in casual disparagement of dogmas and rites and in enthusiasm for what he calls 'open religion', as if to imply that the mysteries can be communicated in the same way as a profane science.[66]

Indeed, it might be added that Radhakrishnan tends to use venerable words like 'myth', 'ritual' and 'dogma' in the pejorative sense, a tell-tale sign in itself.[67]

Coomaraswamy is also distressed by the absence of any evidence suggesting that Radhakrishnan adheres to the traditional belief in the supra-human origins of the Hindu tradition – or any other tradition for that matter. Radhakrishnan's own remarks on the *Rig Veda* in his *magnum opus*, *Indian Philosophy*, only go to confirm Coomaraswamy's suspicions. This scripture, says Radhakrishnan, is composed of '... the impassioned utterances of primitive but poetic souls which seek some refuge from the obstinate questionings of sense and outward things.'[68] Some of the old chestnuts of the nature-myth school paraded yet again with no apparent embarrassment! The Vedas, we note, are neither revealed nor inspired but 'impassioned', composed by 'primitive souls' who have the compensatory merit of being 'poetic' and who are seeking to escape from their incomprehension of the material world. A less traditionalist and more modernist commentary it would be hard to find – lest it be in Vivekananda!

As for the intellectual orientation and methodology of Radhakrishnan, the contrast with Coomaraswamy can be sharpened by considering the implications of the following two passages, the first from Radhakrishnan:

> Although I admire the great masters ... I cannot say that I am a follower of any, accepting his teaching in its entirety ... my thought does not comply with any fixed traditional pattern. For my thinking had another source and proceeded from my own experience ...[69]

---

64 C. Moore: 'Metaphysics and Ethics in Radhakrishnan's Philosophy' in P.A. Schilpp: *op.cit.*; p282.
65 AKC: 'Radhakrishnan' p144 per Stunkel p522.
66 AKC: 'Radhakrishnan' p135 per Stunkel p520.
67 See, for example, Radhakrishnan: 'Fragments of a Confession' p67.
68 S. Radhakrishnan *Indian Philosophy* Allen & Unwin, London, 1931, Vol 1, p71.
69 *ibid.*; p10. Here we might well recall Schuon's question 'What is to be said of a system of "metaphysics" which ponderously places human experience at the centre of reality – as if our intelligence did not allow us to go further ... ?' FS *SW* p19fn. (The question is posed in respect of existentialists but applies no less to Radhakrishnan and others who fall back on 'human experience'.)

Coomaraswamy:

> We write from a strictly orthodox point of view ... endeavouring to speak with mathematical precision, but never employing words of our own, or making any affirmation for which authority could not be cited by chapter and verse; in this way making our technique characteristically Indian.[70]

The contrast could hardly be more explicit.

Despite Coomaraswamy's stringent criticisms of Radhakrishnan's position scholars still tend to confound their approaches to the perennial philosophy.[71] We shall conclude our discussion of Radhakrishnan by juxtaposing a few more quotations which will consolidate the contrast with the traditionalists. Radhakrishnan shares with most modernists the presumption that religious traditions must 'adapt' to the times, find 'new' answers consonant with the findings of modern science. Every religion, he assures us, is '... attempting to reformulate its faith in accordance with modern thought and criticism. Stagnant and stereo-typed religions are at variance with the psychology of modern life.'[72] It seems that there is no doubting that it is 'the psychology of modern life' which must take precedence. How different in tone and temper is this passage from Schuon:

> Nothing is more misleading than to pretend, as is so glibly done in our day, that the religions have compromised themselves hopelessly in the course of centuries or that they are now played out. If one knows what a religion really consists of one knows ... that they are independent of human doings; in fact, nothing men do is able to affect the traditional doctrines, symbols or rites.[73]

Or this, again from Schuon: 'One of the great errors of our time is to speak of the "bankruptcy" of religion or the religions: this is to lay blame on truth for our failure to admit it ....'.[74]

Radhakrishnan tells us that 'no single religion possesses truth compared with philosophic knowledge'.[75] Here he is not talking of a metaphysical doctrine preserved within a traditional framework, in which case his claim may have carried some weight even if its expression were less than felicitous. No, Radhakrishnan is referring to a free-wheeling philosophy tied to nothing but reason and an ill-defined 'intuition'. The kind of knowledge of which he is speaking falls, from a traditionalist point of view, not only below metaphysics but below the various theologies where '... the intrinsically supernatural character of the dogmas and also a certain grace inherent in religion guarantee that theological reasoning when properly used is free from the arbitrariness of profane thought ....'.[76] No traditionalist could speak, as Radhakrishnan so blithely does, of combining 'the best of European humanism and Asiatic

---

[70] Quoted in V.S. Naravane: 'Ananda Coomaraswamy: A Critical Appreciation' in SS *ACRR* p206.
[71] See P.J. Saher: *op.cit.*; pp146–147; L. Hyde: 'Radhakrishnan's Contribution to Universal Religion' in P.A. Schilpp *op.cit.*; p369; J.G. Arapura *Radhakrishnan and Integral Experience* Asia Publishing House, London, 1964, p4.
[72] 'Fragments of a Confession' pp74–75.
[73] F. Schuon: 'No Activity Without Truth' in JN *SG* p29.
[74] FS *SW* p11.
[75] 'Fragments of a Confession' p78.
[76] FS *L&T* p50.

Religion' into a 'philosophy more profound and living than either'.[77] He often disclaims any syncretic intention but it is difficult to see what else his references to a 'universal religion' might entail.[78] What, for instance, is one to make of his plea for a 'higher religion' which is to emerge from a 'collective rational purpose'?[79] Trying to get a firm purchase on Radhakrishnan's ideas about 'universal religion' is akin to trying to drink the water of a mirage. However, what is clear is that his conception of religion is poles apart from that of the traditionalists.

Radhakrishnan may have been some of the things which his many admirers claim – eminent Sanskritist, erudite scholar, statesman *extraordinaire*, a charming personality and so on. None of this has been relevant to the question in front of us which is simply whether one can talk in the same breath about the traditionalists and Radhakrishnan as 'perennial philosophers'. We cannot. Apart from the modernist-philosophic slant of his work, his attitude to tradition as such disallows any such comparison. For Radhakrishnan tradition remains little more than the accumulated weight of the past, a kind of cultural baggage which can be ransacked for its treasures and then consigned to the dustbin of human history.[80]

In the West the term 'perennial philosophy' is most often associated with Aldous Huxley. It is not without irony that Huxley should open his anthology of that name with an error of fact: the term itself was certainly not coined by Leibnitz, being used at least as early as the mid-16th century by Agostino Steuco to entitle his work *De perenni philosophia* (1540).[81] From the traditionalist point of view Huxley's exposition of the perennial philosophy is marred by more than errors of fact. Gai Eaton suggested that Huxley's famous work had, in fact, 'given a dangerously misleading impression of the traditional religious and metaphysical teaching'.[82] This imputation would doubtless be supported by other traditionalists. Without questioning the 'sincerity, intelligence and learning' which Huxley brought to his work, Peter Moore finds his 'moralism and scientific humanism' the key to the disproportions and inadvertencies in his vision of the perennial philosophy.[83] Eaton disparages the spirit of Huxley's work as 'Western through and through', that is, modernist.[84] What evidence might be adduced to sustain such changes?

Firstly, Huxley's approach to different religious teachings, forms and doctrines is both partial and idiosyncratic. As Gai Eaton notes, he approves of Rumi but cannot fathom the doctrine of *jihād*; he acclaims Shankara but has little time for 'popular' Hinduism; he frequently invokes Eckhart but is deeply suspicious of St Augustine. Not without reason did Coomaraswamy write to Huxley saying 'I do not approach the great traditions, as you seem to do, to pick and choose in them what seems to

---

77 'Fragments of a Confession' p7.
78 See 'Reply to My Critics' in P.A. Schilpp *op.cit.*; p812 and *Fellowship of the Spirit* Harvard Uni Press, Cambridge, 1961; p9.
79 'Fragments of a Confession' pp25-26.
80 It might also be noted that Radhakrishnan's understanding of religions other than Hinduism was not altogether convincing. See J. Wach: 'Radhakrishnan and the Comparative Study of Religion' in P.A. Schilpp *op.cit.*; pp445-458 and T.R.V. Murti: 'Radhakrishnan and Buddhism' in the same volume, pp567-605.
81 See A. Huxley *The Perennial Philosophy* Harper & Row, New York, 1970; pviii.; S.H. Nasr: 'Preface' to FS *IPP* pvii; C.B. Schmitt: 'Perennial Philosophy: From Agostino Steuco to Leibniz' *Journal of the History of Ideas* XXVII, 1966; pp502-532; SHN *K&S* pp69-70.
82 G. Eaton *The Richest Vein* Faber & Faber, London, 1949; p167.
83 P. Moore: Review of WP *TTW* in SCR VI, i, 1972; p63.
84 G. Eaton *op.cit.*; p180.

me to be right.'[85] Of course some elements of subjectivity must enter into the shaping of any anthology but the drift of these few examples is clear enough: Huxley has not grasped the relationship between the esoteric and exoteric domains of religion and, like a good many would-be mystics, wants to by-pass the claims of orthodoxy in search of the 'Highest Common Factor' (his own words).[86] He is suspicious of dogmas, rituals and sacraments, of religious forms. He asseverates that Christ and the Buddha both disapproved of 'ceremonies, vain repetitions and sacramental rites' but that the traditions issuing from their teachings have gone their 'all too human way' in developing such forms.[87] Plainly the view of tradition implied here shares very little with that of men like Schuon and Coomaraswamy.

Huxley was one of the prime movers behind a kind of 'neo-Vedanta' in the West, one which attracted other literary figures such as Gerald Heard and Christopher Isherwood. We can assume that Huxley would have shared Heard's ideas when the latter wrote:

> A new religion has come into history — that is Western Vedanta ... the appearance of Vedanta in the West as a living religion ... is inevitable just because the religious heredity of the West has now outgrown the tight Hebrew pot of cosmology ... A faith that taught hell for those who did not get themselves saved in this life was suited enough to put the fear of God into barbarians or men too busy to do much more than make a dash with their last breath for a deathbed repentance. But for people really interested in the spiritual world ... such doctrines were ... a terrible obstacle.[88]

The prejudices with which this is riddled are obvious enough and are characteristic of the neo-Vedantic movement in America and elsewhere. The complacencies of such an outlook are quite repellent to anyone evincing the traditionalist outlook.

Huxley was also entranced by quasi-scientific models which he believed shed light on spiritual matters but which in fact tell us much more about the time which produced them. Given his background and temperament it is no surprise that we should find in Huxley the same evolutionist bias which so characterises modernism.[89] It is by no means neutralised by the fact that it is less starry-eyed than that of some of his contemporaries. It is true that Huxley had a keen eye for some of the more absurd pretensions of modern science[90] but he was no means immune to the seductions of pseudo-scientific models which cannot illumine but only obscure the traditional doctrines with which he is dealing. His lengthy recapitulation of Sheldon's typology of human personalities is a case in point.[91] He gives the game away completely in a piece of foolishness as blatant as the following:

---

85 Coomaraswamy to Huxely, 28th Sept, 1944, quoted in RL *CLW* p220.
86 A. Huxley *op.cit.*; pvii.
87 *ibid.*; pp262–272.
88 G. Heard: 'Vedanta and Western History' in C. Isherwood (ed) *Vedanta for the Western World* New American Library, New York, 1972. Anyone who has read Coomaraswamy's 'Vedanta and Western Tradition' cannot but be struck by the contrast between this commanding essay and the hotch-potch of prejudices paraded in Heard's piece.
89 See, for instance, A. Huxely *op.cit.*; pvii.
90 See his 'Origins and Consequences of some Contemporary Thought Patterns' in C. Isherwood *op.cit.*; pp359–363.
91 See A. Huxley *op.cit.*; pp149ff. See also H. Bridges: 'Aldous Huxley: Exponent of Mysticism in America' *Journal of the American Academy of Religion* XXXVII, ii, 1969; pp341–352.

> In one way or another, all our experiences are chemically conditioned ... Knowing as he does ... what are the chemical conditions of transcendental experience, the aspiring mystic should turn for technical help to the specialists – in pharmacology, in biochemistry ...[92]

Perry and others have anatomised the confusions which run rampant through this kind of literature and there is no point in going again over the same ground. Suffice it to note that the formulation above would be worthy of the most unabashed materialist.[93]

Huxley was also unduly preoccupied with morality and moralism: the almost obsessional concern with ideas about guilt and sin, the 'ambivalent and tortuous attitude to sexuality', the exaggerated antithesis between 'spirit' and 'matter' in one place and their confounding in another – all these are hallmarks of Huxley's work in general. Eaton has mapped out the development of these themes in Huxley's novels, a subject with which we are not here concerned but which does shed some light on his idiosyncratic vision of the perennial philosophy.[94] There are other aspects of Huxley's stance which are quite incompatible with traditionalism and the traditionalist vision of the *sophia perennis*. However, enough has been said to show that any identification of Huxley with people like Coomaraswamy is injudicious, to put it mildly.

Georgi Ivanovitch Gurdjieff (1877–1949) appeared in the West at a moment in history when many European intellectuals had lost faith both in religious tradition and in the extravagant claims of an aggressively materialistic science. He brought with him a teaching apparently derived from ancient sources of wisdom, appropriately exotic but at the same time 'scientific'. He brought, we are told, 'a revelatory release from outdated and claustrophobic notions'.[95] He promised the best of both worlds – of all worlds! It is worth considering Gurdjieff's career and the teachings in a little detail because for many people he represents a kind of 'esotericism' which is all too easily confused with authentic sapiential principles.

Gurdjieff himself was an extraordinarily powerful personality who exercised an almost mesmeric effect on his many followers. He attracted artists, intellectuals and spiritual seekers from all over the world. Peter Ouspensky, J.G. Bennett (who turns up almost everywhere sooner or later),[96] Katherine Mansfield, Maurice Nicol, and Kenneth Walker were amongst his disciples while more recently we find people like Colin Wilson and Peter Brook under his spell.[97]

'The Tiger of Turkestan' magnetised controversy and the whole Gurdjieffian field awaits a scholarly phenomenological inquiry. Here we shall confine ourselves to one general question: does Gurdjieff's claim to a universal esoteric wisdom share anything

---

92 A. Huxley *The Doors of Perception and Heaven and Hell* Penguin, 1959; Appendix II, pp121–122.
93 See W. Perry: 'Drug-Induced Mysticism: The Mescalin Hypothesis' *TOMORROW* XII, iii, 1964; pp192–198. This in an authoritative statement on a subject on which any amount of nonsense has been written in the last three decades.
94 G. Eaton *op.cit.*; pp166–180.
95 A. Bancroft *op.cit.*; p91.
96 Bennett involved himself in all manner of movements, including Subud and Gurdjieffianism. After a colourful career in pursuit of the occult he finally converted to Rome. See C.R. Evans *Cults of Unreason* Harrap, London, 1973; p238.
97 Peter Brook filmed *Meetings with Remarkable Men*, 1979.

with traditionalism? To answer this question we shall consider three issues: his credentials as a teacher, his relationship with his 'disciples', and the content of his teaching. The answer to which these point us is quite unambiguous. We shall in large measure rely on the account by Whitall Perry which Theodore Roszak saluted as 'the best independent, critical evaluation of Gurdjieff'.[98] Perry has drawn substantially not only on Gurdjieff's own works but on the writings of his closest followers.

Many commentators on Gurdjieff have expended a good deal of energy over the question of whether he did, in fact, have access to an authentic esoteric tradition – gnostic, Sufic, Tibetan, Kabbalistic or whatever – and whether the groups with which he came into contact were genuine repositories of ancient esotericisms transmitted through an intact lineage. Such inquiries, while interesting, are somewhat beside the point. As Perry suggests, '... the whole crux of the matter is contingent on whether he was himself a legitimate representative and faithful purveyor of any truths to which he might have been exposed.'[99] One might indeed participate in a properly constituted tradition without being any more authoritative for it. After all, Maharishi Mahesh Yogi's lineage traces back to Shankara, a fact which has not prevented him from betraying the tradition he purports to represent.[100] Furthermore, we need not be 'unduly reverential' in the face of Gurdjieff's claims about 'ancient sages' for 'It is not traditional doctrines alone that go back to antiquity: subversive doctrines also claim a pedigree as "ancient and honourable" as you please.'[101] It is clear from Gurdjieff's teachings – and his books are there for all to see[102] – that whatever the genealogy of his ideas and whatever the proportions of fact and fancy in his claims about his own spiritual apprenticeship, he is neither a 'legitimate representative' nor a 'faithful purveyor' of any tradition whatsoever.

It is well known that spiritual masters in some schools may exceptionally resort to enigmatic behaviour for teaching purposes; the many stories about outrageous Zen masters furnish a case in point. It is also true that those hostile to any and every form of spirituality are ever-ready to seize on phenomena which they do not understand, to wrench them out of context and to interpret them in service of their own ends. One must, then, be circumspect in judgements about these matters. These cautions notwithstanding the dispassionate observer cannot fail to see in Gurdjieff's own role a series of outrages for which no one has been able to offer a cogent explanation consistent with the view that he was a spiritual master. A man who talks frankly of 'shearing' his disciples of their money, who dismisses his most faithful followers in fits of pique, who, in the words of one of his closest associates 'behaved shamelessly over money matters, and with women also', whose lifestyle was positively Rabelesian, whose appetite for sex, food and drugs was apparently insatiable, and

---

98 T. Roszak quoted on back cover of *SCR* XII, i & ii, 1978. Perry's originally appeared as three articles under the heading 'Gurdjieff in the Light of Tradition' in *SCR* VIII, iv and IX, i & ii, 1974–1975. These articles later comprised a book under the same heading, published by Perennial Books. References are to the articles and are hereafter referred to as WP: 'GLT I', 'GLT II' and 'GLT III'.
99 WP: 'GLT I' p212. The same point is made by J.M. Murray in a Letter to the Editor *SCR* XI, iii, 1977; p192.
100 For a sympathetic account of the Maharishi's teachings but one unable to hide their spiritual poverty see J. Needleman *The New Religions* pp128–142.
101 WP: 'GLT I'; p21.
102 *Beelzebub's Tales to his Grandsons*; *Meetings with Remarkable Men*; *Life is Real Only Then, When 'I Am'*; *The Herald of Coming Good*. See also P. Ouspensky's account of Gurdjieff's teachings in *In Search of the Miraculous* and in talks recorded by his disciples in *Views from the Real World*. (Mostly published by Routledge & Kegan Paul, London.)

who, by almost any conceivable criteria, was capable of the most shattering rudeness, insensitivity and grossness – such a man, to say the least of it, hardly inspires confidence in anyone who was not directly exposed to his spellbinding personality.[103] Nor do any of these characteristics suggest a conformity to any traditional conception of the spiritual master.[104]

One of those who knew Gurdjieff well referred to him as 'some sort of self-created, inevitable Messiah' and 'in a very literal, paradoxical sense, the embodiment of that excellent phrase: "a real, genuine phoney"'.[105] The claim takes on its full force in the face of that bizarre mixture of 'dark conundrums, riddles, mystifications and other sundry sophistries' which make up his teaching.[106] It would not be difficult to assemble a collage of Gurdjieff's sayings which would discredit any claim that he gave voice to the *sophia perennis* of which the traditionalists speak. However, suffice it to note a few pivotal ideas in the Gurdjieffian scheme: that man is born without a soul but 'acquires' one in the course of his development; that man is a 'three-brained creature' whose 'evolution' was arrested by the insertion of the 'Kundabuffer' organ by the 'Chief-Common-Universal-Arch-Chemist-Psychicist Angel Looisos'.[107] His attitude to the great religions was one of 'benign neglect'. He evinced some respect for the great founders, conceding that they may have been 'Number Eight Men' (ie. 'cosmic individuals') but showed contempt for most of their followers. He resorted to the threadbare stratagem of claiming that the messages of men like the Buddha and Christ had been completely misunderstood and that it was incumbent on him, Gurdjieff, to 'explain' their teachings. He dismissed the weight of traditional authority without a qualm – his references to the 'criminal wiseacring' of the Church Fathers is characteristic. Traditional spiritual disciplines were travestied in his talk about the ways of 'the fakir, the monk and the yogi' which were to be superseded by Gurdjieff's Fourth Way which would dispose of the clutter of religion, the superfluous impedimenta of tradition. As Perry observes, unless one resorts to the cheap expedient of claiming that the saints and sages were clandestine practitioners of the Fourth Way, Gurdjieff's claim amounts to a condescension to the likes of a St Francis, a Rumi, a Shankara.[108]

Certainly Gurdjieff must have drawn on traditional doctrines – his cosmology, for example, clearly owes something to the Kabbalistic tradition. However, his ideas are often parodies of traditional doctrines. Like the theosophists, Gurdjieff gathered together bits and pieces from here, there and everywhere and welded them into an irretrievably syncretistic and idiosyncratic system which sometimes echoes traditional doctrines, at other times degenerates into a farrago of nonsense. The claim that Gurdjieff's teaching was essentially acroamatic does nothing to hide the fact.[109]

---

103 Evidence for these claims is taken by Perry not from the works of his detractors but his followers. Perry draws extensively on such works as M. Anderson *The Unknowable Gurdjieff*, T. de Hartmann *Our Life with Mr Gurdjieff*, F. Peters *Gurdjieff Remembered*, J.G. Bennett *Gurdjieff: Making a New World*, and P. Ouspensky *op.cit.*

104 See F. Schuon: 'Nature and Function of the Spiritual Master' pp50–59.

105 From F. Peters, quoted in WP: 'GLT I' p232.

106 *ibid.*; p212.

107 See WP: 'GLT II' pp22–35.

108 See WP: 'GLT I' p212. For a discussion of Gurdjieff's attitude to the religious traditions see WP: 'GLT II' pp24–31.

109 For further material on Gurdjieff see, as well as the sources already cited, K. Walker *The Making of Man* Routledge & Kegan Paul, London, 1963; C.S. Nott *Journey through This World* Routledge and Kegan Paul, London, 1969; and C.R. Evans *op.cit.*

The business of comparing the views of various contemporary philosophers, universalists, 'gurus', occultists and the like with traditionalism could be pursued more or less indefinitely. However, enough has now been said to clarify some of the principles which mark off the traditionalist position and which inform its critique of other perspectives with which traditionalism might be confused. Having considered something of this critique we will now turn to some of the criticisms which have been directed at the traditionalist position.

12

Criticisms of Traditionalism

One of the remarkable aspects of the intellectual life of this century ... is precisely the neglect of this point of view in circles whose official function it is to be concerned with questions of an intellectual order   *Seyyed Hossein Nasr* [1]

The modern world tends to be sceptical about everything that demands man's higher faculties. But it is not at all sceptical about scepticism, which demands hardly anything
E.F. Schumacher [2]

Some people may reproach us with lack of reticence, but we would ask what reticence is shown by philosophers who shamelessly slash at the wisdom of countless centuries
Frithjof Schuon [3]

The traditionalist critique of modernism is formidable and inexorable; the modernist response to traditionalism is, by contrast, a paltry affair. There has been no serious and sustained intellectual confrontation such as we might dignify with the term 'critique'. Although traditionalism excites sharply polarised responses we look in vain for any cogent challenge to the work of Schuon and his fellow traditionalists. Such criticisms as have been made tend to be rather scattered and *ad hoc*. Before turning to these criticisms we shall take an overview of the reception of Schuon's work, especially in academic quarters. This entails some discussion of the factors which motivate a resistance to his work and to traditionalism in general.

Schuon's books have, to date, made little impact on the academic community of comparative religionists. Generally they have received only the cursory attention which breeds misunderstanding, or they have been ignored. Take, for instance, Schuon's several studies of the Islamic tradition. S.H. Nasr points out that

> By expounding and elucidating the spiritual treasures of Islam with the clearest evidence, his books have placed before the Western public the most inward aspect of the Islamic message and have explained the deeper reasons whereby millions of men are compelled to accept the Qoranic revelation, making of it their rule of life.[4]

And yet one can search through shelves of scholarly works on Islam and find only the most meagre reference to Schuon's works. Despite acclamations by representatives of the traditions in question,[5] Schuon's books on Hinduism and Buddhism remain all but unknown. Nor are his more general and synthetic works on metaphysics and religion known to more than a handful of Western academics. Some of the reasons for this state of affairs are not hard to fathom. Schuon himself was not a member of the academic community and made no attempt to address his work to this group as such. He did not attend conferences, deliver lectures and seminars or engage in scholarly combat and polemic. He lived in reclusive circumstances and published only in those journals already given over to a traditionalist outlook.

Schuon's material itself is often not easy of access. It demands a concentrated intelligence and a kind of intuitive receptivity before his arguments can be grasped and his insights assimilated. While free of the stridency we sometimes find in Guénon's work, Schuon's tone is implacable and uncompromising. There is nothing of the populariser, pedant or antiquarian in his writings which, at first sight, often appear too abstruse and opaque to those who do not share something of the outlook which informs them. As intelligent a reader as Huston Smith confessed his initial bewilderment on reading *The Transcendent Unity of Religions*. Discussing Schuon's treatment of his central theme, Smith writes, '... he approaches it from a different angle, a distinctive bent. Until this angle is perceived, his entire perspective seems askew;

---

1   SHN *K&S* p67.
2   E.F. Schumacher *A Guide for the Perplexed* Jonathan Cape, London, 1977; p71.
3   FS *SW* p20fn.
4   S.H. Nasr: 'Preface' to FS *DI* p7.
5   See, for example, Dr V. Raghavan's 'Preface' to FS *LS* ppix–xx.

thereafter it falls into place.'⁶ Not everyone has the resources necessary to identify and understand this perspective.

These are cooperative factors in Schuon's comparative obscurity but perhaps the nub of the case lies in his view of knowledge and its purposes. Here he is remote indeed from the assumptions and values shared by most of the international academic community which, in some senses, is rather like a freemasonry with its own rules and regulations of membership.⁷ Schuon is quite indifferent to the liberal-secular humanist ideal of scholarship for its own sake. Much of what passes as 'knowledge' is, for Schuon, nothing more than a familiarity with a mass of information which in itself is neither interesting nor useful. The pursuit of knowledge is, for the traditionalists, a spiritual matter rather than one governed by academic considerations. We remember Schuon's claim that 'It is the spiritual, not the temporal, which culturally, socially and politically is the criterion of all other values.'⁸ This applies no less in the field of ideas and scholarship than elsewhere. Guénon made the same point in writing,

> A strange phenomenon may be noted in the intellectual domain itself, or what is left of it ... namely the passion of research taken as an end in itself ... Whilst the rest of mankind seeks for the sake of finding and knowing, the Westerner of today seeks for the sake of seeking ...⁹

Traditionalists give no support to the idea of a progressive and cumulative knowledge as a goal worth pursuing for its own sake; such a view bespeaks a quantitative, external and profane view of knowledge. Further – and this is a crucial point rarely understood –

> People no longer sense the fact that the quantitative richness of a knowledge – of any kind of knowledge – necessarily entails an interior impoverishment unless accompanied by a spiritual science able to maintain balance and re-establish unity.¹⁰

In much the same vein Schuon warns of the dangers of a cult of 'intelligence' and 'mental passion' which

> ... takes man further from the truth. Intelligence withdraws as soon as man puts his trust in it alone. Mental passion pursuing ... intuition is like the wind which blows out the light of the candle.¹¹

Much of what today is applauded as 'scholarly enthusiasm' or 'an appetite for ideas' or 'a lively and inquiring mind' is often a kind of mental passion. This latter term is by no means a contradiction in terms:

> There are men who believe themselves to be without passions, because they have transferred their

---

6 H. Smith: 'Introduction' to FS *TUR* pix.
7 For some discussion of the International Association for the History of Religions, the 'masonic' institute of comparative religionists, see E.J. Sharpe *Comparative Religion* Duckworth, London, 1975; pp267ff.
8 F. Schuon: 'Usurpations of Religious Feeling' *SCR* II, ii, 1968; p66.
9 R. Guénon *Orient et Occident* quoted in WP *TTW* p732.
10 FS *ITB* p41.
11 FS *SPHF* p132.

whole passional life on to the mental plane, which becomes 'egoistic'. 'Wisdom after the flesh' is, among other things, mental passion with the complement that compensates it – petrification. It is the thinking that goes with a 'hardened heart'.[12]

It would be a wilfully blind academic who would not concede that the charge might be levelled at not a few contemporary scholars.

Schuon's attitudes are no doubt offensive to those of a different outlook. His view of knowledge is likely to be dismissed as 'anachronistic', perhaps appropriate in a mediaeval monastery but not in a modern university. Certainly it is not a view likely to win friends and influence people in high academic circles where the ideal in view so often does indeed seem to be 'a purely external and quantitative form of knowledge'.[13] (It should not be necessary to add that this is not offered as a blanket indictment of all academic scholars, a significant number of whom repudiate a sterile academicism divorced from all values.)

The traditionalist position also runs across the widespread obeisance before a pseudo-scientific ideal of 'objectivity', one behind which, it might be added, hide a multitude of academic sins. Scholars who are prepared to take up a position which goes beyond the 'passion for research taken as an end in itself' tend to be treated with some suspicion, sometimes overt hostility. This, regrettably, applies in the field of religious studies as much as elsewhere. Klaus Klostermaier observes that,

> A scholar whose main concern in studying world religions is directed toward the promotion of mutual understanding, the development of world community, and the strengthening of the spiritual dimensions of the life of mankind has to realise sooner rather than later that the majority of the representatives of *Religionswissenschaft* ... demonstrate indifference, if not outright hostility towards such 'unscientific' goals.[14]

A more melancholy commentary is hard to imagine.

There has been a handful of scholars in the Western academic world who have perceived in Schuon's work a body of ideas and principles of the most urgent relevance to the comparative study of religion. Jacob Needleman, for instance, speaks of the 'completely new perspectives in every aspect of religious thought' opened up by Schuon.[15] Scholars like Joseph Epes Brown and Victor Danner have assimilated a Schuonian outlook into their work.[16] Huston Smith and James Cutsinger have worked to bring Schuon's writings to the attention of the American academic community. Smith wrote of Schuon 'The man is a living wonder; intellectually *a propos* religion, equally in depth and breadth, the paragon of our time. I know of no living thinker who begins to rival him.'[17] Schuon's work did, of course, exercise a decisive influence in the development of traditionalism. As we noted earlier, he was acknowledged within the traditionalist group as its pre-eminent representative. In recent

---

12 *ibid.*; p180.
13 FS *ITB* p44.
14 K. Klostermaeir: 'From phenomenology to meta-science: Reflections on the study of religions' *Studies in Religion/ Sciences Religieuses* (hereafter by former title only) VI, 1976–77; p51. See also Mircea Eliade's discussion of the timidity bred by a misconceived respect for an ill-founded 'scientific method' in *The Quest* Uni Chicago Press, 1969; pp54–71.
15 Introduction to JN *SG* p14.
16 See Chapter 5.
17 Quoted on the cover of FS *SW*.

years efforts have been made to bring Schuon's writings before a wider audience. S.H. Nasr, for instance, has edited an invaluable anthology in *The Essential Writings of Frithjof Schuon* as also the *Festschrift, Religion of the Heart*, dedicated to Schuon on his eightieth birthday. World Wisdom Books have published several collections of his essays in the U.S. However, despite these developments, it seems unlikely, for the reasons already discussed, that Schuon's work will ever have a radical effect on the academic community. We shall return to the relationship between traditionalism and academic studies shortly. First we will direct our attention to some criticisms of traditionalism.

As noted already, there has been little sustained criticism of the traditionalist position and such objections as have been expressed tend to be rather fragmentary. Of the scattered references to traditionalism in contemporary academic literature, those of critical intent are often little more than the disparaging aside, a throwaway cliché, a sectarian prejudice. Most of the book reviews work on a very narrow front: we might find this scholar taking issue with Coomaraswamy over a historical detail, another challenging Schuon's exegesis of a Biblical passage, another expressing scepticism about Nasr's treatment of a particular theme, and so on. Such disagreements can be found within the traditionalist literature itself. Some of the criticisms levelled at traditionalist works are legitimate enough, others simply captious. However, all such criticisms do not, *in toto*, amount to a critique any more than, to borrow Guénon's phrase, a pile of stones makes a building.

We are not concerned here with disputes over details but with such criticisms as suggest a resistance to the basic tenets and purposes of traditionalism. In lieu of any coherent critique we shall have to impose some kind of order on this critical congeries by constructing three general categories: moral and ideological; methodological; epistemological and philosophical, using each of these terms rather loosely. Doubtless there are other schema through which one might marshall disparate critical fragments into some kind of pattern. However, this kind of framework will allow us to move from peripheral to more central criticisms of traditionalism. Our *modus operandi* will be to state such criticisms as have been made as succinctly as possible, to give them a dishonourable discharge when they are spurious, to meet them from a traditionalist viewpoint when they carry some weight, and to concede their legitimacy where appropriate.

It might be noted that, in keeping with some observations made earlier, Coomaraswamy has attracted rather more flak in the English-speaking world than either Guénon or Schuon: this is not because he is any more vulnerable to attack — rather less so than Guénon — but because his work is more widely known. Unlike the other two, he worked in an academic milieu, a fact which accounts for a greater scholarly interest. We can take some of the criticisms of Coomaraswamy's work as representative of more general objections to traditionalism a such.

Guénon and Coomaraswamy have both been reproached for a prejudice in favour of the 'East'. This kind of objection might appear under any one of our three banners but it seems most often to be impelled by socio-political considerations. Its methodological and philosophical implications are, in any case, clear enough. W.T. Chan perceives in Guénon's contrast of Oriental metaphysic and Western science 'a symptom of an intellectual disease that divides the world into two conflicting parts'.[18] He warns of the 'grave consequences' of this malady and rebukes Guénon for 'unwarranted generalisations about peoples'. By way of illustration he cites the hoary chestnut, imputed to Guénon, that the East is 'spiritual', the West 'materialistic'. To help immunise us against infection he appeals to the authority of Radhakrishnan: 'The West is not devoid of mysticism nor the East of science and public spirit. The distinction, if any, is a relative one, as all empirical distinctions are.'[19] Chan chastises people like Guénon for 'lumping' the peoples and civilisations of each hemisphere into 'one piece' and then goes on, somewhat laboriously, to rehearse some of the cultural and religious divisions in the East. He also warns that the kind of contrast made by Guénon between East and West leads, intentionally or otherwise, to 'correlation of moral qualities with race, creed or people'.[20] He closes his case with an appeal to Rabindranath Tagore as an exemplar for those wishing to reconcile 'Eastern mysticism' and 'Western rationalism', which would rather seem to be a case of hoisting oneself on one's own petard![21]

Kenneth Stunkel, discussing Coomaraswamy and Radhakrishnan as mediators of East and West, reproves the former for his Indian 'partisanship' which he contrasts with Radhakrishnan's 'conciliatory spirit'. Referring to Coomaraswamy's critique of Radhakrishnan's general intellectual position, Stunkel writes, 'That Coomaraswamy should chide Radhakrishnan in such partisan terms is a sobering spectacle to men of good will eager to bring diverse traditions and philosophies into some kind of workable synthesis.'[22] V.S. Naravane picks up the same thread in telling us that Coomaraswamy is '... prone to overlook the achievements of modern Europe. The liberating influence of science, the growth of the idea of liberty, the new ways of aesthetic response that modern art and poetry have called forth...'[23] One could find further examples of the same kind but the general point is clear enough. It would be possible to answer each of these criticisms in some detail but here we shall simply make some general points which answer all of them.

The great divide for the traditionalists is certainly not between 'East' and 'West', not between any geographical or ethnic entities, but between tradition on the one hand and anti-tradition on the other. These may indeed have geographical and temporal correlates such as are suggested by the terms 'Westernisation' and 'modernisation' but the heart of the matter is the attitude to tradition. Let us allow Coomaraswamy himself to speak directly to the issue:

> 'East and West' imports a cultural rather than a geographical antithesis: an opposition of the traditional or ordinary way of life that survives in the East to the modern and irregular way of

---

18 W.T. Chan: 'The Unity of East and West' in W.R. Inge et al. *Radhakrishnan: Comparative Studies in Philosophy Presented in Honour of His Sixtieth Birthday* Allen & Unwin, London, 1951; p108.
19 From Radhakrishnan's *East and West in Religion*, 1933; pp45–46, quoted in W.T. Chan *op.cit.*; p108.
20 *ibid.*; pp109–110.
21 *ibid.*; pp110–111.
22 K. Stunkel: 'The Meeting of East and West in Coomaraswamy and Radhakrishnan' *Philosophy East and West* XXIII, iv, 1973; pp518 & 523.
23 V.S. Naravane: 'Ananda Coomaraswamy: A Critical Appreciation' in SS *ACRR* p209.

life that now prevails in the West. It is because such an opposition as this could not have been felt before the Renaissance that we say that the problem is one that presents itself only accidentally in terms of geography; it is one of times much more than of places.[24]

Coomaraswamy was impatient of stereotypical fallacies concerning either the East or the West and, despite the myopic criticisms of some of his detractors, devoted much of his energy towards a reawakening to the treasures of the Western tradition. Few scholars have textured their work so richly with references to Plato and Plotinus, Aquinas and Eckhart, the Fathers, the scholastics and the medieval mystics. The charge of an anti-European slant in Coomaraswamy's work simply will not bear scrutiny. He refers to

> ... that impotence and arrogance which have found perfect expression in the dictum 'East is East and West is West, and never the twain shall meet', a proposition to which only the most abysmal ignorance and the deepest discouragement could have given rise.[25]

Similarly, Guénon was certainly no victim to the sentimentalism that the East was 'spiritual' and the West 'materialistic'. What he did stress was that any traditional society, examples of which still survived in the East, would be oriented to spiritual ends whilst any anti-traditional society, such as can be found anywhere in the modern West, would be governed by other values. Certainly we can discern in Guénon's work a strong reaction against the European civilisation of his own day and it is only fair to concede that this sometimes found expression in a rather extreme and militant denunciation of what he loosely called 'the West'. However, it should always be remembered that

> If Guénon wants the West to turn to Eastern metaphysics, it is not because they are Eastern but because this is metaphysics. If 'Eastern' metaphysics differed from a 'Western' metaphysics – one or the other would not be metaphysics.[26]

Much of the work of the traditionalists is directed towards a demonstration of this last point – hardly an enterprise, one would have thought, prejudiced in favour of the East (Schuon has not been censured on these grounds but it is worth noting his comment concerning the comparative study of Eastern and Western metaphysic and religious phenomena: '... what we have in mind, for the Christian, is a return to his own sources and not an "orientalisation" of the West.'[27])

Criticisms of the treatment by the traditionalists of 'East' and 'West' lead us on to a more substantial point. Roger Lipsey, more intimately acquainted with Coomaraswamy's work, identifies the danger in a somewhat inflexible conception of tradition and modernism:

> 'Traditional' described cultures which, whatever their historical faults, were founded on an understanding of the spiritual nature of man and the world; 'modern' described cultures that have

---

24 'East and West' in AKC *BL* p80. See also Letter to Sidney Gulick, July 1943, AKC *SL* p69.
25 A.K. Coomaraswamy: 'The Pertinence of Philosophy' in S. Radhakrishnan & J.H. Muirhead (eds) *Contemporary Indian Philosophy* Allen & Unwin, London, 1952, rev. ed.; p160.
26 A.K. Coomaraswamy: 'Eastern Wisdom and Western Knowledge' in AKC *BL* pp72–73.
27 FS *LS* p229.

forgotten many truths of the spirit ... 'Traditional' became a word of praise, guaranteeing that a given entity (an idea, a social form, a practice) was true and fitting in itself and related to a larger whole. What was not 'traditional' had deviated from the only real *norm*; it was anti-traditional, that is, modern, and either evil or only accidentally good. This concept of Tradition was presented dogmatically and soon became a rigid means of parting the Cursed from the Blessed.[28]

Lipsey judiciously tempers this by going on to add that

It became so, not because the prophets of traditional thought were by nature narrow-minded, but because the vision of a modern world with little or no true spirituality, torn by vast wars, living under the reign of quantity, provoked a powerful reaction in those who believed they knew of something better that once existed and is now lost.[29]

Nonetheless it must be admitted that the categories of the traditional and the modern do sometimes appear to be too rigid and exclusive, and that the defence of the one and the assault on the other may sometimes seem too combative, especially in Guénon's work.

The attitude of the traditionalists to 'the achievements of modern Europe' has upset commentators other than V.S. Naravane. We might take Coomaraswamy's attitude to modern art as an illustrative case. We have already come across Naravane's regret that Coomaraswamy is apparently impervious to the insights of modern aesthetics. Joseph Rykwert finds it difficult to believe that Coomaraswamy's voluminous art criticism is innocent of any references to Braque or Brancusi, Klee or Mondrian, and that he only refers once in his entire *oeuvre* to Picasso's 'Guernica'.[30] Lipsey finds Coomaraswamy's attitude to modern art to be aggressively unsympathetic and indiscriminate.[31] Herman Goetz spoke of his 'vehement reaction' to modernism and his 'idealisation' of the art of past eras.[32]

We have already outlined some of the principles informing Coomaraswamy's attitude. His position is certainly not to be explained in terms of any ostrich-like head buried in the sands of the past: in terms of the values he espoused his attitude is intelligent, intelligible and consistent. Measured against the traditional criteria of art, the achievements of modernism are, at best, so much chaff in the wind. Remembering Schuon's dictum that 'the only decisive criterion of human worth is man's attitude to the Absolute',[33] we can see why Coomaraswamy should be so 'intolerant' of profane art and why he did not see fit to waste his time on the trivialities of modern art criticism. The achievements of modernism – in the arts or elsewhere – are all tarred with the same brush. 'Criticisms' of Coomaraswamy along these lines are both subjective and normative. We will only point out that Coomaraswamy was concerned to unveil and affirm values sanctified by tradition whilst many of those who deplore his attitude to modern art concern themselves with judgements and impressions which often carry the imprimatur of little more than the fashion of the day.

---

28 RL *CLW* p266.
29 RL *CLW* pp266–267.
30 J. Rykwert: 'A.K. Coomaraswamy' (review article of Lipsey's three volume set) *Religion* IX, 1979; pp104–115. See p111.
31 RL *CLW* pp210ff.
32 H. Goetz quoted in RL *CLW* p211.
33 FS *SPHF* p22.

One of the least plausible criticisms sometimes levelled at the traditionalists is that they want to 'turn back the clock'. Coomaraswamy replied tersely and tellingly to Mr. Richard Florsheim and to another reviewer who suggested 'medievalists' like Coomaraswamy advocated 'a return to a more or less feudal order ... an earlier, but dead, order of things'.[34] (This disapprobation was made in the context of Coomaraswamy's writings about art.) Coomaraswamy's reply, in part:

> These false, facile assumptions enable the critic to evade the challenge of our criticism, which has two main points: (1) That the current 'appreciation' of ancient or exotic arts in terms of our very special and historically provincial view of art amounts to a sort of *hocus-pocus*, and (2) that under the conditions taken for granted in current artistic doctrine man is given stones for bread. These propositions are either false or true, and cannot honestly be twisted to mean that we want to put back the clock.[35]

Others have made the same criticism in more general terms. Dale Riepe, for example, imagines that Coomaraswamy believed he had found a panacea for the modern world 'in a return to a medieval paradise'.[36] Similarly, Guénon has been accused of succumbing to an inappropriate 'cult of the past'.

If we look again at Coomaraswamy's reply to his critics we can discern two points which are of general significance and not confined to art criticism. The intellectual *Zeitgeist* of the modern West militates against an understanding of all things traditional and thus of past cultures. The second point in Coomaraswamy's reply testifies to a concern with the social context of art. The appeal to the past is only in terms of a reaffirmation of traditional principles and not of social and political systems.[37] In any case, none of this can be construed as 'medievalist nostalgia' or 'romantic Utopianism'. Coomaraswamy again:

> I do not in fact pretend to foresee the style of a future Utopia; however little may be the value I attach to 'modern civilisation', however much higher may have been the values of mediaeval or any other early or still existing social order, I do not think of any of these as providing a ready made blueprint for future imitation. I have no use for pseudo-Gothic is any sense of the word. The sooner my critics realise this ... the sooner they will find out what I am talking about.[38]

V.S. Naravane takes up much the same theme when he upbraids Coomaraswamy for obstructing 'social progress' in India and championing the social *status quo*.[39] Riepe refers to Coomaraswamy's 'partially reactionary political doctrine'.[40] Coomaraswamy was certainly never an apologist for the Indian or indeed any other *status quo*. He criticised it in the most acidic terms. What Coomaraswamy was affirming was not a social order vitiated by internal decay and external exploitation but certain traditional social values which he believed worth preserving. Naravane is quite right in pointing out that Coomaraswamy had little time for the assumptions, values and

---

34 Mr Richard Florsheim and the anonymous critic referred to are quoted in AKC *COPA* p86.
35 Note to the *Art Bulletin* in AKC *SL* p47.
36 See J. Lacarriere *The Gnostics* Peter Owen, London, 1977; pp125–127.
37 See AKC *BL* pp 24–25.
38 AKC *COPA* p88. See also AKC *SL* p48, and Letter to Apollo, February 1938, AKC *SL* p49.
39 V.S. Naravane *op.cit.*; p208.
40 D. Riepe *op.cit.*; p126.

methods of the 'progressive', Western-educated 'reformers'. What is surprising is not Coomaraswamy's resistance to these 'reforms' but Naravane's apparently quite untroubled assumption that we will all agree that they were a Good Thing. The general point, of course, is that the values marching behind the flags of 'Equality', 'Liberty', 'Democracy', 'Education' and other such modernist shibboleths, are often quite incompatible with those cleaved to by the traditionalists. They are the outgrowth of a profane, secular social philosophy which ignores or denies man's spiritual nature and our relationship with the Absolute. As we have seen earlier, 'Society' holds no absolute value for the traditionalists. The antagonisms between 'progressive modernists' and traditionalists cannot be resolved – by logic, scholarship, good will or whatever – because they derive from fundamentally opposed *a priori* norms. Furthermore, from a traditionalist perspective, 'politics and economics, although they cannot be ignored, are the most external and least part of our problem'.[41]

Richard Bush launches a criticism that is both ideologically and morally motivated when he writes of Schuon's vision of the transcendent unity of religions:

> I am impressed neither by the unity envisaged nor with the possibilities for communication of it, and moreover, am deeply troubled because of the further division between an elite few ... and the masses of human beings who cannot participate in the transcendent unity. A metaphysical dualism has been avoided at the cost of an epistemological and anthropological dualism, both of which are grounds for a subtle arrogance which is hardly becoming in those who desire religious unity.[42]

This is a veritable hornet's nest of misconceptions, some of which will be left aside for the moment. It might also be noted that Huston Smith has devoted an article to answering Bush's criticisms of *The Transcendent Unity of Religion* and this article is easily available. We shall not here go over Smith's argument.[43] However, a couple of points will not be out of order, especially in view of the fact that the charges of 'arrogance' and 'elitism' have been made by other commentators as well.[44]

Bush loses sight of several important facts in his references to 'the elite few' and to 'an epistemological and anthropological dualism'. He refers here to Schuon's distinction between the exoteric and esoteric dimensions of religion and between the different spiritual types to whom they are addressed. Firstly, it is not a question of satisfying this or that sentimental prejudice (egalitarianism, 'democracy', 'open religion' or whatever) but of dealing with human actualities. To pretend, for example, that everyone is capable of the spiritual disciplines and the metaphysical discernment which the esoteric path demands is to fly in the face of palpable human realities. (There is, of course, that mean mentality which would then argue that esotericism therefore has no right to exist – the-dog-in-the-manger attitude masquerading as some kind of 'egalitarianism'. One is not accusing Bush of this attitude; his misgivings

---

41 A.K. Coomaraswamy quoted in D. Riepe *op.cit.*; p127. See also RG *CMW* Ch VI, pp66–78, and Juan Adolpho Vazquez: 'A Metaphysics of Culture' in SS *ACRR* pp225–237.

42 R. Bush: 'Frithjof Schuon's *The Transcendent Unity of Religions*; Con' *Journal of the American Academy of Religion* XLIV, iv, 1976; pp716–717.

43 See H. Smith: 'Frithjof Schuon's *The Transcendent Unity of Religions*; Pro' in the same issue of *JAAR*; pp721–724. See also SHN *K&S* p319.

44 The charge is lurking, for example, in a remarkably shallow review of Schuon's *Spiritual Perspectives and Human Facts* by R.C. Zaehner in *The Journal of Theological Studies* VI, 1955; pp340–342.

are at least honestly intentioned.) Secondly it should be emphasised that neither salvation nor sanctification has any necessary connection with the esoteric domain: history is there prove it. Thirdly, an esoteric receptivity, like everything else, is a gift from God which neither implies nor confers any particular moral or spiritual merit, this depending on what use one makes of one's endowment. Esoterics are not necessarily more holy or righteous than more exoteric types. Fourthly, the attainment of esoteric wisdom depends on certain 'contours of the spirit' such as preclude arrogance of any kind whatsoever. And finally, the authenticity of Schuon's vision in no wise depends on the quantitative possibilities of its communication.

Whilst on the subject of Richard Bush's rather unconvincing attempt at a critique of Schuon's position as outlined in *The Transcendent Unity* mention should be made of another point: Bush writes that he is 'suspicious of any system which can so lightly brush aside ethical concerns'.[45] The briefest of ripostes will have to suffice here. It is clear that Professor Bush has not ventured past this single work of Schuon's otherwise the following points would have been patently clear: Schuon is not advocating a new 'system' or indeed any system whatsoever; nor is he indifferent to ethical concerns; nor does he wish to subvert but rather to strengthen the moral imperatives properly carried by every integral religious tradition. To accuse him of lightly 'brushing aside' ethical concerns is either to have badly misread him or not to have read him at all. Consider the following sample from Schuon's writings, a few more or less random choices from amongst the hundreds of possibilities that would consolidate the point:

> If metaphysic is a sacred thing, that means it could not be ... limited to the framework of the play of the mind. It is illogical and dangerous to talk of the metaphysic without being preoccupied with the moral concomitances it requires ...[46]

> Intellection ... presupposes conditions that are not only intellectual but moral in the deepest sense of the word ...[47]

> Knowledge only saves us on condition that it enlists all that we are, only when it is a way and when it works and transforms and wounds our nature as the plough wounds the soil. To say this is to say that intelligence and metaphysical certainty do not save ... When metaphysical knowledge is effective it produces love and destroys presumption ...[48]

> ... if metaphysical knowledge remains purely mental, it is worth practically nothing; knowledge is of value only on condition that it be prolonged in both love and will.[49]

This, surely, sounds not at all like a man who wishes to 'brush aside ethical concerns'. Nevertheless, as Smith points out, Bush's contention does signal an important point: morality, in an esoteric perspective, must of necessity appear rather less inclusive and all-important than it does in a formal and exoteric context. The focus of the

---

45 R. Bush *op.cit.*; p718.
46 FS *SPHF* p173.
47 FS *L&T* p31.
48 FS *SPHF* p138. See also FS *SW* p31. This is one of the central motifs of FS *EPW*. See esp. Section III.
49 FS *PM* p15. Similarly: 'The moral exigency of metaphysical discernment means that virtue is part of wisdom; a wisdom without virtue is in fact imposture and hypocrisy ...'. FS *RHC* p86

esoteric will not be on a particular moral code but on virtue as such, the former being in a subordinate position.[50]

Methodological issues cannot be divorced from considerations which go well beyond 'technical' questions about the kinds of procedures followed by scholars in dealing with the data uncovered by their studies. To talk about methodology is to talk about both moral and ideological questions on one hand and philosophical and epistemological issues on the other. There is really no such thing as a 'purely methodological' problem. However, in this part of our discussion we shall consider some criticisms of the traditionalists which might, from one point of view at least, be seen as 'methodological'. Again, such criticisms as one can find tend to be rather piecemeal. Our discussion of traditionalism and the phenomenology of religion in the next chapter will return to several methodological issues in a rather more systematic way. Here we shall briefly evaluate some criticisms directed at the traditionalist attitude to history and historicism, to empiricism, and to the premise of an inner unity of the religions. The discussion will be structured around critical comments made by several contemporary scholars.

One sometimes comes across observations such as the following, from V.S. Naravane: 'Coomaraswamy's insistence upon the contrast between ancient and modern values leads him to overlook the contradictions and sharp differences among the ancients themselves.'[51] He cites, by way of example, Coomaraswamy's emphasis on the continuities rather than the antagonisms between Hinduism and Buddhism. This is really a historiographical criticism which might be brought to bear against the traditionalists generally. It signposts a very important issue which should not be glossed over. It is quite true that the traditionalists are, in general, somewhat indifferent to historical considerations. It is also true that we might find instances – one is thinking primarily of Guénon – where someone appears to be riding roughshod over historical evidence which might compromise their case. This is deplorable wherever it occurs. However, there is a much more important point which cannot be accented too heavily: the primary purposes of the traditionalists are not those which we would expect either an academic historian or a phenomenologist of religion to be pursuing. They are not, in the first place, interested in unravelling the complexities of a particular historical moment nor in relating this or that phenomenon to a dynamic historical process. We remember Coomaraswamy's words with which we opened this study: his purpose is to demonstrate that 'diverse cultures are fundamentally related to one another as being the dialects of a common spiritual and intellectual language' and to uncover 'the common metaphysical basis of all religions'. Although this enterprise may assuredly include a historical dimension it is not, in any central sense, historiographical or empirical but philosophical and metaphysical. Doubtless Coomaraswamy was as aware as anybody of the discontinuities between Hinduism and Buddhism: that he should choose not to emphasise these does not suggest that

---

50 See H. Smith *op.cit.*; pp723–724. Those interested in the distinction between morality and virtue should see Tage Lindbom: 'Virtue and Morality' *SCR* IX, iv, 1975; pp227–228.
51 V.S. Naravane *op.cit.*; p208.

he was a poor scholar – a manifestly absurd proposition – but that the discontinuities were not germane to his purposes.

Mircea Eliade has been subjected to criticisms not unlike those directed at the traditionalist attitude to history. It will not be without some point to digress for a moment to consider his response to some of these criticisms. He offers the following reflections in his journal *No Souvenirs*:

> The principal objection made against me: I 'idealize' the primitives, I exaggerate the importance of their myths, instead of 'demystifying' them and emphasising their dependence on historical events...

His defence:

> ...I have never affirmed the insignificance of historical situations, their usefulness for understanding religious creations. If I haven't emphasized this problem, it is precisely because it has been emphasised too much and because what seems to me essential is thus neglected: the hermeneutic of religious creations.[52]

Now, as we shall see, Eliade's position is by no means the same as that of the traditionalists but this passage raises an important point on which Eliade and traditionalists can concur: to surrender to a purely historical inquiry into religious phenomena is to fall into a kind of reductionism insofar as one imagines that by this procedure one can explain the significance, the *meaning* of the phenomena in question. Elsewhere in his journal Eliade makes another pertinent observation:

> ...I would like to analyse the attitude of historicists of all kinds... all those who believe that one can understand culture only by reducing it to something lower (sexuality, economics, history, etc.) – and to show that theirs is a neurotic attitude. The neuropath demystifies life, culture, the spiritual life... he can no longer grasp the deep meaning of things, and consequently, he can no longer believe in their reality.[53]

In one of the few reviews of Schuon's books which is critical without being silly Shunji Nishi uncovers two obstacles which many scholars are unable to overcome.[54] He points out that Schuon's work rests on epistemological and metaphysical assumptions which not everyone shares. Two specific points vex Nishi: the innateness of metaphysical ideas, and the relationship between the 'ideal' and the 'real'. We can see these two issues as windows onto larger problems. Here is a typical Schuonian formulation on the first point (and this is the kind of thing which troubles Nishi):

> To speak of intelligence is to speak of innateness, for the latter is at the root of every intellectual and mental operation, man obviously being incapable of 'starting from zero' since this 'zero' is non-existent. One cannot replace the optical nerve with some external light, and with all the more reason, one cannot have a substitute for the Self, or God, from whom are derived the notions inherent in the human spirit.[55]

---

52 M. Eliade *No Souvenirs* Harper & Row, New York, 1977; p121.
53 *ibid.*; p144.
54 S. Nishi: Reviews of FS *TUR* and FS *L&T* in *Anglican Theological Review* LX, 1978; pp119–120.
55 FS *L&T* pp57–58 (part of this passage is cited in Nishi's review).

Criticisms of Traditionalism

Nishi's comment:

> One need not be an adherent of any special philosophical stance to recognise that a basic contention such as this flies in the face of the fundamental contributions that the empirical tradition has made to the practice of philosophy over the past two centuries.[56]

No one will deny it! There is little common measure between traditionalism and empirical philosophy. The incompatibility of the two cannot be reduced because of their radically opposed premises. We have already encountered Schuon's claim that a full-blown empiricism is really 'a confession of intellectual impotence'. Rapprochement between traditional metaphysic and empiricism is not possible, the latter holding to an epistemology which confines itself to the material plane. The courts of modern philosophy have no jurisdiction over matters the existence of which they do not even recognise. All that need be said here is that Schuon's claim finds support in all the religious and metaphysical traditions the world over; from this point of view the appeal to the 'fundamental contributions' of empirical philosophy is pretty unconvincing unless one shares the evolutionist assumptions which lie close to the surface of Nishi's commentary.

The second point raised by Nishi is less clearly articulated. He refers to it as a 'methodological' problem but like most such issues it is rooted in philosophy:

> The very manner in which Schuon's fundamental thesis is developed suggests that the theoretical [sic] is the basis for what is. Existence seems to be grounded in ideas. Our understanding of these ideas (which are innate) offers the terms and constructs by means of which we understand existence in all its manifestations. What is posited to be unifying (ie. Absolute Unity or God) is affirmed to be. Whether this is actually the case is surely open to question. Indeed the course of philosophy (and theology, too) over the past two centuries is precisely one of questioning such an approach.[57]

Clearly Nishi is here talking of the doctrine of archetypes which we have already reviewed. Nishi's terms 'theoretical' and 'ideas' are quite inadequate and would be better replaced with 'Ideal' and 'Ideas'. Nishi's formulation reflects a dualistic opposition, fashioned no doubt by materialism and empiricism, between the 'ideal' (which he confounds with the 'theoretical') and the 'real'. An observation from Schuon himself is pertinent in this context:

> Nothing is more false than the conventional opposition between 'idealism' and 'realism', which insinuates in general that the 'ideal' is not 'real', and inversely; as if an ideal situated outside reality had the smallest value, as if reality were always situated on a lower level than what is called an 'ideal'. Anyone who holds this view is thinking in a quantitative and not a qualitative mode.[58]

Nishi also misunderstands Schuon's position insofar as he appears to think that what is 'affirmed to be' is the evolute of some kind of mental process or theorising. Our earlier discussion of metaphysic disqualifies this kind of misapprehension.

Nishi again appeals to the authority of modern philosophy and theology as well.

---

56 S. Nishi *op.cit.*; p120.
57 S. Nishi *op.cit.*; p120.
58 FS *LAW* p27, fn13.

Traditionalism

The dissonance between traditionalism and modernist philosophy is a profound one and not much is to be gained by measuring the former against the latter. Of course traditionalism does not and cannot fit into the framework of empirical, analytical philosophy nor into that of a liberal theology; if it did the traditionalists would remain silent and we could all sit at the feet of a Professor Ayer or a Bishop Robinson!

R.C. Zaehner, reviewing one of Schuon's early books, *Spiritual Perspectives and Human Facts*, dismissed it as 'a disconnected series of private thoughts' and told his readers that

> No effort at all is made to communicate these thoughts to the average reader. In the great majority of cases they are incomprehensible – and this is scarcely surprising since M. Schuon glories in his contempt for human reason.[59]

Two points must be met here. It is perfectly true that the 'average reader' is unlikely to find this or any other of Schuon's works easy of access; as we have already remarked, he demands of his readers a disciplined intelligence and a receptivity such as are not within everyone's reach. However, to say this is a very different matter from asserting that Schuon's ideas are 'incomprehensible'. It would have been better for Zaehner to state frankly that he was unable to understand this book, admittedly dense, aphoristic and sometimes paradoxical, rather than making some vague appeal to the rights of the 'average reader', whoever that may be.

Zaehner's second criticism is even more reckless than the first. The splenetic professor has obviously misunderstood the case. Schuon has written extensively about rationality and rationalism.[60] One can only surmise that Zaehner has been unable to grasp the distinction between reason as such, and rationalism as a philosophy which elevates reason to a position of more or less totalitarian authority. It is the idolatry of reason that Schuon wants to combat, not to deny its legitimate uses. He resists the equation of reason and intelligence but at the same time warns of the treacheries lurking in the assumption that either theology or metaphysics has any rights to illogicality.[61] No intelligent reading of Schuon's work will uncover any 'contempt for human reason': here Zaehner is rather wildly firing off a polemical missile. One does not want to descend to the kind of personal abuse in which Zaehner was apt to indulge but it must be said plainly that this review is, to say the least, ignorant, petty-minded and supercilious. To disagree with what Schuon actually says is one thing, to slander him as an anti-rational, elitist obscurantist is another.

Zaehner again takes up arms against Schuon in two of his own works.[62] In *At Sundry Times* he shows no sign of having moved any closer to understanding Schuon's position:

> ... the co-existence of living religions as utterly different as are Judaism and Buddhism cries for an explanation ... one which ... does not take refuge in metaphysical mystification of the kind now practised by M. Frithjof Schuon.[63]

---

59 R.C. Zaehner: Review in *Journal of Theological Studies* VI, 1955; p341.
60 See, for example, FS *L&T* pp50ff.
61 See FS *EPW* p28.
62 R.C. Zaehner *Mysticism Sacred and Profane* Clarendon Press, Oxford, 1957 and *At Sundry Times*, Faber & Faber, London, 1958.
63 *At Sundry Times* p28.

We find an echo of this in a later book by Geoffrey Parrinder (an unkind commentator might be tempted to an observation about the blind leading the blind):

> ... he [Schuon] maintains that there is 'metaphysical' truth which is one, and 'religious' truths which are many and different manifestations of the inexpressible metaphysical truth. This is rather mystifying, for if the metaphysical truth is inexpressible it is difficult to know what any religion or philosophy can say about it.[64]

At least Parrinder's misgivings are expressed with some courtesy and he certainly does not descend to the kind of foolish assertions of which Zaehner shows himself capable in *Mysticism Sacred and Profane*.[65] Nonetheless, the charge in each case is the same: the dreaded 'mystification'. This seems to be a handy cover-up for a failure to understand: neither Zaehner nor Parrinder undertakes any kind of demonstration of wherein lies the 'mystification'. The substantive point which Parrinder makes is not likely to convince anyone not susceptible to the knee-jerk response which the very word 'metaphysics' is liable to provoke these days, almost as if it were indeed a synonym for 'mystification'. Let us take the related case of mystical literature. Mystics the world over have testified to the ineffability of the plenary experience. Are we then to conclude that we would be better off if none of the mystics had taken up the challenge of trying to communicate something of the experience? Shall we burn our copies of *The Cloud of Unknowing* or consign the writings of St Theresa of Avila to the rubbish-bin?

There is nothing at all mystifying about Schuon's comments on the 'inexpressibility' of metaphysical truths: 'The most explicit metaphysical doctrine will always take it as axiomatic that every doctrine is but error in the face of the Divine Reality in Itself...'. This much Parrinder understands but not what follows:

> ... a provisional, indispensable, salutary 'error' which, however, contains and communicates the virtuality of the Truth. The Divinity is beyond 'knowledge' in so far as this implies a subject and an object. It is for this reason that the divine Essence is unknowable.[66]

None of this is new: it has been said by every metaphysician since time immemorial. Schuon's formulation could hardly be clearer, which is not to say that everyone will understand it.

A good deal of polemical and critical academic literature is pockmarked by the habit of affixing pejorative labels to the thought of one's opponents and leaving it at that, as if nothing more need be said. In the case of the response to the traditionalists we find terms like 'neo-Platonic', 'Vedantic', 'neo-scholastic', 'perennialist', 'essentialist' and suchlike used to close rather than to open debate, as if these were dishonourable epithets which expose a type of thinking now 'outmoded'. Richard Bush tells us in critical tone that Schuon '... would be lost without the language of Christian mysticism, which like Sufism, of course, was profoundly influ-

---

64 G. Parrinder *Comparative Religion* Allen & Unwin, London, 1962; p79.

65 The comments made here are so misinformed that they do not warrant serious discussion. For a critique of Zaehner's own idiosyncratic and provincial view of mysticism see F. Staal *Exploring Mysticism* Uni California Press, Berkeley, 1975; pp67ff.

66 FS *SPHF* pp162–163.

enced by neo-Platonism . . .'[67] – as if it were reprehensible to avail oneself of such spiritual vocabularies as might be adequate to the realities in question! This kind of thing is all of a piece with the psycho-genetic fallacy which we have already discussed.

As we have seen, traditionalism is grounded in the premise of a Primordial Tradition, or Universal Wisdom which, through manifold Revelations, is manifested in the different religious traditions. Further, each of these traditions includes within itself a core of esoteric metaphysical wisdom always shaped by the same principles which constitute the *sophia perennis*. Some scholars have scorned these basic tenets in the traditionalist position. Here we shall consider a few of the lines of attack opened up by these scholars.

We have had occasion to draw several times on the work of Mircea Eliade which shares some ground with that of the traditionalists.[68] It is therefore with particular interest that we come across this passage in his journal:

> What Guénon and other 'hermetists' say of the tradition should not be understood on the level of historical reality (as they claim). These speculations constitute a universe of systematically articulated meanings: they are to be compared to a great poem or a novel. It is the same with Marxist or Freudian 'explanations': they are true if they are considered as imaginary universes. The 'proofs' are few and uncertain – they correspond to the historical, social and psychological 'realities' of a novel or of a poem.
>
> All these global and systematic interpretations, in reality, constitute mythological creations, highly useful for understanding the world; but they are not, as their authors think, 'scientific explanations'.[69]

This is both interesting and seductive. It deserves some detailed commentary.

Firstly one would be more than a little interested to be furnished with evidence that any of the traditionalists have ever claimed that the Primordial Tradition is an historical and empirical datum amenable to any kind of 'proof'; we have already met with Coomaraswamy's statement to the contrary (see Chapter 6). One must assume from the use of the singular and the definite article that Eliade is here referring to Tradition rather than the various traditions. Tradition is, in Coomaraswamy's words, an axiom or first principle: in this sense it might be compared to a mythological paradigm whose *locus* is not historical but *in illo tempore*, to mobilise one of Eliade's own favourite phrases. However, this is quite a different matter to the implication, clearly carried by Eliade's remarks, that the traditionalist vision of the Primordial Tradition is an imaginative 'speculation' that can fruitfully be compared to the 'systematic interpretations' of Freud and Marx. Moreover, Eliade's contention becomes doubly misleading if we allow it to apply to the work of the traditionalists on the traditions where they *are* writing about palpable historical realities.

Eliade's reference to Freud and Marx is more than a little puzzling. Elsewhere in the same work he observes, quite rightly, that 'to think like a materialist or a Marxist

---

67 R. Bush *op.cit.*; p719. Nasr comments on the abusive mis-use of the term 'neo-Platonism' in his Gifford Lectures. See SHN *K&S* p230.
68 These affinities should not be exaggerated. See Chapter 13.
69 M. Eliade *No Souvenirs* p291.

Criticisms of Traditionalism

means giving up the primordial vocation of man. Consequently to disappear as man.'[70] Yet he also likens his own discipline of the history of religions to the method of Marx and Freud, as if the enterprise did indeed demand a denial of our 'primordial vocation'.[71] We are not concerned here with a critical review of Eliade's journal but one mentions this apparent contradiction, or at least tension, because it is reflected in Eliade's ambivalence towards Guénon. He says that the 'speculations' of the traditionalists are 'true' if situated in the realm of 'imaginary universes' rather as if Guénon might usefully be compared to, say, Dostoyevsky. Eliade does claim that 'we have more creative possibilities in imaginary universes than we do on the level of history'; his judgement of Guénon is therefore, in his own terms, not uncharitable. Nevertheless, it simply will not do from a traditionalist standpoint. The traditionalists' own perception of their work has little to do with the personal creativity which Eliade values so highly. Indeed, personal creativity in the metaphysical realm is a contradiction in terms. The primary purpose of the traditionalists is not creation but explication and transmission. Schuon:

> In reality, the *philosophia perennis*, actualised in the West by Plato, Aristotle, Plotinus, the Fathers and the Scholastics, constitutes a 'definitive' intellectual heritage, and the great problem is not to replace them with something better – but to return to the sources, both around us and within us, and to examine all the data of contemporary life in the light of the one, timeless truth.[72]

This is a repudiation of all relativistic notions of truth and of the idea that new 'systematic interpretations' of the human condition, such as those offered by Marx and Freud, could have anything whatsoever to add to the perennial wisdom.

Eliade himself is clearly sceptical about the existence of the *sophia perennis*.[73] Given this attitude Eliade's 'interpretation' at least allows him to discern some significance in Guénon's work. However, this 'tolerant' and 'open-minded' attitude is something of a two-edged sword. In some senses it represents an evasive compromise and puts one in mind of Schuon's remarks:

> ... if there is a shortage of arguments for excusing the falsity of an opinion, consolation is sought in declaring that it constitutes a sample of 'human effort', or a 'contribution to culture', and so on, as if the aim of intelligence were not the discernment of truth.[74]

Eliade's concluding remarks about 'mythological creations' and 'scientific explanations' also leave the reader somewhat bemused. One would have thought Eliade innocent of any supposition that an authentic myth can ever find its provenance in individual thought. Eliade's reference to 'scientific explanations' can only refer to the empirico-historicist modes which he has severely criticised himself. He is right in suggesting that traditionalism cannot be accommodated in these modes but if this is a reproach – the intention is not clear – it comes strangely from one who has

---

70 ibid.; p86.
71 ibid.; p83.
72 FS *SW* p43.
73 See *The Quest* p36.
74 FS *SW* p42.

justly castigated his colleagues for their supine capitulation to the enfeebling demands of an illusory 'scientific objectivity'.

In another context Eliade makes a useful point which bears repetition here: one does not have to accept the traditionalist position as a whole to profit from a close study of works by traditionalists. Discussing one of Coomaraswamy's books Eliade notes

> One may or may not agree with Ananda Coomaraswamy's personal conviction with regard to *philosophia perennis* and the universal, primordial 'Tradition' informing all premodern cultures; what ultimately matters is the unexpected light that Coomaraswamy throws on the Vedic and Buddhist religious creation.[75]

The writings of not only Coomaraswamy but of all the traditionalists are textured with the most penetrating insights and flashing intuitions about specific religious phenomena: a rejection of their metaphysical framework is no reason to close oneself to their writings on such phenomena. However, from a traditionalist viewpoint this is rather back to front: ultimately what matters is not this or that phenomenon but the timeless principles and truths which lie behind it.

Alan Watts takes up the question of a 'universal tradition' in a more specific objection to the traditionalist position. In *Beyond Theology* he explains why, after being significantly influenced by both Guénon and Coomaraswamy, he came to reject the whole traditionalist position: '... there is not a scrap of evidence that the Christian hierarchy was ever aware of itself as one among several lines of transmission for a universal tradition ...' whereas 'the so-called "traditionalist" school ... regards every orthodox spiritual tradition as a more or less deliberate adaptation of the *philosophia perennis* to the needs of different cultures.'[76] The use of the word 'deliberate' here is quite misleading and proof enough that Watts has failed to understand the relationships in question. Several points: firstly, such 'adaptation' as there is, is to be found in the Revelations themselves, from which the traditions issue, and not in any self-conscious and *ad hoc* doings of the formal representatives of these traditions according to their own lights; secondly, the fact that the formal custodians of a religious tradition may not be aware of the relationships of the traditions to the *philosophia perennis* is only to be expected given that their function is the protection of the formal integrity of the orthodoxy in question; thirdly, the concomitant exclusivity is the prerogative of each and every tradition which quite properly demands an all-or-nothing commitment from its adherents; fourthly, there remains the testimony of those sages, to be found within every tradition, who have providentially recognised and affirmed the supra-formal unity behind the divergent formal manifestations found in the different traditions.[77]

There are those, of course, who believe that the whole principle of the transcendent unity of religions and of a universal exoteric wisdom is a mirage in the minds of

---

75 M. Eliade *The Quest* p36. See also 'Notes on the *Theosophia Perennis:* Ananda Coomaraswamy and Henry Corbin' *History of Religions* XIX, 1979; pp167–171.

76 A. Watts *Beyond Theology* quoted in W. Perry: 'Anti-Theology and the Riddles of Alcyone' *SCR* VI, iii, 1972; pp176–177. For Watts's earlier attitude see *The Supreme Identity* Random House, New York, 1972; p15.

77 It must, in fairness, be conceded that Guénon's work does leave room for some confusion about the relationship of Tradition and the traditions.

well-intentioned but misguided 'idealists'. This implication is carried by the criticisms of several of the commentators we have already discussed. It is perhaps worth reinforcing a point made earlier in this study: it is a grave mistake to imagine that one knows what the traditionalist position is simply because one has encountered something superficially similar elsewhere. One only compounds the confusion by rejecting the traditionalist vision of the *sophia perennis* because of some inanity uttered by someone who claims to be speaking in the name of the timeless wisdom. To the contention that there is, in fact, no perennial philosophy, the simplest rebuke is Whitall Perry's overwhelming demonstration of it in *A Treasury of Traditional Wisdom*. No one who has not read this magnificent compendium is in any position to deny the existence of a timeless wisdom. The evidence is there for those with eyes to see and ears to hear.

A tenacious misunderstanding which bedevils a good deal of discussion was given voice by Philip Sherrard in an earlier period before he aligned himself more completely with the traditionalist position:

> ...while it is one thing to say that all traditional forms ultimately express the same universal truth, it is quite another to say that they all express it to the same degree ... one is still left with the question of determining where it is in fact best represented.[78]

Two points of clarification are necessary here. Firstly, the traditionalists do *not* assert that each and every religion expresses universal truth to 'the same degree'; the efficacy of the forms and doctrines used to relate the contingent to the Absolute can and do vary. However, and this is the second point, because each tradition finds its source in a Divine Revelation it must include within itself an adequate if not exhaustive account of the relationships of the relative and the Absolute, proportioned to the needs of the collectivity in question, and it will thus also 'extol and actualise a spirituality that is equal to this doctrine and thereby include sanctity within its ambit both as concept and reality'.[79] In this light the problem of determining the 'best' evaporates: it is always a question of the spiritual temperament and receptivity in question. It is quite meaningless to say, for instance, that Islam 'better' represents universal truth than Buddhism: it does so for Muslims only.[80] This mania for artificial discriminations and false hierarchies is symptomatic of the either/or type of thinking which tends to tyrannize the modern mentality. One might just as well argue about which is the 'best' geometric form.

All this notwithstanding it is possible to make discriminations concerning the comparative comprehensiveness of different religious and metaphysical doctrines. Thus Schuon has no hesitation in telling us that Shankara's doctrine is more profound and inclusive than Ramanuja's which it subsumes but does not invalidate;[81] similarly he endorses St Bonaventura's attribution of 'wisdom' to Plato and 'science' to Aris-

---

[78] P. Sherrard: 'The Tradition and the Traditions: the Confrontation of Religious Doctrines' *Religious Studies* X, 1974; p409. Similarly Parrinder who writes 'The notion that all religions are of equal truth and value is one of the commonest misconceptions.' *Comparative Religion* p83.

[79] FS *IPP* p14.

[80] This position is shared by many Hindus. See A. Sharma: 'All religions are – equal? one? same? A critical examination of some formulations of the neo-Hindu position' *Philosophy East and West* XXIX, i, 1979; pp59ff.

[81] See FS *SPHF* pp103–104 and FS *SW* p18.

totle.[82] Or again, he states that the *Advaita* Vedanta perspective and that of Platonism, are amongst the 'most adequate expressions possible of the *philosophia perennis*'.[83] These few examples show that the traditionalists assert no such thing as the formal 'equality' of the different traditions. However, these kinds of discriminations can only be made by those fully qualified to do so and without any wish to construct some kind of meaningless 'ladder' of the religions which could only sow the seeds of confusion and strife.

This brings us on to another problem posed by Sherrard. He points out that in order to answer the sorts of questions which have just been under discussion it is necessary to be 'in possession of the knowledge according to which they can be answered', a knowledge which is 'the highest humanly possible'.[84] Quite so. But at this point Sherrard falls into a trap of his own contrivance:

> It is precisely here that what one might call a *petitio principii* is involved ... For the degree of knowledge one possesses will be that represented in the tradition from which one has obtained it: otherwise one would not be in possession of it. To say then that this is the highest degree of knowledge, the fullest expression of it possible ... and consequently that the tradition through which one has obtained it is a universal tradition in the full meaning of the words, is simply to argue round in a circle. It is to use as one's criteria of what constitutes the highest degree of knowledge, and hence of where this is represented, precisely those principles enshrined in the tradition from which one has obtained them in the first place.[85]

Prima facie this looks persuasive but the passage really announces Sherrard's failure to understand the relationships between the exoteric and esoteric domains, and between Revelation and intellection. It is also an irremediably dualistic and rationalistic piece of argumentation. The principles in question have been expounded earlier in this work but a little recapitulation is perhaps in order to expose the flaws in the argument. It should also be pointed out that Sherrard is trying to meet the traditionalists on their own ground: this makes it all the more important that we should not be snared in the same trap.

Under the traditionalist understanding esoteric wisdom can indeed only be nurtured within the cadre of an integral tradition. (The rare exceptions are of no moment in the present context.) Orthodoxy opens 'inwards', as it were, on to Truth:

> ... orthodoxy is the principle of formal homogeneity proper to any authentically spiritual perspective; it is therefore an indispensable aspect of all genuine intellectuality; in other words, the essence of every orthodoxy is truth, and not merely fidelity to a system that might be false. To be orthodox means to participate, through the medium of a doctrine that can properly be called 'traditional', in the immutability of the principles which govern the Universe and fashion our intelligence.[86]

---

82 FS *SW* p43 fn1. Note also: '... two doctrines may be opposed to one another either because of a legitimate difference of perspective, or because one of them is erroneous, or because both are but in different ways; care must be taken to avoid putting mere discrepancies of form on the same level with fundamental contradictions.' *SW* p18.
83 FS *EPW* pp21–22. For an explication of Sankara's metaphysic, drawing heavily on Schuon's work, see my own article 'Sankara's Doctrine of *Maya*' in *Asian Philosophy* II, ii, 1992; pp131–146.
84 P. Sherrard *op.cit.*; p411.
85 *ibid.*
86 FS *SW* p13. I am indebted to Dr. William Stoddart for pointing out an error in the original English translation of this passage.

This alone is an answer to Sherrard's problem: 'the essence of every orthodoxy is truth'. However, we might also note that the sources of esoteric wisdom are not exhausted by the formal elements of the tradition in question: esotericism is concerned with intellection, that is, the direct apprehension of truth as such. Intellection is intellection and not 'Christian' or 'Muslim' intellection, and, as such, it dissolves all dualities and liberates one from the confines of any particular perspective. Thus Sherrard's objection falls to the ground.

In conclusion we might recall a remark from Schuon to forestall further objections along the lines opened up by some of the critics of traditionalism :

> There will be those, no doubt, who will question how the effectiveness and existence of this knowledge can be proved: the only possible reply is that such proof is given by the expressions of Intellection themselves; just as it is impossible to prove to every soul the validity of a given religion, a fact which in no wise detracts from that validity, so it is also impossible to prove the reality of the Intellect to every understanding, which again proves nothing at all against the said reality.[87]

---

87 FS *L&T* pp31-32. See also p33fn.

13

The Phenomenology of Religion

... the scientific pursuit of religion puts the saddle on the wrong horse, since it is the domain of religion to evaluate science, and not vice versa
Whitall Perry[1]

The passionless reason of... 'objective' scholarship, applied to the study of 'what men have believed', is only a sort of frivolity, in which the real problem, that of knowing what should be believed, is evaded
Ananda Coomaraswamy[2]

The term 'phenomenology of religion' was perhaps first used in the late nineteenth century by the Dutch theologian, P.D. Chantepie de la Saussaye. It now has a wide currency in academic circles and has become something of a rag-bag into which have been stuffed philosophical concepts, methodological principles and scholarly aspirations. It is at once a rubric, a motto, a cliché, a smokescreen. As one commentator has rightly observed, '... phenomenologists of religion have always been a little difficult to pin down, and even to identify satisfactorily. Like mystics, saints and bushrangers, they are more often taken dead than alive.'[3] In the hands of some of its earliest practitioners the term 'phenomenology of religion' referred to typological constructions and systematic classifications deriving from cross-cultural, comparative study of religious phenomena perceived to be of the same generic type. This kind of 'descriptive phenomenology' was exemplified by the Hastings *Encyclopedia of Religion and Ethics* (1908–1921) in which one could find entries under such headings as 'prayer', 'sacrifice', 'ritual' and so on, each drawing on a wide range of data.[4] Thus 'phenomenology of religion' was

> ... a systematic counterpart to the history of religion, an elementary method of cross-cultural comparison of the constituent elements of religious belief and practice, as opposed to their treatment in cultural isolation or in chronological sequence.[5]

Under the influence of scholars like Nathan Söderblom,[6] W. Brede Kristensen,[7] and Gerardus van der Leeuw[8] the term took on more epistemological and philosophical weight by implying a kind of systematic study which would reveal structures, relationships, patterns of meaning and essences in the comparative data.

The term 'phenomenology' pre-dated Chantepie; it had been used by Kant, Fries and Hegel to denote an epistemological theory. However, it came to be most closely associated with the philosophy of Edmund Husserl whose ideas had some antecedents in the work of Franz Brentano. Husserl's own ideas were modified by later philosophers such as Martin Heidegger and Jurgen Habermas to form a loose phenomenological school.[9] Husserl set out to bridge the gap between positivistic epistemologies which stressed the primacy of the object, the thing known, and idealistic philosophies which accented the primacy of the subject, the knower. Husserl was in search of a

---

1 Whitall Perry in a review of Ninian Smart's *The Phenomena of Religion* in *SCR* VII, ii, 1973; p127.
2 AKC *BL* p22.
3 E.J. Sharpe: 'Universal Religion for Universal Man', *Charles Strong Memorial Lecture 1978*; printed in *Colloquium*, Journal of *ANZSTS* 1978; p23.
4 T. & T. Clark, Edinburgh, 1908–1926.
5 E.J. Sharpe *Comparative Religion* Duckworth, London, 1975; p223. See also W.E. Paden *Religious Worlds: The Comparative Study of Religion* Beacon Press, Boston, 1988; Chs 1 & 2.
6 On Söderblom see E.J. Sharpe: 'Nathan Söderblom and the Study of Religion' *Religious Studies* IV, 1969, and *Comparative Religion* pp154–161 & 226ff.
7 On Kristensen see E.J. Sharpe *Comparative Religion* pp227–229, and A. Sharma: 'A Reconstruction of the Phenomenological Method of W. Brede Kristensen' *Milla Wa Milla* XVIII, 1978; pp6–12.
8 On van der Leeuw see E.J. Sharpe *Comparative Religion* pp229–235, and F. Struckmeyer: 'Phenomenology and Religion: Some Comments' *Religious Studies* XVI, iii, 1980; pp253–262.
9 For a survey of the phenomenological school of philosophy see H. Spiegelberg *The Phenomenological Movement, A Historical Introduction* 2 vols, Martinus Nihoff, The Hague, 1960.

'scientific' epistemology which centered on the relationship between subject and object. The 'phenomenology of religion', as usually understood in the discipline of comparative religion, has only tenuous links with Husserlian phenomenology. There are philosophers (rather than comparative religionists) who have applied Husserl's ideas to the study of religion – Max Scheler is one. Amongst comparative religionists Van der Leeuw is perhaps the only one to attempt a genuinely Husserlian methodology.

We are not here concerned primarily with phenomenology as a strict philosophical system but a comment from Schuon will perhaps not be without interest:

> ... an intuition so right as that which forms the basis of German 'phenomenology', inevitably remains, for lack of objective intellectual principles, fragmentary, problematical and inoperative. An accident does not take the place of a principle nor does a philosophical adventure replace real wisdom. No one has, in fact, been able to extract anything from this 'phenomenology' from the point of view of effective and integral knowledge, such as works on the soul and transforms it.[10]

This fact is not always remembered by those who draw comparisons between phenomenological philosophy and Oriental metaphysic – between, for example, the ideas of Heidegger and Nagarjuna.

If comparative religionists have not really applied a Husserlian methodology as such it remains true that they have taken two concepts of critical importance from phenomenological philosophy: *epoché* and *eidetic vision*. *Epoché* is the identification and 'suspension' of one's own presuppositions, attitudes and commitments in the face of the phenomena one is studying; '... it emphasizes the need to abstain from every kind of value judgement, to be "present" to the phenomena in question purely as an impartial observer, unconcerned with questions of truth and falsehood.'[11] *Eidetic vision* is a more slippery term but suggests a perception of critical inter-relationships, forms and essences through a sympathetic and receptive study of comparative data, a capacity to discern in the phenomena themselves the essentials of a religious structure or situation. The point needing some emphasis was made by van der Leeuw: 'Phenomenology is concerned only with "phenomena", that is with "appearance"; for it, there is nothing whatever "behind" the phenomena.'[12] Thus the 'essence' is to be perceived in the phenomena themselves. *Epoché*, then, provides a context for the observation of phenomena while *eidetic vision* is a mode of perception. These, generally speaking, are now seen as the constitutive elements in the 'phenomenological method' as practised by comparative religionists. Certainly there have been all manner of conflicting methodologies which have sought respectability under the canopy of 'phenomenological method' and there remains a lively if somewhat inconclusive debate on this subject. We will not here enter into the intricacies of this debate but confine ourselves to a few general remarks before going on to consider the traditionalist position on some of the issues raised.

It has not escaped the notice of several commentators that there is a fundamental contradiction, or at the least a very considerable tension, between the ideals of *epoché*

---

10 FS *SPHF* p15. See also FS *SW* p43.
11 E.J. Sharpe *Comparative Religion* p224.
12 G. van der Leeuw quoted in F. Streng: 'The Objective Study of Religion and the Unique Quality of Religiousness' *Religious Studies* VI, 1970; p215.

and *eidetic vision*. The first marks a striving after a kind of scientific 'objectivity', almost as if the scholar's mind could be a *tabula rasa* on which the phenomena themselves could spell out their significances. *Eidetic vision* however, allows a degree of subjectivity in through the back door, as it were. The debate about 'phenomenology' is in reality a debate about the place and the limits of scholarly objectivity, about commitment and neutrality, and about the role of hermeneutics in religious studies. It is not difficult to see why the 'phenomenological method' proved so attractive to the European scholars who pioneered it: not only did it liberate religious studies from the tyranny of an excessively historicist approach underpinned by evolutionist assumptions but it also seemed to provide a means of reconciling 'scientific' scholarship and personal religious commitment. For men who were, after all, mostly Christian theologians, phenomenology allowed them 'to "suspend" their faith without denying it ... to be open and uncommitted as phenomenologists while maintaining their allegiance to a particular tradition'.[13] In the academic climate then prevailing this was important for other reasons which need not be canvassed here.[14]

Within the discipline variously called 'comparative religion', 'religious studies', 'history of religions' and so on – the plethora of terms itself indicates confusion over the proper identity and methodology of the discipline – there has recently developed some feeling that the 'phenomenological method' is something of a phantom. Some scholars now believe that 'phenomenology' has raised more questions than it has answered, or indeed can answer. Thus H. Penner:

> Anyone who desires to find out what 'phenomenology of religion' is, and how the approach is applied, will find the search a frustrating experience ... In some cases the term ... appears as a metaphorical word for work that lacks methodological rigour.[15]

Or Klaus Klostermaier:

> If one examines what 'phenomenology of religion' is supposed to mean in the context of our discipline ... How this ... could be called a 'method', capable of supporting a 'science of religions', is an unanswered and unanswerable question. It is a cover-up for methodological confusion.[16]

However, if the term itself be somewhat nebulous or ambiguous the issues which are at the centre of the debate are very real ones.

The participants in the methodological debate can be divided into two main camps which for purposes of convenience we can call 'conservative' and 'radical'. The conservative camp has its stronghold in Europe, the radical in the U.S.A. – the British try to maintain a non-aligned position and maintain friendly relations with both blocs. (Whether one wants to see this as an 'honest broker' position or one of timid compromise depends on one's point of view.) The issues over which the two groups part company include the place of 'objectivity' in religious studies, the former

---

13 K. Klostermaier: 'From phenomenology to meta-science; reflections on the study of religion' *Studies in Religion* VI, v, 1976–1977; p553.
14 See E.J. Sharpe *Comparative Religion* Ch X, pp220–240, and C-M. Erdsman: 'Theology or Religious Studies' *Religion* IV, 1974; pp59–74.
15 Quoted in C. Davis: 'The Reconvergence of Theology and Religious Studies' *Studies in Religion* IV, iii, 1974–1975; p215.
16 K. Klostermaeir *op.cit.*; p554.

group tending towards a 'scientific' and empirical ideal of impartial scholarship, the latter leaning more towards a morally-committed 'creative hermeneutics' which allows of normative judgements and assessments. Needless to say our picture of these two opposing camps is very generalised and over-simplified. However, it does help to clarify some of the issues. Let us listen for a moment to a few claims by representatives from each camp.

C.J. Bleeker articulates the 'conservative' position when he writes 'the history of religions in principle is an empirical science. It does not produce any value-judgements....'.[17] R. Zwi Werblowsky remarks that

> It is no secret that comparative religion is, in many respects, an awkward subject. One of its difficulties stems from the fact that many of its practitioners seem unable to make up their minds whether the subject of their studies is theology (viz. philosophy of religion) or simply that particular type of religious manifestations [sic] indicated by the somewhat vague term 'religious phenomena'.[18]

He goes on to suggest that the latter is the proper pursuit of this discipline, that it should rigorously exclude any normative considerations, theological or otherwise. (These remarks are made in the context of a critique of the ideas of Joachim Wach.) As well as Bleeker and Werblowsky one might cite Ake Hultkrantz,[19] Kurt Rudolph,[20] and Ugo Bianchi[21] as representatives of a school of thought which stresses an objective, scientifically constituted and predominantly empirical approach to religious studies.

Across the Atlantic we find a significant number of scholars who, for one reason or another, were disenchanted with the objectivist approach and who assigned a more creative role to the subjective resources of the scholar: Joachim Wach, W. Cantwell Smith, Mircea Eliade, Joseph Kitagawa, W. Oxtoby and Klaus Klostermaier were amongst the most prominent. Few of these scholars see themselves as 'phenomenologists' and certainly they do not share any single methodological or philosophical platform. However, they all believe that comparative religion must free itself of a sterile imitation of the natural sciences. They point out that even in the most rigorous of the sciences – physics for example – the ideal of 'objectivity' as it has been understood is now under serious question and disrepute.[22] Thus, for instance, Mircea Eliade championed a bolder and more interpretative approach:

> Such a creative hermeneutics does not always seem to guide the work of historians of religions because, perhaps, of the inhibition provoked by the triumph of 'scientism' in certain humanist disciplines. In the measure that the social sciences and a certain anthropology have endeavoured to become more 'scientific', the historians of religion have become more ... timid ... Neither the history of religions nor any other humanist discipline ought to conform ... to models borrowed from the natural sciences, still more as these models are out of date ....[23]

---

17 C.J. Bleeker: 'Comparing the Religio-Historical and the Theological Method' *Numen* 1971; p11.
18 R. Zwi Werblowsky: 'The Comparative Study of Religions, A Review Essay' (on Wach) *Judaism* VIII, iv, 1959; re-print p1.
19 See A. Hultkrantz: 'The Phenomenology of Religions: Aims and Methods' *Temenos* VI, 1968.
20 See K. Rudolph: 'Basic Positions of *Religionswissenschaft*' *Religion* XI, 1981; pp97-107.
21 See U. Bianchi: 'The Definition of Religion: On the Methodology of Historical-Comparative Research' in U. Bianchi et al. *Problems and Methods of the History of Religions* E.J. Brill, Leiden, 1972.
22 See Chapter 10.
23 M. Eliade *The Quest* Uni Chicago Press, 1969; pp60-61.

Similarly W. Cantwell Smith, concerned with the experiential dimension of religious faith, warns against the stifling effects of a false objectivity: 'Objectivity drastically fails to do justice not only to the known but to the knower, not only to the object of knowledge but to the subject.'[24]

We cannot here reconstruct the philosophical and methodological platforms of these scholars or rehearse the agendas they envisage for the discipline. However, we might mention in passing the morally-impelled concern with fostering inter-religious understanding (Klostermaier, Smith), the attempt to find in religious studies a basis for a new 'planetary humanism' (Eliade), the effort to reconcile theology and comparative religion on something other than a 'phenomenological' basis (Wach, Charles Davis, Tillich), the interest in philosophical issues in the study of religion (Paul Ricouer).[25] All of these developments testify to a feeling that phenomenology, in pursuit of a scientific method, has not altogether answered the needs of the case.

At this juncture it is perhaps worth mentioning two points which have surfaced in the on-going debate about methodology: the emphasis on the self-perception of the believer; and the notion that the study of religion can, in itself, be a spiritual pursuit. Some time ago W.B. Kristensen suggested that 'If our opinion about another religion differs from the opinion and evaluation of the believer, then we are no longer talking about their religion. We have turned away from historical reality, and are concerned only with ourselves.'[26] This notion, very much in vogue in some quarters, is sometimes encapsulated in the dictum 'the believer is always right'.[27] W. Cantwell Smith is one scholar who has been concerned with the applications of this principle. In one of his essays he asserts that '... no statement about a religion is valid unless it can be acknowledged by that religion's believers.'[28] This is a little more subtle and flexible than Kristensen's formulation but the general thrust is the same. Some commentators have gone so far as to identify this as a keystone in the phenomenological method. Michael Pye, for instance, sees it as a *sine qua non* and suggests that theories which import 'modes of understanding which go far beyond the self-understanding of particular believers or participants' are thereby not strictly phenomenological.[29]

The fact that the issue of the existential effect of religious studies on the student is now receiving more ventilation also shows that the debate about the discipline goes well beyond technical and procedural questions. Mircea Eliade has written persuasively about the crippling effects of treating religious phenomena as 'objective data' and no more. He is worth quoting at some length on this point:

---

[24] W.C. Smith: 'Objectivity and the Humane Sciences' in W.Oxtoby (ed) *Religious Diversity: Essays by Wilfrid Cantwell Smith* Harper & Row, New York, 1976; p168.

[25] For some of the literature in this field see, as well as sources already cited, K. Klostermaier *In the Paradise of Krishna* Westminster Press, Philadelphia, 1969; essays by W.C. Smith, Kitagawa and Eliade in M. Eliade and J. Kitagawa (eds) *The History of Religions: Essays in Methodology* Uni Chicago Press, 1959; W.C. Smith *The Meaning and End of Religion* SPCK, London, 1978 and *Questions of Religious Truth* Victor Gollancz, London, 1971; J.C. Wach *The Comparative Study of Religion* Columbia Uni Press, New York, 1958.

[26] Kristensen, quoted in E.J. Sharpe *Comparative Religion* p228.

[27] This is taken so seriously in some places that a thesis about a particular religion will not be accepted without the imprimatur of a representative of the tradition in question.

[28] W.C. Smith: 'Comparative Religion – Whither and Why?' in M.Eliade & J. Kitagawa *op.cit.*; p42.

[29] M. Pye: 'Problems of Method in the Interpretation of Religion' *Japanese Journal of Religious Studies* I, ii & iii, 1974; pp113–114, quoted in A. Sharma: 'Towards a definition of the Phenomenology of Religion' *Milla wa Milla* XVI, 1976; p14. (Pye offers Jung, Levi-Strauss and Eliade as examples of scholars who import precisely such theories.)

> ...the majority of the historians of religion defend themselves against the messages with which their documents are filled. This caution is understandable. One does not live with impunity in intimacy with 'foreign' religious forms... But many historians of religions end by no longer taking seriously the spiritual worlds they study; they fall back on their personal religious faith, or they take refuge in a materialism or behaviourism impervious to every spiritual shock.[30]

The kind of engagement which Eliade calls for will, by contrast, make the researcher more receptive to the spiritual messages of the phenomena under study: 'Creative hermeneutics *changes* man; it is more than mere instruction, it is a spiritual technique susceptible of modifying the quality of existence itself.'[31] Likewise: 'To the degree that you *understand* a religious fact (myth, ritual, symbol, divine figure), you *change*, you are modified – and this change is the equivalent of a step forward in the process of self-liberation.'[32] W.G. Oxtoby draws attention to the fact that, far from being a value-free and quasi-scientific pursuit, the phenomenological method as practised by most of its exponents confers approval in principle on the faith of others and thus helps preserve the value of one's own faith. He argues that

> Phenomenology's chief potential clientele is among religious committed persons as an appreciation of religious commitment... The individual scholar enters into a reverent extension of knowledge which strengthens his own private or shared attitudes towards a transcendent reality. In phenomenology, the science of religions has in effect become a religious exercise in itself.[33]

Eric Sharpe makes the same point in writing, '...phenomenology may be not only reconciled with religious faith, but may indeed be a peculiarly contemporary expression of it.'[34] Klaus Klostermaier goes further and talks about 'the religion of study' which, as he understands it, 'is not only one more theory of religion – it is in itself a way'.[35] We have isolated a few of the issues and ideas which have been at the centre of the debate about the 'phenomenology of religion'. We shall now turn to a commentary on these developments from a traditionalist point of view. The traditionalists themselves have remained aloof from the academic jousting so we shall have to proceed by inference.

For the traditionalists the debate about objectivity and commitment is something of a non-issue: to be a traditionalist is to be committed to a specific religious tradition and to a pursuit of an understanding of the *sophia perennis*. The traditionalists, for the most part, are not interested in an empirically-based scholarship for it own sake but only insofar as it finds a place in what, in the first place, is a spiritual way. Their vocation is to make intelligible the perennial wisdom and to preserve the forms and values vehicled by each integral religious tradition. In other words the whole orientation of the traditionalists is quite different from that of most academic scholars:

---

30 M. Eliade *The Quest* p62.
31 *ibid.*
32 M. Eliade *No Souvenirs* Harper & Row, New York, 1977; p310.
33 W.G. Oxtoby in an article entitled *'Religionswissenschaft* Revisited', quoted in E.J. Sharpe: 'The Phenomenology of Religion', unpublished paper; p9.
34 E.J. Sharpe: *ibid.*; p10.
35 K. Klostermaeir: 'The Religion of Study' *Religious Traditions* I, ii, 1978; p65.

academic pursuits can find a place in this framework but they will always be governed by 'extra-academic' considerations. This notwithstanding, it is worth considering some of the issues which have been under discussion in a traditionalist light. As we have seen, a primary idea associated with the phenomenology of religion is the belief that the 'essences' of religious manifestations can be discerned, through *eidetic vision*, in the phenomena themselves. In other words there is no 'essence' separable from the concrete forms which express it. The phenomenologists' procedure, from a traditionalist point of view, is a case of putting the cart before the horse. The approach of traditionalists like Guénon, Coomaraswamy and Schuon starts at the opposite epistemological pole: it is only through a grasp of universal principles which reveal the essence of religious forms that one can make sense of the disparate phenomena, these being contingent expressions of the principles in question. As Nasr states, 'Only in understanding the essence of a religion can its forms become understood as intelligible symbols rather than opaque forms.'[36] Thus the traditionalists proceed from a set of axiomatic principles to the phenomena; the phenomenologists proceed from the myriad and chaotic data, through *eidetic vision* or 'creative hermeneutics', to some kind of understanding of the significance and meaning of religious phenomena. From a traditionalist point of view the latter enterprise is doomed to fail.

The two ideals of *epoché* and *eidetic vision* are quite unsatisfactory from a traditionalist viewpoint, as are the objectivist-scientific and the hermeneutical-interpretative emphases to which they lend themselves. The whole notion of a scientific 'explanation' of religious phenomena is anathematised in this perspective: 'To attempt to explain or to account for Religion in modern scientific terms is simply an attempt to explain the greater in terms of the lesser, which is impossible.'[37] This applies not only to those degrading reductionisms already discussed but to each and every pretension that religious phenomena can ever be meaningfully explained within an empirical and quasi-objective framework.

If the usage of the term 'eidetic vision' is subjected to critical scrutiny we find that, in itself, it really means very little. Its real significance is as a gateway for subjective interpretations. Let us take Mircea Eliade, one of the most interesting and influential advocates of a 'creative hermeneutics', as a kind of test case. In one of his essays he tells us – and it is a characteristic formulation – that 'It is only insofar as he succeeds, through hermeneutics, in transmuting his materials into *spiritual messages* that the historian of religious faiths fulfils his role in contemporary culture.'[38] The traditionalist would not, I think, quarrel with this. Certainly Eliade repudiates a barren scholarship which appears to have no other aim than the accumulation of a quantitative and external mass of information about religious phenomena; he is deeply concerned with significances, meanings, messages, and would doubtless endorse Joachim Wach's claim that '... if *Religionswissenschaft* [the academic and comparative study of religions] is only an aesthetically interesting or purely academic matter, then, indeed, it has no right to exist today.'[39] Again, the traditionalist would

---

36 S.H. Nasr *Sufi Essays* Allen & Unwin, London, 1972; p130.
37 Lord Northbourne *Religion in the Modern World* J.M. Dent, London, 1963; p49.
38 M. Eliade *The Quest* p36.
39 J. Wach, quoted in E.J. Sharpe *Compartive Religion* p238.

be the first to agree. However, there remains an intractable problem: on what epistemological and philosophical basis is this 'creative hermeneutic' to be carried out? Eliade's critics have not been slow to point out that his whole 'hermeneutic' rests on certain metaphysical and ontological assumptions which are implicit and somewhat camouflaged in his work because they are not stated openly or supported with any argumentation.[40] We would seem to have a case in point of Charles Davis's claim that 'The failure to follow through the logic of inquiry from history and science to philosophy produces unacknowledged metaphysics.'[41]

It is clear that any interpretation must depend on certain assumptions and values. The problem, of course, is that comparative religionists do not and cannot agree on the philosophical and normative base on which interpretation can be built. This is less a problem for theologians who can investigate 'other religions' in the light of 'the religion'. Such a procedure is entirely proper to theologians but, as one scholar remarks,

> It cannot be so when the aims of study are understanding and explanation of any and all religious phenomena ... To the extent that 'theology' is concerned with the tenets of a particular Religion, its assumptions cannot provide methodological principles. By the same token they cannot provide a unifying centre for the disciplines which together make up the study of religion ...[42]

The upshot of all this is that comparative religion finds itself in an inescapable impasse, flanked on one side by those still hunting the unicorn of a 'scientific method' and on the other by a bewildering array of interpretative paradigms which are drawn from the subjective resources of the scholars in question. Let us return for a moment to Eliade.

From a traditionalist viewpoint the 'spiritual messages' with which Eliade is properly concerned can only be deciphered through a metaphysical discernment which transcends the limits of any particular philosophical or theological outlook. Anything less will produce an interpretation coloured by the subjective evaluations of the scholar in question. A traditionalist reviewer of Eliade's journal, *No Souvenirs*, had this to say:

> One has the impression of an uprooted and genial academic of broad sympathies and expert scholarship busily drifting from article to article, book to book, without inward centre or the intellectual [ie. metaphysical] discrimination to master his prodigious mental fertility.[43]

These words might apply to a good deal of the discipline as a whole. The 'inward centre' and 'intellectual discrimination' is precisely what no methodology can ever provide: it is to be found through Revelation, tradition, gnosis. Bereft of these, academic scholarship must inevitably fall prey to the Scylla of a dead and quantitative empiricism or the Charybdis of a subjective relativism. Nasr states the traditionalist

---

40 See, for example, R. Baird *Category Formation and the History of Religions* Mouton, The Hague, 1971; pp88–89.
41 C. Davis: *op.cit.*; p213.
42 E.H. Pyle: 'Reduction and the Religious Explanation of Religion' *Religion* IX, 1979; p198. (This contention is challenged in an interesting and provocative article, already cited, by Charles Davis.) See also P. Heelas: 'Some Problems with Religious Studies' *Religion* VII, 1978; pp1ff.
43 D. Lake: review of Eliade in *SCR* XII, iii & iv, 1978; p244.

position in a nutshell: 'Once man rejects revelation and tradition there is little virtue in religious open-mindedness [so highly valued by the "phenomenologists"] because there is no longer a criterion for distinguishing the true from the false.'[44] The situation of the academic scholar is precisely analogous to that of the post-medieval artist who is thrown back on to subjective resources whilst the traditionalist may be compared to the medieval artist whose work derives its 'objectivity' from the tradition and the vocabulary which shapes his work.

Nasr's remark brings us to another issue. It is generally agreed in academic circles that *religionswissenschaft* cannot concern itself with questions of truth and falsehood, that this is not its province. This would no doubt be the retort to Nasr's statement. However, not only does this condemn the discipline to impotence in the face of the questions which naturally present themselves to anyone with an 'existential' interest in religion, it also closes the door on any and every normative judgement and evaluation. (This point will be elaborated in the next chapter). Here the gulf between phenomenologist and traditionalist widens into a veritable chasm: for the latter the nature and manifestation of truth is at the very centre of study while the phenomenologist is obliged to steer clear of this troublesome area.

The two subsidiary ideas which we mentioned earlier – the emphasis on the self-understanding of the believer, and the notion that religious studies can, in itself, take on a religious and spiritual dimension – also call for some commentary from a traditionalist viewpoint. Doubtless Kristensen, W. Cantwell Smith and others who have affirmed the principle of the critical importance of the self-understanding of the believer did so as an antidote to the Eurocentric assumptions of some of their predecessors. A concern for the ways in which the believers themselves see and understand and experience their religion is, in itself, entirely laudable. However, as a methodological principle it is not without its ambiguities. The very enterprise of cross-cultural study makes it inevitable that the scholar will uncover significances of which the ordinary believer must be ignorant. It is true that, as many understand it, the principle does not demand that the scholar's perception be identical to that of the believer but only that it does not contradict it. Nevertheless, there remain problems: which believers are we to consult? Who will give us an authoritative view? Are we to take an opinion poll? One does not wish to lampoon an entirely well-intentioned idea but surely the difficulties are obvious enough. From a traditionalist viewpoint it might also be added that only an understanding of the relationship of the exoteric and esoteric realms and a firm grounding in immutable metaphysical and cosmological principles can ever give an adequate account of religious forms: this kind of understanding will, in the nature of things, only be shared by a small minority of the believers in question, namely those with the same credentials. For the traditionalist it is precisely these qualifications which give the works of Guénon, Coomaraswamy and Schuon their authority and which enable them to penetrate doctrines and forms from a wide range of different historical situations and from different spiritual climates.

Oxtoby, Klostermaier and others are on firm ground in suggesting that the study of religious forms can take on a spiritual dimension, as it does in the work of all the traditionalists. However, the contention that such study can itself become a spiritual

---

44 S.H. Nasr *op.cit.*; p127.

discipline would be disavowed completely by the traditionalist. The forms and disciplines of the spiritual life are drawn from Revelation and tradition and cannot be improvised in any *ad hoc* and subjective kind of way, as if the human individual is able to draw all things needful out of himself. Without doubting the sincerity of Klostermaier's own convictions one must suspect that comparative studies more often serve as a substitute for a lukewarm and faltering faith. One is put in mind of Martin Buber's words: 'it is far more comfortable to have to do with religion than to have to do with God'.[45]

No one will deny that many of the developments in the study of religion in recent decades mark real and important advances: a growing awareness of the limits of historicism and empiricism, the resistance to subversive reductionisms, the search for underlying meanings and spiritual significances, the attempt to enter into other spiritual universes in an attitude of respectful sympathy, the recognition of the existential involvement of the student, the concern for the experience of the believers themselves, the attempt to reconcile personal commitment with a rigorous scholarship – all of these are developments which any traditionalist can applaud. Nevertheless, in the traditionalist view, none of this can lead to a full understanding of religion, of the religions or of religious phenomena without recourse to the traditional principles which have been under discussion in the present work. This imperative will be one of our concerns in our final chapter.

---

45 M. Buber *A Believing Humanism* Simon & Schuster, New York, 1967; p110.

14

Religious Pluralism and the Study of Religions

The passion for research taken as an end in itself [is] ... 'mental restlessness' without end and without issue ... this substitution of research for knowledge is simply giving up the proper object of intelligence ...
René Guénon[1]

The essential problem that the study of religion poses is how to preserve religious truth, traditional orthodoxy, the dogmatic theological structures of one's own tradition, and yet gain knowledge of other traditions and accept them as spiritually valid ways and roads to God
Seyyed Hossein Nasr[2]

... the only possible ground upon which an effective entente of East and West can be accomplished is that of the purely intellectual wisdom that is one and the same at all times and for all men, and is independent of all environmental idiosyncrasy
Ananda Coomaraswamy[3]

Some of the implicit antagonisms between any purely academic study of religion and the traditionalist approach have already been laid bare. We shall round off this theme with a few general observations about *religionswissenschaft* and then focus on the problem of religious pluralism and the light shed on it by traditionalism. A few concluding remarks about the ways in which traditionalism can enrich the comparative study of religion will bring the present work to its end.

One commentator, Kurt Rudolph, considering the state of the discipline some years ago, had this to say:

> *Religionswissenschaft* is in every fibre an offspring of the eighteenth and nineteenth centuries ... the characteristic features both then and now have been tolerance, criticism, objectivity, history and humanity.[4]

This is an unexceptional statement. Not everyone would agree that this is a desirable state of affairs or that this formulation should be prescriptive, but as a loose description of the discipline over the past century it can hardly be disputed. The most significant general point, in a traditionalist context, is that the discipline is indeed a child of its times. It might be argued that traditionalism too was parented by recent European history but as a rebellious rather than a conforming child. Certainly traditionalism is, in some senses, a reaction against the mainstream of European thought in the post-medieval period; its appearance would hardly have otherwise been necessary. This fact also explains why traditionalism must sometimes appear rather combative and militant: in the prevailing intellectual climate the traditionalists have been forced to play the role of the advocate and could not always fulfil the function of the judge with the impartiality and sobriety becoming the latter. Here we are concerned not with the genealogy of either *religionswissenschaft* or traditionalism but with the catalogue of disciplinary characteristics listed by Rudolph in the quotation above, considered from a traditionalist point of view.[5]

Tolerance: this, in fact, is a sentimental attitude germinated in the soil of European liberalism. That it may comprise some healthy and positive values no one will deny. However, in the religious field it can easily cloak an insolent condescension on one side or, worse, an impious indifference to each and every religion on the other. 'Tolerance' can often signify nothing more than a vacuum of any firmly-held beliefs or pieties. One is reminded of Joachim Wach's observation that 'There is something pathetic about the modern historian of religion who uses strong words only to convince us that he has no strong convictions.'[6] Tolerance is no substitute for a

---

1 R. Guénon *Orient et Occident* quoted in WP *TTW* p732.
2 S.H. Nasr *Sufi Essays* Allen & Unwin, London, 1972; p127.
3 A.K. Coomaraswamy: 'The Pertinence of Philosophy' in S. Radhakrishnan & J.H. Muirhead (eds) *Contemporary Indian Philosophy* Allen & Unwin, London, 1952, rev. ed.; p160. Cf.: 'I am in fullest agreement about the necessity of recognizing a common basis of understanding, but see no basis ... other than that of the philosophia perennis ....'. Letter to H.G.D. Finlayson, December 1942, AKC *SL* pp285–286.
4 K. Rudolph: 'Basic Positions of *Religionswissenschaft*' *Religion* XI, 1981; p100.
5 Rudolph is not here being set up as a straw-man: his formulation has been chosen more or less at random as a convenient way of structuring our discussion of several key issues.
6 J. Wach *The Comparative Study of Religion* Columbia Uni Press, New York, 1958; p8.

properly-constituted understanding of the inner unity of formally divergent and sometimes antagonistic religious traditions. As Coomaraswamy remarked '... the very implications of the phrase "religious tolerance" are to be avoided: diversity of faith is not a matter for "toleration", but of divine appointment.'[7] Certainly a well-intentioned tolerance is preferable to an atheistic hostility or a materialistic scepticism about religion; to say as much is to say very little! Nevertheless, tolerance as nothing more than a vague and undemanding sentimentality is, from a traditionalist vantage point, not a firm foundation on which to construct any comparative study.

Criticism, of course, has an honourable place in any scholarly study. A critical sifting and weighing of evidence, a scrupulous respect for the data, the suspicion of the facile generalisation and the over-tidy schematisation, the exposure of the faulty hypothesis and the spurious argument, the finely-honed discrimination and the incisive analysis – all of these should be stock-in-trade for the comparative religionist. But is 'criticism' enough? What of synthesis? To what end is a ruthlessly critical inquiry to be directed? We remember Perry's distinction between traditional learning which is concerned with 'integration, composition and unity' and a quantitative scholarship whose 'nature is to criticise and decompose' and which works by 'fragmentation'.[8] Is it not time to redress the imbalance?

As a methodological ideal *objectivity* has been a tyrannical master. As we have seen, a growing number of comparative religionists are no longer prepared to chafe under this yoke. We have already discussed the inadequacies of this ideal and there is no point in recapitulation here. However, it is worth nothing that the sciences which helped lure us into paying homage to this false idol are abandoning it more readily than many scholars in the so-called humane disciplines. A recent commentary by an American scholar underlines the sad irony of the present situation:

> The social sciences are, or aspire to be, sciences; they have a scientific methodology ... the majority of social sciences have adopted a form of radical empiricism ... This methodology was borrowed from the teachings of the logical positivists. Logical positivism was given up long ago by most scientists and philosophers ... Yet this positivistic doctrine ... has taken firm root in the social sciences. It has done so because it provides a simple (if over-simple) distinction between fact and value which allows social scientists to make the (sometimes bogus) claim of scientific objectivity.[9]

The only genuine objectivity – that is to say, freedom from the conditioned idiosyncrasies of an outlook rooted in a specific spatio-temporal situation – comes from a 'perfect adequation of the knowing subject to the known object'[10]: this is the goal of esotericism and the fruit of intellection. It has nothing whatever to do with any kind of empiricism modelled on the modes of the natural sciences.[11]

The relationship of *history* to other dimensions of the study of religion has been the subject of a good deal of debate in the past few decades. Phenomenology arose,

---

7 'Sri Ramakrishna and Religious Tolerance' in AKC *SPII* p42.
8 WP *TTW* p731.
9 Alton Chase, quoted in H. Smith *Beyond the Post-Modern Mind* Quest, Wheaton, 1982; p82. On this subject see also G. Trompf: 'Social Science in Historical Perspective' *Philosophy of the Social Sciences* VII, 1977; pp113–138.
10 FS *EPW* p15fn1.
11 See FS *EPW* pp15–45.

in part, as a protest against the inadequacies of an excessively, even obsessively historical approach in the late nineteenth century. Traditionalism is also, in one sense, a reaction against historicism. Some might argue that it has erred too far in the opposite direction and that a greater concern with historical scholarship would give more credibility to the traditionalist perspective. Be that as it may, the reasons for the reaction against historicism, both within the discipline and by the traditionalists, are clear enough. An exclusively historical approach leaves a formidable array of questions not only unanswered but unasked. The traditionalists are concerned ultimately with transhistorical realities: thus history itself must remain a limited auxiliary tool rather than an epistemological platform.

Rudolph's list of the salient features of the discipline is completed by the rather fuzzy term *humanity*. In the case of Rudolph himself the term apparently signals a kind of Marxist humanism such as would not be shared by most comparative religionists. He concludes his article this way: 'Thus the science of religion brings forward a humanist concern, which is not surprising because it itself is a child of humanism.'[12] This claim is, to say the least, open to dispute. However, insofar as comparative religion is fuelled by a 'humanist concern' it must, under a traditionalist view, remain quite inadequate to its task. A humanistic *credo* may be adequate to the enterprise which reduces religion to the purely phenomenal level where 'data' can be collected, scrutinised, collated, manipulated and typologised and which satisfies itself with an 'explanation' of the socio-political and psychological 'functions' of religion. However, 'the exclusive concentration on the exterior aspects of a spiritual universe is equivalent in the end to a process of self-alienation.'[13] Furthermore, any view which sees religion as merely another 'cultural creation' is, from the outset, a reductionism quite unable to say anything about religion as such and utterly unable to answer the most profound and urgent questions about it. If such a view conforms to reality then the traditionalist vision is made of straw.

It is now a commonplace that we are living in an unprecedented situation, one in which the different religious traditions are everywhere impinging on each other. There has, of course, always been some intercourse in ideas and influences between the great religious civilisations. Nevertheless, each civilisation formerly exhibited a spiritual homogeneity untroubled, for the most part, by the problem of religious pluralism. For the vast majority of believers in a traditional civilisation the question of the inter-relationship of the religions was one which was either of peripheral concern or one of which they remained unaware. The homogeneity of Christian civilisation has long since been ruptured by secularist ideologies of one kind and another; we have had occasion to make mention of these earlier in this study. In the last few centuries European civilisation has, in turn, been the agent for the disruption and sometimes extirpation of traditional cultures the world over.

The academic discipline of comparative religion was, in part, motivated by the cultural contacts to which an aggressive European imperialism gave rise. Since then all manner of changes have made for a 'smaller' world, for 'the global village'. For

---

12 K. Rudolph *op.cit.*; p106.
13 M. Eliade *The Quest* Uni Chicago Press, 1969; p60.

some time now it has been impossible to ignore the presence of religious cultures and traditions different from our own. The question of the relationship of the religions one to another and the imperatives of mutual understanding take on a new urgency both for comparative religionist and theologian, and indeed, for all those concerned with fostering a harmonious world community. This problem has especially disturbed some Christian thinkers conscious of the excesses and brutalities to which an aggressive exclusivism sometimes gave rise.[14] Klaus Klostermaier, Cantwell Smith, Bede Griffiths and Thomas Merton are amongst some of the better-known Christian writers who have recently pondered this question. Furthermore, in an age of rampant secularism and scepticism the need for some kind of inter-religious solidarity makes itself ever more acutely felt.

The 'philosophical' question of the inter-relationship of the religions and the moral concern for greater mutual understanding are, in fact, all of a piece. We can distinguish but not separate questions about *unity* and *harmony*; too often both comparative religionists and those engaged in 'dialogue' have failed to see that the achievement of the latter depends on a metaphysical resolution of the former question. The problem of resolving the apparently conflicting claims of different religions has been put in the 'Too Hard' or 'Too Controversial' or 'Too Unscientific' baskets by comparative religionists: the task cannot be shirked for ever.[15]

In its early days the discipline was unable to meet this problem because it was too enmeshed in the pervasive evolutionism of the period. It also disqualified itself from a consideration of this kind of issue when it surrendered to a methodology which aped that of the natural sciences. The historical, philological and typological approaches to religious phenomena assuredly uncovered and collated an invaluable mass of raw materials but sidestepped any questions which could only be answered from some normative base. To this day scholars have been properly sensitive to the dangers of allowing 'comparative religion' to become 'competitive religion', of opening the gate to an anarchic contest of conflicting truth claims, norms and beliefs. The phenomenological approach sought to overcome the limitations of a purely descriptive approach and emphasised a more morphological study. However, once again, any questions about the truth claims of the religions or about the ways in which formal antinomies and contradictions might be resolved were ruled out of court. Today the discipline is in a state of ferment, perhaps of crisis. The apparently endless debate about methodology, about the role and purposes of the discipline go on. However, there seems to be a groundswell, in some quarters, in favour of a bolder approach to some of the questions which have previously been exiled from the domain of comparative religion. The debate is enlivened by philosophers, theologians and others concerned with the implications of the collision of religions in the modern world. There is a good deal of talk about ecumenism and dialogue, and about fresh theological and phenomenological perspectives which might serve the

---

14 In this context it is important not to be duped by the simplistic picture of an all-destroying missionizing juggernaut. As Eric Sharpe has pointed out, it was often the Christian missionaries who, under the pressure of circumstances, were amongst the first to discover the spiritual riches of other civilisations and to question a rigidly exclusivist stance. See E.J. Sharpe: 'The Goals of Inter-religious Dialogue' in J. Hick (ed) *Truth and Dialogue: the Relationship of the World Religions* Sheldon, London, 1974; pp78ff.

15 See J.F. Kane: 'Pluralism, truth and the study of religion' *Studies in Religion* IV, ii, 1974–1975; pp158ff. (Kane's diagnosis of the problem is much more convincing than his cure.)

ideals of world community, of inter-religious understanding and the revitalisation of religious and spiritual life generally.[16] From a traditionalist viewpoint, the vexed issues of ecumenism, dialogue and the inter-relationship of the religions are all strands in the same web. Let us consider a few of the most significant implications of the traditionalist view.

Firstly, it should be noted that the recognition of the proper status of traditions other than one's own depends on various contingent circumstances and does not in itself constitute a spiritual necessity. As intimated already, in some respects a religious intolerance is preferable to the kind of tolerance which holds fast to nothing: '. . . the Christian saint who fights the Moslems is closer to Islamic sanctity than the philosopher who accepts everything and practices nothing.'[17] Secondly, traditional orthodoxy is the prerequisite of any creative intercourse between the traditions themselves. To imagine that dialogue can usefully proceed without firm formal commitments is to throw the arena open to any and every kind of opinion and to let loose a kind of mental anarchy which can only exacerbate the problem. Thirdly, and this is the most crucial point, the question of the relationship of the religions to each other can only decisively be resolved by resort to traditional esotericisms and by the application of trans-religious metaphysical principles. But here we are back with the somewhat sensitive relationship of the exoteric and esoteric dimensions of religion. Schuon's argument, in effect, amounts to this: the problematic relationship of the esoteric and exoteric domains is more fundamental than the relationship of the traditions one to another; if this relationship were clarified and understood, then many of the questions about the inter-relationship of the religious traditions would simply dissolve. Or, to put it differently, the 'problem' of religious pluralism can only be resolved through a penetration of the exoteric barriers which each tradition has erected.

A proper understanding of the exoteric-esoteric relationship, along with other principles which we have discussed in this study, would put an end to all the artificial and quite implausible means by which attempts have been made to reconcile formal divergences. As Marco Pallis, starting from a Buddhist perspective, has suggested,

> Dharma and the dharmas, unitive suchness and the suchness of diversified existence: here is to be found the basis of an inter-religious exegesis which does not seek a remedy for historical conflicts by explaining away formal or doctrinal factors such as in reality translate differences of spiritual genius. Far from minimising the importance of these differences in the name of a facile and eventually spurious ecumenical friendliness, they will be cherished for the positive message they severally carry and as necessities that have arisen out of the differentiation of mankind itself.[18]

---

16 For a sample of the literature on dialogue see the following: Masao Abe: 'Christianity and the Encounter of World Religions' *The Eastern Buddhist* New Series, Vol 1, 1965; E.J. Jurji: 'Religious Convergence and the Course of Prejudice' *Journal of the American Academy of Religion* XXXVIII, 1969; E.J. Jurji (ed) *Religious Pluralism and World Community* E.J. Brill, Leiden, 1969; K. Klostermaeir:'Hindu-Christian Dialogue' *Journal of Ecumenical Studies* V, 1966, and 'A Hindu-Christian Dialogue on Truth' *JES* XII, 1975, and 'Hindu-Christian Dialogue: Its Religious and Cultural Implications' *Studies in Religion* I, ii, 1971; T. Merton: 'Ecumenism and Monastic Renewal' *JES* V, 1966; R. Pannikar: 'Inter-Religious Dialogue: Some Principles' *JES* XII, 1975; E.J. Sharpe: 'Dialogue and Faith' *Religion* III, 1973; and Bede Griffiths *Vedanta and Christian Faith* Dawn Horse Press, Los Angeles, 1973, and *The Marriage of East and West* Collins, London, 1982.

17 FS *L&T* p182. See also SHN *K&S* p291 & 307fn28.

18 M. Pallis *A Buddhist Spectrum* Allen & Unwin, London, 1980; pp109–110. See pp102–120. (The essay from which this excerpt is taken can also be found in R. Fernando (ed) *The Unanimous Tradition*.) See also V. Danner: 'The Inner and Outer Man' in Y. Ibish & P.L. Wilson (eds) *Traditional Modes of Contemplation and Action* Imperial Iranian Academy of Philosophy, Tehran, 1977; pp407ff.

There have been several attempts to reconcile these formal antagonisms under an array of different philosophical and theological canopies – theosophy, 'anonymous Christianity', 'natural religion', 'universal religion' and so on. For reasons already discussed at some length the traditionalists find all such attempts to resolve the problem of religious pluralism quite unconvincing; they are symptoms of the confusion of the times rather than an answer to it.

The outlook implied in the passage from Pallis depends on a recognition of the exoteric-esoteric relationship and a subordination (*not* an annihilation) of exoteric dogmatism to the metaphysical principles preserved by traditional esotericisms. The main obstacle on this path is the tenacity with which many representatives of an exoteric viewpoint cling to a belief in the exclusive claims of their own tradition and to other 'pious extravagances'.[19] Schuon goes to the heart of the matter:

> ... if exoterism, the religion of literalism and exclusive dogmatism, has difficulty in admitting the existence and legitimacy of the esoteric dimension ... this is understandable on various grounds. However, in the cyclic period in which we live, the situation of the world is such that exclusive dogmatism ... is hard put to hold its own, and whether it likes it or not, has need of certain esoteric elements ... Unhappily the wrong choice is made; the way out of certain deadlocks is sought, not with the help of esoterism, but by resorting to the falsest and most pernicious of philosophical and scientific ideologies, and for the universality of the spirit, the reality of which is confusedly noted, there is substituted a so-called 'ecumenism' which consists of nothing but platitudes and sentimentality and accepts everything without discrimination.[20]

For many scholars the dilemma has been this: any 'theoretical' solution to the problem of conflicting truth claims demands a conceptual platform which both encompasses and transcends any specific theological position; it must go beyond the premises of any particular theological outlook but at the same time not involve a compromising of the theological position to which one might adhere. Traditionalism shows the way out of this impasse. It neither insists on nor precludes any particular religious commitment. Once the necessity of orthodoxy is accepted, and the principles which govern the relationship of the exoteric and the esoteric are understood, then one can remain fully committed to a particular tradition while recognising the limits of the outlook in question. Traditionalism requires neither a betrayal of one's own tradition nor a wishy-washy hospitality to anything and everything. The observation made by an early reviewer of *The Transcendent Unity of Religions* might be applied to traditionalism as a whole. It presents 'a very concrete and specific philosophy of religion for an ecumenical age ... It opens one possible way for discovering a basis for coexistence for the different creeds.'[21] We might add that it provides not *a* way but *the* only possible way.

We recall the words of Coomaraswamy with which we opened this study, calling for 'a revision of the principles of comparative religion' whereby the discipline could

---

19 The phrase is from Schuon's essay 'Deficiencies in the World of Faith' *SME* p125.
20 FS *L&T* p4.
21 F.H. Heinemann in *The Journal of Theological Studies* VI, 1955; p340. One might add the proviso that the kind of ecumenicism envisaged would necessarily have to be esoteric. As Seyyed Hossein Nasr has recently pointed out 'Ecumenism if correctly understood must be an esoteric activity if it is to avoid becoming the instrument for simple relativization and further secularisation.' SHN *K&S* p282.

serve the end of demonstrating 'the common metaphysical basis of all religions'.[22] The possibilities of this demonstration are more or less endless but the principles on which the undertaking can be based and the framework within which it can be pursued have been reconstructed by Guénon, Coomaraswamy, Schuon and the other traditionalists. Their work is there for those who seek a vision of religion adequate to the needs of the age.

Traditionalism addresses itself to the inner meaning of religion through an elucidation of immutable metaphysical and cosmological principles and through a penetration of the forms preserved in each religious tradition. The sources of the traditionalist vision are Revelation, tradition, intellection, realisation. It is neither a vestigial pseudo-scientific methodology nor a subjectively-determined 'hermeneutic' but a *theoria* which bridges the *phenomena* and the *noumena* of religion; it takes us 'from the forms to the essences wherein resides the truth of all religions and where alone a religion can really be understood'.[23] It provides an all-embracing context for the study of religion and the means whereby not only empirical but philosophical and metaphysical questions can be both properly formulated and decisively answered.

It would be sanguine in the extreme to imagine that comparative religion as a discipline will harness itself to the enterprise outlined by Coomaraswamy. Nor can traditionalism itself ever be primarily an academic discipline. Nevertheless, there remain considerable possibilities for the discipline of comparative religion to assimilate at least something of the traditionalist outlook or to accept it as one of the perspectives from which religion can be studied. Clearly there are some spikey questions which attend any attempt to reconcile a traditionalist vision with the demands of an impartial academic scholarship. The present work harbours no pretension that all of these questions have been confronted here, let alone resolved: this study is intended as an introduction to traditionalism and as an attempt to explore some of its implications.

The argument that traditionalism is too normative to be allowed to shape academic studies is no argument at all. As currently practised by many of its exponents comparative religion is quite clearly normative anyway. As soon as we are prepared, for instance, to talk of 'sympathy', of 'mutual understanding', of 'world community', and so on, we have entered a normative realm. It is time scholars ceased to be embarrassed by this fact and stopped sheltering behind the tattered banner of a pseudo-scientific methodology which forbids any engagement with the most interesting, the most profound and the most urgent questions which naturally stem from any serious study of religion. The question is not whether the study of religion will be influenced by certain norms – it will be so influenced whether we admit it or not – but to what kind of norms we are prepared to give our allegiances. The time has come to nail our colours to the mast in arguing for approaches to religion which do justice to the traditional principle of adequation, and which will help rescue the discipline from the ignominious plight of being nothing more than another undistinguished member of a disreputable family of pseudo-sciences.

---

[22] A.K. Coomaraswamy: 'The Pertinence of Philosophy' pp158–159.
[23] S.H. Nasr *Sufi Essays* p38.

The discipline of religious studies will never have any integrity so long as it is pursued as a self-sufficient, self-validating end in itself. As Klaus Klostermaier has so acutely observed,

> The study of religions can no longer afford the luxury of creating pseudo-problems of its own, of indulging in academic hobbies, or of acting as if religion or the study of it were ends in themselves. The one thing that might be worse than the confusion and uncertainty in the area of religious studies would be the development of a methodology of religious studies, by scholars of religious studies, for the sake of religious studies: playing a game by rules invented by the players for the sake of the game alone.[24]

If this is not to be the fate of the discipline then, at the very least, there must be a much more radical debate about philosophical, theological and metaphysical questions generated within the discipline. E.O. James many years ago observed that 'The study of religion . . . demands both a historical and a scientific approach and a theological and philosophical evaluation if . . . its foundations are to be well and truly laid.'[25] A serious consideration of the works of the traditionalists and of the whole traditionalist perspective would, at least, open the way for a fruitful reconvergence of philosophy, theology, comparative religion and metaphysics.

Those who accept the traditionalist position can reap a richer harvest. The explication of the *sophia perennis* and its application to contingent phenomena shows the way to an outlook invulnerable to the whim and fancy of ever-changing intellectual fashions and armours one against the debilitating effects of scientism and its sinister cargo of reductionisms. It annihilates that 'neutrality' which is indifferent to the claims of religion itself and removes those 'optical illusions' to which the modern world is victim. For those who see religions as something infinitely more than mere 'cultural phenomena', who believe them to be the vehicles of the most profound and precious truths to which we cannot and must not immunise ourselves, who wish to do justice to both the external forms and the inner meanings of religion, who cleave to their own tradition but who wish to recognise all integral religions as pathways to God, whose pursuit of religious studies is governed by something far more deep-seated than mental curiosity – for such people traditionalism can open up whole new vistas of understanding. Ultimately, for those prepared to pay the proper price, it can lead to that 'light that is neither of the East nor the West'.[26] A rediscovery of the immutable nature of man and a renewed understanding of the *sophia perennis* must be the governing purpose of the most serious comparative study of religion. It is, in Seyyed Hossein Nasr's words, a 'noble end . . . whose achievement the truly contemplative and intellectual elite are urgently summoned to by the very situation of man in the contemporary world'.[27]

---

24 K. Klostermaier: 'From phenomenology to meta-science: reflections on the study of religion' *Studies in Religion* VI, iv, 1976–1977; p563.
25 E.O. James, quoted in E.J. Sharpe: 'Some Problems of Method in the Study of Religion' *Religion* I, i, 1971; p12.
26 from the *Koran*, quoted by S.H. Nasr: 'Conditions for a meaningful comparative philosophy' *Philosophy East and West* XXII, i, 1972; p.61.
27 *ibid.*

Epilogue

'Tradition' is the keystone in the works of the authors whose writings have been the subject of this study. It is perhaps appropriate to conclude with a profoundly suggestive passage on this theme from one of Frithjof Schuon's most magisterial essays. If our inquiry into traditionalism has helped anyone better to understand the implications of this message then it has served its purpose. Schuon's words carry a teaching over which we cannot ponder too long or too deeply. They will serve better than any encomium of Schuon to draw this study to its end.

> Tradition speaks to each man the language he can comprehend, provided he wishes to listen. The latter proviso is crucial, for tradition, let it be repeated, cannot 'become bankrupt'; rather it is of the bankruptcy of man that one should speak, for it is he who has lost all intuition of the supernatural. It is man who has let himself be deceived by the discoveries and inventions of a falsely totalitarian science ... man has ended by being submerged in his own creations; he will not realise that a traditional message is situated on quite a different plane or how much more real that plane is ... Tradition is abandoned, not because people are no longer capable of understanding its language, but because they do not wish to understand it, for this language is made to be understood till the end of the world ... an affirmation of the truth, or any effort on behalf of truth, is never in vain ... every initiative taken with a view to harmony between different cultures and for the defence of spiritual values is good, if it has as its basis a recognition of tradition or of the traditions. 'When the inferior man hears talk about Tao, he only laughs at it; it would not be Tao if he did not laugh at it ... the self-evidence of the Tao is taken for a darkness.' These words of Lao-Tse were never more timely than now. Errors cannot but be, as long as their quite relative possibility has not reached its term; but for the Absolute errors have never been and never shall be. On their own plane they are what they are, but it is the Changeless that shall have the final say.
>
> from: 'No Activity Without Truth',
> in *The Sword of Gnosis*, J. Needleman *ed*

Bibliographical Note

The following works and bibliographies provide details on the work of the traditionalists.

Burckhardt, Titus	*Mirror of the Intellect* Quinta Essentia, Cambridge, 1987; edited by William Stoddart. (Burckhardt bibliography compiled by William Stoddart).
Chittick, William	*The Works of Seyyed Hossein Nasr Through His Fortieth Birthday* Research Monograph No 6., Middle East Center, University of Utah, Salt Lake City, 1977.
Coomaraswamy, A.K.	*Coomaraswamy 1: Selected Papers, Traditional Art and Symbolism* ed. Roger Lipsey, Bollingen Series, Princeton University Press, 1977.
	Coomaraswamy 2: Selected Papers, Metaphysics ed. Roger Lipsey, Bollingen Series, Princeton University Press, 1977.
Coomaraswamy, Rama	*Ananda K. Coomaraswamy Bibliography/Index* Prologos Books, Berwick-upon-Tweed, 1988.
Coomaraswamy, Rama & Alvin Moore, Jnr *ed*	*Selected Letters of Ananda Coomaraswamy* Indira Gandhi National Centre for the Arts, New Delhi, 1988.
Crouch, James	*René Guénon: A Chronological Check-List of His Published Writings, 1909–1986* privately published, Melbourne, 1987.
Désilets, A.	*René Guénon: Index Bibliographie* Bibliothèque philosophique No 4, Quebec, Presses de l'université Laval, 1977.
Kelly, Richard	*Index to Studies in Comparative Religion* privately published, Melbourne, 1986.
Laurant, Jean-Pierre	*Le Sens Caché Selon René Guénon* L'Age D'Homme, Lausanne, 1975.
Lipsey, Roger	*Coomaraswamy: His Life and Work* Bollingen Series, Princeton University Press, 1977.
Nasr, S.H. & William Stoddart *ed*	*Religion of the Heart* Foundation of Traditional Studies, Washington DC, 1991. (Schuon bibliography compiled by William Stoddart).
Schuon, Frithjof	*The Essential Writings of Frithjof Schuon* Amity House, New York, 1986. (Schuon bibliography compiled by the editor, Seyyed Hossein Nasr.).

Major Traditionalist Writings in English

The following list is not intended as a detailed bibliography but only as a guide for interested readers. For full publication details of various editions and the names of translators and editors, and for some details on the extensive periodical literature by traditionalist writers, see sources listed under Bibliographical Note on the preceding page. For periodical material readers are directed particularly to the journal *Studies in Comparative Religion*, published in England from 1967 until the early 1980s. In general the editions listed here are those to which reference is made in this study.

More accessible works recommended for readers coming to traditionalist writings for the first time are marked with an asterisk *.

Brown, Joseph Epes
    The Sacred Pipe Penguin Books, Baltimore, 1971.
    * *The Spiritual Legacy of the American Indians* Crossroad, New York, 1982.
    Animals of the Soul: Sacred Animals of the Oglala Sioux Element, Shaftesbury, 1993.

Burckhardt, Titus
    An Introduction to Sufi Doctrine Thorsons, Wellingborough, 1976.
    Siena, City of the Virgin Oxford University Press, 1960.
    * *Sacred Art in East and West* Perennial Books, Bedfont, 1967.
    Alchemy: Science of the Cosmos, Science of the Soul Penguin Books, Baltimore, 1972.
    Art of Islam: Language and Meaning World of Islam Festival, London, 1976.
    Fez, City of Islam Islamic Texts Society, Cambridge, 1993.
    Mirror of the Intellect: Essays on Traditional Science and Sacred Art Quinta Essentia, Cambridge, 1987.
    Chartres and the Birth of the Cathedral World Wisdom Books, Bloomington, 1996.

Coomaraswamy, Ananda
    Hinduism and Buddhism Philosophical Library, New York, 1945.
    Figures of Speech or Figures of Thought: Collected Essays on the Traditional or 'Normal' View of Art Luzac, London, 1946.
    Time and Eternity Artibus Asiae, Ascona, 1947.
    * *Christian and Oriental Philosophy of Art* Dover, New York, 1956.
    The Transformation of Nature in Art Dover, New York, 1956.
    The Dance of Shiva and Other Essays Noonday Press, New York, 1957.

Coomaraswamy 1: Selected Papers, Traditional Art and Symbolism ed. Roger Lipsey, Bollingen Series, Princeton University Press, 1977.
Coomaraswamy 2: Selected Papers, Metaphysics ed. Roger Lipsey, Bollingen Series, Princeton University Press, 1977.
* *The Bugbear of Literacy* Perennial Books, London, 1979.
Sources of Wisdom Ministry of Cultural Affairs, Sri Lanka, 1981.
What is Civilisation? and Other Essays Golgonooza, Ipswich, 1989.
Spiritual Authority and Temporal Power in the Indian Theory of Government Oxford University Press, New York, 1994.

Coomaraswamy, Rama — *The Destruction of the Christian Tradition* Perennial Books, London, 1981.

Cooper, Jean C. — * *Taoism, the Way of the Mystic* Aquarian Press, Northamptonshire, 1972.

Eaton, Gai — * *King of the Castle: Choice and Responsibility in the Modern World* Bodley Head, London, 1977.
Islam and the Destiny of Man Islamic Texts Society, Cambridge, 1986.

Fernando, Ranjit *ed* — * *The Unanimous Tradition* Sri Lanka Institute of Traditional Studies, Colombo, 1991.

Guénon, René — *Man and His Becoming According to the Vedanta* Oriental Books Reprint Co., New Delhi, 1981.
East and West Sophia Perennis et Universalis, Ghent, 1995.
* *The Crisis of the Modern World* Luzac, London, 1975.
Introduction to the Study of Hindu Doctrines Luzac, London, 1945.
The Reign of Quantity & the Signs of the Times Penguin, Baltimore, 1972. Reprinted by Sophia Perennis et Universalis, Ghent, 1995.
Initiation and the Crafts Golgonooza, Ipswich, 1974.
The Symbolism of the Cross Luzac, London, 1975.
The Multiple States of Being Larson, Burdett, 1984.
The Great Triad Quinta Essentia, Cambridge, 1991.
Fundamental Symbols: The Universal Language of Sacred Science Quinta Essentia, Cambridge, 1995.
The Esoterism of Dante Sophia Perennis et Universalis, Ghent, 1996.

Lings, Martin — * *A Sufi Saint of the Twentieth Century: Shaikh Ahmad al-'Alawi* University of California Press, Berkeley, 1971.
* *Ancient Beliefs and Modern Superstitions* Allen & Unwin, London, 1980.

	* *What is Sufism?* Allen & Unwin, London, 1975. *The Quranic Art of Calligraphy and Illumination* World of Islam Festival, London, 1976. *Muhummad: His Life Based on the Earliest Sources* Allen & Unwin, London, 1983. *Symbol and Archetype: A Study of the Meaning of Existence* Quinta Essentia, Cambridge, 1991. *The Eleventh Hour: the spiritual crisis of the modern world in the light of tradition and prophecy* Quinta Essentia, Cambridge, 1987.
Nasr, Seyyed Hossein	*Ideals and Realities of Islam* Allen & Unwin, London, 1966. *Science and Civilisation in Islam* Allen & Unwin, London, 1968. * *Man and Nature: The Spiritual Crisis of the Modern World* Allen & Unwin, London, 1976. *Sufi Essays* Allen & Unwin, London, 1972. *Three Muslim Sages* Delmar, New York, 1975. *Islam and the Plight of Modern Man* Longmans, London, 1976. *Islamic Science, An Illustrated History* World of Islam Festival, London, 1976. *Knowledge and the Sacred* Crossroad, New York, 1981. *Islamic Art and Spirituality* Golgonooza, Ipswich, 1987. *The Need for a Sacred Science* SUNY, Albany, 1993. *Religion and the Order of Nature* Oxford University Press, New York, 1996.
Nasr, S.H. & William Stoddart *ed*	*Religion of the Heart: Essays Presented to Frithjof Schuon on His Eightieth Birthday* Foundation of Traditional Studies, Washington DC, 1991.
Nasr, S.H. & Katherine O'Brien *ed*	* *In Quest of the Sacred: the modern world in the light of tradition* Foundation of Traditional Studies, Washington DC, 1994.
Needleman, Jacob *ed*	* *The Sword of Gnosis* Penguin Books, Baltimore, 1974.
Northbourne, Lord	* *Religion in the Modern World* J.M. Dent, London, 1963; Perennial Books reprint in the mid-70s (no date given). * *Looking Back on Progress* Perennial Books, London, 1970.
Pallis, Marco	* *Peaks and Lamas* Cassell, London, 1939. *The Way and the Mountain* Peter Owen, London, 1960. *A Buddhist Spectrum* Allen & Unwin, London, 1980.
Perry, Whitall	*Gurdjieff in the Light of Tradition* Perennial Books, London, 1979. *The Widening Breach: Evolutionism in the Mirror of Cosmology* Quinta Essentia, Cambridge, 1995.

	Challenges to a Secular Society Foundation of Traditional Studies, Washington DC, 1996.
Perry, Whitall *ed*	*A Treasury of Traditional Wisdom* Allen & Unwin, London, 1971.
Schaya, Leo	*The Universal Meaning of the Kabbalah* Allen & Unwin, London, 1971.
Schuon, Frithjof	*The Transcendent Unity of Religions* Harper & Row, New York, 1975.
	Spiritual Perspectives and Human Facts Perennial Books, London, 1967.
	* *Gnosis: Divine Wisdom* Perennial Books, London, 1979.
	Stations of Wisdom Perennial Books, London, no date given; reprint of John Murray edition, London, 1961.
	Understanding Islam Allen & Unwin, London, 1976.
	* *Light on the Ancient Worlds* Perennial Books, London, 1966.
	In the Tracks of Buddhism Allen & Unwin, London, 1968.
	Dimensions of Islam Allen & Unwin, London, 1969.
	Logic and Transcendence Harper & Row, New York, 1975.
	Islam and the Perennial Philosophy World of Islam Festival, London, 1976.
	Esoterism as Principle and as Way Perennial Books, London, 1981.
	Sufism: Veil and Quintessence World Wisdom Books, 1981.
	Castes and Races Perennial Books, London, 1982.
	From the Divine to the Human World Wisdom Books, Bloomington, 1982.
	Christianity/Islam: Essays on Esoteric Ecumenicism World Wisdom Books, Bloomington, 1985.
	The Essential Writings of Frithjof Schuon ed. S.H. Nasr, Amity House, New York, 1986
	Survey of Metaphysics and Esoterism World Wisdom Books, Bloomington, 1986
	In the Face of the Absolute World Wisdom Books, Bloomington, 1989.
	The Feathered Sun: Plains Indians in Art and Philosophy World Wisdom Books, Bloomington, 1990.
	Roots of the Human Condition World Wisdom Books, Bloomington, 1991.
	The Play of Masks World Wisdom Books, Bloomington, 1992.
	Images of Primordial and Mystic Beauty: Paintings by Frithjof Schuon Abodes, 1992.
	* *Echoes of Perennial Wisdom* World Wisdom Books, Bloomington, 1993.
	Treasures of Buddhism (revised and enlarged edition of *In the Tracks of Buddhism*), World Wisdom Books, 1993.

	The Transfiguration of Man World Wisdom Books, Bloomington, 1995.
Road to the Heart: Poems World Wisdom Books, 1995.
The Eye of the Heart: Metaphysics, Cosmology, Spiritual Life World Wisdom Books, Bloomington, 1997.
Sherrard, Philip	*The Rape of Man and Nature* Golgonooza Press, Ipswich, and Sri Lanka Institute of Traditional Studies, Colombo, 1987.
* *The Sacred in Art and Life* Golgonooza, Ipswich, 1990.
Human Image, World Image: the death and resurrection of sacred cosmology Golgonooza, Ipswich, 1992.
Stoddart, William	*Sufism: The Mystical Doctrines and Methods of Islam* Thorsons, Northamptonshire, 1975.

Other Suggested Reading

Austin, R.W.J.	*Sufis of Andalusia* Allen & Unwin, London, 1972.
Berry, Wendell	*Standing on Earth: Selected Essays* Golgonooza Press, Ipswich, 1991.
	What Are People For? North Point Press, San Francisco, 1991.
Coomaraswamy, Rama & Alvin Moore, Jnr ed	*Selected Letters of Ananda Coomaraswamy* Indira Gandhi National Centre for the Arts, New Delhi, 1988.
Cooper, J.C.	*Yin and Yang* Aquarian Press, Northamptonshire, 1981.
	Symbolism, the Universal Language Aquarian Press, Northamptonshire, 1982.
Cowan, James	*Mysteries of the Dreaming: The Spiritual Life of Australian Aborigines* Unity, Lindfield, 1989.
Cutsinger, James	*Advice to the Serious Seeker: Meditations on the Teachings of Frithjof Schuon* SUNY, Albany, 1996.
Eaton, Gai	*The Richest Vein* Faber & Faber, London, 1949.
Eliade, Mircea	*Shamanism: Archaic Techniques of Ecstasy* Bollingen Series, Princeton University Press, 1964.
	A History of Religious Ideas 3 vols, University of Chicago Press, 1978, 1982, 1985.
Ibish, Y. & P.L. Wilson ed	*Traditional Modes of Contemplation and Action* Imperial Iranian Academy of Philosophy, Tehran, 1977.
Kelley, C.F.	*Meister Eckhart on Divine Knowledge* Yale University Press, New Haven, 1977.
Lings, Martin	*Shakespeare in the Light of Sacred Art* Allen & Unwin, London, 1966.
Lipsey, Roger	*Coomaraswamy: His Life and Work* Bollingen Series, Princeton University Press, 1977.
Merton, Thomas	*New Seeds of Contemplation* New Directions, New York, 1972.
	Zen and the Birds of Appetite New Directions, New York, 1968.
Neihardt, John	*Black Elk Speaks* Pocket Books, New York, 1972.

Quinn, Jr, William	*The Only Tradition* SUNY, Albany, 1997.
Raine, Kathleen	*Defending Ancient Springs* Golgonooza, Ipswich, 1985.
Roszak, Theodore	*Where the Wasteland Ends* Doubleday, New York, 1972.
Schumacher, E.F.	*A Guide for the Perplexed* Jonathan Cape, London, 1977.
Sharma, Arvind *ed*	*Fragments of Infinity: Essays in Religion and Philosophy* Prism, Bridport, 1992.
Sharpe, Eric	*Comparative Religion* Duckworth, London, 1975.
Sherrard, Philip	*Athos, the Holy Mountain* Sidgwick & Jackson, London, 1982.
Singam, S.D.R. *ed*	*Ananda Coomaraswamy: Remembering and Remembering Again and Again* privately published, Kuala Lumpur, 1974.
Smith, Huston	*Forgotten Truth* Harper & Row, New York, 1977.
	Essays on World Religions ed. M. Bryant, Paragon House, New York, 1992.
Smith, Wolfgang	*Cosmos and Transcendence: Breaking Through the Barrier of Scientistic Belief* Sherwood Sugden & Co, La Salle, 1984.
	The Quantum Enigma Sherwood Sugden & Co, La Salle, 1995.
Snodgrass, Adrian	*The Symbolism of the Stupa* Cornell University, Ithaca, 1985.
Staveley, Lillian	*The Golden Fountain* World Wisdom Books, Bloomington, 1982.
Sworder, Roger	*Mining, Metallurgy and the Meaning of Life* Quakers Hill, Sydney, 1995.
Ware, Kallistos	*The Orthodox Way* Mowbray, Oxford, 1979.

Acknowledgments

It is a pleasure to acknowledge at least some of the debts incurred in writing this study. My mentors at the University of Sydney enlarged my view of religion and helped me to see comparative religious studies in new perspectives. I thank Professors Arvind Sharma, Eric Sharpe and Garry Trompf, and the late John Cooper. I am also grateful to my colleagues in the Department of Arts at La Trobe University Bendigo. I particularly thank Roger Sworder and Rodney Blackhirst for their support and encouragement.

Several people familiar with the traditionalist outlook have been both gracious and generous in their help. Ranjit Fernando and Dr. William Stoddart deserve special mention while Cecil Bethell, the late Francis Clive-Ross, James Crouch, Richard Forsaith, Richard Kelly, Alvin Moore Jr., Professor Seyyed Hossein Nasr, John Paraskevopoulos, Whitall Perry, Lyndon Reynolds, Professor Huston Smith, James Wetmore, and Graeme Vanderstoel all came to my assistance in ways too numerous to catalogue here. To these, to my family and to others who must remain unmentioned I am beholden.

K.O.

Index

Abdel Wahed Yahya (René Guénon) 13
Abraham, 59, 63,
Absolute, the 25, 64, 72, 73, 77, 79, 81, 82, 86, 88, 95, 107, 145, 146, 171, 173, 174, 183, 207
Abu Bakr Siraj Ad Din (Martin Lings) 47, 66n, 104n
Advaita: see Vedanta
Adler, Alfred 136
Aesop, 81
aesthetics and aestheticism, 31–33, 111–113, 169
Ahmad al Alawi, Shaikh 38, 47
    Alawi order 38n
alchemy, 46, 62, 111
Almqvist, Kurt 133
Ambrose, St 2
Amelius, 3
American Indians, 6, 35, 38, 39, 40, 51, 69, 92, 100, 108
Andrae, Walter 32, 103n
Anguttara Nikāya, 8n
Anizan, P. 13
Anthony, Metropolitan 133n
Appleyard, Bryan 118
Aquinas, St Thomas 33, 54, 82, 84, 89, 96, 107, 111, 139, 156, 170
archetypes, 103–106, 177
Ardrey, Robert 124
Aristotle, 139, 181
    Aristotelian science 122
Arnold, Matthew 27
ars sine scientia nihil, 45, 111
art, 32–35, 40, 41, 46, 63–64, 102–113, 196
    American Indian 33, 108
    'art for art's sake' 31, 91, 108
    nouveau 31
    Arts and Crafts Movement 29
    baroque 102, 113
    Buddhist 32, 37, 40, 63
    Christian 32, 34, 45, 112
    Egyptian 109
    Greek 112
    Indian, Hindu 28, 32, 33, 34, 108
    Islamic 47, 50, 55
    liturgical 108, 110
    modern 33, 108, 111–113, 171, 195
    naturalistic 109–110, 112
    'originality' in art 8, 33, 111

    Plato on art 32, 34
    Rajput 32
    Renaissance 102, 112–113
    Sinhalese 32
    surrealist 113
    Tibetan 33, 109, 110
    traditional 32–35, 45, 46, 63, 64, 102–113, 196
Ātman, 148
Attar, 2
atheism, 80, 84, 138
Augustine, St 8, 33, 59, 60, 108, 132, 159
Aurobindo (Ghose), 143, 148
Austin, R.W.J. 54
Avatāra, 93, 107
    Kalki 153
Avaloka, 52, 54
Ayer, A.J. 178

Bacon, Francis 118
Baha'i, 146
Bando, Shojun 52, 54
Basham, Arthur 27
Beauty, 42, 43, 105, 107–113
Beethoven, Ludwig van 5
Bennett, J.G. 160, 162n
Bhagavad Gītā, 37, 59
bhakti, 96
Bharati, Agehananda 149
Bhave, Vinoba 149n
Bianchi, Ugo 190
Bible, 74, 93, 98
biography, attitudes to 3–9, 27
Bishop, Donald 54
Black Elk, 6, 8, 39, 51, 103
Blake, William 29, 31, 89
Blavatsky, Madame H.P. 52
Bleeker, C.J. 190
Bodhisattvas, 37
Boehme, Jacob 103
Bonaventura, St 184
Book of Kells, 45
Boston Museum of Fine Arts, 31
Bournoure, L. 125
Bradley, F.H. 85
Brahman, 87n, 90, 148
Brahmananda, Swami 152n
Brahmo-Samaj, 74, 149, 152
Brentano, Franz 187

Bronowski, Jacob 131
Brook, Peter 161
Brown, Joseph Epes 35, 39, 48, 50, 51, 54, 100
Buber, Martin 71, 196
Bucke, R.M. 148
Buddha, Gautama 7n, 63, 72, 75, 92, 93, 153, 154, 159, 162
Buddha, Amitabha 83
Buddhism 6, 7,15, 18, 34, 35, 40, 46, 47, 51, 63, 72n, 74, 77, 103n, 165, 175, 176, 179, 183, 203
    Buddhist art: *see under* Art
    Mahāyāna 83
    Pure Land 83
    Tibetan 47, 83, 105n
    Zen 145, 146, 161
Burckhardt, Titus 35, 45–46, 50, 51, 52, 53, 54, 64, 111, 124, 129, 134
Bush, Richard 173–175, 180

Campbell, Joseph 27, 35
Capra, Frithjof 20n
Carlyle, Thomas 29
caste, 70
Catholic Church, 13–15, 51, 133
Ceylon Reform Society, 28, 29
Chan, W.T. 169
Chesterton, G.K. 133
Chinese tradition, the 15, 40, 77, 92
Chittick, William 49n, 52
Chou Li, 59
Christ, Jesus 6, 59, 71, 72, 93, 139, 153, 154, 159, 162
Christianity, 15, 35, 60, 64, 77, 111, 140, 144
Church Fathers, 162, 170, 181
civilization 28, 37, 44, 58, 64, 66, 67, 116, 132, 201
    modern 16, 18–19, 21–22, 52, 67, 172
    traditional 2, 16, 37, 38, 65
Clive-Ross, Francis 53, 54
coinage, 109
colonialism, 28, 31n, 131
comparative religion, viii, 35, 165, 186–196, 199–206
Confucianism, 18
Coomaraswamy, Ananda K. viii, ix, 6, 8, 9, 11, 24–39, 41–44, 46–48, 50–52, 54, 60, 66, 69, 80, 87, 88, 91, 103n, 105, 107, 108–111, 113, 116, 133, 135n, 143, 144, 150, 154–157, 159, 160, 168–173, 175, 176, 180, 182, 186, 193, 195, 198, 204, 205
Coomaraswamy, Doña Luisa 6n, 27n
Coomaraswamy, Rama P. 46, 50, 54, 133n
Coomaraswamy, Sir Mutu 28

Copernicus, 118
cosmology,19, 20, 21, 46, 47, 50, 51, 52, 53, 99, 106, 134, 146, 159, 195, 205
'cosmic consciousness', 148
crafts, 19, 21, 64, 108–109, 111, 113
Cragg, Kenneth 120n
Crazy Horse, 103
Creationism, 124, 128n
Crick, Francis 122
Critchlow, Keith 54
Cutsinger, James 52, 136n, 165, 167
cycles, doctrine of 16, 19, 98, 100, 129n, 130

Danner, Victor 52, 54, 167
Dante, 18, 125
Darwin, Charles 5, 118
    Darwinism: *see* evolution and evolutionism
Da Vinci, Leonardo 112, 125
Davis, Charles 191, 194
de Chardin, Pierre Teilhard 124, 133, 145n, 146
Deed, Dorothea 54
de Fremond, Oliver 13
de la Saussaye, P.D. Chantepie 187
Denton, Michael 125n
Descartes, René 22, 118, 119
Dewar, Douglas 125
dharma (*dhamma*) 35, 94, 203
Dickens, Charles 29
Dolmetsch, Arnold 46, 47
Dostoyevsky, Fyodor 180
Durkheim, Emile 66

East and West, 16, 23, 28, 49, 154–155, 169–170, 198, 206
Eaton, Charles le Gai 15, 21, 41, 50, 54, 55, 116, 158, 159, 160
education, 28, 29, 30
Eckhart, Meister 33, 37, 43, 85, 86, 95, 96, 103, 147, 159, 170
ecological crisis, 119–120
ecumenicism, 202–204
ego, egoism, 3
eidetic vision, 188–189, 193
Einstein, Albert 5, 118
Eliade, Mircea 12, 17, 35, 71, 104, 106, 109, 112n, 120, 137, 154, 176, 180–182, 190–194
Eliot, T.S. 27, 40, 50
empiricism, 19, 117, 119, 175, 177, 196, 200
Encausse, Dr ('Papus') 17
Enlightenment, the 3, 117
epistemology, 187, 201

epochê, 188, 193
eschatology, 13
esotercism (esoterism), 12, 13–17, 39, 40, 42, 43, 68, 75–83, 94, 95, 99–100, 151, 152, 161, 173–175, 184, 185, 195, 200, 203, 204
Eternal, the 62, 88
    Eternity, 34, 64, 103, 130
Et-Tahawi, 153
Ettinghausen, Richard 27
Études Traditionnelles, 13, 14, 39, 51, 52, 53
Evans, Christopher 19n
evolution, 123–133, 155
    and archetypes 129–130
    evolutionism 49, 118, 123–135, 139, 140, 146–149, 155, 159
    mega-evolution 125–126, 129
    "missing link", 127
    palaeontology 124–129
    transformism 126, 128
    social evolutionism 130–133
    and religion 124, 127, 128n, 131, 155, 159, 202
Existentialism, 4, 91n, 117, 118n, 138, 157n
exotericism (exoterism), 43, 68, 75–83, 94, 95, 99, 144, 152, 173, 195, 203, 204

faith, 90–91, 94–96
Feer, Catherine 38
feminism, 136
Fernando, Ranjit 51, 55
Ficino, Marsilio 107
Florsheim, Richard 172
folklore, 15, 52
Fondi, Roberto 125
Form, 102
    forms 37, 60, 64, 71, 76–83, 94, 103–112, 118, 129–130, 142, 150–151, 159, 183, 193, 196, 205, 206
Foundation for Traditional Studies (USA), 54, 55
France, Anatole 11
Francis, St 162
Frankl, Victor 120
Freemasonry, 11, 14, 15, 17
Freud, Sigmund 5, 118, 136, 180, 181
Fromm, Erich 5

Galileo, 118
Garrett, Eileen J. 53
'genius', 5
Ghazali, 97
Gide, André 22
Gifford Lectures, 50
Gill, Eric 35

gnosis, 15, 40, 47, 77, 80, 85–86, 92, 94, 98, 121, 144, 148, 155, 195
gnosticism, 15, 86
God, 64, 66, 76, 78, 80, 83, 87, 93, 96–98, 103, 107, 108, 110, 112n, 122, 133, 138, 139, 140, 145, 153, 154, 159, 177, 196, 206
    Godhead 87n
Goetz, Herman 27, 171
Golgonooza Press, 55
Goodness, 43
Gopi Krishna, 146
Govinda, Anagarika 41n, 66n, 104, 110, 137
grace, 62, 64
Grangier, T. 25
Griffiths, Bede 202
Guénon, René viii, ix, 7, 9, 11–25, 27, 28, 31, 33–39, 41–43, 46–48, 50–54, 58–61, 63, 66, 69, 75, 86, 90, 103, 104, 109, 111, 117, 118, 120, 135, 138, 143, 145, 165, 166, 168–172, 175, 180, 180–182, 193, 195, 198, 205
Guild and School of Handicraft, 29
Gurdjieff, G.I. 48, 74, 143, 145, 160–163

Habermas, Jurgen 187
Heard, Gerald 143, 146, 159
Hegel, G.W.F. 92
Hehaka Sapa: *see* Black Elk
Heidegger, Martin 187, 188
Heisenberg, Werner 119
Heraclitus, 6
Hesse, Herman 143
heterodoxy, 73–74
Himmelfarb, Gertrude 131n
Hinduism, 7, 12, 18, 23, 34, 35, 40, 51, 77, 93, 103n, 148–154, 155, 156, 158n, 159, 165, 175, 176
    neo-Hinduism 63, 73, 74, 143, 148–154
    reform movements 74, 98, 148–154
historicism, 3, 135, 175, 176, 189, 196, 201
Hofstadter, Richard 131n
Hultkrantz, Ake 190
humanism, 3, 74, 117, 118, 120, 123, 138–141, 146, 158, 201
    humanitarianism 139–140
Hume, David 93
Humphreys, Christmas 34
Husserl, Edmund 187
Huxley, Aldous 27, 48, 143, 146, 154, 158–160
Huxley, Julian 138

Ibish, Yusuf 54
Ibn 'Arabi, Muhyiddin 8, 45, 147
Imperial Iranian Academy of Philosophy, 49, 54

imperialism, 131, 201
Incarnation, 72
individualism, 3, 5, 9, 111–112, 117
Infinite, the 62, 64, 65, 84, 88, 107
initiation, 13–16, 64, 77, 111
inspiration, 63, 71
Instituto Estudios Tradicionales (Peru), 54, 55
Intellect and intellection, 16, 21n, 40, 45, 46, 63, 85, 80, 92, 93, 95, 103, 105, 119, 122, 155, 174, 184–185, 200, 205
Intelligence, 79, 89, 110, 166, 176, 178, 184, 198
Irenaeus, St 116
Isherwood, Christopher 143, 159
Islam, 12, 13, 14, 23, 37, 38, 39, 50, 51, 54–55, 63, 64, 71, 77, 183, 203
Islamic Quarterly, 39
Izutsu, Toshihiko 52

James, E.O. 206
jihad, 159
Jili, 45
jñāna, 15, 96, 151
John, St 8, 70, 132
Johnson, Phillip E. 125n
Judaism, 7, 40, 71, 77, 179
Junayd, 82
Jung, Carl 103n, 106, 134n, 136, 191n

Kabbalah, 15, 51, 99, 161, 162
Kali Yuga, 19
Kant, Immanuel 187
karma, 129
Keeble, Brian 54, 61
Kelley, C.F. 43n, 95n
Kelly, Bernard 13n, 22, 23n
Kitagawa, Joseph 190
Klostermaier, Klaus 167, 189–192, 196, 202, 206
Knowledge, 36, 89, 92, 94–95, 97–98, 116, 166–167, 174, 179, 184, 198
Koran, the 63, 70, 73
Kramrisch, Stella 32
Krishna, 59, 153
Krishnamurti, 74, 143, 145, 146–147
Kristensen, W. Brede 187, 191, 195
Kung-sun Lung, 103

Lacarriere, Jacques 23
La Gnose, 12
Laing, R.D. 6, 120
Lao Tzu, 6, 33, 207
Laurant, Jean-Pierre 11n, 14, 41
Leibniz, G.W. 158n

Le Voile d'Isis, 13, 52
Levi, Sylvain Fr. 24
Levi-Strauss, Claude 191n
liberal theology, 73
Lindbom, Tage 175n
Lindisfarne Gospels, 45
Lings, Martin 47, 50, 53, 54, 55, 62, 89, 124, 125
Lipsey, Roger 22, 24, 27n, 34, 59, 170–171
Locke, John 118
logic, 88–92
logical positivism, 200
Lorenz, Konrad 124

Macnab, Angus 54
Madhava-Vidyaranya, 7n
Mahadevan, T.M.P. 95n, 149n
Maharishi Mahesh Yogi, 145n, 161
Mansfield, Katherine 160
Maritain, Jacques 12
Marx, Karl 138, 180, 181
  Marxism 3, 73, 132, 138, 201
Mary, Holy Virgin 136
Maslow, Abraham 136
materialism, 19, 99, 117, 118, 121–123, 128, 133, 133–134, 150, 181, 192
Matheson, D.M. 54
Matthew, St 74
māyā, 6, 148
Meher Baba, 145
Merton, Thomas 9, 47, 81n, 110, 137, 202
Messengers, Divine 71–72
metallurgy, 19
metaphysics, 15–17, 21, 22, 23, 33, 34, 35, 36, 39, 40, 42, 52, 77, 84–99, 134, 146, 149, 156, 157, 158, 165, 170, 173–182, 194, 203–206
  and certitude 22, 24, 64, 87–88, 94, 96, 97
  and culture 30
  immutability of 88, 91
  and logic 89–92
  moral concomitances of 87, 91, 92, 95, 174–175
Michelangelo, 5, 112
Michon, Jean-Louis 45n
Middle Ages, 65, 172
Mignot, Jean 111
Milhaud, M. 12
missionaries, 202n
modernism, viii, 4, 14, 16, 31, 41, 67, 116–141, 159, 165, 171
  modernisation 149n, 150, 169
monasticism, 40
Montague, F.A. 124n
Moore, Charles 156

Moore, Peter 158
morality, 77, 87, 91, 92, 95, 160, 174–175
Mormonism, 74, 146
Morris, Desmond 124
Morris, William 29, 31
Moses, 153
   Mosaic Revelation 63
Mozart, Wolfgang Amadeus 125
Muhummad (The Prophet), 6, 47, 72, 73, 153
Mulay al'Arabi ad Darqawi, 45
Müller, Max 70, 145n
mysticism, 51, 77, 80, 86, 88, 145, 146, 148, 169, 170, 179, 180
   and drugs 49, 160
   mystics 3, 33, 34,
mythology, 52, 80, 176, 180, 181

Nagarjuna, 33, 65, 92, 93, 147, 188
Naravane, V.S. 27, 169, 172, 175
Nasr, Seyyed Hossein 10, 18, 36, 39, 41, 42, 49–50, 53, 54, 55, 71, 72, 87, 93, 104, 111, 117, 140, 164, 165, 168, 193, 195, 198, 203n, 204n, 206
Nature, 38, 50, 51, 109, 120n
Needleman, Jacob 27, 54, 120, 145, 165
Negus, Michael 124
"New Age" movements, 136, 145
Newton, Sir Isaac 5, 118, 119
Nicea, Second Council of 108
Nicholson, Richard 46, 47, 145n
Nicol, Maurice 160
Nietzsche, Friedrich 91
nihilism, 120
Nishi, Shunji 176–178
Northbourne, Lord W.E. 50, 52, 58

O'Brien, Katherine 55
occultism, 11–12, 17, 111n, 137–138, 143, 145
Orthodox Churches, 13, 51
orthodoxy, 40, 54, 65, 68, 69, 73, 74, 76, 79, 80, 95, 145, 146, 149, 153, 182, 184–185, 198, 204
Ouspensky, Peter 160, 161n
Oxtoby, Willard 190, 192, 196

Pallis, Marco 18, 21, 22, 35, 42, 46–47, 51, 53, 54, 60, 61, 62, 64, 65, 75n, 85, 94, 95, 109, 145n, 204
Parabola, 54
parapsychology: see psychology
Parrinder, Geoffrey 179
Paul, St 65
Peilleaube, Fr 12

Penner, H. 189
perennialism: *see* traditionalism
Perry, Whitall 11, 12, 14, 24, 25, 27, 35, 41, 43, 48–49, 50, 53, 54, 120, 128, 137, 142, 146, 147–148, 161, 162, 183
Perry, W.J. 106
philosophia perennis (also *sophia perennis*) viii, 33, 43, 48, 59, 118, 143, 145, 149, 151, 154, 158, 160, 162, 180–184, 192, 199n, 206
philosophy 31, 35, 81, 85, 87–92, 97–98, 155, 157, 158, 177, 194. 202, 206
   traditional viii, ixn, 87–98
   modern 9n, 88–92, 97, 119, 155, 157, 177, 178
physics, 20, 123
Pio, Padre 112n
Plato, 33, 37, 43, 45, 84, 103, 139, 147, 170, 181
   Platonism 32, 48, 144, 151, 184
   neo-Platonism 179, 180, 184
Plotinus, 3, 33, 60, 89, 170, 181
Polanyi, Michael 120
Porphyry, 3
positivism, 4, 117
'Progress', 46, 50, 131–132, 155
prophecies, 73
psychology, 49, 123, 133–138
   parapsychology 53
   psychism 63, 106, 134–138
   psychoanalysis 19, 27, 134–137
   psycho-genetic fallacy 4, 180
   psychologism 2, 4, 93, 117, 118
   traditional 34, 134
Pye, Michael 191
Pythagorean tradition, the 62

Quinta Essentia, 55

Radhakrishnan, Sarvepalli 9, 143, 149, 150, 154–158, 169
Raghavan, V. 27
Raine, Kathleen 54
Rajneesh, Bhagwan 74, 145
Ramakrishna, 34, 72, 105–106, 143, 149, 151–153
Ramana Maharshi, 46, 95, 149
Rammohan Roy, Raja 149
Rama, 153
Ramanuja, 96, 184
Rampa, Lobsang 19n, 145n
Rana-Hoseyni, Karamat 54
rationalism, 4, 19, 90, 97–98, 112, 117, 118, 155, 169, 178
Real, the 64, 72, 73, 77, 79, 86, 88, 91, 96, 122
realisation, 77, 80, 95, 150, 205

reason, 88–92, 95, 97, 122, 178
Red Cloud, 39
reductionism, 4, 120, 176, 196, 205
Regnabit, 14
reincarnation, 49
relative, the 72–73
relativism, 4, 117, 135, 136, 146, 181
religion, religions 42, 43, 52, 62, 66, 67, 68–83, 87, 91, 93, 94, 99, 135, 137, 142–163, 165, 177, 179, 180, 186–196, 198–206
   and science 121–124, 127, 128n, 131, 186–196
   counterfeit 142–163
   Encyclopedia of Religion and Ethics 187
   inter-religious dialogue 202–203
   natural 204
   phenomenology of 175, 186–196, 202
   pluralism 198–206
   Religionwissenschaft 167, 194, 195, 199
   religio perennis 40, 43, 68, 81
   transcendent unity of 40, 68, 76–77, 80–83, 97, 173–175, 182–184, 202, 203, 204 (diagrams 76, 77)
   universal 143–144, 151, 153, 158, 204
Renaissance, the 3–6, 102, 106, 112, 112, 170
Revelation, 15, 60, 62–66, 68–73, 76–78, 81–83, 94, 95, 97, 119, 121, 122, 135, 145, 149, 195, 196, 205
Reynolds, P.L. 14, 41
Rheims, Archbishop of 13
Ricouer, Paul 191
Riepe, Dale 172
Robinson, Bishop John 178
Rosicrucianism, 17
Roszak, Theodore 21, 22, 89n, 120, 122, 132, 148, 161
Rothko Chapel Colloquium, 54
Rousseau, Jean-Jacques 140n
Rudolph, Kurt 190, 199
Rumi, Jalal ad-Din 84, 162
Ruskin, John 29
Russell, Bertrand 138
Rykwert, Joseph 171

Sartre, Jean-Paul 138
Shankara, 33, 43, 54, 88, 90, 96, 147, 154, 159, 161, 162, 184
Schapiro, Meyer 26
Schaya, Leo 50
Scheler, Max 188
Scholasticism, 85, 170, 181
Scholem, Gershom 64
Schumacher, E.F. 120, 131, 140, 164
Schuon, Catherine (neé Feer) 38
Schuon, Frithjof viii, ix, 2, 4, 7, 8, 24, 25, 36–43, 46, 48, 50–55, 58, 62–100, 102–113, 116–119, 121, 122, 128, 132, 140, 142, 143, 146, 150–153, 157–159, 162, 164–168, 171, 173, 174, 176–181, 183–185, 188, 193, 195, 203–205, 207
science, 116–137
   traditional 19–21, 84, 86, 92, 106, 111, 120–121
   modern 19–21, 46, 118–123, 133, 137, 154, 157, 159
   Scientific Revolution, 3, 117
   scientism, 3, 17, 19–21, 89, 90, 117, 118–123, 206
   evolutionary science 123–133
   and religion 121–123
Scientology, 19n, 145
Scriptures, 59, 70, 71, 73, 98, 121
secularism, 202
Sen, Keshab Chandra 149
Sendivogius, Michael 89, 103
Sermonti, Guiseppi 125
Sertillanges, Fr 12
Shadilites, 13
Shah, Idries 145
Shakespeare, 47, 49, 125, 132
shamanism, 19, 40, 69
Sharma, Arvind 148
Sharpe, Eric 38n, 143n, 192, 202n
Shelley, Mary 120
Sherrard, Philip 50, 51, 54, 183–185
Shute, Evan 125
Skinner, B.F. 136
Smith, Wilfrid Cantwell 190, 191, 195, 202
Smith, Huston 52, 75, 76n, 78, 79, 165, 166, 167, 173
Smith, Wolfgang 20n, 52
Snodgrass, Adrian 52
Söderblom, Nathan 187
societies
   traditional 45, 64–67, 108
   modern 64–67, 172–173
Sophia, 52, 54
sophia perennis: see *philosophia perennis*
Sophia Perennis, 39, 49, 52, 54
Sophia Perennis et Universalis, 15
Spencer, Herbert 123
spiritualism, 16, 17, 19, 53, 135
Sri Lanka Institute of Traditional Studies, 54, 55
Steiner, Rudolf 145n
Steuco, Agostino 158
Stoddart, William 41, 46, 50, 51, 52, 185n
Studies in Comparative Religion, 39, 48, 52, 53, 54
Stunkel, Kenneth 155, 169
Subud, 74, 145, 146n, 160n
Sufism, 13, 15, 39, 45, 47, 49, 51, 62, 77n, 88, 161, 180

Suhrawardi, 103
Supreme Identity, 87
swadeshi movement, 29
symbolism, 2, 18, 21, 33, 53, 77, 79, 81, 91–92, 97, 102–112, 120–121, 157
syncretism, 16, 17, 52, 87, 142, 143, 144, 148, 163

Tagore family, 28, 149
    Rabindranath 169
Tao, the 87n, 207
    Taoism, 12, 18
Tarthang Tulku, 105n
Tauler, John 86
technology, 119
Temenos, 54
Temple, William 71
Theresa of Avila, St 179
Theresa of Lisieux, St 96n
Thubden Tendzin (Marco Pallis), 46
theology, 64, 65, 85, 87, 93–98, 157, 158, 177, 178, 194, 198, 202, 204, 206
theosophy, 16, 17, 19, 73–74, 143, 162, 204
Thomism, 65
Thompson, F.R.S. 127
Tibet, 46, 47, 69
Tillich, Paul 191
time, 19–20, 34, 62–63, 64
tolerance, 199–200
Tolstoy, Leo 5
Tomorrow (later *Studies in Comparative Religion*) 39, 53
Tourniac, Jean 42
Tradition 6, 10, 15, 58–67, 95, 124, 170–171, 180–183, 193, 195, 196
    Primordial 15, 59, 60, 63, 180
    Tradition and traditions viii, 7, 15, 53, 58–67, 75–83, 149, 151, 157, 180, 182
    Unanimous 55
Traditionalism, viii–ix, 6, 8, 9, 24, 25, 37, 41, 50–55, 59, 138, 143, 150, 161, 163, 175, 182, 199, 201, 204, 205, 206, 207
    criticisms of traditionalism 164–185
    traditionalists viii–ix, 9, 25, 44–55, 75, 150, 153, 158, 196, 199, 205
Transcendental Meditation, 145
Truth, 2, 7, 8n, 43, 45, 59, 60, 61, 64, 69–70, 76–82, 84, 87, 88, 93, 94, 96, 142, 144, 145, 147, 157, 179, 183, 195, 207
    truth, beauty and goodness 106–107, 113
Tylor, E.B. 130

UFO-ism, 19n
Uncertainty Principle, 119
universalism, 52, 76, 143, 151
Universality, 77
Upanishads, the 92, 98, 148
Urs Graf Verlag, 45
Utopianism, 132–133, 172

Valsan, Michel 14, 25
van der Leeuw, Gerardus 187, 188
Vasari, Georgio 112
Vasquez, Juan Adolpho 30
Vedanta, 11, 12, 15, 16, 17, 18, 34, 35, 48, 88, 95, 148, 151, 152, 154, 159n, 184
    neo-Vedanta 159
Vedas, 35, 103n, 149, 156, 182
Versluis, Arthur 54
virtue, virtues, 95–96, 106–107, 112, 175n
Vivekananda, Swami (Narendra) 72, 143, 148–154, 156
Voltaire, 118

Wach, Joachim 190, 191, 194, 198
Walker, Kenneth 161
Wetmore, James 55n
Waterfield, Robin 6n
Watts, Alan 143, 145, 146–148, 182
Werblowsky, R. Zwi 190
West, the 16, 23, 28
    Westernisation 150
    West and East: *see* East and West
Wetmore, James 55
Williams, Raymond 29n
Wilson, Colin 161
Wilson, Peter Lamborn 54, 62n
World of Islam Festival, 54
World Wisdom Books, 55, 168
World Parliament of Religions, 148

Zaehner, R.C. 128n, 146, 173n, 178–179
Zimmer, Heinrich 32, 33, 34, 35
Zolla, Elémire 52